COMING HOME

another special girl Kathleen Magee from Co. Mayo.

*These are the stories of people who left Ireland
as young men and women and,
after many years in exile,
closed the circle of emigration by
coming home again.*

Compiled by Frances Browner
and produced by
The 'Safe-Home' Programme

ORIGINAL WRITING

© 2008 The 'Safe-Home' Programme Ltd.™

'Safe-Home', Mulranny, Co. Mayo
www.safehomeireland.com
Cover image courtesy of National Library of Ireland

ISBN: 978-1-906018-71-9

A CIP catalogue for this book is available from the National Library.

Published by Original Writing Ltd., Dublin, 2008.
Printed by Cahills, Dublin.

TABLE OF CONTENTS

INTRODUCTION

"Actions speak louder than words" is a truism that comes to mind, as I ponder on the origins of The "Safe-Home Programme". Many years ago, as a young family doctor appointed to serve the medical needs of a remote corner of County Mayo, I became aware of the neglect of two groups of older Irish people. One I termed the sad silent migration of elders in my locality to faraway institutions in Ireland when they could no longer live alone. Establishing St. Brendan's Village not only ensured that they would not be compelled to leave the area, but reversed that trend, by allowing them a place to come home to. The other group were Ireland's very own older emigrants spread throughout the world. Many yearned to return to spend their final years in the land of their birth, but lacked the means to do so or perhaps were in poor health. Others were told they could not be considered for local housing. I established Safe-Home to repatriate those people.

The Programme has ensured that hundreds of senior emigrants, who would not otherwise be able to do so, have been repatriated to as near as possible to their county of origin. It has secured safe accommodation for over eight hundred returnees. A similar number have been counselled from returning, as coming home is not for everybody. Safe-Home must ensure that repatriation is a positive experience, as the Ireland these people left has changed beyond recognition. Another thousand remain on our list, anxious to come home. A window of opportunity remains to do more for them, but that opportunity will not always be there, so we must act now. Those economic migrants had every reason to forget us, but they did not. Considering the major contribution made to our country through the Emigrant's Remittances, amounting to billions of euro, which sustained entire communities, and kept our National Debt in check, we owe our emigrants a debt which we have just begun to repay. This repayment of an honourable debt, though never sought, is owed to them in justice, not charity.

Our emigrants return to secure sheltered accommodation in the bosom of an often rural community. They have breathed new life into those areas helping to sustain and regenerate them. I owe a debt of thanks to all those who continue to provide accommodation for our returnees. A small minority are terminally ill or are suffering from end stage chronic severe illness and have a deep desire to die in their own country. They are repatriated to the High Support Unit in St. Brendan's Village, under my care, where they spend their final days. It is always a singular honour to serve them.

Safe Home is now a national organisation, with international connections, based in St. Brendan's Village, Mulranny, County Mayo, which assists older Irish born emigrants to return to their homeland. Established in 2000, The 'Safe-Home' Programme is a 'not-for-profit' company with charitable status, overseen by a Board of Directors, and managed by an excellent staff. We would not function without the financial support we receive from the Irish Government through the Irish Abroad Unit, the Department of Foreign Affairs, the Department of the Environment, Heritage and Local Government, the Department of Social and Family Affairs, and from private donors. Nor would we function without the Irish Voluntary Housing Associations; the Irish Welfare and Information Centres and all the workers abroad both lay and clerical who assist us in our task, and who do such an excellent job with our emigrants still resident overseas.

I thank Her Excellency Mary McAleese, President of Ireland, who honours us by being our Patron. I thank all who assisted me in the past including ex Housing Government Minister Robert Molloy for the special amendment to the Capital Assistance Scheme which helped greatly. I am grateful for the encouragement of the Mayo Associations including Mr. Tom Biesty and Prof. Seamus Caulfield along with my colleagues in the Irish Council for Social Housing.

I would like to commend our own excellent staff on a job well done, the Safe-Home Programme Director, Máirín Higgins, Administrator, Mary Ann Fadian and Development Officers, Brenda Fleming and Noreen Mulrine, as well as our committed volunteers, and my fellow directors (including ex-directors) Dr. Tom Collins Mrs. Teresa Cowley, Fr. George Ennis(deceased), Michael J. Ginnelly, Mrs. Teresa Hanley, Mrs. Ruth Heard, Mrs. Phoebe Masterson, Mrs. Annie Nixon, and Dr. Nessa Winston.

With my fellow directors I would like to take this opportunity to compliment Frances Browner for her considerable skill in documenting this virtual treasure of amazing personal experiences, which illuminate a dark economic period in our nation's history. Our returnees' stories leap out from the pages that follow – larger than life. Their passionate desire to come home is a common theme among them. Their generosity towards us still knows no bounds and their unrivalled spirit has enriched our communities further since their return. Their life stories speak for themselves and are now part of our heritage. What wonderful people – it is a privilege to know them. *Ní bheidh a leithéidí ann arís*. I know you will be touched by and enjoy reading the very special accounts that follow.

Dr. Jerry Cowley. Chairman/Founder Safe-Home,
The National Repatriation Centre,
St. Brendan's Village,
Mulranny, County Mayo.

COMING HOME WITH WILLIAM
by Frances Browner

My mother always said she stood on deck until Dun Laoghaire was a dot in the distance. For David Sinnott it was like going to Croke Park – once off the train you just followed the crowd. Suitcases tied in twine had been dragged from the roof of the CIE bus, a regular feature of the Irish landscape in the Fifties and Sixties according to Edward Cullen. The bus brought them from every town and village in Ireland, as thousands left to find a better life elsewhere. Everyone back then was bound for the boat to England.

Their last sight of Ireland would have been the row of Georgian houses flanking the seafront; Killiney Hill in the background, clearer then without the cranes and modern marina; and Bulloch Harbour devoid of its new sea view apartments. The two church spires would have been visible, but not the shopping centre sandwiched in between. The Dublin Mountains would eventually have risen out of the mist, shielding the travellers from their homes in the West while Bray Head to their left would provide a barrier from the South-East.

They would tell tales of thatched cottages and sitting around the turf fire; card games at the table and learning to play the melodeon by an oil lamp; fiddles fixed to the kitchen wall and candles lit in the window at Christmastime; and the hurling match that will be played without them like so many other events in their families' lives. Laurence Marley laments now on all the local history he missed whilst absent from his village of Kilsaran in County Louth. Stories are abandoned then, as Ireland fades into the fog and the boat starts to sway. Day-old sandwiches discarded, stomachs start to heave and for the next few hours all that consumes the passenger is trying to stay well. Finally, the only road to Ireland is a trail of white surf. How did that ultimate wrenching from homeland feel? They just got on with it, they tell me, and made the best of it, because there was no other choice but to go.

The hill of Holyhead jagged and majestic sprouts from the waves just like Howth Head in Dublin. Wales seems like a continuation of Ireland except for the small matter of the Irish Sea. There is even a lighthouse at the end of the pier to remind one of Dun Laoghaire. The boat enters the harbour, doors open onto the quay and there is no going back. How did the stone houses huddled together on the dock appear to the Irish traveller long ago? Were they cold and bleak and unwelcoming, even on a sunny day? Or was the emigrant too heavy of heart to care? Did they mechanically lunge forward towards yet another train that would transport them into the English heartlands where they would be swallowed up for yet another year until it was time to go home again?

There were those who were glad to go too; glad to leave the poverty, hunger and isolation of the Irish countryside behind. Mary Caffrey maintains that no matter what town or city they went to, once they mixed in with the people, they were fine. And of course the bright lights would have beckoned; the dance halls and the pubs; the café and the *craic*; not forgetting the money, which is the only reason they went, wasn't it? Seamus Roddy reminisces about the great day out in London that could be got for seven shillings and six pence. Not bad for a country boy from Roscommon. They formed families there, forged friendships and the camaraderie amongst Irish communities abroad was powerful. Martin Cawley even goes so far as to say that the real Irish people are the ones who went away; they're even more Irish than the ones who stayed behind. Bridie Collins agrees. "We always kept up the old values and traditions. It was what bound us together."

It wasn't until they got older that the desire to come home became strong. Sometimes it was retirement; an illness; the death of a spouse; or the longing to be buried amongst their people that inspired them. No matter, many immigrants harbour the hope of one day coming home.

Today I am going over to bring one of them back. William Gibbons left Aughagower in County Mayo in 1960 and spent the next forty-seven years in London. Now he has decided to come home.

We first met in May 2007 when William came back to Westport to be interviewed by Cluid Housing Association for one of the new apartments on Altamount Street. "I'm ready, I think, and I'd like to

be offered one of these flats, even though there's nobody left in Mayo belonging to me. There were four of us in the family; we all went away and now everyone is back, but me. I'm the black sheep. My brother and sister returned in the Seventies and settled in Dublin and Meath. My mother sold the farm in Aughagower when my father died and bought a house in London where she lived for many years. She also came back, but died in 1998 when she was ninety-four years old. There's no one left in the West for me, except in the graveyard. Nevertheless I'm thinking of coming back. I don't really know if every Irish person in England wants to, but I do."

William returns in November to sign on with Cluid for Apartment Number 5, Firestation Close, on Altamount Street. "It took a long time," he sighed. "I was starting to get anxious when I didn't hear. There's so much to be done and now we have Christmas on top of us. I don't know how I'm going to manage. I have to move my stuff; transfer my pension; organize my medical card and give notice to the landlord. I'll be cleaned out paying rent over there and paying it here. It's all happening so fast. Maybe I won't move at all."

It's now December and we're at the London Irish Centre in Camden Town where Welfare Advice Worker, Jerome Duffy, is helping William to sever his past in London, literally. He arranges to have electricity, gas and telephone services cut off on William's day of departure and for his final energy bills to be paid by direct debit before he closes his account with Abbey Bank. He contacts the landlord, *Peabody Trust*, to have the meters read on Wednesday and to discuss final rent payment. "I didn't realize there was so much work to moving," William whispers as Jerome talks on the telephone to yet another bureaucrat about transferring his pension. "I couldn't have done it without Jerome."

The Centre was started by two priests back in the Fifties as a hostel for newly arrived emigrants from Ireland. They bought the building on the corner of Murray Street for two thousand pounds in 1950 and it housed twenty to thirty people. Gradually it developed into a meeting place and subsequently provided employment services and advice on social welfare benefits when they became available. "All told there are about thirty of us working here," Jerome updates us. "We've got four advice workers, outreach workers, and a separate staff who deal with people who grew up in institutions. They're involved with getting them compensation from the Redress Board. We have a cultural centre where there is always something going on like tea dances and boxing matches. St. Pancras boxing club holds their fights there. Every September the Centre holds a *Return to Camden* festival, which celebrates the Irish tenancy in North London. There's lots of Irish music and dancing in McNamara Hall, named after one of the founders, and it's a great laugh."

William had come to the Centre on and off through the years, mainly for social events. The dances used to be great one time," he recalls. "There was *The Round Tower* on Holloway Road and *The Gresham*. Then there was *The Half Moon*, which had the best music and was a great place back in the Sixties. We used to all end up in *The*

Boat train (courtesy of National Library of Ireland)

Half Moon on Holloway Road. It's called *The Quays* now. Then there was *The Buffalo* in Camden Town. That was a rough place; you could get a right-hander when you walked in the door and it was often from a woman too. They could be a rough lot.

I haven't time to think about whether I'll miss London or not; that's why I'm spending so much time in the pubs lately; trying to forget. It was two o'clock Saturday night before I got to bed and I missed Mass the next morning. I always try and get to Church on a Sunday. I was in *The Lion* on Archway last night. It's been my local for quite a while. People are calling to the flat all the time and all the mates want to say goodbye and keep insisting on another drink. I can't sleep then thinking about it all and whether I'm making the right decision or not. I must be an awful idiot going home. And it's not going home either; it's like emigrating all over again. My family is there though, and my sister in particular wants me back, but I have an awful lot of good friends here and they all think I'm mad to be leaving. Then again, maybe they'll come back after me."

Jerome reckons he'll have them all over on holiday. He then announces that everything has kicked in and their tasks concluded. "The pension credit letter will be sent to me and I'll fax it over to Mary Ann Fadian in the Safe Home office until the benefits come through in Ireland. It will then be transferred over to the new Irish bank account as of your next payment and all the energy services will be closed down Wednesday. Insurance policies are sorted, and the only thing left outstanding is the electricity. As soon as the caretaker comes around and you get the reading, ring me. I'll ring them, and have the final bill, same story, sent to Altamont Street, your new address. It should be a smooth sailing I think. Give us a ring, then Will, and let us know how you're doing."

William is dubious. "Won't it take a long time to get the phone installed?"

Jerome assures him that Ireland is very good at all that sort of thing now. The line will be installed already and it's just a matter of buying a telephone and signing on with Eircom for a number. "It's a lot of work" Jerome is sympathetic, "but I knew we'd get to the end of it eventually. People have enough to think about when they're moving so we're happy to help with the rest of it. Keeps us busy, doesn't it? We deal with a lot of Irish people wanting to go back, but this is the first time I've carried a case to this stage of the process. Will is the first person I have actually witnessed physically going home. Every week we get enquiries about The 'Safe-Home' Programme. Right now I have about eight or nine clients on waiting lists for houses throughout Ireland. All four welfare workers at the Centre probably have the same number of applicants waiting. It's a very popular scheme and it works wonders. There isn't really a replica and I can't find fault with it. It's amazing."

They shake hands and we step out onto Camden Square armed with a bag of *Quality Street*, complements of administrator, Maria Connolly.

"I met a fellow from Fermanagh one day and he said to me, I'm getting out of this place," William recalls as we head towards the bus stop. "I'm with a crowd called Safe Home, he said, and they're helping me to get home. So that's how I first heard about it. He's back now about three years; maybe I'll get in touch with him." Bus number 253 hurdles along Camden Road towards Holloway. Lovely

London July 1962

London accents resonate in the crisp December air. I try and imagine how this city must have seemed to a boy from rural Ireland all those years ago.

Going home to Ireland now will be just as daunting. "It probably won't really hit me until January when I realize that I'm not coming back after Christmas. Even that can be stressful. I never liked Christmas, not even when I used to go back to Ireland on holidays. I didn't go back at all for twenty-two years. All of my family were here so I didn't need to. It was all new to me again after being away for so long. It was like going into a strange place. I had broken up with a lady friend and I was on the drink, so it was a double dose. It's a good job I had friends here when I came back. I had no interest in visiting anybody when I was there; I'd rather go to the pub. That was in the Seventies and my mother was home by then with my sister. I was working with a chap from Tyrone at the time, a good friend, and he kept saying, you're going back this Christmas. I was glad I did in the end and I went every year after that and a few times in the summer too. I hadn't really thought a lot about Ireland in the twenty-two years, but it didn't half affect me when I got there. It was a very emotional time. Just like this."

We stroll along Holloway Road in the borough of Islington, pass the Kebab shop and Thai take-away; the *Sainsbury* branch where Will likes to shop, *Paradise Cafe* and *Ambassador Cars* taxi service, the *Odeon* cinema and finally we reach *The Quays*. "This place would have been packed with Irish people long ago. They've completely changed it," Will exclaims, as we enter the bright blue premises.

The atmosphere is warm and welcoming, festive decorations collide with vintage pictures of The Quays in Galway, from where its former owners hailed; Sky Sports competes with Christmas carols and Irish accents abound. The waitress is from Cork; the barman from the Midlands and four young Dublin girls eat lunch and chat animatedly at an adjoining table.

William and I order roast beef and discuss the social scene in the Irish pockets of London versus that in Ireland. The pub scene is slowly dying over there, I tell him. That's been my experience since I returned from New York twelve months previously. It's harder now to find a place where when you walk in the door you would know everyone. The Irish pubs in North London would be more similar to those in the Bronx, I would say, rather than their counterparts in Ireland. I'm afraid William is going to miss that. "Well, there's good music in *The Castlecourt Hotel* in Westport on a Sunday night; and on a Saturday you have Hoban's. So that's two nights sorted," he laughs. The Irish people abroad have not changed to the same extent that they have in Ireland he admits, and I agree. There was no Celtic Tiger wagging his tail in Kentish Town or Woodlawn. "My mother always said that there are an awful lot of good Irish people, but they all came over here." William laughs nervously and I assure him that people in Ireland still retain a genuine spirit of generosity and friendliness. At least that's what I have found. And many of the returnees I interviewed for this publication have remarked on how everyone speaks to them on the street and in the supermarket; on how helpful local Welfare Officers and Public Service employees have been in making their transition easier; and on how supportive family members have been in welcoming them home. It's not the same country they're going back to after a fifty-year absence, but some returned emigrants have found it just as good, or even better.

From interviewing them over the last year I've learnt that you have to become involved, I tell William, like Bridie O'Connor you have to embrace the local community if you want them to embrace you. It's a lesson I've learnt from many of the returnees; instead of complaining that my social life has plummeted since leaving New York, perhaps I should explore my North Wicklow environs and investigate possibilities there. That should be easy in Westport, I try to convince William, where there are so many activities.

"I suppose I could climb Croagh Patrick;" he tries to sound enthusiastic. "A lot of people here would miss the big shops and the buses; they wouldn't be interested in moving to a remote town in the West of Ireland. The cost of living over there puts people off too. I won't be saving any money, that's for sure."

We lather the roast beef with horseradish, good for arthritis ac-

cording to William, if you boil the root
and drink the juice, and we delve into the
Yorkshire pudding.

"Then again, I wasn't saving any
money before I left either; wasn't even
making enough to keep me. There was
nothing for a young fellow like me back
in Mayo in 1960. I had worked in a few
places, helping people out on farms, but
there was no money. Where we came
from the land was bad so there wasn't
much to do. I had worked for a while at
home, helping my father with the cattle.
He walked miles driving them to Ballina
and Ballinrobe; he even took them on the

The Quays

train to Dublin and across to Wales on the boat. He always had a
drover and a dog with him. Everyone knew him by the dog, Coolie,
because you had to have a really good dog for the cattle. He bought
another place back in Galway where the land was better and he always took a little lad out of the orphanage at Letterfrack to help on the
farm, but we had no idea they were so badly treated. So even though
my father would have been considered quite well off at the time, there
still wasn't enough work for me. A lot of people were coming back on
holidays saying how great it was in England, so myself and my cousin
decided to bugger off to Manchester.

We took the train to Dublin; then the boat from Dun Laoghaire.
The new boat isn't too bad; the old ones were terrible altogether. Everyone was getting sick; you couldn't walk around at all, not even to
go to the toilet. We took another train then to Manchester, but sure
we were all so young, we didn't know what was happening. We got
digs in Plymouth Grove and a job with a building firm by the name
of *Bailey's*. They were a small crowd and the money wasn't good. It
had been a terrible winter, with frost and snow and fog and a lot of
the building sites had closed down so we came and went, in and out
of different jobs, my cousin and I. In the meantime, my brother had

come down to London, to Edmonton, and after six months, I decided to join him. I moved into the same lodgings and we shared a room for many years.

My first job in London was with *The United Kingdom Engineering Company* laying cement troughs for underground cables on the first electrified train line in England. It ran from Liverpool Street station to Waterloo and out to Bovington. It was hard work, but it was nice because we were in the country a lot and it was steady. It was all steam trains that time that had to be stoked with coal. We had a great time riding the steam trains through all the railway stations with a driver and stoker. Then I went with *Westinghouse,* a brakes and signals outfit and after that I went on the building sites. I stayed then with one contractor, an English crowd, for fourteen years. The Irish were the worst to work for. I worked with *Murphy's* for the summer one time on an Oil Tanker down on the Thames that was being converted into a hotel and finally I went with the Gas Board mainly for the health benefits.

I was homesick at first and I didn't like the food. There was no meals from the landlady where I stayed. There'd be a cooker in the room and that was it. Then when I got to know a lot of people and established a social life, I loved London. We used to walk from *The Buffalo* in Camden Town to Harringey at three o'clock in the morning, and it was so safe. I had one mate from Aughagower and we had a great time together, dancing, and drinking, the usual stuff. Then he met a lady from Tourmakeady, got married and that was the end of that friendship for a while. My brother and I had hooked up with these Cork chaps in the lodgings and we ended up renting a house together on Station Crescent off West Green Road in Tottenham. There was some *craic* in that house, I can tell you, whistling out the window at the women and drinking in the nearby *Black Boy* pub. You must remember we were so young; I was only nineteen when I came here."

We talk about Catherine Connelly and how at the great age of eighty-four she had made the move back to Ireland last April and has settled in already. William is optimistic that it probably will be alright once he gets there; it's the thought of moving that is upsetting him. For the past few weeks he sometimes hasn't got to sleep until five o'clock in the morning, worrying about the shipping of his belongings; saying goodbye to everyone; wondering is he doing the right thing. "One of my friends tried it once and only lasted eight weeks. It's not the Ireland we left, she said, and she didn't have a car. Are you sure, she said, you know what you're doing. I think so, I told her. I'm going to give it a try anyhow. Sure what would I be doing on my own here in London? None of my family is here. I had a cousin I used to have a drink with on a Sunday, but he's dead now; he died shortly after his wife.

It's just that there's so much still to do. The caretaker is supposed to come around and have a look at the electricity box. The removal people are coming to get my stuff tomorrow. Two hundred and fifty pounds they're charging; that's not bad. They're leaving the bed behind so as I'll have somewhere to sleep. I can't close down my bank account if I'm not in the country; it's got to be done in person. I'll have to fly back again to do it. Maybe I'll stay then. It's a nice flat I'm giving up too, in a quiet area and I've been living there just over sixteen years. Am I mad to be leaving?

If I'd known all the bills I'd have to pay today, I wouldn't have had the heating on so much. You'd think they'd give me a rebate, when you think of all the money I've given them over the years! I should have told British Telephone to get stuffed and British Gas. They have me cleaned out before I go home. I can't close my bank account until all these bills are paid, can I? And I don't want them to turn off the phone before I go. There's so much to think about."

Two hours later we venture once more out onto Holloway Road where the temperature must have dropped at least ten degrees. "It's not as cold as this in Ireland is it?" William sounds sceptical. "Hopefully my furniture will be in the new flat, wouldn't that be great? I'll have no bed to sleep in otherwise. My sheets and that are coming with the shipping. Will there be any shops open when we get into Knock? My flight is at five to three and it only takes a little over an hour. *Heatons* and *Dunnes Stores* in Castlebar should still be open. They're great for sheets and stuff like that. Will we have time to stop on the way to Westport? I've booked into a B&B for the first night, but I'd prefer to move into the flat as soon as possible." We part at the junction with Archway Road and I promise to visit again the next day. I watch him struggle against the wind through a town that was home for almost fifty years and I wonder how the streets of Westport will compare.

"Any port but Westport," William chuckles, as we sip tea at 132b Junction Road the next day. "Only joking," he tells his friend, Billy, who has dropped in to say goodbye. "It won the Tidy Towns a few times; can't be a bad place. Surrounded by hills so as the robbers couldn't get out. It's nice down at The Mall though."

"London is lovely too," says Billy, "especially around September, down by the Thames."

"It is," William agrees. "I'm going to miss it and this flat too. It's only about twenty years old and run by *The Peabody Trust*, a housing association. Peabody was an American who came over here to help the homeless. It's hard to get one; you could be a long time on the list. I got this because of the arthritis in my heels; because where I was living I had to climb stairs. That was in Harringey. It used to be Harringay, but they had to change the spelling in order to be politically correct. Ridiculous really when one time gay used to mean happiness."

The removal men didn't make it yet because a driver has fallen ill and another one has to come in from Wales. There's a phone call from Margaret in Westport to say that a cooker and hob has been delivered to Altamount Street and from a local man with a van for hire who can't be there until nine in the morning. William tells him he must be on time, "because I'm going home tomorrow. I'm emigrating." He replaces the receiver. "Forty pounds he wants to move a couch and an armchair down to Crouch End. My bank balance is a bit lighter now. There'll be no need to close it at this rate.

I haven't eaten a damn thing all day, waiting for the removal guy to come. I will have to leave the key with Billy or with another friend, Tom, who lives down a side road here, if they don't come by tomorrow. My rent is paid up to the 30th so I have until then to get my stuff out of here. I can't eat. I can't sleep. I'd be more relaxed if I knew my belongings were shipped out of here. The antique shop is open until seven tonight; I might bring some more things up there. They've already taken a wardrobe off me. It was heavy wood, solid, and they gave me thirty pounds for it. They took that and the chest of drawers.

"This is my last cup of tea on Junction Road." There's a knock on the door. "This could be Mary now or is it Angela coming? I know her knock, or it could be Sheila for the wardrobe. No? It's Bernie."

Bernie bustles into the living room already crammed with boxes, suitcases and odds and ends of furniture still looking for a home. "It's hard to believe you're going, Will. Known you for years I have. From *The Lion*, from all over; we drank all over didn't we lovey?"

"We certainly did. Do you need a lamp, Bernie?"

"No, lovey, my flat is choc a bloc with stuff already. I'm so tired. There was a big night in *Mother Redcaps* Saturday, wasn't there, a memorial for that fella from *The Pogues*, who died last year. You couldn't move in it. Shane McGowan was there and Bono. It's all about it in *The Irish World* newspaper. All set Will? You know there's a lot of storms in Mayo today. The electricity lines are down in Belmullet. I hope your plane can land in Knock."

"I hope so too. It was wicked stormy when I flew over in November to sign up for the flat. Maybe I'll stay where I am! I'll start unpacking now, will I, Billy? Do you want a mirror, Bernie?"

"No thanks, lovey. You have to go now, Will, its all arranged. I'd like to live in Ireland too because all the family are there aren't they? My Dad's from Mayo and me Mum's Galway. I spent all my holidays there, still do. I'm over and back all the time. I'm going over to see Big Tom in *The Traveller's Hotel* in Castlebar in February. I'll be in *Digger J's* in January. There are great dances there; showbands and all. It's about seven miles outside Westport in a place called Ayle. There's a lot of good bands coming for Christmas and the New Year. Do you ever go there, Will?"

"I do and I'd give you a dance, but do you know I don't dance. I don't know why, I just never learnt. I did the odd *Siege of Ennis*, but I wasn't good at it. A gang of us would be drunk and we'd get up. I never waltzed in my life. I'm the only one in the family that never danced and I'm the only one who is musically minded. I went to the dances hoping that somebody would drag me out. When I was only about seventeen I was at a big dance back in Westport one night and they announced a ladies' choice. Is there still such a thing? And this one came straight for me. I didn't run, but I had to refuse her. She could have got me thrown out see. That right, Billy?"

"That's right. You were not supposed to refuse a woman if she asked you to dance, even though she could refuse you. All the dance-halls are closing down here now, aren't they Bernie?"

"They are and all, lovey. Dad had his Christmas party in *The Galtymore* in Cricklewood last week. There's only one hall left in it now; it's supposed to be closing down in the New Year because nobody goes there anymore, do they Will?"

"Not many. There used to be three halls in *The Galty* in my day. In the Sixties they'd have céilí on one side and modern in the other. You could go from one to the other if you wanted. It was a great place. That's all gone now. There's nobody left here anyhow; they're all dead. Sure all the dancehalls are gone now."

"I think *The Forum* is still going."

"It is, Billy, but not for the Irish. Now, I have an accordion here, but I don't know if I'll be allowed to bring it on board because I have a briefcase as well. Maybe I'll bring it down to The Mall in Westport one day, down to the river - the river of no return. I could be a busker. I never learnt how to play it properly. When I was about sixteen, I could play *The Sally Gardens* and all that. I'll play ye a tune now, *Curtains of Night* (drawn back by the stars) by the McNulty family. For years when I had arthritis I couldn't even pick the thing up. The jigs and reels are too fast for me. *Take this message to my mother* is another one I like. I do sing that when I have a drink."

"*Bring down the lamps*, do you know that one Will?"

"No, Bernie, but I have a nice lamp here to get rid of and curtains too. What do you think of them curtains? Any offers for the gramophone? I have the records there and all, about a hundred, forty-five's. I have a lot of John McCormack. When we were young at home my father bought one of the first in that area, a *Decca*. Your man who made the light bulbs was the first one to make them, Edison. This one was advertised in a *Loot* out in Romford one time, it's like the *Buy Sell* paper in Ireland or *Pennysaver* in the States. I paid £130 for it. The man who sold it said it belonged to his father and he didn't want it. We always had one when I was a kid. A lot of them had *Master's Voice*. I should display it in a glass cabinet because it's a beautiful piece. There was a family near us in Aughagower who were in a band and we'd hear them practicing on a Sunday evening when I was a young fellow so the records remind me of that. I was only joking about selling it; I wouldn't part with it for the world."

"You're right too, lovey. I must be off now. When you get a telephone number, Will, give it to Tom and I'll get it from him. It takes four or five months to get the phone installed in Ireland. My friends in Castlebar are waiting that long for Broadband."

"I won't worry about the phone for a while. I don't want anybody ringing me anyhow."

"We have another holiday stop now in Mayo, don't we lovey?" Bernie bustles out again. "And don't leave it too late in the morning. The traffic here is dreadful. From six until nine in the morning you can't move."

"I will, Bernie, might see you later in *The Lion*," William closes the door behind her. "I need a drink, but I'm bloody starving. I haven't eaten since my porridge this morning. I usually eat at home; I haven't been to the café in years, but all the meat I have now is in the freezer. I wouldn't have a drink unless I had a meal first; not on an empty stomach; I'd die. I won't sleep tonight worrying about the shipping. If he'd come today it would have taken a load off my mind. I think I might need counselling after all this. In the meantime, let's go to the caf."

We walk along Junction Road, peer in the window of the *Squawk* Antique shop and wonder if they'll take Williams's lamp. We pass by the Church that has been converted into apartments and a pub called *Drum & Monkey*. William stops to chat to Pat the bus driver and pops into a neighbouring house to drop off a box of *Maltesers* to the kids.

"He's a great mixer," said Billy, as we enter *The Golden Café*, "he'll have no problem fitting in anywhere." We sit at a Formica topped table and study the walls papered with menus – Fish 'n Chips; Jacket Potatoes and Meat Pies; Bubble and Squeak for only £3 and the milkiest coffee. "We would have been here every day of the week one time, for breakfast, dinner and tea sometimes." William and Billy reminisce. "All the men did it – into the café after work and then to the pub. We did it for years. From the Caf to the Pub; that was our journey until we hitched up with a lady friend who would take care of us. I was too scared to get married though. Women often told me I was selfish. I'm sorry in a way. I think life is easier for married people; I might have a son or daughter now to look after me."

Two Dublin women flurry in for chip butties; they stop to chat in genuine North Wall accents despite their forty-four years in Islington.

Tim from Kerry stops in for a steak. "Going home for the Christmas, Will?"

"I'm going for good," William replies with a confidence he does not feel, I am sure. "Maybe I'll be back," he whispers from behind his knife and fork. Fair play to you is the response all round. "When you've him settled," Tim calls after me before we step out into the cold London night, "will you come back for me?" I assure him I will and his laughter rings in our ears for many yards up Junction Road.

We bundle into *The Lion* and take a seat beside the roaring fire. The place is packed for a Tuesday night and there is still a smattering of young Irish around, despite the notion that nobody is leaving anymore. God is Watching Us chants Nancy Griffith over the RTE radio airwaves while we are joined by another friend, Annette. She envies William his new beginning and would love to be going back to the home of her ancestors; Mum from Offaly and a Kerry Dad. The Vodka and lemonade tastes good, as I listen to the local gossip. Every now and then I ask William how he's feeling. "If I keep talking, I won't have to think about it."

People stop by to say hello, goodbye, others will arrive later for the real farewell. Maybe there'll be a song; *Take Me Home to Mayo* is suggested, but not favoured by William, *Mother MaChroi* being his usual party piece. He never even joined The Mayo Association when he was here. "They used to have a Westport Association in Willesden one time and I went there a few times." We discuss which taxi I'll take to Enfield, whether I'll be ripped off or not. There seems to be a general distrust of them, although this has not been my experience so far. *Ambassador Cars* must be used to me by now and my new address at another lion, *The Red Lion* on Hartford Road where Offaly man Ray Bell is the Governor. *A Return to Camden* poster catches my eye as I exit. They all want to return to Ireland right now, how many will return to Camden?

Photo courtesy of Bloomberg News

"I might be back," William glances over his shoulder the next day, as the cab speeds along the M11 to Stansted Airport and Essex fields roll by the window. The line snails along to check in for Ryanair Flight FR805, but luckily we still have thirty minutes before the desk closes. How did the first half-hour of this voyage compare? William's case is too heavy; he has to go to another desk to pay extra so we have to run that final lap up to Departures. We are not sitting together, but I think maybe he would prefer to be alone on the last leg of his journey. It's so different by air. For the *Ryanair* generation there is not the same feeling of being wrenched away from a place. We'll be in Knock in an hour's time. There is not the same feeling of finality that there is on the boat; not the same goodbyes that there would have been fifty years ago. Friends will shoot over to see him; he might come back to visit. There is much more movement now. Thank God for *Ryanair* is echoed throughout these memoirs and for Monsignor Horan who opened up the West of Ireland to the world.

I ponder on my own departure for New York in 1987 on an Aer Lingus jet with a rucksack on my back. I'd only intended spending the summer there and stayed for twenty years. I always came back on holidays though and my mother said she was dizzy looking at the revolving doors at Dublin airport; that one time when someone left for America, you never saw them again. In the 1990's crossing the Atlantic became as casual as hopping on a bus. We were always in touch by telephone too, and in later years by text and email. We always felt close to home. As we soar over the Irish Sea today, I'm struck by how much nearer England is and yet some of the people recorded in these pages; people who spent half a century there, felt so distanced from their homeland.

The Red Lion, The Lion, The Quays and Camden Town all seem a lifetime away, as we disembark at Knock, and indeed they are. I saw Irish faces everywhere, on Holloway Road, in Enfield, at the Seven Sisters tube station, waiting for the bus in Croydon, travelling by train from Crewe to Euston. They came from every county and you could still see it in their Irish eyes. In New York you can change who you are, but not in London.

Take me home to Mayo, there it is.

Welcome home Will.

Old Head and Croagh Patrick Co. Mayo

CATHERINE CONNELLY

I came home to Ireland in April 2007 after forty-eight years in Australia. I enjoyed it there, but I couldn't stay because of the heat. I would have stayed if my husband, Jimmy, had lived, but in the end I didn't have anyone, only looking at the four walls. Darwin is not like Kerry; there were wire doors and we had to keep them locked all the time because strangers would be knocking at them looking for drink and smokes. It was a terrible way to live. I always loved Ireland and always dreamt of it. I never thought I would come home though and even threw away my Irish passport when I became an Australian citizen.

When I left Bunaneer National School, I went working in Waterford in Dan Greene's shop where I stayed for seven years. In 1949 I left for London and cried and cried watching my mother holding on to the bonnet of my cousin's car, as we drove down the lane from our house in Castlecove. Irish people never want their families to leave; it was poverty made us to roam, I always say. Poverty brought us all away in the end. They had to send me home after three months, I was that homesick, but, when I went back a second time I became friendly with this Limerick girl from Newcastlewest. Bessie was her name and she spoke Irish and she would ring me up and ask me if I wanted to go to Church and instead we'd head off to a dance! Our employers wouldn't understand a word when we spoke in Gaelic. I knew a little of the language, not much, but I could understand Bessie. My sister, Mary, was there too, and her husband used to laugh at all our stories. I had such a gay life, you know.

Another sister, Eileen, was a chef on Baker Street and I got a job there as a parlour maid. We had a great time there and went dancing seven nights a week. The master of the house, Commander Garner, was lovely, as was his wife. They had something to do with *Gold Flake* cigarettes. They'd go away for three months and we'd invite our boyfriends to the house. She trusted us and we never touched anything belonging to her. We were there seven years and then Eileen met Ted and they went to Australia. My mother got sick and I came back to mind her. I was here two years when she died on St. Patrick's Day. I could have stayed at home then and could even have married a local man. He became very wealthy after; with caravans and everything, and married a girl who was in the same class as me. She had a shocking temper and threw a stick at the teacher one time. I had a date with him one night, but I left him waiting beside the bush because I thought to myself how could I leave my poor sick mother. Then this girl was home from England and she picked him up after. Every time I came home he'd put his arm around me and give me a big kiss. She'd give me a look! My nephew, Jeremiah, says to me now, there's your boyfriend up there, pointing at his land, you could have had all that.

We grew up on a farm very near here; where we had four or five cows. We were very happy, but still I went back to Australia with Eileen and Ted after my mother's funeral. That was in 1958 and I was thirty-four years old. We travelled on *The Iberia* that sailed out of Southampton. It was lovely. I met a lot of people. There was dancing and bingo for the six weeks it took to get to Melbourne. We stopped in Port Said in Egypt and in India. And the poverty there, the poverty. If you were ever in Port Said you'd never throw away another piece of bread. They were so poor. It was an awful place.

The Iberia

When I arrived in Melbourne I went working as a barmaid for this

Clare woman and she was terrible. Oh! She was terrible. I worked from half past seven in the morning until half past seven in the evening and when I was finished I'd be sitting down reading a book and she'd say, Kitty, she'd say, there's ironing there to be done. So you can imagine, I never got a break, no never. I worked in that bar, *The Four Courts*, for nine years. We met lots of Irish. There was an Irish girl with me and she was married to an Irish man there. She told me there wasn't a cup left in the dresser that he hadn't broken. I couldn't believe it when she told me. Then she went off with a Dutch fellow. She was a lovely girl and she had two lovely children. But, he was a drunk you know, the husband. He didn't mean it; it was the drink. I liked Australia at first; I liked working in the bar. I met a few Irish boys, you know. We had a lovely Australian barman, Jack who'd look at my tip glass and say "Kitty how did you make all this money?" I made good tips because I was nice to everyone, you know. When the boss would come around I used to hide them, as I didn't want him to know how much I was making. I'd chat away to keep him happy and we always got on well. My daughter always says I'll definitely get into Heaven. I'll talk myself in there.

I was never homesick really, especially after I met my husband who was a customer in the bar. James Connelly was his name, like the rebel. I fell madly in love with him; he was so good looking. He was Scottish, but had been a long time in Australia. We got married in 1961 in St. Pat's in Melbourne and the reception was in God I can't think. I lost my first baby because I stayed working in the bar for the first three months lifting heavy stuff. Then I was blessed with two more children. My daughter, Caitrionna, was born in 1963, and my son, Jimmy, was born the day *The Beatles* come to Melbourne in 1964. There wasn't much difference between them. I was forty years of age when I had my first child, which was considered quite old at the time. They're having them when they're fifty now! Caitrionna works for the Government and she's married to Bruce. He's a wonderful husband to her, a wonderful husband. My God he does everything for her. You'd think they were only married yesterday. It's lovely to see them like that. He works in an oil company and has to go away every fortnight.

Caitrionna had a good job in Alice Springs teaching the Aborigines, but Bruce got this job then so she had to give it up. She didn't mind, she's happy there now.

Kitty in Aussieland

My husband, Jimmy, was a rigger in the buildings when I met him first, and then he joined the Air Force where he became a Lieutenant. The Air Force was a wonderful life when we were younger; to anyone I'd say it was a wonderful life. You'd meet different people and you could go to the pub on the Base and there was a great social life. You'd meet people from all over the world. There weren't many Irish in it. I stayed working after I was married. I sent the two kids to a crèche while I worked in the bar and in a factory that made motor parts. I worked then for the Jesuits as a waitress, which I loved. And I worked in the University of Melbourne for four years. I used take the kids to school in the morning and then I could work and come home in the evening. We had a great time there. Then Jimmy got posted to Darwin. It was a different lifestyle to Melbourne. It was a wild life. You couldn't keep your kids in. They went out to discos and everything. I tried to keep them close and keep control over them, but it was harder in Darwin. It was harder still when I was left there on my own.

Jimmy died suddenly nearly nineteen years ago. He went to work one morning; dropped the boss off and said he had a pain. He asked for some tablets, and then he sat in the chair and died. My granddaughter was born the 4th of October, 1988, and he died on the 6th. I could have married again, but I never bothered. I'd only have married an Irishman anyhow. On the ship going over this man told me to never marry an Australian because they go to the football, he said, and you'll be left at home with your kids. And I always remembered that. It was very lonely on my own. I used to play lawn bowls, and I loved that. I never won anything; I was always the bridesmaid; always the runner-up, never on top. Then I had my two grandchildren. Kerryanna and

Loughlin for company. My grandson, Loughlin, was fourteen years of age last Tuesday. He had to write a history essay recently and he asked me what I used to do in my younger days. I was telling him I used to go to the dances in the evening to the platform. We used to cycle into Caherdaniel and to Sneem and our clothes would be drenched from the rain, but we'd still dance.

I came home on my first holiday after fifteen years. And Oh! I couldn't believe the briars had grown up around the house and the curtains were gone. My brother just had a string across the window with a piece of material thrown around it. You think it should be the same, but everything had changed. When we went to Mass I could hear them all whispering, do you know who's home from Australia? Katie O'Leary. I laughed you know. I came back on my own that first time, but I often came back afterwards with the children. Then I brought my daughter when my husband died and the baby with her. We went to Scotland too. My husband had eleven in the family and we spent a week with every one of them. We had a lovely time there.

I decided to come back to Ireland for good when I was living in Darwin. The heat and the humidity would kill you. We couldn't even wear a top with sleeves or a pair of pants. We'd have a little light frock and a panties and bra on us and the heat was terrible. I had one friend, a Scotch girl, but I used to find it very lonely after my husband died. I came home every year then to spend the summer here in a caravan out by my homeplace in Castlecove. I loved it so much I thought, I'll make a break and go back. When I heard about the care houses here, I put in an application. My daughter wasn't very happy when I was offered a house in Waterville and she tried to talk me out of it. She's still upset, but I arrived home on the 16th of April and I love it. At the moment I'm living in Glenmore with my nephew, Jeremiah, while I wait to sort out the superannuation pension from Australia. When I move into Waterville I'll miss the mountain here because this is what I was used to. The house there is all newly painted and I'm hoping the Council will put in a carpet for me. I'll have a washing machine and won't need much turf on the fire to heat the water. I'll be happy there. I'll have my curtains and my plants.

The great thing about being back is that I am close to the home of my childhood. I grew up in Castlecove, in County Kerry, in between Sneem and Cahirdaniel. A nephew took it over after my brother died and sadly it's not ours anymore. I have no family in the area except Jeremiah. I'm the last of the O'Leary's now. Castlecove is such a beautiful place. There's a lovely castle down the road, with a lovely legend attached to it where we used to play as children. There was a notch across where they used to hang people and their bodies would fall into the sea.

My father died when I was only fifteen. He went fishing for salmon and he collapsed at my brother's feet. He was a wonderful man who worked very hard. He died as he lived too because the sun shone at his funeral. They always say happy is the corpse the sun shines on. He killed himself working, because every time there was a knock at the door, if a cow was calving, or a horse was in trouble, no worry, off he'd go. They don't do that anymore. Except Jeremiah, he's very good. He's very honest. He put up the curtains and all for me.

There's no neighbours around here and I don't know anyone anymore. I had three or four school friends here one time, but most of them are dead now. I don't know hardly any of the younger ones, but I hope to make new friends in Waterville. I met the woman who lives next door to my new house there and she was very nice. I would tell anyone to come back though. My mother used to always quote that old Irish poem, *The Bard of Ballycarry, 1770-1816*, by James Orr, which begins: *The savage loves his native shore, Though rude the soil and chill the air, Well then may Erin's sons adore Their isle, which Nature formed so fair!* I think it's something in the Irish; they always want to return to their native country. It's always inside you. Maybe everyone isn't the same as me. Ted thought I was mad. My sister, Eileen, is dead now and he's over there yet. He's a lovely man, but he said he'd never come back to Ireland. My son Jimmy thought I was crazy too, but he said it's up to you Mum. He's a fitter and turner and works in Korea now.

I always kept up my religion in Australia and always stayed in touch with Irish culture. I think that helps in settling back, also the fact that I visited very often in recent years. As a result, I'm not a bit lonely. Glenmore is very isolated, but that doesn't worry me. There's nothing much on television. I love the football and I follow Kerry, of course. I loved football in Australia too where I followed the Australian Rules, but I didn't like the way they treated the Irish boys when they were over here last year. They always want to win. Like the golfer, Tiger Woods, he always wants to win too. And the Dublin football team, they always want to win. I know you'll say it's the same with Kerry, but it's not. They'll win the All-Ireland this year again, I'll guarantee you that.

Since I came back I have my life signed away filling up forms. I have to get a recycle sticker for my car; I have to apply for the grant from the ESB and the free telephone allowance. Safe Home has been very good with all of that. There's another form to have the phone connected. Then I'll have to ring *Eircom* for a phone with big letters. I need to buy furniture, but I have to wait on my money from Australia for that. I only brought curtains and saucepans and things like that with me. They charged me two hundred euros at customs. I've found everyone very nice; the people in Social Welfare, the housing association, Brenda Fleming in Safe Home, all the different people I've had to deal with have all been very nice. I was told they'd be odd, but they weren't. I take people as I find them anyhow. I don't like nastiness; I'm not nasty myself. My mother was a very quiet woman so probably I brought it from her.

She had the most beautiful handwriting too. I didn't bring that from her. We were only taught Irish, religion, and the Fenians at school. What good was it to us? When I went to London I couldn't read. You'd be surprised. They didn't give us any education. It was all Irish. What difference was it going to make for us? I love the way they speak it now on that TV channel, TG4, and I love the songs. I don't understand them, but I love them. I love that programme *The Melting Pot* at half past six. I think the Irish are great writers. I met a man in Brisbane and he was Irish and he'd written a book. They've wonderful brains, but they don't work them. I worked hard all my life; that's what keeps me young. We all worked hard all of our lives, not like the young people today.

Ireland is not the same as it used to be. When I came home on holiday two years ago I was waiting for the candles in the window at Christmastime, you know. There was a bridge across the way from us in Castlecove and we used to mark out our tree and the holly bush. And there was a big river we used to cross and we'd get a jam jar and fill it up with sand and stick a candle in it. They were beautiful. We'd get up at half past six in the morning and we'd all go to Mass. Four miles walk to Caherdaniel and four miles back. And we'd have all new shoes and everything, all the best clothes we got in parcels from America. Oh! It was beautiful with all the lights in the windows, as we walked to Mass. And nothing would be done on Christmas Day. Everything would be prepared from the day before, the vegetables and the goose or whatever it was. It was all done. No-one worked on Christmas Day. I remember it well. I missed that the last time, the lights in the windows. It's all electric now. Still.

I'd never go back to Australia. Travel wouldn't worry me anymore. I've been all over; to Singapore, India, Egypt and England and I've travelled all over Australia, even to Adelaide. It wouldn't bother me if I never went anywhere again. I'm eighty-four now and my travelling days are over. I did enough moving around with Jimmy when he was in the Air Force. My daughter is coming next year with her husband and two children. They've good wages the two of them. I flew back by myself in April. I stopped in India again, which was still dreadful. There were police everywhere; of course security is strict all over now. I met a man from Northern Ireland on one of my trips back, Jack is his name. He writes to me still and I think his wife is dead since. I haven't written to him yet to say I'm back for good. I think he might be interested, but I wouldn't get married again.

Another time I was coming home and I met this French girl who read my Tarot cards and she said you're going to meet this man and he'll change your life and I'm thinking who it could be, but I never met him. Then again, it could be any man, it mightn't necessarily mean marriage; it could mean changing my life in another way. On one of my trips home I had met Jeremiah out playing cards and I knew he was a relation and he said any time you want to come home you can stay with me. So maybe he was the man who was to change my life.

If it wasn't for Jeremiah I couldn't have come back this soon. I needed somewhere to stay until the house was ready.

There's plenty of social life here if I want it. There was a lady here one day from the Gaeltacht (Irish speaking region) and she wanted me to go to Dingle on a bus, but I wasn't interested. I don't go out that much. They have bingo in Cahersiveen, but I'm happy here in Glenmore and I don't care if I never left it. Listen to the sounds of the lambs. They're not selling so well now what with competition from New Zealand. I spend my day with housework and gardening; I'm never idle. That's one thing about me. Jeremiah tells me sit down, but there's always something to be done. I cook for him every day; he'll miss me when I'm gone into Waterville and I'll miss him too. I was lucky to be able to stay here with Jeremiah. Maybe he was the man who changed my life after all.

Interviewed at the home of her nephew, Jeremiah Hallesey, in Glenmore, County Kerry, on Wednesday, August 29th, 2007

Cahirdaniel – my home town

MARY ANN KELLY

I came home in March 2007 because I had no where else to go. I was being evicted from my residence in New York and was going to have to move somewhere so I thought, why not Ireland? I was very ill at the time and the transition proved very traumatic. But, thanks to Safe Home, my cousin, Anne, my Franciscan family and my newly-found friends in Kilorglin, I am slowly settling in. Although Kerry is not my county of origin, I was very fortunate to be offered a house here.

I was born in Birr, County Offaly, but lived in Sandycove, County Dublin, for a few years before returning to my mother's home in Crinkle when my father died. He had contacted pneumonia at a very young age and my mother said she went out to make him a cup of tea one day and when she came back he was dead. I don't know how much of that is fantasy or not, but that's what she told me. It was 1946 and I was four years of age; my little sister six months. As a young widow with two young children, my mother had to work and she got a job as a housekeeper for a while, which she thought was beneath her. Then a cousin of her employer came back from New York on a visit and offered to bond her into America. What was she to do? She had no choice. You must remember in the Ireland of 1950 people didn't have choices. Maybe America was great and maybe it wasn't; but it was better than what she had here. She grasped the opportunity and went.

My sister and I stayed on in Crinkle where my mother's family owned a shop that was uniquely Irish. One half was a grocery store and the other side a bar. My father's people also had a shop in Kilbeggan, and his father was an auctioneer. Both sides of the family seemed to have thought my parents were too young and immature to get married and hadn't given their consent. My father, a commercial traveller, was happy go lucky. He liked gambling and having a good time.

I think he disappointed his father, yet when he died his family came very quickly to Sandycove and took his body back to Kilbeggan to be buried. There is some mystery attached to it all that I've never really got to the bottom of, but you can't carry all that anger and resentment around with you. You have to bury it and move on. Meanwhile, my mother had found work as a housekeeper on Long Island and within a year she sent for my sister. I did not follow them for another ten years. I try not to blame my mother for something that happened in my childhood. She would often say maybe she shouldn't have left me.

After my sister left for America my grandfather decided that I should stay with him in Kilbeggan and not be bounced around from one family to another. Even though he hadn't approved of my parents' marriage he was always nice to me. We had a beautiful garden when he was alive where we would go picking strawberries. It was full of flowers and vegetables. He had studied to be a Jesuit during the 1800's and was going to be ordained a deacon, but ended up marrying his brother's fiancé, whom he had met on a visit home. Nonetheless he had got the education, and was very successful in the grocery and real estate business, which was unusual for a Catholic at that time. He would also write letters for all of the people in the locality, and after he died we learned of how he had helped them; how he loaned money for someone to go to England, to get an education, whatever. When he got older he lost his sight and had to have an eye removed. I used to read the newspapers to him and if I was sweeping the floor he'd say, "I might only have one eye, but I can still see the bits you're missing." I stayed on in Kilbeggan, finishing school in the convent with the nuns and passing my Leaving Certificate.

On November 11th, 1959, a couple of months before my eighteenth birthday, I went to America. I flew out on the very last propeller plane, a week before the jets came in. It took eighteen hours via Gander (Newfoundland) and I was sick every hour on the hour. I would loved to have waited for a jet, but my mother wanted me to fly on Veteran's Day, which was an American holiday and she would have the day off. She met me at the airport and put up bond for me. I think that was a very good idea back then that you had to be sponsored by someone already living there. You also had to have a medical and prove that you were not a criminal. I had been christened Mary Philomena Ann and Josephine is my confirmation name, but everybody called me Anne. The doctor at my medical examination said I should simplify it so when I became an American citizen I cut it down to Mary Anne. At first I got a job in *Woolworth's* until my Leaving Certificate came through and then I got hired by a bank, but I was the worst teller they ever had so I had to abandon that for *Metropolitan Life Assurance* on Madison Avenue where I stayed for about six years. All of the young Irish girls started either in the Telephone Company, a bank, or Met Life. They even targeted the Catholic schools for obedient young girls. We had to wear high heels to work, as sneakers didn't become acceptable until after the transit strike in the Sixties, during which everyone had to walk to work.

I lived with my mother in Incarnation Parish on 175th Street and St. Nicholas Avenue which was mainly Irish, Italian and Jewish. It was also a pretty tough neighbourhood and when I was a member of the Legion of Mary we would accompany the local children to Mass. My mother was embarrassed by this. I also joined the Gaelic League at their Bronx branch until it moved up to Westchester, and I danced in *The Jaeger House* ballroom and afterwards frequented the all night coffee shop, *Wrights*, on 86th & Lexington Avenue. There was the German dancehall too, *The Laurel Eye*. Back then we could travel home on the subway at all hours of the night and thought nothing of it. There would always be a group of us together.

After many years I got married, but that ended in annulment. I met Jimmy in this store called *Scottish Products*. My maternal grandfather was a Scotsman who came to Ireland with the Leinster Regiment and I was always interested in Scottish culture – their music and dancing –because of that. Jimmy played the bagpipes. He was Scots American and a non-Catholic. His mother hated Catholics. Her first husband was Italian and every month when she wasn't pregnant he would beat her, so she hated Catholics as a result. She had a mouth on her like a long shore fisherman.

Jimmy and I started dating and after three years we got married at

Thanksgiving. We had a great time at first and I loved going around to all the céilí where he was playing the pipes, but soon things began to go downhill. I knew him for three years, but I didn't really know him at all. After Christmas he announced that his friend, Danny, was moving in with us for a while. Danny was just back from Vietnam and was very much damaged from it. I think Vietnam damaged a lot of people then. He seemed to exert a lot of influence over Jimmy and followed him wherever he went; he was very controlling. I found him two apartments, but he wouldn't leave, and Jimmy didn't insist either. He was completely dominated by this Danny. One night when I came home and found them sitting close together on the couch they made me feel like an intruder in my own home, so I left. I was terribly innocent back then. I was thirty years old so I should've known better, but I hadn't a clue. It didn't occur to me that there was anything strange about it. Danny arrived in January and I left in May. I was working at

Baby Anne in Birr, Co. Offaly

St. Vincent's hospital in the admissions office by this time and it was very upsetting for me. I couldn't tell anyone and my mother was embarrassed that the marriage had ended at all; much less why. I hired a lawyer and started divorce proceedings. It was the lawyer who picked up that Jimmy might be homosexual, but he never admitted it and it was never established that he and Danny had that sort of a relationship. I also tried counselling on the advice of the nuns at the hospital and it was there that I came to realize what the real basis of their friendship might be, but I never had any real proof of it. I had made a huge mistake; a huge error in judgement. He got evicted after I left as they couldn't pay the rent and we lost touch. I got a divorce and eventually an annulment, even though I knew I wouldn't marry

Photo of Mary Anne as a young girl sent to mother in New York

again. In the end it was alright. There are always people who will slide through the cracks. We all make bad choices, but we have to invest in ourselves; in how can we make our lives better.

I moved into a furnished room after my divorce. There was social life for separated women at the time if you could afford it, but I had too many debts. The dancehalls were all finished by then. I was still attached to the Gaelic League and still marching in the St. Patrick's Day parade with them; and I was still involved with the Legion of Mary. I was also a member of the Offaly Association for a while and an officer with the United Irish Counties. It was at this stage too that I registered at Fordham University and started studying for a B.A., which made a big difference to my life; it gave me so much confidence. But, it wasn't until I joined the Franciscans that everything improved. I made loads of friends and enjoyed a great social life with them.

Holy Name Province has its headquarters on 31st Street in Manhattan. The Franciscan Order was established by St. Francis and he also invited secular members to help them with the poor out in the field, as he realized that not everyone could give up everything and leave their families to join the Order. His group was male only and the men built the churches and helped care for the lepers and the sick. St. Clare came along afterwards and started a female sect. Their common belief was that religion was about actively helping others in need; they did not subscribe to the pomposity that governed most other religious orders. That is also the reason I became a secular Franciscan. As well as being a member I worked for the Friars for eight years in their pilgrimage office. Their pilgrimages were a lot of fun; with sing-alongs and music; not just prayer. Eventually they had to close it down as they were not running it as a business, which they should have done. They were not making a profit, as they are too reality oriented. They've also run a bread line since 1932, and operate residences for the homeless particularly those who are certified as mentally ill. They're so action orientated. If someone is hungry, the Franciscans feed them; if they're sick, they try to cure them; if they're homeless, they find them somewhere to live. That's how they operate. Prayer alone is not the answer.

It was St. Francis who stood by me too when I got raped. I had just left St. Vincent's, where I was passed by for promotion, and had moved into an apartment in Queens. The guy who came in to do a paint job raped me for three hours. It was St. Francis who stood by me then. My mother thought it was a shame and didn't want me to press charges; she didn't want me to bring any attention on the family. She said my aunts who had raised me in Ireland would never talk to me again. She'd said the same when I got my annulment, as the Church at home where I had been baptized and confirmed would have been notified and she was horrified that everyone would know. I was lucky I had the Friary; I had my Paternity. They helped me to find a new home; they took me out socially and were always there if I needed someone to talk to.

After that I moved into residential accommodation in The Salvation Army hostel, as I couldn't live by myself anymore. The hostel was in a beautiful location on 39th Street and Lexington Avenue. About 350 people lived there; it was like a college dorm. There was a nice dining-room where we got breakfast and dinner, but we had to share the bathrooms, as an en suite would be $150 more a month and the rent was already $950. I was attending meetings by *New York Women against Rape*, but I found them too negative with women talking about how they couldn't go outside the door. I had to go out because I had to work. Some while later a woman was walking home from Queen of Angels bingo in Sunnyside, a neighbourhood in Queen's, New York, and this fellow grabbed her purse and knocked her down so that she was badly hurt. She reported it and one Irish cop in the precinct put it together that it was the same person as had attacked me. They would never have found him otherwise. I felt I had to go to court for closure, so I did. I testified against him, and he was found guilty. You can either go crazy feeling sorry for yourself or you can say that this too will pass. I didn't have the luxury of giving up work. I didn't have the luxury of feeling sorry for myself. I got the help I needed from the Franciscans. Sure I was angry. Anger is helpful at the beginning but if you hold onto the anger it destroys you. Once he was put in jail that was it for me. It was over.

I graduated in 1980, but never got into social work, which had been my ambition. I had a series of jobs including two years as a reservations clerk with *Aer Lingus* at their office on 42nd Street. Then they moved out to Melville on Long Island and I didn't go with them because it would have been too much hassle getting out there on the railroad. It would have been impossible at the weekends when the LIR (Long Island Railway) were forever rerouting. I left then because I had no choice. The last job I had was for the ASPCA where I was given redundancy instead of disability. I had to have my knee replaced in 1999 and that is when everything started to go down. I was then in an automobile accident and the judge decided that it was not the other driver's fault and denied me compensation, but that's OK too. It was hard to get a job while walking with a cane; there is discrimination even though they say there isn't. It took about a year to get disability and all that time I had no income so that is when I went through all of my money.

New York is a great place, but when you're sick and trying to get on disability and all that nonsense it's very hard. My social security check just about paid the rent. My IRA (Individual Retirement Account) and other pension benefits were dried up with medical bills. I think it was harder for women to make it on their own there. If two of you have an income then basics are covered. Not everyone lives the American dream. I was unfortunate because of my annulment/divorce, the rape, my illness and education, which cleaned up all of my income. It is very expensive in America – I was working full-time and studying at night. I had to take out a student loan, which I've since paid back. It's very hard for people unless they have a lot of money; when you're sick and on disability, it's a mess.

It had been hard for my mother too. She had left a large family behind in Ireland and only knew that one woman who brought her

44

Mary Ann (right) with sister, Carmel

over. She never remarried; she was never interested. She liked New York, and worked many years in a hospital, but she never had the opportunity to return home. She did not have a choice. She was not educated enough to get work in Ireland and it was expensive to travel back and forth. That's one of the great changes in Ireland now; that education is available to everyone and there are more opportunities for people than there were before. I think people who went that time were very brave, as they left their families knowing they might never see them again.

My mother died three years ago aged eighty-four and weighing only eighty-four pounds. She had moved out to my sister, Carmel, in New Jersey and spent her last few months in a nursing home where she needed full-time care. Carmel and I weren't all that close growing up, as my mother always came between us, but now we get on better. We talk to each other every week.

I was living on 39th Street on September 11th, 2001, and saw on television the first plane flying into the World Trade Center. After breakfast I went upstairs to the 17th floor roof garden with some of the other residents and watched in horror as the second plane crashed and the building subsequently collapsed. The Franciscans immediately went downtown to help the victims; providing bottles of water and offering counselling. I wanted to help, but was due to go into hospital a few days later to have my knee replaced for the second time so I couldn't stay on my feet for very long. Nevertheless, I wanted to be with people who understood so I went down to 4.30 Mass that afternoon where Father Russel Becker was celebrating. When he prayed for Father Mykal Judge, a member of our Church and Chaplain to the Fire Department who had been killed that morning while administering the Last Rites at Ground Zero, it was like the world stopped. Mykal Judge was the craziest man on two feet. You could tell him anything. He was so popular and loved wherever he went. Hilary

Clinton spoke at his funeral, which was covered by close circuit television. She said she'd never forget his kindness to her when her husband was going through hard times. He knew she had very little support and like a true Franciscan he was there to do what he could. That's why I love my crazy, lovely family.

Last September I suffered my own personal dilemma when The Salvation Army decided to sell the hostel. It was prime property and prime location and worth millions of dollars. The previous February they were planning a reunion party for all past residents; in September they decided to sell. I came home one day and there was an eviction notice pinned to my door. They were actually closing down the building. It was a shock. It had been so convenient; everything was within reach especially my doctors and the Franciscans. It was horrifying to lose my home. Where was I going to go? My cousin, Anne, back in Ireland, came up with Safe Home. I always had that sort of relationship with Anne where I could pick up the phone and tell her I was coming over and that was never a problem. That often happened when I worked with *Aer Lingus* and I might get a last minute stand-by flight to Ireland. She would always be there to pick me up at Dublin airport no matter what time I was arriving. My cousin, Tom, in London, was the same. For some reason there was always a connection there. She asked me if I'd like to come home and I said the Celtic tiger's blood is too rich for me. She said hold on we might be able to work something out. She told me to get on a plane and have my friends clean up my room and save anything they thought I would want. I never though of coming home before, because I just couldn't afford it. Moving around was not going to be an option for me with my leg, and I was going to have to move somewhere, it might as well be Ireland. Father Colm Campbell at The New York Irish Center on Long Island helped me with all the paperwork at that end and never charged me. It's unbelievable all the help I got; it's like a miracle. I'm so grateful to all these people.

I came back to Kerry to be near Anne and have settled here in Kilorglin. I miss my friends in New York, but the people in Kilorglin have been wonderful to me. I'm having a great time. I go to Mass and everyone says hello. I've made a very good friend, Colette, and her husband. We go to bingo every week on a little bus and the driver, Johnny, leaves us back to the door. Last week I won one hundred euros so my luck must be turning. Then Sunday night at *The Manor Inn* there's dancing and you can go along and dance or just listen to the music or whatever you want, all for five euros. I joined the choir in the church so I've made friends through that too. I also joined a writer's group in the local library and I'm going to take part in the Christmas pantomime. I'm one hundred percent better now. I was a mess when I got here first because I had been given such little notice when they sold my building. I think the air is better here and the fact that I'm not under stress.

Being a member of the Franciscans has also helped me in my move to Ireland. The Franciscans are a real family. For instance my friend, Kevin, contacted the Provincial here in Killarney and told them that a secular Franciscan was coming home from America and asked them to look out for me. When I walked into Killarney Priory, I was greeted with, "Oh, you're the lady we've been waiting for." They told me there was a meeting on the first Friday of every month and I've been going there ever since. I was able to transfer membership; it was no problem. We support each other; we look out for the other; it's a family affair. It's not like as my mother used to say, "Threepence looking down on tuppence." Everyone is the same. I miss those people. That's what I miss most about New York, my friends and the Franciscans.

Mary Ann (left) with her crazy lovely Franciscan family before leaving New York

Before my return last February I hadn't been home in a while because I was so sick. There are a lot of changes, but who'd want it go back to the way it was in the Fifties? People didn't have choices then about emigration; they just had to go. There was nothing here. I went to America because my mother and sister were there. People get nostalgic about turf fires and all that, but they forget about how hard they had it. Trying to live in the past is useless. We can learn from the mistakes of the past, but we can't live there. People say now that everyone had better values back then, but so what when they were starving, and the house was freezing in the winter? And they didn't all have values; not even some of the clergy.

Being near Anne now is wonderful. I sometimes spend an afternoon with her in Carralake. I love to sit there and look out at the mountains and the lake; it is so tranquil. Her brother-in-law moved a couple of months ago and his furniture became available. Another relative put them in a truck and brought them over to me. I had everything. And it was all done for me. I came home not knowing if I'd have anything and now I have everything I need. Safe Home was so helpful and I'm very grateful to that programme. They applied for me to get a subsidy on my rent, which I received, and helped me apply for a PPS (social security) number. There is a lot of paperwork at first and the welfare officer only comes to Kilorglin on a Wednesday and Thursday so you have to nab him then. When I get my travel pass it will be easier for me to get to Killarney. I can't afford seven euros a day to go there by bus. The cost of living is high here, but you have to learn to manage it. My biggest expense at the moment is medical, which is a major problem until I get my medical card. The way I look at it is, if you want something in life you have to put yourself in the way of getting it, and you have to do what people want in order to facilitate getting what you want.

It is very stressful having to move from one home to another, but I had no choice, I was being evicted. I was going to have to move somewhere and no matter where I went I imagine it would have been as hard as coming here. Then I was in very bad health and I was without my medication for some time so that was very worrying too. I think the main thing I would say to anyone moving back is to make sure you will be near family and friends, as you are definitely going to need help to settle in. Then you will need to sort out Social Welfare and you will need help with that, as it can be very complicated. And you have to forget about the place you are leaving behind, because more than likely you won't be going back. We can't change history and we can't compare today with yesterday. I just feel that it is a miracle for me, given that I had nowhere else to go, that I've come home and the fact that everything has worked out so well so far must mean it was meant to be for me. It might not be meant for everybody.

The last day I spent in New York was Ash Wednesday 2007. I was at the Friary for ashes and we went to lunch afterwards. We were all very sad because I was thirty years in that Church; it was home. Now I have had to create another home here. We have to create a safe space for ourselves where our spirit is nourished, because when your spirit is nourished it can grow. I can do that again here in Ireland, I hope.

Interviewed at The Mount Brandon Hotel, Tralee, County Kerry, on Friday, June 8ᵗʰ, 2007

DAVID SINNOTT

I came home in January 2007, but it was on a Saturday evening in March 1955 that we left Wexford, my friend and I. We cycled into Ferns and left our bikes at the station to be picked up later. Then we took the train to Dun Laoghaire to link up with the boat to Holyhead. It was like going to Croke Park. When you asked someone in Dublin how to get to Croke Park, they'd say follow the crowd. Well it was the same in Dun Laoghaire. Everyone getting off that train was going for the boat. It was absolutely packed. We could hear the cattle roaring down below. They'd be going over to England for the slaughter. I suppose it was as strange for them as it was for us. That time I used to take a few bottles of Guinness, so that helped me a little with the leaving, but the bloke who came with me never took a drink in his life. Even on the boat he was never tempted. He was only seventeen at the time and he told me he'd left without telling his mother and father. I was dumbfounded. When his father died years later I explained to the mother that I didn't bring him with me; it was his own idea. I don't know if she believed me or not.

After getting off the boat, after travelling all night, you'd be completely stupefied, as green as the grass in the field. I had been up to Dublin a few times to see the Gaelic games when the county would be playing, but that was the farthest I'd been until I landed in England. I had the sister's address written down and there were about five busstops where we got off the train. I asked this bus conductor for directions. He told me to take the Number 31. We were standing at the first stop we came to until the conductor shouted at us, "It's the third one." And when we looked up sure enough there was the Number 31, written on the third stop, but sure we'd never even seen a bus before, never mind a stop. We asked the conductor where to get off and found ourselves in front of a greengrocery shop. We had the right address, the right road, how could it be a greengrocer's? Now I couldn't figure this out. The shop was closed too because it was a Sunday so we didn't know what to do. A lady came along eventually and told us we had to go down a side street where the door was and take a stairs up to the flat above the greengrocers where my sister lived. We stayed there only one or two nights, as she didn't have the room to put us up.

We moved from there into a massive, great big house full of lodgers, where we had our meals and all like. The landlady was a complete and utter alcoholic. She used to come in legless and she had two daughters who were nearly as bad as her. One thing she did do, however, was get both of us a job in a dairy. She knew one of the Governors and he took us on. We worked in it for a while and the money was great, but it wasn't for us. We had both worked on farms in Ireland so we were more used to the outdoors. Eventually we got a job with a small builder. It was what we wanted, with more wages. We were happier doing that; it was harder work, but we were happier doing it. The money on the buildings wasn't all that great but a lot better than it was here. I'll tell you what I was getting now before I left, working on a farm up the road here in Ballyregan, not far from Boolavogue, owned by English people. I got three pounds ten shillings in the old money, and I had to feed myself on it.

Manchester was fine, but I liked to keep on the move like; I had to keep moving, I don't know why. The bloke that I started working for was a gentleman. He had a small business building garages and we got on great. He'd promise you the earth, but give you nothing, but he'd give you the week's wages like, you were sure of that. He came from outside Manchester and when that job was done he had another couple of jobs down in Stockport and he asked us if we'd like to carry on working for him and we did. We stayed with two sisters from Cavan and they had two big houses with about thirty-five blokes in each, lodgers like. Massive, massive houses they were. And they had families in them as well. This woman now where we lived, she and her husband had split up and she had three kids and this other man was living with her. The three kids were all belonging to the husband, but she was just living with this bloke now. They were sort of trying to keep it quiet, you know, because there'd be a poor view of that.

There was great camaraderie that time among the Irish. There was never a bit of bother. People drank. They were working very hard especially on the railway, maybe seven days a week maintaining lines and all that sort of stuff and they'd have to travel miles, but they were on good money. At the weekends then they'd go to the pub. We drank mostly in Irish pubs where you'd always meet someone from home. There was the odd one looking for trouble after a few drinks, and there might be a fight; then again the next evening they'd go drinking again and be the best of friends. When you're away like that you'd become closer. Stockport was about eleven miles outside Manchester and it was full of Irish. There were plenty of Irish girls around too. We used to go back to the Irish dancehalls in Manchester especially to *The Astoria*; that was the best. We used to get a bus up there and they'd run a coach from the dancehall for people who were coming back to Stockport. The dancehalls were everywhere, even in the Church halls there was dancing that time, Irish dances like you know. It went mad for a few years, and then it all died away again. I believe there's only the odd one left now. In London you had *The Galtymore* in Cricklewood. That's all knocked down now, but they have a new one built up the back. All of the Irish bands were there. It was 1955 and you might as well have been back in Ireland. When I was dancing here all the top bands used to be there in Arklow. That ended up as a bingo hall. There was another one down at Courtown Harbour called *The Tara* and a pub beside it with the same name. The dancehalls were massive back then. There was no such thing as a bar in the hall, only tea or coffee or soft drinks were served; lemonade and stuff like that. After years I went back and they had a bar in it. I was surprised.

I'll tell you how I left Stockport now. There were blokes who used to work for this firm putting pipes in the ground for the telephone company. They were stopping in the house we were in and they said they were leaving Stockport for Coventry and they needed eight people. They told us if we came with them we'd get the lodging money paid. Once you moved with them from one town to another you'd get the lodging paid. We moved to Coventry with them anyhow and worked with them for years. Coventry was alright; full of Irish again.

Everywhere in England was full of Irish, from every county. It's funny but I was one of those people who should never have left Ireland, you know what I mean. My heart and soul was here; sure all my memories were here. Even now like, I think back, all my memories go back to where I came from.

I was born in Ferns, over the road there, on the 4th of February, 1934. There were six of us and we lived in a little cottage belonging to a farmer. I came third with two girls in front of me. We had a little brother who got double pneumonia and died at eleven months. I remember it to this day, you know, because he had just started to walk. My father was a cobbler. He could do anything. I don't know how none of it rubbed off on me, but the man could turn his hand to absolutely anything. He was gifted in every department, but repairing boots was his main livelihood. That time it was a big thing because nobody could throw away old shoes and buy new ones the way they do today. People used come from miles around up to the house with their boots. We had piles of them. When I was starting to grow up like and had a bicycle, I used to have a carrier at the back where I would tie the boots and travel miles on the bike dropping them off to the customers and they'd give me a couple of pence.

During war time I often looked out the door and saw the German and English boats aflame out in the sea. In later years I told blokes in the pubs in England that I had a war injury. There was this hill near us and I'd be up there snaring rabbits and one evening didn't a German bomber come around the side of it, and I'd never seen one before in me life. The pilot was after being shot over the Irish Sea and had only three wheels left. He was down that low I could see him and he was waving at me to shift the cattle below in the field so that he could land and now I think he might have been trying to get rid of the bombs before he landed. He eventually crash landed down near the sea here and was later taken prisoner to the Curragh. I, meanwhile, got such a fright that I ran and dived into a big ditch of bushes and briars and got all cut and scraped. That's how I got wounded in the Second World War.

I stayed at home until I was twenty-one because that was sort of the done thing. Once you turned twenty-one you could do what you liked. That was what I understood anyhow. My two sisters had gone over to an aunt of mine in Manchester and neither of them was married by the time I was ready to leave so I wrote to one of them and told her I was coming. A while later I was at the pictures in a town about sixteen miles from here with this bloke and I told him I was thinking about going to England. He said if you hang on another month I'll be along with you. That was it then. But, I can't believe sometimes when I'm driving around with my friends here the length I used to come on the bike. You might see one or two cars on the road that time; the odd person might have a car, like. When I think of all the miles and miles I travelled on the bike, it was unbelievable.

The drink blanked out the memories. I suppose that's why a person did drink. I thought myself that I couldn't live without drink. I had to have a drink to even socialize with people. I thought it was a way of life. And once you were drinking then you just concentrated on working to get money for drink. It wasn't until I had a treble by-pass in 1991 that the doctor told me to give it up. He said that the smoking and drinking was eighty percent of my problem, clogging up the arteries. He said if you want to have a couple of pints it's not a problem, if you want to have a small whiskey, that's fine. But, I said to tell you the truth I'd never touch a drink or cigarette again as long as I lived for the simple reason that I was never a man who could have one or two. If I went into a pub at all I'd stay till closing. I'd have no chance now because they're open twenty-four hours a day, I'd be dead long ago. Once I started I couldn't stop. People wouldn't admit it that time, but a lot of us were alcoholics. There's no two ways about it.

I left Coventry with a bloke from Meath. We left one morning on the train and we didn't know where we were going. We ended up in Luton, not far from London. I stayed around that area for a good while working mostly on the buildings again, and in a few factories too. Once you got the hang of it, it was easy. You'd go in for an interview and personnel would see you. There could be fifty people waiting. There was a young fellow interviewing me one time, and as soon as he heard I was from Ireland he said sure you only want to be in here for the winter months and I said no, I want a job to stop in. But, he knew from experience that the Irish men just wanted to be indoors for the winter; that they'd be gone again in the summer. They'd be out on the buildings again. Do you know what you could do and I done it myself? You could walk out of a job there and walk fifty yards up the road and get another one.

I was all over London, but spent most of my time in Kilburn. Little Ireland they used to call it, County Kilburn. There were Irish from every county there. There are still a lot of them there; I'd still know a good few. But one time you'd meet new people every week, young people. I was always straight with them and they always respected me for that. I met a bloke from Carlow the next county up. He was as green as I was when I went over, as honest as the day was long, you know the way we were brought up like. I'd often meet him in the pub and he always respected me for the advice I gave him, which was sometimes you have to tell a little white lie, you can't be too honest. If someone came up to me and said will you give me a fiver till tomorrow I'd give it to him and then he'd be gone. I'd never see him again. So I had to learn how tell the little white lie. I never got married. I think the drink sort of took care of that too. I had plenty of girlfriends and all that and I think the drink put them off. From what people said to me when I was on the drink I wasn't a very nice person. At least they had the

David (left) with Lucy and friends in Kilburn Park

guts to tell me. When I went off it then I could see it for myself. You're not the same person with the drink, but you can't see that. Moving around would put the girls off as well. I had loads of girlfriends before I went to England. A couple of them I wouldn't have minded settling down with. You'd never know, I might bump into them now again!

I used to follow the county in the games; I'd be up like a lunatic to Dublin to see them. But I wouldn't blow a gasket over them now. I listened to the game last Sunday driving around in my friends' car; they were getting hammered by Kilkenny in the first half and I said turn it off for the second half. I used to be interested. I used to know fellows up from Buffer's Alley, the Doran's, who played. Some of their sons are playing now. I used to play up in their field. I went to school in a place I couldn't even spell for you. For education I got none. The problem was they spent too much time teaching us Irish. We didn't speak it at home. I couldn't pick it up; I might as well have been learning French, but I spent all my time trying to learn that like and I used to get the head beaten off me over it. Then when I left school at fourteen I couldn't read or write. I was often ashamed like, I couldn't read the newspaper or anything. Now I can; just picked it up myself. I went to work right away. I even worked before I left school. As far back as I can remember I never did anything but work. In the summertime my father would take us out to thin turnips, mangles and beet; we'd take on fields of them. Then you'd have to get sticks for the fire; there was no electricity that time or gas or coal.

I came home on a holiday the first year and then for years I didn't come at all. Then I was in a place in London one time, stopping with a Mayo woman who was married to a Pole. She was a terribly nice woman. If I was sitting in the room on a Wednesday night she'd come up and ask me if I wanted a couple of quid for the pub. There was no telly that time. She'd say give it to me Friday. I met some great people and I met some bad ones too. Some of your own could be bad. I was in this place anyhow and one Monday night I went to bed early, I'd had a heavy weekend, and a knock came to the door and it was the landlady. She said there was some bad news for me; there were policemen at the door. I said I didn't do anything wrong but she said, no, it wasn't like that, it was news from Ireland. Can you tell me, I said, before I go down to the door. Your mother is dead, she said. That was 1961 and that was my next time home. It was a sad time, but the drink deadens the sadness. I think that's why a lot of people drink. A long time after that my father died in London. He was one of the first people that had the heart by-pass performed by an Egyptian doctor there in Harefield. He was in bad health and my sister talked him into going over. He only got a couple of years out of the plastic valve and stayed in London the whole time until his death. My younger brother came over with him and there was nobody left in the home place. There was nobody left in Ireland. All six of us emigrated, three boys and three girls. Two of the girls are dead now, the eldest and the youngest.

The turning point in my life was when I had the operation in 1991. I was drinking heavy at the time and working hard. I often heard it said that you have to go through a bad experience to get good. What happened to me changed my life anyhow. I took bad one Christmas when I was stopping with my friends. They rushed me in an ambulance to Norwich Park hospital where I immediately went into cardiac arrest. The doctor said it was fifty-fifty whether I'd be there by morning. I was in Intensive Care for a few weeks and I told the doctor that I was having the same symptoms my father had before his by-pass. She said by telling her that, I might have saved my life. She made an appointment in the Royal Free Hospital for me to see a heart specialist who told me I'd have to have major surgery. He had a real bad stutter, but he was a gentleman. He said you'll have to have an angiogram, after which he told me I'd have to have a by-pass. While I was recovering, I was down in the basement of the hospital and there were two people being wheeled out every hour. It was the most frightening experience of my whole life. There was a young girl there from Wales looking after us; she was only seventeen years of age and she took care of eight of us, all on monitors. I thought she must surely be an angel. When I was her age I was out going mad. She was absolutely one hundred and twenty five percent. After a couple of weeks they took me up to a ward and there was a Jew and an Arab and they hated one another's guts; it was like they were going to war. I lost the head with them

Back home in Gorey, at last

one night; here we all were practically dying and they were going on about something that happened hundreds of years before. It's the same today with Iraq; all that killing for nothing. What does the suicide bomber get out of life? Why doesn't the man who brainwashed him go down and do it?

There was an awful lot of brainwashing in this country too, through religion. I am not a devout Catholic. I didn't give it up; I just never started. Even when I was a kid it never got through to me. And I'll tell you what really knocked it on the head altogether. As I said already my two sisters went over to England before me. When she was eighteen the eldest girl came back one Saturday evening with a two week old baby boy. Nobody knew she was having a baby. She took a taxi out to the house and I seen it come down the road. My mother and father took her in and I remember the next morning they went off early to see the priest before Mass. I was only about twelve or thirteen, and there used to be a bunch of us down the back of the Church planning where we'd go that afternoon like, what match we'd be watching, whatever. I could hear the priest getting louder and louder and saying something about all the young Irish girls going to England to have babies and the next thing he let a roar, "This is the first bastard to come into my parish." I'll never forget it. It was the very same as if the roof of the church had come down on my head like. I thought to myself this can't be real. I was dumbfounded. Later that day he came down to the cottage and couldn't apologize enough. I don't know what changed his mind, but it never changed mine. After that I was finished with religion. I still say my prayers and that; I pray for all my friends, but I'm not a practicing Catholic.

After the operation I started to think that I'd have to have a base in life. Even if I won the lottery and travelled all over the world, it wouldn't be a life, I'd still need a base to come back to. Coming home

58

is everything. Somewhere you can-turn the key and it's yours. I went most of my life without that. Stopping in digs you're so controlled by everybody. I always either stayed in digs or a room; never got around to getting a flat. The easiest thing that came to me was what I took. My life was surrounded by drink. I didn't have money for anything else. The majority of blokes I met in England were the same. They wouldn't admit it, but they were alcoholics, and I think we would have been the same no matter where we went. A certain amount of it was from loneliness, there was no television in the room at that time, nowhere to sit and chat, so the pub was an outlet. You went down there and met friends or maybe had a game of cards or darts or something. And the people who were there if they'd money in their pockets they'd buy you a drink to keep you there. Ireland has a lot to answer for as regards alcohol and now it's getting to the women too.

The reason I finally came back to Ireland for good was because of these friends I had in Kilburn, Frank and Peggy Murphy, who had come home to Ferns when they retired. They'd been in England the same length as me and they invited me over on a holiday. It was twenty-seven years since I'd been here and I fell in love with the place all over again. I came over for two weeks and stayed a month. It was the scenery that did it for me. You see when I was drinking I didn't notice it. After you had your breakfast you'd go straight to the pub. When people would ask you about the holiday all you could tell them about was the pub. We never appreciated the scenery. Frank and Peggy drove me all around on that holiday revisiting all of the old haunts of my youth. We went to the seaside at Courtown and to the place where *Saving Private Ryan* was filmed, near Curracloe. As far as you could see on either side of you was sand. Two little boys were building a turtle and a mermaid while I was collecting seashells. I looked around and I thought I'd really like to live here. When I went back I went down to the Irish Centre in Camden Town and discovered this Safe Home place. There was a girl working there and her father was from Ferns. We got on the same as if we knew one another all of our lives. She did everything for me; it was unreal. She even let me use the phone to ring the Murphy's and she rang the local Council here looking for a house for me. It took about five years for me to get back. But, I didn't follow it up as much as I should have done because of Lucy.

I was stopping with these people that time; he was from Laois there up the road and she was from Belfast. They were both on their second marriage and they had some grandchildren. They had a friend who had been back in Ireland where her brother bred Jack Russells and she picked out the smallest of the litter and brought it back to the grandchildren. I was out walking one night and when I came back there was the little pup, only a few weeks old, lying there on the floor. I picked it up and fell in love straight away. That was Lucy. I started bringing her down to the park every night for a walk and every time she saw me she would run to me. The little children couldn't understand how she was so fond of me. And that was the reason I stayed, for that little dog. We'd had her for nine and a half years until she had to be put down. The Vet gave us a little box and a blanket and we buried her in the back garden. Then I walked across the road to where I was staying and there was a letter on the floor from the Safe Home people with a photograph of this place here.

When I told Frank and Peggy about it, they came over and met Matty and phoned me up and told me it was beautiful. Then Matty, (Matthew Lacey) who is in charge here, rang me up and said I was to come over and take a look around. I was coming on a holiday anyhow so I stopped off to see the place and I thought it was like an oasis. I sat down with Matty, who is one hundred percent, and had a cup of tea here and he said it's yours if you want it. I couldn't believe it. I went back then to England to sort myself out. It took a while to get everything done; to sort out the pension and that, and I was ready to come back just after Christmas last.

When I had my health I never thought of coming home. I suppose you get into a way of life. My father wasn't here anymore and the younger brother sold the home place for a couple of hundred quid. If he had to leave it a bit longer we'd have made a fortune. The woman who owns it now, she's a hundred percent like, and you wouldn't believe the changes she's made to the place. The only thing I recognized were the trees I had planted myself. Lord Save Us they were up to the heavens. They're up about fifty foot in the air now. What I'm trying to say is there wouldn't have been any reason for me to come home when I had my health because I didn't have any family here and I didn't have any home here either.

I always regretted leaving Ireland. I think the changes are great; you've got to come up with the times, heven't you, like? England never crosses my mind now, even though I have friends there and all like. I don't know if I'll ever go back. I had a lot of friends when I was drinking and then when I stopped they were not the friends I thought they were. Not like the Murphys.

The way I take life now is one day at a time. Since the operation I don't even think ahead or behind me, what I've done, I've done. Maybe if I hadn't my friends in Ferns to go around with it would be a different story but the people here I get on great with them. There's no problem there like. And I've been feeling great since I came back, getting the best of grub and everything. I fed myself always when I was in the digs and things. I had to look after myself. The doctor said you shouldn't eat this and you shouldn't eat that and here I'm eating everything. I go for walks now. I go down the road and come back and have my dinner at one, then supper at five. I have my own room with the television and all.

Life is good in Gorey. Life is what you make it anyway, no matter where you go and you can't take it for granted. It's a great plus having Frank and Peggy; having friends from England. They've been back about five years now and couldn't settle at first. They nearly sold up and went back one time, but now they're glad they didn't. It takes a while. I wouldn't leave this place now; I'll finish my days here. Everyone says hello, how are you, nice day. If you spoke to someone in England like that, they'd run away from you; they'd think you were after something. When you get close to dying you start thinking there's more to life than drink, and work, and stopping on your own. Life is good in Gorey because I don't take it for granted.

**Interviewed at his home in Gorey, County Wexford,
on Friday April 20th, 2007**

ELLEN ANN GÖTZNER

I grew up in Gurranabraher at the top of Cork city. That time it was fantastic. We used to play up in the Shandon graveyard and all we were afraid of was seeing a man going to the toilet. But, I love it here on White Street too, where I've been since I came home from Germany in January 2007. I had become homesick for Ireland after my husband, Con, died in 2003. Then my dog died and I was very lonely altogether. I had no children you see and I always said I'd come home when Dusty died. We were out shopping one day and he was knocked down by a car. I brought home *seine eschen*, (his ashes) after having him cremated and was happy enough then. I brought Con's remains home even though he was German and he's buried up in St. Catherine's.

My father died in 1961 and my mother in 1964. I was only fifteen years of age and had to take care of my nine brothers and sisters. There were eleven of us altogether, but my eldest sister grew up *bei* (with) my grandmother. I went to school in St. Vincent's Convent, but, I didn't stay there too long, as my father had motor neuron disease and I was kept out of school a lot to help my mother. I was up before the Courts twice for that and fined a shilling the second time. I eventually left school when I was fourteen years of age and started work in the Cork Shoe Company, which my father, a shoemaker, had started with a Mr. Duggan. Then my mother who was asthmatic died of a heart attack and I had to take over the housekeeping altogether. I don't remember playing outside at all when I was a child. I was always working.

When the children had all gone to school I started working in the Orthopaedic Hospital, which was just up the alley from us. At first I only went in cleaning when they were short and then I got a full-time job in the canteen. It was a great way for me to meet some girls because I had no social life up to that. We would go dancing in the ballrooms, to *The Arcadia* and *The Majorca*, and I loved all the big bands, especially Dickie Rock and Joe Dolan.

Then Konrad (Con) came along. I met him in a bar called *The Bodega* up on Oliver Plunkett Street; that time it had a very bad name, but there was always a good sing-song. I had got talking to a German girl there called Barbara and I was to meet her for coffee one day, but the boat on which her husband used to *kapitän* (captain) had to go out early and she sent Konrad and another man down with a note to me. I didn't fancy him at first because he was big, you know, but he was nice so I agreed to go out with him. You don't hurt a person that's nice. I was about twenty-four years of age and he was the same age. He was also an orphan like me, and had the same name as my father – Con, as did his father before him. His mother was called Annie like mine. We were tangled up from the very beginning.

Con was lovely. His English wasn't great at first, but he wrote straight away and I still have every letter he sent me. As time went on his English got better and after three months it was almost perfect. He worked on a ship called *The Visor* that brought cars over from the *Ford's* car plant in Dagenham, outside London. They would dock in Cork once a week. I hadn't the nerve to say I wouldn't meet him and after a while he grew on me then. He was someone I could trust and he never tried to do anything to me, you know what I mean. We met in February and got married in December. When he proposed I said I have to meet your family first, as how can I marry you when I don't even know who you are? He brought me home with him to Bremen that July. He only had a stepmother there really. I was afraid because I'd never slept with him, but he said that was alright; that she was Catholic and didn't believe in things like that either. My friend, Barbara, had already told me about the anti-baby pill, but I said not to worry that there'll be nothing happening. Con used to often tease me about that. He'd say, "There'll be nothing happening," and I'd say, "No, there'll be nothing happening." Back then I wouldn't even stand with a fellow too long kissing him in case something happened. I knew the babies came from inside, but I didn't know how they got there and how it happened, I didn't know. I always saw my mother with a big belly, so I knew there was a baby in there, but that was all I knew. My husband had to explain everything to me on my wedding night. There was nobody in Ireland that time to explain. It was awful.

We got married in the Church of the Ascension, on December 7th, 1974, and all the patients from the Orthopaedic came in their wheelchairs to see me. The reception was in *The Country Club Hotel* in Montenotte, and cost one hundred and seventy six pounds for forty-four people, which included the toast. A round of drink for everyone afterwards came to £51.40. Con paid for it all. I have the album here and all of the bills, even for the honeymoon night in *The Imperial Hotel* in Cork city, which cost £7.29. There was a bible beside the bed and I pretended to be reading it half the night! I got a loan of my dress and I got a present of the cake. My uncle gave me away and a very nice man, Fr. Cashman, married us.

I had a very happy marriage and I was very lucky. At first Con came to stay with us because I couldn't leave until all the children had finished school. We had a great laugh. He loved living here and he always said we'd come back when he retired. He found it hard to get a job, as he didn't have a work permit, and could only stay six months at a time. He did work for a while in a metal factory in Blackpool, but he cut his hand on one of the machines and had to leave. He didn't want to go back to Germany, but felt he had to. He wrote then to say he was too lonely on his own and I'd had a miscarriage, so I took some time off work and went over in September 1975. I said I'd be back in a few months and I stayed for thirty-two years.

I loved Germany. We lived in a lovely seaside town in Cuxhaven, by Hamburg. I had brought nothing with me, not even a spoon. I had to go to *Karstadt* (a department store) and buy basic kitchen utensils and a blow-up mattress. We only stayed in that first flat about ten months because the man across the road was always drinking and we moved into another where we spent eight years. After that we rented a house. Con wanted to buy, but I wouldn't, because I never thought I was staying there, ever. Sometimes we looked at houses, but

I'd say, "No, Con, I'm not staying here." I liked it and the people were friendly, but I never thought I was staying. I worked in a tin factory by the next town, Sahlenburg, for fifteen years, packing tins. I earned very good money there, as I'm not afraid of work at all. I went looking for the job myself; walking into the factory and insisting on speaking to someone who spoke English. I had a rabbit coat on me and it was pouring rain so I looked like a drowned rabbit when I got there. A man came out to speak to me and I said I needed a job there because I'd heard they paid well and I had to pay the rent. I used to speak that way you see, I was very forward, and what do I know? He took me on straight away. I heard after he was the head fellow; that he wouldn't normally meet the workers, but it was on account of the English that I was brought to him. So I met the wrong fellow in one way and the right fellow in the end.

Con first worked in *Rathaus* (the City Hall) as a *büromensch* (office clerk), but he didn't like being on land so much. He enquired at the *Arbeitsamt* (job centre) about going back to school and at first they said he didn't stand a chance. He wasn't very outspoken, but I was. I was recovering from a miscarriage and I got up out of my bed and went down to the job centre and insisted on speaking to someone

My beautiful Bavaria

65

in English. I met the top man, again, and he said he'd see what he could do. Sure enough Con got accepted to study engineering. First he had to learn tool making; then he had to go to sea for two years practice and then do some more semesters at school. He eventually qualified as Chief Engineer and got a job with *The Viking Bordeaux*, a 180 passenger ship, which was based in the Canary Islands. We had a good life even though there wasn't always much money, especially when he was studying. I would go down to the market on a Saturday just before it closed when everything would be much cheaper.

It was very hard at first. I used to have my bags packed every day and if Con even said boo to me I'd tell him I was gone. I missed everything. Cork was a lovely city then and I missed the way of the people. Although I'm after getting out of that way now and I'm not getting back into it. In Germany I learnt to save and not to spend above my means. I budgeted every month and paid my bills first. Here they take out a loan from the Credit Union even for a holiday. I didn't come home one time for seven years because I didn't have the money and I wouldn't take out a loan, even though I had homesick. Every time I saved up to come home, the car broke down or something else happened and I had to get it fixed. The Germans are very friendly but they're very straight. They're not as hospitable as the Irish, but they're more genuine. Here they'd feed you, but they talk about you after. I goes mad with that.

We lived on a lovely street in Cuxhaven with only six houses and we were very friendly with all of our neighbours. We'd meet to celebrate birthdays and socialized mainly in each other's homes. Somebody always had birthday. When we were younger we'd go to the pubs and have a laugh, but after thirty we'd mainly go out eating and then of course I travelled a lot with my husband. I went on river cruises with him to Denmark, Sweden, and Finland, and we took the Baltic Odyssey cruise to St. Petersburg in Russia several times. Another time I flew to Greece and met up with him there. That was a fantastic trip. A pilot boat took me out to the main ship and these two dogs were barking at me, as I tried to climb up the ladder in a short skirt. In the end I had to hoist the skirt up and run up the lad-

Der Kapitän

der to get away from the dogs. I love animals, but was terrified of these dogs. The men were shouting "Götzner, only your wife would do that." I forgets some of the trips now but I loved them all. I was in Russia twice, Bornholm in Denmark and Oshiwaya, the furthest town in the world. You have to cross over the *Aquator* (Equator) to get there. I always had homesick for Dusty though, as he couldn't travel with us. One Christmas Con was docked in Hamburg and I went on board for dinner with him. I snuck Dusty in with me and there were TV cameras everywhere and I trying to hide the dog! Another time his ship was docked in Ireland on Christmas Eve so I got to eat Christmas dinner at home in Cork.

German food is lovely and I loved cooking there. I can get most of the ingredients in the English Market over there on Patrick and Prince's Streets; there's about four or five doors into it. I cooks sauerkraut sometimes, and bratwurst, a German sausage, and this dish with mincemeat and onions, paprika and other spices mixed in with breadcrumbs and an egg. In Germany we always beat up an egg and spices and *knoblauch* (garlic), and dip the chop in it before frying on the pan. It was like a schnitzel; it tastes better and looks nicer on the plate and everything. When they makes the chop here there's nothing on it. You have to use sauce then to get a taste out of it. I much prefer the German way of cooking. And of course now they have *Lidl* and *Aldi* here. I used to do all my shopping by them in Germany. Food is much cheaper over there anyhow and you get much more for your euro in general.

I never really drank, but I do smoke, preferably German cigarettes. I'm on my second book now to give them up – *Help me I'm Smoking* – but it hasn't worked yet. I was probably drunk once. They drinks a lot of wine in Germany and a good bottle would cost two fifty, three euros. I always bought German beer for Con, as there are no chemicals in it. Over there they always have drink in the house and you'd always offer alcohol to a visitor, but I don't like doing that here unless I know the person can go around with it; handle it or what do I know. There is a lot of alcoholism in Germany too, but most of them I knew were dry now; that means they don't drink no more. But, they're very open about it there, whereas here they'd be hiding it and they don't get over it then. Here they just drink and drink and drink. I have no mind for going into bars, but I like a glass of white wine with water, which we called *wein shorle*. Vedle then, I don't know how you say it, was wine without water. I knew a lot of Scottish there, but not Irish. It was only in the last few years that they started celebrating St. Patrick's Day. I used go see this group called *The Irish Paddies*. Con came one time, but he didn't like that it was in a bar, but I loved their singing, so I would go with one of my neighbours. We'd have a good old laugh. They used sing good old Irish songs and the place would be black. We'd have to go to the bar two hours before they started just to get a corner, and we daren't go to the toilet or we'd never get back in. You couldn't fall down because you'd be all scrunched in together. They were all German fellows in the group; two of them lived a few streets away from me so they were practically my neighbours.

It's hard to remember how to pronounce all the words. Our V is their W; and our F can be V and F. It's hard to recall it all; an educated person would do much better than I can, but our 'e' is pronounced like an 'i' over there, and 'i' is pronounced 'e'. They also talk from the throat. If I was on my own now I could get clear with it, but I get confused when someone asks me to translate. I can't always find the right English word at the right time. I learnt German from just speaking to people and was probably fluent when I lived there because I never had any trouble and people never knew I was a foreigner until I opened my mouth. They'd all say then they'd never tip that I was from Ireland; they thought I was Swedish or Danish. I think in German all the time still. I dream in German too and I have to look up the English words on the computer and what do I know.

I thought the Germans spoke very loudly when I went over first and I thought they were always arguing. They'd be waving their hands and everything and I was sure they were fighting with one another. Con used to laugh at me. Then they think the Irish are very loud, but they love us. When I went over first there was a lot of talk about the war. Konrad's father's first wife was killed during it. He wouldn't have remembered that much himself, as he wasn't born until 1948. But his stepmother, the father's third wife, was friendly with this old man who used to be the *bürgermeister*, (Lord Mayor) of their town and this old neighbour would point at him and say right in front of him, "See him, he got a lot of fellows shot." She said they were hiding Polish people one time and that guy gave them away; he got them knocked off, she said. The ordinary people didn't know what was going on; people like you and me, they hadn't a clue and they can't be blamed for what happened. No more than we can be blamed for what the IRA done or what happened in the North of Ireland. Like us the Germans were just trying to survive.

I was in East Berlin when the Wall fell and there was great excitement altogether. I had a friend from East Berlin, Volker, who had escaped through Prague and he wanted to go home to see his mother. I had arranged to go with him and then my Aunt Esther came over on holidays with her husband and three children and they all wanted to come too. Because we were Irish we had to get visas. We had a great weekend there, grilling on the terrace, and all the neighbours came to see us because they'd never met Irish before. They visited me later when they were allowed to travel and their jaws dropped when they saw what we had in the West, because they had nothing. They

had beautiful homes, but nothing in them. Anyhow after the Wall
came down we had difficulty leaving. Volker told me to stay close
behind him going through the checkpoint, as he said there might
be problems with us being foreigners. Only Germans were being
allowed out. I said what am I going to do with all them, pointing at
Esther and her family? But, we managed it in the end. East Berlin is
a beautiful part of the city now, you should see it, a beautiful part
of the city altogether.

Con always said the minute he had his pension we'd come back.
And he'd have been finished when he was fifty-eight, so I'd have been
here by now anyhow. He was just after coming home from work that
day. In fact I had picked him up in Holland and was lying on the chair
after giving him his dinner. He looked over at me at one stage and
there was an awful look in his eyes. But he ate his dinner and enjoyed
it; it was lamb. I never ate lamb since. He said that was lovely, you
know, but he had an awful lot of work to do so he went into the sitting
room to the computer. I sat back on the couch and fell asleep. Later
he made coffee and on his way out to the kitchen he saw a neighbour
through the window trying to carry in something and he went out to
help her. Next thing I heard the neighbour screeching. Con had collapsed suddenly and died. An ambulance came, but they said there was
no point in taking him into hospital. That was about half past three
in the afternoon and they left him there with me then until about nine
o'clock that night. His aunt came then and two stepbrothers. I didn't
know what kind of funerals they had there, as I'd never really been to
one so I didn't know what was in front of me. His uncle was a priest;
a very nice man, but he had met a girl and fallen in love with her and
went over to the Old Catholic vernacular. The family were all very
religious, but my husband had nothing to do with the Church. In Germany they take taxes out of your earnings called *kirchensteuer* and
Con let them take the money, even though he didn't use the Church.
What family he had came to the funeral and some of my family too.
I asked in the Catholic Church in our area if his uncle could perform
the ceremony and they said they'd have to ask the Bishop. I said don't
bother and had him laid out in the Protestant Church instead with the

ceremony celebrated by a priest from the old vernacular. The Catholic priests wouldn't do it. They said I couldn't bring his body back to Ireland either, but I did.

It was sad. I misses him terrible. Not a day goes by that I don't talk to him. A few weeks before he died he said that he was after achieving everything in life that he wanted. And he said, listen, girl, I'll always look after you, because I'd never have done it without you. We used always go for walks together and we used to talk a lot. And even though we had the telephone there we still used to write letters to one another. I think letters are lovely. There's a difference between sitting down in the morning talking to someone on the telephone and sitting down with a letter to read over breakfast. Con always wrote in English not German.

> *Dear Nellie darling, We are just leaving Madeira and are on our way to Las Palmas where we will arrive tomorrow. Nellie, darling, there is nothing really to tell because we spoke already on the telephone .... My lovely wife, I love you so much and I miss you. You are the only love of my life and will always be, I always have you in my heart and in my mind, my lovely darling. I*

> *am looking so forward to coming home to you soon again and that I can hold you in my arms and kiss you. My sweetheart, you are such a good wife and I am so happy that I married you. I think when I got to know you that was the best day of my life ....*
> *Hope to see you soon.*
> *A thousand kisses.*
> *Say hello to Dusty ....*

Our wedding day

He was only fifty-four years of age when he died. It was too soon. I'm fifty-eight now, and I don't think I'll ever get married again, unless to the same man. Unless lightening strikes. Sure I didn't even want to get married back that time. When I used to see how the men would come home to their wives, drunk and everything, I knew I didn't want that. I always prayed to St. Anthony that if I got married that I'd get a good husband. Well he gave me that. They used to say to me in the Orthopaedic, are you praying for a husband again? And I'd say I'm praying for a good one. Because what you have at home, I don't need. I didn't want to get married but what I saw around me was that everybody does. And they all had loads of children. One woman I knew had twenty-two! When I met my husband, I said, Con, I said, I don't want more than six children. If I've more than six children I said, I'll be gone. He used to say SIX? In Germany they never had more than two. I would love to have had children. The doctor said in my heart I wanted them, but not in my head.

After Con died I moved 800 kilometres away because the rent in Cuxhaven was too high and I couldn't afford to pay it by myself. I was paying eight hundred euros a month and my small pension wasn't enough to cover that. One time I went to visit my friend, Maria, in her little village in Bavaria. There was a flat for rent in a house across the road from her for only three hundred euros and I decided to pack up and move there. I loved it. It was like something out of a story book with the Alps in the background. For the dog it was fantastic, as we could walk miles and miles. There were loads of fields around and we would walk through seven different villages. I walked so much that in the end I knew more about the place than Maria who had lived there all her life. There were timber huts, like an inn, where we could go in for wine, and bread served on a timber board like a small tray. I have them here and they're better for bread and cheese than a plate. The crumbs gather in a little ledge and you wash it then like a cup and saucer. My sisters love them and they say they'll take them off me. That's where I lived then for the last four years of my life in Germany.

I was back there on a holiday three weeks ago. I flew over for one euro with *Ryanair* and spent four days with Gertie whom I rented the flat in Bavaria from. She hadn't wanted me to leave and offered to come down in rent, but I said no, Gertie, I have homesick and I want to go home as soon as I haven't Dusty. Her husband was the blacksmith in the village so there was always something going on in their house. That's why I got used to not going out to bars and that. Somebody always had birthday or on a Sunday then we'd go eating and we'd always have a good old laugh. There was a thousand people living in the village and I knew everyone of them. They still enjoyed a village-style existence. I also went to visit another friend, Petra. It was great seeing old friends again and that's what I miss most here – my friends. I'm still friendly with Barbara that girl from *The Bodega* all those years ago. She lived by us in Cuxhaven for a long time, but she's after moving away now.

I miss Germany. I miss the way of life there too. But, Ireland is lovely and the people are lovely too. It was always home. I loved Germany but my heart was always in Ireland. And my husband's too. It's hard to describe, but when you emigrate you're always between two worlds. I am happy here now because I have my family close by and I have my way of life back, but it was very hard at first when I was living with my sister. It wasn't her fault; she's a very loving person, but I found it very hard to be in someone else's house and not my own. Then I moved to a flat in Cobh and I didn't like that either. I was very bad at first because I missed my old way of life and I missed the friends I had there. I liked the way it was in Germany. You knew that when you had an appointment, you kept the time. If they say they'll be there at three, they'll be there at three. Here it could be five or six o'clock. If they don't come today, they'll come tomorrow. And sometimes they don't come at all, and they don't even ring. If I've to meet someone now at three, I say to them if it's half past don't bother coming at all. And they look at me and say, "You should go back to Germany."

I love the shops though, they have beautiful clothes here. I didn't like the style in Germany at all; I found they were very altmodisch (old-fashioned). Oh! There's a German word again. I was the same at school this morning: I kept lapsing into German, and I said to the teacher, "You'll have to forgive me because I was thinking in German all weekend."

73

I see an awful change in the young people here. They have their own minds; we didn't have that before. I think it's good that they know more than we did and that they all get the chance to learn. We were out working so young; now they go to school longer. Nobody cared whether I went or not. When I was finished school I still had to go down to the Convent for religious instruction in order to make my Confirmation. I have nothing against religion, but if they'd taught me how to read and write; wouldn't I have been better off? I didn't always go to Church in Germany and I haven't been to confession in thirty years and I'm OK with that. At this stage what have I to confess? I go to Mass here when I have a mind to. I go more often here than I did in Germany. I pray the whole time to St. Anthony and often pop into St. Augustine's to light a candle to him. I don't know why I pray to him in particular.

My niece saw the ad for Safe Home on the computer. She printed out the information and sent it to me. I wrote to them and they sent me

At home on White Street

a lovely letter back. It all took about one year. I told them I couldn't come home until the dog died because she would have never survived without me. Now I'm settling in here and I'd love to go to school again and learn something. Esther does say, what do you want to learn? And I say, I dunno, but I just want to learn, because I have nothing; nothing in life. I say I never learnt nothing. My niece says if she could make curtains like me; if she could do what I'm after doing here with this flat, putting up shelves and every-thing, she'd be happy. But, I say, I haven't a paper for one thing. I don't want to work. Sure who'd take me on? I'm too old and I had operations on my hands for carpal tunnel, probably from all the work in the factory and I done an awful lot of crotchet and knitting. I can't do anything like that anymore. I can still do the sewing though; I bought a new machine and gave the old one to my aunt. I've taken up computer classes in St. John's College and I love that. We have a bit of a laugh and the teacher, Eleanor, is very nice.

I was expecting it to be much worse here. Cork was a small city when I left it, surrounded by fields, and Patrick Street was the one main thoroughfare. Now it's expanded so much. I like it well enough though; I like my class and I like my flat and I sit out there on the balcony and have a smoke and at seven o'clock I'm in then for the evening. I don't like going out after that. I have a car. I'm getting used to the other side of the road. I can visit my husband's grave, which I couldn't do in Germany. I don't mind the traffic. I've always been used to that, as I drove everywhere to meet him, to Holland, to Belgium, anywhere at all really. I drove one time from Ireland back to Germany. I thought too it would be much harder to get set up here, because in Germany they're so strict. The social welfare people here made sure I knew exactly what I was entitled to. I had to have all of my papers translated from German. The welfare officers were very nice and helpful. I couldn't say I've had any bad experience since I came home. I don't regret not buying a house in Germany because there's no selling there now. Nobody's buying houses at the moment. Germany's not like before. The people are not worse off; I wouldn't say that, but they're not booming like they are here. Germany used to be booming too. When things got bad, it was the poor who missed out. The rich still got richer, but the poor got poorer.

When I read *Ashen Meine Mutter* (Angela's Ashes) it reminded me of where my grandparents lived in O'Brien's Place, on a lane like Frank McCourt's, but I never remember it being dirty, although it was always freezing. My grandmother had a lovely little house with a kitchen, living room and a loft. We used to sleep up in the loft and it was very cosy and the mattresses were stuffed with fresh hay. I wouldn't say we had a hard life growing up, but it was sad. The pain hurt, but it passes faster when you're young. They were happy days even though I know it was sad that our mother and father were dead, but I have it in my head that ours was always a happy home. I understand a hard life as being when you've no food and you're cold and hungry, that's hard; whereas I think we had everything. I was only twenty-five when I went away; I was still very young. I often ask the others did they lose out on anything when they were younger and they say no. It goes through my head sometimes that I didn't do enough for them, but they say no. I hope that's true, *und was weiss ich*? (And what do I know?)

**Interviewed at her home in Cork City
on Wednesday, July 11th, 2007**

Dusty takes a back seat

JOHN CONNOR

People in Ireland have a different sense of humour than they used to. Remember I've been away from County Monaghan for fifty years now. I came back in October 2006, but went out to New York in 1957 when I was only eighteen years old. I even have the ticket for the train from Blackstaff out the country there that took me up to Dublin. There's no railway line there now. But, I can see the date here; it was the 18th of April, 1957. I must have taken another train after that because I flew out from Shannon. It was only a propeller plane and I think it took thirteen hours to get out to America. We came down in Gander (Newfoundland) and I remember it the same as if it was yesterday. I went to a sister who was there twelve months before me. She's dead now, Lord Have Mercy on her. The superintendent from the building where she lived gave me a lift from the airport and I was going to open the door in the middle of the street. I saw the sister and I was in a hurry to get out and speak to her. It's a wonder I didn't get knocked down. I never thought of the traffic. Sure we'd no cars around here that time, only an ass and cart; you'd be lucky to have a bicycle. Sure I thought they were all half mad up in Dublin. I was up there for the first time when I went for the medical and I didn't know what they were doing with all the cars. Look at them today.

It was very hard to get work in New York. You had to take the first thing you got. I started off taking care of the vegetables in the *Safeway* supermarket and I as green as the cabbage myself. Everybody was calling us greenhorns. Sure they called us County Cabbage, we were that green. I then got a job as a porter on Fifth Avenue in a big department store – *Bergdoff Goodman*, but you were working all the time and you never got a Saturday or a Sunday off. You'd be working nights until three or four in the morning and then back in again the next morning. Then I went on the buildings and sure come November you'd be laid off. You'd be off then for the winter. I stayed with my sister and her two friends; the three of us stopped in a flat down there on 149th Street. I wouldn't like to live there now. I think it was on the Number 4 subway; the Jerome/Woodlawn line. Ah! Sure we'd be packed into the train like cattle; I wouldn't like to be on it now. I can't remember the name of the parish but there were a lot of Irish in that neighbourhood. I ended up living on Dekalb Avenue in the Bronx beside this big Polish Church.

What with working nights all the time and never being off at the weekends we ended up going on the drink. There was a rake of pubs there on 149th Street. We went to one in particular there on Melrose Avenue, but I can't remember the name of it. We used to go to *The Jaeger House* dancehall and then you had *City Centre*, wasn't it? I think they're all closed now. We used listen to this band; the lead singer used to play the accordion; I can't think of the name now. Sure it was nearly all Irish girls we met. You'd never meet an American one; you'd be afraid to talk to them. I was afraid to talk to any of the Americans. I read in one of the recent Safe Home newsletters about a woman who was saying how she was afraid to talk when she went over first in case they wouldn't understand her. I was the same. We used to go up to Gaelic Park and do you know what we used to do? To tell you the truth now we used go into the bar and spend the day there. I never seen a match in it at all; never. Sure it was ridiculous really. I don't think Monaghan had a team there, but I was never interested in

Train ticket from Blackstaff

Gaelic games anyhow. I never played. I used to go to the beach on a Sunday instead. I don't know how I didn't die one time. My sister and her mates had moved up to Fordham Road and I went off to the beach by myself in nothing only me shorts. I called into the girls after and I sat down on the chair and I couldn't get up when it was time to go. I couldn't move. There were bubbles on my back, bubbles and blisters all over it. I had to sit there for the night. I couldn't lie down or nothing. I still went to work the next day, but sure I couldn't do a bit. I couldn't even put on a shirt. That was an awful doing I got. I'm lucky I didn't end up in hospital and if you did then you'd pay for it.

I came back to Ireland for a visit after four years and then back to New York again. Sure you'd be off for nearly the whole winter. And all you'd get was fifty dollars a week on the social welfare or whatever they called it; you wouldn't get no rent money or anything like that. The pay was OK at that time, but you'd have to go down every day to the Union when you weren't working and you'd be stuck at the back of the queue and if there was no work you'd have to come away again. I came home that first time on the boat. I don't know if it was the Queen Mary, was it? It was OK. I came back because of the drink. I worked in England for a short time and went back again to New York, for the adventure, I suppose. I had loads of adventure. I liked New York well enough when I was working. I waited six years for a permanent job and then the next brother came out and I gave it to him. It was in a school, as a custodian, that's what they called it. He kept it until he retired. He's over seventy now and he done better than me. It was the only job he ever had. He got married over there and had a big family and they all have their own houses and everything now. I missed out by not keeping that job.

With sister, Alice, New York 1957

I came back to England, to Leeds, in November 1963 and was there a week when Kennedy was shot. I'll never forget it. I'd been in America all through the elections and all the Irish were following him. Then Bobby came along and we were all for him too. Now you have Ted and he's still alive. Isn't it hard to believe? He was going to go for President too, but sure he couldn't as they'd have assassinated him. I went to Leeds because the brother was there, working on the buildings as well. We were doing mostly ground work, pipe laying and that. It was nearly all hand building, with *Murphy's*. We thought it was great. John Murphy was one of the biggest contractors there. We did all kinds of work for him; they wouldn't do it today. It was alright at times.

After that I was in Germany in a place called Stuttgart for a couple of years. Germany was very good that time; it's no good now. It was booming then; there was an awful lot of buildings going up. We were living in huts with our own bedroom and shower. The contractor you were working for would put you up. But, you were really working for an agency; it was the agency that paid us. There were a lot of English working there, not Irish, and there'd be signs up in the pub – No English Allowed. The English used to cause trouble you see. When we'd say, "We're from Ireland," they'd say, "Come, come." There's nothing in Germany now; the Germans are all coming here.

I came back to Shepherd's Bush in London and said I'll stop here now. It was OK when I was young, but lately there I got mugged three times and had my nose broken and the police would want to know now't. Nevertheless, I spent the last twenty years there. The rent wasn't bad; of course I wasn't paying it; Social Welfare did that. Somebody gave me Safe Home's information and I wrote to them and they wrote back and told me this and that and the other and that was it. They were getting me a flat in Castleblayney first and I came home to see it, but you'd be looking into a graveyard and I thought I'll be in there long enough, so I turned it down straight away. Then I got the flat here and I came back for good last October. This little flat is grand. I put down all the wooden floors in a couple of hours. There's nothing to it, just tap them in there with a hammer; it's simple. There's a few things wrong with the flat. The sink is leaking; the new boiler is leaking, but apart from that the flat is fine. I feel safe here in a way. Sometimes I leave the windows open at night time, but anyone can come up there on a ladder.

The bloke from Social Welfare gave me a hard time altogether. It was hard trying to get the few bob out of them. It was him that got on to me about the pension. Safe Home told me to go down to see the one in the housing association, Respond, and I showed her the papers and this man down in Carrick looked into it and to make a long story short they got me a pension. Sure half the time we weren't working on cards over there and sure we took no notice. There's a Community Centre here and they've put things in the door to come to meetings, but I don't bother. Sure it's all families and that and I wouldn't know anybody. What's in the Community Centre for me? There's a communal garden too, but I don't use that either.

I'll be back twelve months in October and I can't understand them here at all now. There's a different attitude. There are eight flats here in this complex and the neighbours are not that friendly. There's only one man there who'll talk to me. I have a brother there in the town and another one out in the home place. We're from Inniskeen where the poet, Patrick Kavanagh, is from. I didn't know him; nobody did until he died. It's only then that he came into the spotlight and there's people coming down from Dublin in bus loads for his anniversary. He's buried up there in the Church in Inniskeen and big bus loads come down every year to visit his grave. I grew up on a farm. There's three sisters dead and one brother dead, and there's three still alive. I used to work on a neighbouring farm, but there was nothing there that time. I tried to get a job here in Carrickmacross, but sure there was no work here either. There was no work at nothing. My parents had nothing. I used to go working on the bog a few days a week and whatever money I got I gave to the mother. Even when I went to America that time I sent my money home to her, as did my sister who had some sort of office job.

I've no other choice now but to stay here since I gave up the flat in London. I haven't joined any social activities; it's only the pub now you'd get. Everyone knows me, but I don't know them. Sure how would I know them? I'm fifty years gone; fifty years gone now last April. I met a bloke there one day that I went to school with; but sure how would I know him? As for

John's father, Owen (2nd left, kneeling) & brother, Jim (back left) with neighbours

81

school, sure there was no heat there; no nothing. We'd light a fire in the morning and by the time the place would be heating up you'd be going home. It was away out in the country. It's well gone now. I liked the teacher; I tried to visit her grave, but I couldn't find it. She used to cycle all the way out there on a bicycle from Carrick even when there was snow on the road; sure it was a terror too. I stayed there until I was fourteen, I think. You'd be working then at home; working a bit with the father. Next door then there was a farm and you'd be gathering spuds there for them, but sure it would only keep you so long. You wouldn't be working full-time like.

So I'm back now, but if I could have my flat in London, I'd be gone in the morning. I do a lot of walking here. I was out there at quarter to seven this morning and I walked about eight miles. Around Christmas I did more; the weather was better then than it is now. Then all that rain came. This is the mildest winter gone by that I ever remember and this is the worst summer, sure everybody knows that. When I left first for New York the sister, Lord Have Mercy on her, and her friend would say, "Well, would you go home now in the morning?" And I'd say I would not. I knew well they were testing me out, but sure what was there to come home to? There was nothing here. There was no work here for us at all. It's not like today.

I can't understand Ireland at all now. I think the banks must own all the cars; they're all new. You'd see very few cars here that are ten years or older. And look at the houses they're building? Sure the banks must own all that too, and the building societies. And then in another few years time when they want to get the houses re-decorated they'll have to get another loan. Sure look what happened down the road from here. See all them flats over there? Do you know what happened? The subbie that started the building went bust; they reckon seventy million euros gone bust. The flats are only half built and they're left like that now for this year. I wasn't here when it started up, but there was a lot of pile driving done down there and it cost millions. They had to go down deep with a machine; it was all bad land. You could see it coming. I'd be up here looking down at them. There'd only be three or four working on it and then when a Bank Holiday or anything would come along they wouldn't work at all. There's none of the flats finished. The building has two stories and a car park underneath. There's another lot of houses going up down the road too. I don't know what all this building is for, but they're still not working as hard as we did.

I worked with one crowd in Heathrow Airport for four years. We built the tunnels where the trains went in and out. There were hundreds and hundreds of Irish there and we used to be winding up the foreman. We worked long hours from seven o'clock in the morning until six o'clock at night, and until one o'clock on a Saturday. The van would collect us in the morning and bring us home at night. You wouldn't get many to do it today. I couldn't work here because all they do is sit down, fold their arms and look at it. Machines do everything. I wouldn't work anywhere really; I've worked long enough. You wouldn't get work here anyway without the cards. I see a man next door to me and he's up and down every day trying to get bits of work.

I go out to Inniskeen sometimes to visit the brother and to see the parents' graves and that. The brother still has the home place. He's not married at all so then one of the nephews will get it. I never got married either because I travelled too much. That was an awful going in England one time. A lot of the lads used to do that. That was the way it was; pulling in and out of towns. We were young and mad for adventure. If I had to get a steady job in New York I would have stayed. Yet when my brother came out there, I gave it to him. I can't write much; I can write a bit, but he was even worse. He couldn't have filled in a form or nothing. When he was young he got TB and he went into hospital. I can remember the hospital room well; my mother and father were there, Lord Have Mercy on them; there were three doctors and the priest who anointed him. They were told if he dies before morning, don't be surprised. They wanted him to be brought to the sanatorium and my mother said no, we'll bring him home. So they did and he's still alive today.

I went out to New York there two or three years ago to a friend from Ballybay who has a flat in Yonkers. It was the 17th of March and we went down to watch the parade with only a suit of clothes on us and sure we were freezing; no coat, no jacket, nothing. I went down one day then on me own, down to Fifth Avenue to see *Bergdoff Goodman's*. I wasn't sorry I hadn't stayed, not at the time anyhow. I can remember St. Patrick's Day and the lines along Fifth Avenue would be painted green. I often marched in it for Monaghan and the parades were longer then too. You'd always get the day off. That was one thing you'd be off for. If we had the sense we have now we'd have probably settled down more, but we were too young. Imagine me going off that time at eighteen years of age?

You'd have friends in England from meeting them in the pub and that and from working with them. You'd have friends from different counties. I went to the dancehalls in England years ago. We'd go to *The Shamrock* in Leeds and *The Galtymore* in London, which is closed now I

Trashing Mill, Drumneil

think. I knew Cricklewood like the back of me hand. I lived in Kilburn too and knew people all over. I'd never have thought of coming back only that things got so bad. They were getting drugs outside my door. In the end up it's the same here. I go down the town there and it's drugs, drugs, drugs, in the town of Carrick. It's going to come the same here. They're getting too much money. You'd want to be down that town when the school kids are around. They're fighting there between themselves. There are hundreds of them and the guards do nothing. They go into the shop and they all have fifty euros to spend. I seen three or four young fellows there on a waste patch, a walk away down there, drinking and breaking bottles. I met a bloke there the other morning at about a quarter to eleven, a young fellow and he was stoned out of his mind. They're up there drinking first thing in the morning. You'd never have seen that in Carrick before I left.

I'd say a lot of the Irish lads would like to come home, but they can't because they don't have the fare. I knew two houses near where I lived and there was thirty-eight Irishmen in one and twenty-eight in the other. There'd be ten sharing the one kitchen, a little small room, one would have to get up to let the other one in, and its Irish men that own them too. An awful lot of them are on social welfare. I told them to put their names down with the Council for a flat, but they wouldn't listen to me.

That flat of mine was only £68 a week. The one underneath me was £1,600 a month plus council tax, gas and water rates. I'd say they were glad to see me going because then they could put the rent up. They were privately owned. There were a lot of Irish in it, rightly. A lot of them can't come home and that's it. If you're married with a family there's nothing to come home to. I wasn't going to stay there all my life. Things were getting bad all the time. It was time to go.

I'm not sorry I drank; sure you had to do something. I smoked one time too, but I gave them up when the sister died from lung cancer. I started smoking small cigars and then I smoked a pipe, and then I gave it all up. I wouldn't smoke again. A woman knocked on the door the other night looking for a cigarette and I offered to go down the road to get her a packet. It wouldn't take me long to get down to the shops on the bike. I used to cycle in England too. I had a car one time, but I nearly got killed in it. I never drove since. Sure you can't drive here anyway if you have a couple of pints. I don't think the anti-smoking ban stops people going to the pub here. They're smoking out the back and smoking in the toilet. It's the drinking driving that's killing the pubs. There's only two in Inniskeen now and they're mostly closed during the day. There's nothing there now. Not like when I left.

I never threw that train ticket away, from my first journey up to Dublin on my way to America. I always kept it. I threw some pictures away and burnt others, even though my mother said you never should burn photographs, but I always kept that ticket. I used to write home regular. Oh! It used to be lovely to get a letter. There was a row of little boxes at the end of the stairs and you'd break a leg to get down and see if there was any post. You wouldn't now. My mother used to always write and I have to say she was a lovely writer. I missed her

Stony grey soil, Inniskeen

terrible, but we had to go and that was it. She lived until she was ninety-four. She died twelve months after my sister and I think it was from heartbreak. My father died a long time ago, when I was in Kilburn. Ah! They had hard times. My father grew up on the farm we had. Sure they had nothing. I remember my father would smoke turf in the pipe when he couldn't get tobacco. You couldn't get nothing in the shops unless you had the money to pay for it. There was nothing, no welfare, nothing, not a penny, not like now.

They wouldn't believe the way this country has gone. I don't know how they keep going and I don't know what will happen the next generation at all. They're all drinking so young; when they get older all you'll see is a pile of drunks. What about all them drugs that were caught in Cork the other week? They only caught one load, but the other nine got away. I was in my twenties when I started drinking in New York and it was nearly all shots there, wasn't it? There was no pints of beer, only glasses. I never missed a day from work though, that was one thing. The foreman on the job would tell us to come in anyhow. That only lasted so long too.

I might go to London on holidays for a week or two. I have a few pound over there and plenty of places to stay. I miss England. You'd always meet someone walking down the road and they all know you. The people are different here. There's a different atmosphere; a different way altogether. After a while talking to someone here I get carried away and think I'm still back there. The crowd here don't know what to say to me; they don't know what I'm talking about. I don't think I'll be able to mix up with them at all.

Interviewed at his home in Carrickmacross, County Monaghan, on Wednesday, July 25th, 2007

LAURENCE MARLEY

I came over on the 23rd August last and had a look at the flat here and I thought I'd get nothing better. I'd come to a dead end kind of thing in England, you know what I mean? I had the idea of coming home for good, but I couldn't afford to buy anything in Ireland. That was out of the question. I had a lovely flat in South-ampton, and I wouldn't have left it for anything less than this. When I got the opportunity to come to Castleblayney, I took it and came back in October 2006. It's only fifteen minutes from where I was born in Castlebellingham, County Louth.

I left for England in 1958. It was August the 24th and when I got to Dagenham there was a thunder storm; you know the August thunder-storms they get? And I thought, well that's a good start. My intention was to work in *Ford's*, the car manufacturers. A neighbour from our little village of Greenmount was home on holidays and he told me there was a job for me in there if I wanted it. I went for the adventure I suppose, just to see what it was like. I was working on a farm and I wasn't making a lot of money and there were people coming home from England every day telling us how good it was there. I went over by boat from Dun Laoghaire and I headed straight for Dagenham where I stayed for about two years. Then I met these chaps and they said there was more money in industrial painting. I got tied up then in the painting trade and stayed at it until the day I left. I painted every-thing. You name it, I painted it.

The industrial painting was hard work and risky work. But, I was young, see, and I didn't mind. We'd have to sit in *Bolson* chairs and cradles and we'd be three hundred feet up in the air mainly on the sides of these ships and tanks. *Bolson* chairs were little seats with a rope attached and we'd swing up and down in them. When I was in Dagenham I was only working sort of locally. We got the jobs from meeting fellows, through word of mouth. The first question you'd ask is how many hours. A fellow told me one time that there'd be twelve hours a day in this place and I said, that's an awful lot, and he said, but you won't be working the whole twelve. That was the secret you see, you'd only be working six or seven hours, but you got paid for twelve. It was all dangerous work. Then I met this chap from Cork who was in the

The Carroll girls. My mother (4th from left) with her sisters andnephew outside their family home in Co. Louth

trade and he said come along with us, there's more money, so I did.

From 1961 to 1972 I travelled the whole of England up and down painting gas holders. There was good money in it then and being a single chap you got your lodgings paid, plus your wages, and then 'away from home money', and the craic was good. You were in a different town every four to five weeks. I started off in Leicester, then I went to Bolton, Lancashire, and London. This is all now in one year. You'd always be based in London because it was a London firm we worked for – *Yeoman's*. They had their offices outside Euston Station and all you had to do was get off the train and say, "I'm back" Then they'd fix you up with another job. Caernavon in North Wales was the next stop and me and this Kerry man spent a few weeks down there. That was great. There were lovely girls there, all single, and no men because they were all away working. North Wales that time was poorer than Ireland, and that's hard to believe, I know. There were two girls working in the hotel where we were stopping and their wages was about £32 a month, which was about £8 a week wasn't it? Now we were getting twenty to twenty-five pounds a week, so that was the difference. We went into the pub the first Wednesday night and it was full of women, young and old. "Where's all the fellows?" We said. "Working," they replied.

They treated Wednesday night the same way we treated Friday.

They'd celebrate the half-week whereas we only celebrated the week-end. There were one or two Irish living there. No matter where you went you met the Irish.

It took me three days then to get from Caernevon to Seton in Devon, where our next job was, from one end of the country to the other, then it was back to London again. No matter where I was sent I always wrote home straight away to let them know. I was staying with these friends in Ilford, famous for the films, and we had a big job coming up in West London. We were going to be there for the winter. I was only back a week from Seton and I went into the job one morning in Fulham and the chap that I was staying with handed me the telegram that my mother had died. So that was it, I had to go home then for her funeral. I was lucky though because if I'd still been in Seton they wouldn't have known where to contact me because it was the one place I hadn't let them know of. I didn't think I'd be there so long.

A lot of times I went home around Christmastime and stayed six or seven weeks, because most of that work started around Easter. I used to like that. That's what kept me there, I think, because if I hadn't been doing that, I wouldn't have stayed away from Ireland as long as I did. In the middle Sixties then I hurted my leg and I was in hospital for six weeks in Falmouth in Cornwall. I was off work from the middle of October until the following April. I have a huge scar on my leg still and I wear a special sock to protect it. I burnt it with this paint that we had to heat until it turned liquid. If you can picture cart grease; the thick stuff you used to grease cart wheels long ago, that's what it was like. It was so strong we'd have to throw away our clothes at the end of every work day because it was very dangerous. Anyhow one day my trouser leg caught fire and burnt my leg. I had to have a skin graft and still have a nine by four inch scar. I had plenty of rest when in recovery and I was getting paid workman's compensation, which wasn't great, but it was better than nothing. I wasn't missing out on money, but when you're off work like that you spend more. We also worked down in Roefun painting these tanks that were all under the ground and camouflaged by trees. They store the petrol there ready for wartime and keep it hidden from bombers or attack from the enemy. It was a big estate with a massive big fencing around it and we got the contract. It was 1966 and England won the World Cup. You always remember those sort of things don't you?

When I finished all the travelling I stayed local for a while in London doing house painting and that. In 1977 I painted the gates of Wimbledon Tennis Club. That was a good job. Money was no object there trying to get it finished before the tennis tournament began. I was working right up to the last minute on the Sunday night. The foreman would come along and say, "Larry, there's another little piece needs doing, I'll give you an extra fifty quid if you stay." Everything had to be painted green, except the gates, which were always black with a grey undercoat. The craic was there though. You'd have tourists coming along every day just to see where the place was. This American couple came up to me one day and asked me to take a photograph, but my hands were full of black paint and you know what the Americans are like? She said, I'll take one of you then, and she asked me for my name and address to send it to me. She was groping in her handbag for a pen and for the craic I said my name was Leonardo DaVinci and she said can you spell that for me please? Well I didn't know which way to look. I wanted the ground to open up and swallow me so that I could have a good laugh. I felt sorry for her in the end and told her that's what me buddies call me and I gave her my real name then. She never did send that photo though.

We had a great craic and a great social life too. Sure I was in every dancehall in London. We danced in *New Cross* and *The Shandon* when we lived in Dagenham. We used to go an odd time to *The Shamrock* in Elephant & Castle. It was owned by Irish wrestlers and there was always trouble there. You must remember there was no alcohol at these dances; only a tea bar. Then we used to go up to Cricklewood, to *The Broadway* there, and if you wanted to hear the big bands you had to go to *The Galtymore*. I seen Big Tom, Larry Cunningham and all them there in the Sixties. There'd be crowds of people and half the time we'd be looking for the bar. But, it would be good craic. Then you had *The Garryowen* in Hammersmith, which was a fairly big dancehall, but then that all died away and the pubs started up. If you go into Shepherd's Bush or Hammersmith or anywhere like that now it's all Irish pubs. They're all Irish owned, Irish staffed, and groups of Irish people drinking in them. You'd think you were in Ireland really. I'd say I met more Irish people in Shepherd's Bush say than I'd met here. If you went out for the whole weekend you'd meet the whole of Ireland in three nights. You name it, you'd meet them.

I never danced an Irish dance until I went to London; until I went to *The Harp*. For the craic we'd get up for *The Siege of Ennis; The Walls of Limerick*; and *The Sixteen Hand Reel*, or whatever you call it. They'd always have a couple of céilí dances during the night. There were people there who could do it; people from Clare would know all about that; but up our way I never seen an Irish dance. There was a céilí in Ardee alright when Dermot O'Brien was starting out, but there was nothing around Castlebellingham. I did a bit of singing in

Celebrating St. Patrick's Day in London, 1961

a band, but we were only getting thirty bob a night in a pub called *The New Cross House* in Southeast London and in *The Shepherd's Bush Hotel*. We never had a proper name, but were sometimes called The Mike Smith Trio. Mike played the accordion, there was a drummer and I did the singing.

When me father died in 1978 I stayed at home for a month and I came back to me bedsit in London. I was living in Shepherd's Bush at the time. That was one of the things I never liked about London was that it was hard to get a decent place. The uncle of the man who owned the house lived next door to me and he told me the nephew was going to sell the house. I was sitting on the bed, the suitcase wasn't even unpacked and I thought to myself I'll go to Southampton. I knew the run of the place, as I'd worked there on jobs on and off and you'd never be out of work painting in Southampton, ever. You had the docks, the oil refinery plus all the home decorating. I took my case the way it was and my toolbox and the rest of my stuff the landlord offered to store for me in his house in Hammersmith over there by the big *Hoover* factory. You know the bits and pieces you'd pick up. I headed off anyhow for Southampton and I found work with a small company, painting and decorating. I stayed there for twenty-eight years.

The name of the firm was called *Town or Country* and they built flats for serviced rental accommodation. It was the alternative to a hotel; you could rent the flat for the length of time you were going to be in town and everything was included, even the toilet paper. Cleaning services were offered too. The owners were from the town of Ipswich and I was from the country so that's how I came up with the name for them. I often thought of setting up a business of my own, spray painting vehicles. I completed a course and have a certificate for it. But, when I found out that I would need £25,000 to start up, I changed me mind. There was a lot of work with *Town and Country* and it was constant work. The farthest I ever had to travel was eight miles to Burlesdown near Hambel, the yachting marina. It's about half way between Southampton and Portsmouth where all the marinas are. I decided then that that was going to be it. Whenever that job finished I was going to retire. And I did.

With friends in Bolton, 1964

The only regret I had was that I hadn't gone to Southampton years before that. I shouldn't have gone back to London in 1972 when I stopped travelling. I got a lovely flat through the Irish Club in Eastleigh, a nice little Irish centre, nothing like the ones in London, but a nice little place. I met this chap one night and he told me about this flat that he knew about, self-contained, up one flight of stairs. At the time I was in a bedsit where I had to share the bathroom and facilities with the other residents. There wasn't that many people there though; whereas in London there could be ten sharing. That was the thing about the bedsit wasn't it? You always had to share something. I often said to myself if I'd stayed in London a hundred years I'd never have found a flat like the one I got in South-ampton and it was only twenty pounds a month in rent. It was 1982 and I was about four years there at the time. The social life was good. I joined the clubs mostly - The Workingman's club and the Labour Club. I met a chap in Kilkenny who worked in *Rank's* over there; *Hovis* and that; and I'd often go to the pub with him. He was married to a Sligo woman. There was also the British Legion Club, which I was in one day and the secretary asked me if I'd do a job for them. I agreed and got well paid for it. Of course you're in then and I didn't even have to join the club. For the last eight or nine years I never used the pub in Southampton; I always went to the clubs.

My passion was for Country & Western music. I visited Nashville, Tennessee last year and Alabama to see the home of Hank Williams in Montgomery. I love his music and his statue was right outside the hotel where I was staying. The trip was organized through a small travel agent in Southampton and I flew from Gatwick to Charlotte in Virginia, from Charlotte to Montgomery in Alabama and from there I travelled by coach to Nashville so as I could see some of the countryside. That took six hours. I stopped off in Birmingham, Alabama, to visit the Country Hall of Fame where they have Elvis Presley's piano and his gold plated car. His museum in Memphis wanted to display them there, but the Country Hall of Fame wouldn't give them back because he was a country singer before he ever became a rock star, you know. They also have some of the clothes Porter Wagner and other famous singers wore. The only white people you'd see were coming out of the Municipal offices; everyone else was black. I was there at the end of March and it was eighty-five degrees. Nashville was about ten degrees below that. I went to loads of shows in *The Grand Ole Oprey*, to see Ricky Scaggs and some others that wouldn't be household names here. One night I was lying on the bed when an announcement came over the speakers, "Please stay away from the windows because we're expecting a typhoon." Turns out about twelve miles away from us, in a place called Huntsville, about twelve to fourteen people were killed that night. I could see the lightening flashing alright, but we still went off to the *Oprey* and the show still went on.

All that's in Alabama is churches and banks although I visited an Irish pub and met a Mayo couple there. The streets were so clean you could eat your dinner off them and there were people all over town with a little brush and a pan picking up things off the sidewalks, especially outside the shops. Montgomery was founded by an Irish man, Brigadier General Richard Montgomery, and only has a drugstore, a pawn shop, a deli and a small university. You had to go out miles to the shopping centres. Hank Williams was born in a little village outside the town. Although he was famous and one of the greatest singers that ever lived, he never fitted in with *The Grand Ole Oprey*. They were a real click and he thought they were using him. There was a bit of friction there over the years. I visited his grave where his first wife is buried beside him in a massive big cemetery. There's a couple of empty beer bottles beside it because he liked his booze, and a hat because he always wore a hat. In fact, there is only one picture of him in the museum without his hat and that's when he was kissing his bride. I flew from Nashville to Philadelphia and had to walk about three miles from one gate to the other for my flight to Gatwick. Oh! That was a killer that was. My next big trip was coming home to Ireland.

I always had it on me mind to come home. If I hadn't been doing what I was doing in the Sixties I probably would've come back then. I enjoyed all that travelling. I mean I probably seen the whole of England. I seen more of England than I have of Ireland so far. And there are some lovely places; Essex, Kent, Cornwell, Devon, Somerset, and the North of England. There are a few interesting places too. I didn't miss Ireland then, but later on when you're sitting around at night and all the work is finished, you'd start thinking about home. I retired officially in 2001. That's when I got my pension and then I started doing part-time work for people, but not a lot, as I'd enough of it by then. In the latter end of my stay then you could say I was sort of self-employed you know. You get to know the feel of the land and all that eventually, don't you?

Years ago I thought about buying a house, but not in the latter end I didn't, because I thought to myself, I'm not going to put myself in a position where I have big bills over my head. I did think about buying in 1985, but there was a chippie working with us at the time and he

Home for the holidays – Mullingar Fair 1965

was paying £400 a month mortgage on a little house and that put me off. The banks were charging 17% at the time and the fellow we were working with was paying 21%. I preferred to have the money in my pocket than someone else's. Of course now you couldn't afford it. There were houses going up in Southampton before I left, over where the football grounds used to be, and they were charging £160,000 for a one-bedroom flat. The last I heard they were £190,000.

I never got married. That was another thing about the travelling. I had loads of girlfriends around the place. I went out with a Kilkenny girl in London for a while, and I went out with a Cork girl long-term. There's a picture of one of them there in *The Harp*. She has the real Sixties look with the short skirt and white boots. I met a couple of nice girls on me travels too. I'll tell you what, there were very nice girls in Sheffield, and Bolton. But, I didn't want to get tied down to be quite honest. I am quite happy on me own.

I like being back well enough. I miss England on a Saturday night with the craic in the clubs and all that, but I'm getting used to it here now. Sure Ireland is a different country altogether, isn't it? It's not like

95

it was when I went to Kilsaran National School where I stayed until I was fourteen years of age and then went straight to work on the farm next door. My father worked for the Board of Works. He was on the drainage for years going around the country working on the levels before the dredgers took the stuff out. My mother was from Annagassan. One of her nephews was Noel Carroll, the Irish champion runner. I met him in London in 1963. She had four sisters. Two of them, Monica & May, went to London when they were young girls and the other two went to work in factories in Belfast. We're only four miles from the border; I go over to play the lotto all the time. We never seen any trouble at all growing up; it never bothered us. The relations used come down all the time and we'd go up to them. I have more relations up in Belfast than I have down South. We were in a pub in Belfast once, after being up at a wedding in 1971, and it was bombed after. They left the bombs on the window sill. We were sitting right beside those windows where three or four days later a bomb was left and it blew straight in and killed the chap who was cleaning the glasses. The Church in Ardoyne where the wedding took place was also bombed a few weeks later.

I never seen much trouble in England either. We had to leave the pub one night in Southampton where there was a bomb scare, but that was only a crank. I never had much trouble for being Irish, certainly not in London anyhow. You'd be wary at first, but I found the English people very welcoming. I always thought they were very tolerant of foreigners, but I don't think they are now. The Irish always stuck to themselves and if you didn't go outside Hammersmith or Shepherd's Bush you might as well say you were in Ireland. It was that

Dancing the night away in The Harp, Newcross London, 1967

simple. A place like Southampton was more conservative, even in their politics; it was always conservative country until Tony Blair changed the whole landscape. I remember the two Labour MP's when they just started out – Denham and Whitehead– they'd be in the Club that time. Next thing Tony Blair came on the scene and the two of them got in and they're still in. Hill had been the local conservative MP for years. Even with the docks there and Unions and everything it was always very conservative. Margaret Thatcher was worshipped down there. You couldn't say a word against her. So Blair changed everything dramatically.

I suppose I would go back to England on holidays. I still know a few chaps there. I keep in touch with Peggy who used to work with *Town or Country* and I hear about the owners, the Batley's, from her. I also had a nice neighbour, Elizabeth, and I ring her a lot and she keeps me informed with what's going on in the flats where we lived. I had a nice life there, but still probably wouldn't have left if I could have found a good job here. There was more money to be made in England fifty years ago; that was the main difference between the two countries that time. Now it's the other way around and there's more money here. It's unbelievable.

I've joined the Blayney golf club. It actually joins the graveyard there. If you're walking along the course you're looking into the graveyard at the same time. They have a small clubhouse, no big deal really. I go out on my own mostly because I want to get some practice. I've only been out with another chap once. It's still early days and I suppose it will take a while to get to know people here. All the old friends are gone. My niece, Kim, just qualified as a Social Worker from Aberdeen University in Scotland. She used to come down to Southampton for weekends and I told her not to stay there too long; that she'd lose all her friends back in Ireland. I told her to give it five years and then to come back. That's the hardest thing about staying away so long, trying to make friends when you come back. But, I have family close by and that's been a great help. Also I drive and that makes a big difference because you'd be lost in Ireland without a car. I went to Dundalk today to get a foot pump because someone was letting the air out of the tyres around here. I had one, but you lose a lot of things when you're moving so I had to go into *Argos*. There isn't a lot of things you can get here; if you want something special you have to go to Dundalk. The shopping is very limited in Castleblayney. There are only two very small supermarkets. They'd started building a bigger one and it's stopped now all of a sudden. The crane hasn't moved in three months and nobody knows what's going on.

I have a book here on our local history in Kilsaran and when I look through the pictures in it, I feel very left out. There is a picture of the Castlebellingham Junior Team in 1928 with my father, Joe Marley. I would have known all of his team mates when I was growing up. There's another photo in it of the Bellingham Brass Band in 1890 with my uncle, Jack Marley. His wife is still alive and she's ninety-four now. There's an article about the Castlebellingham brewery where my grandfather worked. It closed down in the 1920's. During the 1914-18 War the twenty-three workers employed there joined up, so that was the beginning of the end for them. There's a picture of my sister taken in 1959 with *Kay's* ladies football team. I was gone by then you see. All this happened when I was away. This is where I missed out. That all went on when I was away. Sometimes I look at this book and I feel a bit left out, you know what I mean? There are no pictures of me in this book, because I was gone.

When I came back in 1961, I thought Ireland had changed dramatically in only three years. It had prospered so much. Our local pub, *The Crowing Cock,* was extended and they had music. The craic was ninety. It appeared in a tourist guide because it was so well-known and when they built it up there used to be petrol pumps and all outside. A big concrete firm had started up here too; it's in Dublin now. If you were driving through Tallaght you'd see a big, big, sign with *Kilsaran Concrete* on it. That was originally in our little local village. So in three years the town had prospered. If only I'd stayed, I'd probably be in that book there – it would be my claim to fame.

I was on a radio programme in Southampton once called *Claim to Fame* and listeners had to call in and guess your occupation. At the time I was painting the gas holder at the Oval Cricket Ground. It's a famous landmark that you'd see it if you were watching cricket on the television. The final clue was "my work should have been admired by thousands, but many wouldn't have noticed it at all." One woman eventually guessed it. But, how true that is. My handiwork can be seen all over England, as can a lot of Irishmen's, and it is probably never noticed and hardly ever admired.

Interviewed at his home in Castleblayney, County Monaghan, Wednesday, August 1st, 2007

Me and my friend, Hank. Montgomery 2006

MARY AND JOE McCORMACK

Mary: Joe and I came home for good in August 2006 and it was a big change. It's not the Ireland I left as a young postulant over fifty years ago. A Sister Hubert had come to the Mercy Convent in Templemore looking for applicants. She showed us pictures of these poor little children in Africa and you know me heart went out for them and I made up my mind to go and help them. I put up my hand that I wanted to be a nun. I was only about fourteen and a half years of age. I had great grandaunts who had been teaching nuns in Australia and I just had the feeling that I might like it too. My parents thought it was a great thing. I then entered St. Joseph of the Apparition, a French nursing order in Manchester, where I stayed for the next eight years until I decided to come back into the world again.

I was professed Sr. Mary Raymond in November 1946, when I was nineteen years old. They never trained me to be a nurse in the end, as I hadn't the full qualifications, but I loved helping the sisters look after the patients in Whalley Range Hospital. There was a lot of Irish girls there; including three sisters from Limerick. They were nice enough to me, but I think I was a bit lonesome and I wanted to come home. When I went first every time I'd hear a cow moo in the field I'd start to cry because it reminded me of Ireland. Then they were going to send me on a mission to Marseilles in France and I think I got a bit scared. I thought, God! I don't want to go there. I think that's what made me come out.

We hadn't been allowed go out of the grounds all that time. We were allowed to have letters, but the ones we wrote had to be looked at by the Rev. Mother before they went out. I didn't see my mother for eight years. Sad, wasn't it? That was wrong, wasn't it? You wouldn't get people to do that now. Long ago it was a big thing to have someone in a religious order; they wouldn't agree to it now. The only member of my family that I saw in all that time was my father. Daddy came over, God rest him, to see me being professed and he came over again to bring me home. When I wrote to say I wanted to come out, Daddy wrote back, "Mary, you're as welcome as the flowers in May." So there was no hindrance in that respect. Mother Emily, the founder of the Order and Reverend Mother, Sr. Gabriel, was nice about it too. I felt in my heart that I wanted to go and they all understood that.

It was great to see my mother and brothers and sisters again. I stayed around Templemore for a while and then I thought I'd apply for a job. There was no work in Ireland for me so I went then to the Daintree Hospital in Northampton looking after patients. I didn't mind leaving home the second time, but I worried that I wouldn't be up to the standard, being a nun for so long. I didn't think I'd have the experience that the other girls would have; having been enclosed so long and not used to the outside world. I didn't really know anyone over there, but I had loved looking after the old people.

After a while when I had a bit of confidence, I wanted to become more independent so I left the hospital and went working with *Boots Chemists* in their big factory on Island Street, Nottingham. We sat on a bench, rows of girls on each side, examining all the tubes of penicillin on a conveyer belt and any damaged goods had to be put aside as a disregard. It was a nice job, but the belt would go so fast sometimes. I stayed in a lovely flat in Sneaton Vale belonging to a Polish man and his wife. I had a big double room and there was a cooker on the corridor. We got discount with our *Boots* card and I made a lot of friends in the factory. We had good laughs. The girls were always sneaking out to the loo for puffs of a fag. They were nice people to work for too; we'd clock in and clock out. I remember one girl clocked her friend in one day and she never showed up, so the girl had to go. They were very keen on things like that, you know.

A friend of mine was working in *The Midland Bar* at the railway station and she said, would you come, and I said well, I'll try it. There was live-in accommodation and there'd be always a night guard policeman at the station in his little hut. You knew you were safe. All of the railway stations had bars that time. They used to call them saloons where travellers would go in and have a cup of tea or a sandwich, or a drink. And that time a lot of the celebrities used to travel by train so I met quite a few famous people, and got some good tips. The biggest tip I ever got was from a Londoner who was in there to complete an agreement on a house and he ordered a double whiskey. After his business associate had left he said to me, you must have brought me the luck of the Irish, and he gave me a fiver. He must have done a good deal. If you gave a good pint with a big froth on it, a lad might let you keep the change, which you put on a shelf above the till. The customers were mostly Irish. The workmen would be coming down from Newark-on-Trent and other places like that in Nottinghamshire and as the train stopped they'd come in and participate in a drink. I liked it there very much. I liked everything I did except I was a bit lonesome in the Convent, so it was better to be truthful to the Lord and say I wanted to go home.

I wasn't able to dance, but I used to go and watch everyone else dancing. I met Joe in Nottingham. Was it at a dance?

Joe: I'll tell you what happened, she had brought a nephew over from Ireland and she was looking for digs for him. This was in 1959 and her father was after dying, and she came into the digs I was in, bed and breakfast, you know, and that's how I met her. The first time I saw her I said to myself, that's the woman for me. Her nephew got the digs anyhow and I learnt from him that she was working at the railway bar, so I went down to see her there, and that's how we met up.

I had a date with another girl that night and I went along to the dance to see her alright, but I took on with Mary then and that was it. I was only after coming over earlier that year, 1959, and I was driving a steam roller at the time. I done everything, construction work and all, you know. Then I went table jointing after that. But, I'll always remember Mary when I met her first because she was dressed in black. Her father was after dying, you see, and back then you had to stay in mourning for a year.

Mary: That's right. I went to *Colliers*, a big drapery shop in Nottingham, to get a black coat made. Daddy was only sixty-five when he died of a heart attack.

Joe: Her father was Arthur Carroll who used to play football for Tipperary in the 1920's. There was an article in *The Tipperary Star* that described him as the "custodian of the Tipperary net between 1917 and 1926." He was originally from Forrest, outside Templemore, and won his first medal with Templemore in 1913. He was also on the last Templemore team to win a county senior football championship in 1936. He collected seven mid senior football championship awards and played in five Munster football finals, for which he had three Munster champion medals. Alternating between full back and goalkeeper he played in seven county finals and was on the winning team on two occasions, in 1925 and 1936. He was also on the Tipperary

Sr. Mary Raymond

All-Ireland team that was beaten by Wexford in 1918 and was supposed to be playing on Bloody Sunday in 1920, but his mother had died that week.

Mary: Imagine, he could have been shot like Michael Hogan, the Tipperary Captain, who died that day. There was loads of spectators killed too.

Joe: The Black and Tans had stormed the pitch in Croke Park when Tipperary were playing a challenge match against Dublin. They were retaliating against executions carried out by Michael Collins and his men the previous night. Because of Bloody Sunday that year's All-Ireland couldn't be played until 1921 when Tipperary beat Dublin. Mary's father's played that day and got a medal. *The Irish Independent* report on the match called him a "massive man who could fist a clearance farther than the average kicker."

Mary: My nephew in Australia has the All-Ireland medal and my son has one of his Munster medals. We divided them up among the family. I remember when Daddy passed away God rest him. The funeral was miles long and they had a sixty second silence on the wireless before a match that was being played in Croke Park and the commentator was Michael O'Hehir. He used to speak very quickly.

Joe: There's a waxworks of O'Hehir inside the door of the GAA museum in Thurles and you'd swear it was him. Thurles, in County Tipperary, is where the organization was started by Archbishop Croke. Croke Park was called after him and the Hogan Stand was called after Michael Hogan who died on Bloody Sunday. Another Templemore man, Bill Grant, also played in 1920, and he and Arthur Carroll were the two representatives of the local club that marked out the site of the present pitch in 1922. It's called The Carroll and Grant Pavilion, after the two of them. There's a great history attached to Mary's family tree.

Mary: I had two grandaunts out in Australia, both nuns. They were before my time, but they never came back. They were great singers, I believe, and used to sing in a choir. My relations all have headstones in the graveyard up the road there dating back to the 1800's. Mammy didn't die until she was eight-five. It's very hard coming back for funerals.

Our wedding day

Joe: That's the hardest part about going away. It's very sad. Me mother died at fifty-two so my father went to England then. He worked over there and he had a house of his own. He must have been over fifty years of age when he went first. It was hard for him at the start, but he got used to it. He got friends and that. When he died we brought him back to Ireland to be buried with the mother.

I'm from Mullingar in County Westmeath and I went to school in St. Mary's College, right beside the Cathedral of Christ the King. I went to the convent first for national school and then up to St. Mary's for the primary. I left when I was thirteen and a half, when I passed my Primary Certificate. I was a messenger boy and things like that, anything I could get me hands on, until I went on the oil lorries when I was sixteen, working for *Shell*. They used to deliver paraffin all over the country. It was all paraffin then; there was no electric in places, you see. We'd go all over the country with it, out into the real rural farming places bringing them paraffin for their lamps. They let you go then when you were eighteen because they'd have to pay you a man's wages, you see. If you were lucky you'd be kept on.

Then I went putting down television cables for *Jenning's* of Dun Laoghaire in County Dublin. There were laying all the cables for RTE from Dublin to Galway and when they came around by Mullingar I got a job with them for about twelve months. I went on the railway then in 1954. I worked for CIE in the locomotive department as a spare fireman for five years. You done spare fireman first before you'd be appointed full-time. I'd be working the fire for the steam engines and when they done away with the steam and brought the diesels in, I was made redundant. I was working all the time, you know, I didn't have to go to England. I applied everywhere. Loads of my mates went to Canada so I applied there to the uranium mines and that. There was loads of money in it. There was a scheme to go to Australia, the ten pound passage, and I tried for that too. I applied for work on the buses in Melbourne but, I didn't go. I'm glad now, as it's too far away. People who went never came back. It took six weeks to get there by boat. They died on the boats to America during the Famine; it took that long. The world is much smaller today. My grandfather was in America with his sister. He worked on the railways out in the Wild West for parts of it and he came back then and worked on the railways in Mullingar. His sister stayed over there and never came back. My mother had sisters and she never seen them again after they'd gone to

America. They even went to England and never came back, for some unknown reason. I had aunts and uncles in Greenford in Middlesex and they never came back, never, not even for a holiday. I don't know how they did that.

I decided to go to England anyhow when I was twenty-four years of age. I went to Leicester first, to me sister. A lot of people from my town were living there then. I loved it at first when I was fancy free. I lived in a place called Thurmaston where I stayed in digs. They were very good; she was a very good woman, the landlady. She was English, but she had all the Irish staying with her. *Murphy Brothers*, big contractors, were not far away and she had all their workers as well, you know. But, she was very good. We had a rip-roaring time. On St. Patrick's night we used to go around all the houses, having a drink, partying. I went to all the dances in the town centre of Leicester - I forget the name of them now, but in Nottingham it was *The Queens* and they knocked down that and took it to America stone by stone as some heritage building. Then we had *Cathedral Hall* on Derby Road in Nottingham. The ballroom of romance it was called. There was loads of romance there too, I can tell ya.

Mary and I were three years courting. I was courting a girl from Galway first and then Mary done her out. She used to love that song, *The Galway Shawl* after that. We came back to Templemore to get married in that Church across the road there, the Sacred Heart. We had the reception in *The Castle Hotel* in Thurles. It's closed down now. Her sister, Josie, was the bridesmaid, and my brother, Michael, was best man. We went on our honeymoon to Killarney and back to England then where we settled in Nottingham. We had two children, a boy and a girl, Angela and Arthur.

Mary: Arthur after my father, God rest him, and Angela we just picked ourselves.

Joe: We lived in a flat first and then we got a house. Houses were very scarce that time when you'd no money to buy one. Not like today. I was doing construction first and then I got on the electricity board laying the underground cables. Mary was suffering with her leg by this time and couldn't work.

Mary: I had an ulcerated leg for thirty-four years before I had two knee operations and then I had to get the fuse because didn't I get the MRSA, the bug, when I was in hospital. I have a stiff leg now; I can't bend the knee. There's a steel pin in it, the whole way down from the hip, all because of the MRSA, all because of that infection I picked up in the hospital.

Joe: After I retired, we were living in warden-aided accommodation. It's for old people so as they don't have to go into homes, you know, and there's a warden there to help you. But, Mary always wanted to come home to retire here; she always wanted to come back to Templemore.

Mary: Josie, my sister, is here and I wanted to be buried with my father and mother, and my three brothers in the graveyard just up the road there. I have a sister still in Nottingham. Our children are in England too.

Joe: We read about Safe Home in a magazine one St. Patrick's Day in Nottingham. We applied for the forms and that and that's how we went on about it. It went on about two years before we got things sorted. Waiting for accommodation was the problem, you see, but then we were offered this place and we liked it. Moving was a horrendous job though. We engaged a

With our granddaughter, Molly

van to bring over all of our stuff, and we brought as much as we could, including Mary's reclining chair. They had a big farewell party for us in our parish and presented us with a plaque of Nottingham City depicting all of its well known areas, including Nottingham Castle; the statue of Robin Hood; *Ye Olde Trip to Jerusalem*, the oldest pub in England; Wollaton Hall, which is situated on a five hundred acre deer-park; and The Council House. Nottingham is also a very industrial city. *Players* cigarettes and *Raleigh* bicycles are manufactured there, and of course, *Boots Chemists* was founded there.

The children thought it was great that we were coming back, but they miss us and we miss them too. We have a granddaughter, Molly, who will be nine in January, and they've all been over to see us. Molly is lovely. She loves dancing and skating.

Mary: Sometimes I want to go back to live there again. I don't know why, after being there so long and mixing with the people, you'd miss them. And I find I don't know too many here and that makes it hard. It means a lot when you know people. And there's all new generations growing up here; they don't know me either.

Joe: Oh! I'm alright here; I'd settle anywhere. I used to drive, but Mary won't hear tell of it now. Sure the driving here is horrendous, isn't it? They're so impatient, up behind you, tailgating and every-

With our son, Arthur

thing. Well, they wouldn't last five minutes in England, you know. They're very bad drivers here. They don't care. They've no regard for the other road users either. Anything goes, don't it? If you look at all them accidents; it's speeding that's causing them, overtaking on bends and everything, you know, things you're not supposed to do. That road from Nenagh to Borrisoleigh is fierce bendy altogether and it gets flooded too when it rains and they whiz along it. They're doing bits to straighten it, but sure they're taking so long. It's beautiful countryside around here though with the Slieve Felim mountains. We've been up to Mullingar for a week. I've sisters and nieces and nephews still there. And I've two sisters in Leicestershire. There were thirteen of us in the family; eight lived and five of us died.

Mary with Angela and Molly back home in Templemore

Ireland has changed, but it's for the good; there's better conditions here now. Back then we had a two or three-roomed house for ten children; today they have a ten-roomed house for two and three children. Ridiculous isn't it? Back then you had ten and eleven children and they had to get out of it as soon as they grew up, and emigrate or whatever. It was sad when you think of it. It's not the place we left and the people are different. Well, the young generation has changed all over the world; they're not like the old people, they were great. They were more friendly and everything. You see all the murders we have here, it's horrendous, isn't it?

Mary: It's very scary, and it's very expensive too. The cost of living is very high here. There's not much crime in Templemore though.

Joe: Oh, no, this is a quiet town. It's an agricultural town, you know, very quiet. It's lovely here in that respect. Of course it is the home for the Gardaí training depot, which is bigger than ever now. It's a great boost to the town. They don't believe in progress here at all though. They object to everything. *Tesco's* were to come in, but they were rejected. Up in Mullingar they've shut down all the petrol stations because the big stores like *Asda* and *Aldi* are selling petrol that cheap. They're objecting to them coming in here too. I mean they can't stop progress. We would have seen those changes in England too when we were there.

Templemore has been a great town to us though. There's people coming in here to help us all the time, Fás you call them, and we have home help too, which is great. Everything we looked for, we got, so we can't say anything wrong about that.

Mary used to bring the children home every year even if I couldn't come and they always liked it here. They didn't really get involved in the Irish dancing and that over in England, but they were educated in Catholic schools. There was an Irish Centre and we used to go to it sometimes; it was very good. And then there was all dancehalls around and parish halls as well. There were Irish everywhere.

Not everyone who went over wants to come back. They have their families there and that would be a big thing to keep them. Grand-children is a big thing for people. We seem to have more time for our grandchildren than our children for some unknown reason. You can spoil them I suppose and then hand them back. Another friend of ours did come back to live in Geashil outside Tullamore in County Offaly. She was down here the other week. Some of our friends from England have come to visit us as well. We haven't been back yet to visit as trav-elling is hard for Mary. She has to have two seats on the plane.

I am glad I went away; it was a great experience. It's best to travel, to widen your outlook. It does you good. It's nice to go and it's nice to come back. Sometimes you'd wonder what would have happened if you'd never went.

Mary: Yes, you would sometimes, wouldn't you? There's an old prov-erb that travel is an education. They always used to say that long ago. It's a change, I suppose and I'm glad I went too. But, I'm also glad to be back.

Interviewed at their home in Templemore,
County Tipperary, on October 15th, 2007

MARTIN CAWLEY

My wife, Carole, and I came back to Ireland in January 2006, and it was very hard at first. Ireland is nothing like it was forty, even twenty, years ago; absolutely nothing like it. I found the quietness and the slowness of the place a bit strange at first. We couldn't sleep with the quietness. But, I generally tend to take things in my stride. What's the point in getting excited about anything? Just get on with it, I always say.

Amenities, however, are very scarce here. The public transport system around here is very poor so if you don't drive you're knackered. There's a bus goes once a week. The main Sligo Dublin bus passes by on the N4 out there but you're taking your life in your hands waiting for a bus because you are literally standing on the side of a main motorway. And it would be so easy for it to come in through the village here and so convenient for the villagers too. It's very dangerous for old people and for children to be standing out there on the main drag especially in the dark; it's just lethal. The nearest doctor is in Boyle, which is about six miles away, so you definitely need a car. I've had a bit of a problem with arthritis so that's curtailed me a lot and then I got carpal tunnel in both hands and had to have them operated on in Sligo hospital. Our sons came over from England at different times and stayed a while to help us get around, as Carole doesn't drive. But, I'm alright now. Today is the first day that I can stretch out my fingers.

The neighbours around here are very helpful, as is the woman who runs the post office. We have a couple of German neighbours. There's also a few back from London, all from Sligo town, and a few lads on the road that I went to school with. We knew everyone within a few weeks. But, I find that people here don't pop into one another's houses like they used to or the way we did in England. They're a bit more reserved than what you would have had in an old Irish village long ago. But, they're always there if you need them. They always offer to take us places. They have a little car pool going and are always telling us not to be stuck. The thing is if you really are ill; by the time they get an ambulance out you'd be better off trying to get a lift. The health system in general seems to be very bad, waiting to see a consultant and that. Once you do get to see them, they're good. But, it's getting there is the thing. Letters go missing from your doctor and that. I think the dampness here brought on the arthritis too. Maybe it had been dormant all along, but the dampness in Ireland brought it out. I'd been gone forty-five years so I'd forgotten really how damp it was.

It was Manchester I went to originally. I was working with the North-West cold storage in Sligo town and I used to get the odd day on the coal boats. I was walking down the docks one Sunday with two other boys who were complaining that there was nothing here; that they were heading off to England. One of them, Joe, said he wanted to go to Birmingham, and the other, Noel, said he wanted to go to London, and out of the blue, I just said that I'd choose Manchester because there was nobody I knew there, whereas the whole of Sligo was in Birmingham that time. If you did anything wrong, they'd be writing home about you! So we tossed a coin and didn't I win. Manchester then it was. They went the following Wednesday and I waited until Thursday to pack in the job and get me wages. I left on the one o'clock train the following Saturday and the boys met me Sunday morning. I'll never forget it. It was raining, as we headed for a house in Old Trafford where the boys had got digs.

It was 1961, we were eighteen years old, and we hadn't a clue. We didn't know how to cook or nothing. We didn't know what it was like to eat in a café or anything like that. At first all we ever ordered was steak and chips because it was the only thing we knew. We'd hear fellas on about curry at work so one night we decided to try it with rice and God we didn't like it at all. We had to order a pint of milk to wash it down. The other lads were laughing at us, but sure we weren't used to it at all. We moved into full board then and that was a lot better. It was a lot cleaner and of course you had hot water; you could go and have a bath, but you'd have to be quick about that too because if someone got in before you, there might be no water left. We found

Sherlock's dance hall that first night and we met a lad who told us we'd get a job with *Bovis* contractors no problem. Fair play, we went down the next day and they started us off straight away. The foreman, a Limerick man from Newcastlewest, showed us the ropes and I'll never forget him. Every second week we got a bonus and he'd take us down to the post office in Spring Gardens and make us send the extra money home to our mothers. He came down with us the first three or four times and then he said now you can do it on your own. He also made us get a post office savings book to put away a few shillings for ourselves and he showed us how to get sorted out with new clothes and that. He was a sound man.

The social life was great. You could nearly go dancing every night of the week. We had *Sherlock's* on a Sunday afternoon and Sunday night, and you had the RAOC hall on a Monday and Wednesday and sometimes the odd Friday night. These Irish men used to hire out the halls and hold dances there. Coen, a Galway man, was big into promoting the dances and the O'Connell brothers, big contractors in Manchester, used to bring in all the big acts to *Sherlocks*. They had Bridie Gallagher and The Bachelors and Ruby Murray and of course all the big showbands especially The Royal, which was the main one. It could be very lonely though as well. You could be stuck up in a room, just the two of ye looking at the bare walls. Joe went home after a few months; he was too homesick. Sure we didn't know how to wash clothes or anything. We'd sooner buy a new shirt than wash one. Then we'd hit the hairdressers every Friday night for a shampoo and a blow back. That used to be all the craic them days. We'd get a trim then into the square neck, that was all the go. Then with your white shirt and red tie you'd be all set for the dance.

We were making good money alright, that was the reason we were there, but we were spending it just as quick. I was with *Bovis* for about three years and then I went on to another firm called *Jarvis* and then of course, *Murphy's*, who were paying a lot more money than anyone else. A lot of the firms only wanted us to work, work, work, with no commitments, no stamps or nothing, and of course we didn't listen when we were warned about them. We'd go on anyway and try and of course some of the jobs you wouldn't get paid for and some of the lads would move on then to another town. Some of the employers treated the Irish very bad. After a while with *Murphy's* I went back to *Bovis* again. What had happened was they had gone out of town for a while because there was no work in Manchester and then they came back to build a new *Sainsbury's*, I think it was, in Stockport, and then that job finished and I went back to *Murphy's* again. I stayed with them then for a good while and then I was with a bricklaying company. That's the way it was going, you were on the move all the time. That's how it was in the building trade.

I came home regularly on holidays and always travelled by boat. It was all boat that time. We'd sail into Dun Laoghaire, and then take the train to Westland Row in Dublin where you'd have the breakfast and a few pints before boarding the train to Sligo town where I grew up. My father was a docker. He was in the Army first and then he came out of that and did any bit of work he could get his hands on; a day here and a day there, and then he was with the ESB for a while putting the poles down and then me grandfather retired. He was working on the docks and me father took over from him

My father with Josephine

like. The dockers always passed the job on from one to another; that was the way it used to be. There was ten of us in it and we all emigrated although not everyone stayed away. Mary only went as far as Dublin to do nursing, and she's still there. Josephine only stayed a few months in London and then went straight back to Mammy! Margaret went to Manchester and Theresa to Denmark where she is still. One of my brothers left home when he was fourteen after having a row with the auld lad over smoking. He went off on one of the potato boats going over to Scotland and now he's finished up in Brighton. He'll never come back.

I always knew I'd come back; I was just waiting for the opportunity. I always thought about Ireland even when I was younger, listening to the matches and that. My mother used to always send me *The Sligo*

Champion. We could go in and read the papers in the Irish Centres, but we couldn't buy them anywhere over there. The first Irish Centre in Manchester was St. Brendan's up near City Road in Old Trafford; then they opened one in Cheetham Hill and now they have an Irish Heritage Centre which attracts visitors from even America and they're going to build an even bigger one with a hotel. It's going to cost millions. The Irish Centres are great though because that's where everyone congregated, especially families. They would be full of second and even third generation Irish people, the children and grandchildren of the emigrants.

I was only there a couple of years when I got married, foolish again then, you see because we were so young. She was a Kerry girl who had moved over with her family, parents and all. They just upped sticks and left. We finished up and divorced in the early Seventies and then I met this woman here, the love of my life. Carole is an English woman, a Birmingham woman at that, but her ancestors are Irish. I needed a good Brummy to sort me out. My brother introduced us; he had known her first husband who was also Irish and who died very young. There was a do in the pub one night, a big charity do and we met there. Between us we have nine children who were all very immersed in Irish culture and all educated in Catholic schools. Carole thinks there's a closer Irish community in Manchester than there is here. The thing is you're all living very close to one another over there. If you only went around the corner you'd bump into another Irish person; if you went down for a pint you'd always run into the Irish lads because that's where the craic was, but the Irish are not as plentiful over there now as they used to be. When I go back now to visit, I see a hell of a difference. I look at lads now and I see how old they're getting, with their little carrier bags with their little bit of bread in it and I think to myself, the poverty is still there. They're going back then to their little room, you know what I mean, to their empty little bed-sit. And you'd hear of them being found dead after months.

One year we were over here in Sligo on holiday and I seen this lad that I knew from Manchester. He'd come back long years before. Now his older brother was still over there and I asked how he was and he told me that he was found dead above in his flat and he'd been dead about six weeks. He said there'd been no sign of him for a long time. He wouldn't come back on a holiday or anything. I had known him in the early years and he used to say to me, sure what's over there for me now, Martin? Yet his mother and brothers were here. And yet he said there was nothing here for him? The family asked me to find out where he was buried, as they didn't want him in a pauper's grave. I enquired in the cemetery in Manchester when I went back and the girl there told me it was very hard to find anyone because they all went under different names. When people went over first they sometimes changed their names and put up their ages in order to avoid the tax man. You could get a set of cards when you were eighteen years of age, but they were youngster's cards, probation cards or something like that, which meant that you could only earn a certain amount of money, and you were only meant to work so many hours. The legal requirement that time was twenty-one years of age; then you were considered an adult and could earn higher wages. When you'd start work first, you'd get a set of cards that you had to bring down to the employment exchange. They knew right well what the Irish lads were up to; they were well used to it. That's the way it used to be. They'd stamp your card and you'd take it back to the foreman and he'd keep it then until you moved onto the next job. We had no birth certificates or passports or any form of ID whatever so they had no way of check-ing. As a result, the woman who worked in the cemetery told me that they don't know who's in there half the time. It was harder to trace people who died alone and had no one to identify them. She said I could try in the crematorium, but it would be the same there. And she was right. Then the local priest in his parish had moved on and I couldn't find any record of his death there either. So that was it.

There was no need for anyone to be isolated in Manchester like that because as I said, there was a very close-knit Irish community. If somebody was off sick and couldn't work, everyone would help in to support the family. We'd hire the local hall and a band and there'd be a raffle and we'd make a collection for the person. As an Irish man pointed out to me one day, you'd never see any of the other nationalities doing that for one another. So there was no need for anyone ending up alone there, although I can understand them thinking sometimes that there's nothing for them here because it has changed so much.

Oh! You'd see a lot of changes. The manners in people, I think that's gone, especially in the young ones. There's no helping one another anymore. The community is gone and there is terrible violence. The two things I'd really have a problem with are the health system and law and order. The things I read in the local paper would make you wonder. You never heard tell of rape or anything like that long ago in Sligo. If somebody's car window was broken one time or somebody's house window was broken, that was a big thing. You'd have the Sergeant up and he'd get to the end of it. Now cars are stolen and people are stabbing each other on the streets and it's ridiculous. The guards don't seem to be taking the law seriously at all; they seem to be restricted or something. Drivers are on the roads with no taxes and no insurance and they seem to be getting away with it. There was two murders there in Sligo in the last twelve months and nothing is being done whatsoever about them. The guards know who did it, but they maintain they haven't enough evidence because witnesses are too afraid to come forward with information. Then for minor offences you can get off if you know the guards in the area or are related to them. I've seen them give warnings to people not to drink and drive after they're gone off duty. If they do stop them and they know them, they'll let them off. But, when you see the politicians getting away with things, what can you expect? That sends out a message to the people. I'll tell you one thing; you wouldn't see that happening in England.

Another thing that has changed a lot is the rural pub. When our children come over, now when I say children, they're in their forties, they go into Sligo town for a drink and they have a great time, but not like they'd have in the Irish pubs in Manchester. The pubs here and the restaurants are all money orientated and they're there to make as much as they can. The old traditional pub is gone. There's the odd one still around, but they're closing down too. There's a pub up the road there and he's doing nothing. Nobody goes into it. We're off the beaten track here and people don't want to drive unless there's music on a Sunday night or something. I miss the pub. Friends of ours come over every year and they're always looking for somewhere to have a bit of craic and a bit of traditional music. There is one place in Sligo, but they don't start until eleven o'clock at night and that's too late for us. You're waiting all night for it to start. Then there's no atmosphere because half the pub is outside smoking. You're sat at the table on your own unless you go out and join them. Smokers and non-smokers agree that it's breaking up the company all the time. Often they have better craic outside than we're having inside.

There used to be great craic in the pubs years ago, even before I left. I never drank that much, but I used to love going into the local to have a pint with the auld lad and maybe there'd be a game of darts going on. Now the young lads only want to listen to the jukebox. Plus people don't have the money for the pub now. They all live in big houses and spend big fees on children's schooling; they don't have any left to go out for a drink. They prefer to drink at home. Everyone seems to be wary of each other too. They seem to be looking at each other and weighing one another up. The curiosity is still there.

My father always drank in *Conmey's* on Hogan Street and then there was *The Angler's Rest*, and *The Rendezvous*; that used to be called *Water's*. Drink was the scourge of a lot of people that time too. I know a lot of men in England wore the pioneer pin, but there was plenty of drinking done in this country. I saw a lot of it in Sligo, especially among the dockers. Sure there was one pub called the early house and it would open at five or six in the morning for the dockers and they'd go in for a few pints on their way to or from work. It catered for the sailors and navigators too. The only one that's still there from our time is *Conmey's*. They've spent a lot of money doing it up and it's full of students and that. The old style pub is pushed out. It's a pity because it's a culture of its own gone. There's no communication at all now. In the Irish communities abroad you're all the one, no-one's a stranger. Even at work there was a great atmosphere; great camaraderie among one another. We were all the one. But, I've noticed now for a good while that the Irish areas in Manchester are dwindling. Shoreton, Old Trafford, Stratford, Longside, and All Saints were the basic areas in Manchester for the Irish communities. The Irish have either come back or fallen by the wayside. There's not as much of the present generation coming in either. Then of course the building of Manchester University done away with a lot of the old neighbourhoods.

I'm still glad I came home for the peace if anything because crime is getting very bad over there too. The quietness would drive you mad sometimes here though. It drives Carole mad. Bobby keeps us going. He's half Yorkshire terrier and half Tibetan spaniel and he's been great company for us. We often drive into Strandhill and take him for a walk along the beach. We love *The Strand Bar* in there too and it's only about twenty minutes away. We have the Internet and we like going on that for a bit of craic. To be honest I wouldn't want to live in a small village like this if I was twenty years younger, or if I was single. Oh! God I'd be gone! I'd say to a single person coming back to Ireland to definitely go into a town where there'd be people around them and where they'd be looked after because they wouldn't survive out in the sticks. I'd say make sure you're a driver because you can't depend on public transport over here. Carole can't drive and that never bothered

My Father (centre) with the Sligo Dockers

119

her over in England because I did all the driving and there were buses at every corner. When I was ill with my hands and we couldn't get into the chemist or the doctor for a prescription we really noticed the difference then.

I'd say to anyone thinking of coming back to think very carefully and weigh up all the pros and cons. And to make sure that all the paperwork is completed, because that's one thing they're spot on with here is the paperwork. It depends on why someone is coming home too. If they think they're coming back to the place they left behind, they'd be better off staying where they are. Plus the people they once knew may not still be here. A lot of the people I grew up with in Sligo have either moved out of the town; moved out of the country altogether and not come back, or they've moved into the cemetery. I've met a few of my friends up in the graveyard! Only that we came back twice and three times a year for years and we've kept in touch with everyone here and everything that's going on, we wouldn't have fit in at all. It would have been terrible if we'd had no back-up. I knew what I was getting into. I had a PPS number sorted out and everything. The outreach workers with Safe Home are spot on though and they'll help with that.

We don't get much chance to miss England, to be honest, because one or other of the children are always over here. We have a daughter married in Milltown in County Galway and we have grandchildren here, so that makes a big difference. My family was delighted I came home, especially my sister, Josephine. They all knew it was going to happen. Margaret had come back from Manchester before me. She was there a long time as well. I always talked about coming back. Margaret used to always say to me, I can see you coming back to live on The Hill. And she was almost right, wasn't she? The Hill in Sligo town is where we grew up, in Number 16, St. Edward's Terrace, and I still have the key to the door; every one of us does. My brother lives there now. If you go out the Bundoran road there you'll see all the houses up on a hill, along by the river. Anyone I ever knew in Manchester that was coming home to visit in the area, even as far as Bundoran or Ballyshannon, I used to tell them to call into Number 16 and they always would. Or if it's daytime call into *Conmey's*, I'd say to them, and you'll see the auld fella there.

I have never found any resentment among people about the fact that I've been away. You might get more of that in the villages, but not in a big town. But, you see I never really went away. I was always coming back; always drank in the same pub; always kept in touch with my friends and family; and then of course nearly everyone else had emigrated at some stage too, even if it was only for a couple of months. Nearly everyone in Ireland went, didn't they? They had no choice. The only resentment there might be would be from other people who are waiting for houses and they wonder how someone who'd been away for so long might get one ahead of them. Some people then don't even know we're home for good. If they see us in town or calling into my sisters, they say, are you back again, Martin? You must have plenty of money, they say.

We felt it was meant to be when we saw this place first. We came down on a winter's night and when we drove in around by Ballinafad Castle, Carole said, there's our Padraig's castle. Our son had made a castle in art class when he was fourteen, which we've always kept, and it's an exact replica of The Castle of the Curlews around the corner there. Then the street here was all lit up with street lights and Carole looked at me and said, Martin, I want it. The girl from Cluid Housing Association, Eileen O'Hara, contacted us the night we were returning home. When the call came through to tell us we had the house, Carole started crying. I had to pull in beside the statue of The Chieftain overlooking Lough Arrow there and hold Carole until she calmed down. She always knew since the day she met me that we'd be coming back and she always loved Sligo. We brought our furniture home. Our son-in-law came over with a van and moved everything back for us. I had come back a week earlier with my son and gave it a major clean up and a bit of paint and that was it. You'd be better off bringing your own things with you, especially if you knew someone who had a wagon and could take them over, because the cost of living is very high here. We have been back to England twice on holidays since we left. We took the car and travelled by boat because we still had bits and pieces to bring back. But, you can fly from Strandhill now into Manchester for only about sixty euros.

The cost of living here throws a lot of people off coming back. I'd suggest to them if they had a few pounds to spare they should come over for a week or two and have a look around; go out and socialize a bit and see what's going on. Then again it might be easier in that we have a lot of foreigners here now and people coming from England would be used to that, although the ones here have not really integrated with the Irish yet. Some people though who have not been back in thirty years still think it's the country they left behind and they won't believe you when you tell them otherwise. I suppose it's depends on your attitude too. If you've got the appetite for it; if you're longing for it, then you should try it.

Martin (left) with brother-in-law Michael, sister Nora and friends in Manchester

It's great to walk down the street and hear someone shout your name. Some people might interpret their friendliness as nosiness, but it depends on yourself how much personal information you give out. After the operation I needed someone to change the dressing on my hands and somebody told us there was a district nurse based in the village. We found out her address from the post office and Carole wrote her a note with our telephone number and shoved it under her door. The next morning she phoned us up and she was so friendly. There was no formalities; it was like we already knew her. When she came up here the first time, she made herself at home straight away.

And that is lovely about the people around here. What Carole especially likes is that they call you by your first name the minute you meet them. There's no airs and graces. For instance, the pharmacist talks to us like he's our own son. He's a great fellow, great craic, and he's back from London himself. There's still a lot of local family businesses in the small villages, even our local doctors are a husband and wife team. They go by their first names too. It's a great way to break down barriers.

I was delighted with Sligo winning the Connaught Championship, but they've an awful lot of work to do yet. Sligo is not really a GAA county; it was mostly soccer always, wasn't it? I always followed the soccer. I had an uncle playing for Sligo Rovers, Coogan McLaughlin was his name. They won the Free State Cup that time in 1937. I always followed them over in England too; always followed the results every week on the paper because I knew a lot of the lads playing. The original Sligo Rovers team was built from the Hill. All the early players came from there; they were nearly all dockers.

Emigration should be part of every history course in Ireland. There are so many stories out there, many of them heartbreaking. My mother was devastated when we all left. She'd be out looking for the postman every morning, "Anything for me Mattie?" She'd call to him. Her heart would drop, she told us, when he'd say, "Not today, Mam." And I'd say all the mothers were at that craic. And that time the postman came twice a day and once on a Saturday so that's a lot of heartache in one week if there was no letter from abroad. Another person they'd be waiting for is the wire boys who brought home the money. They'd come along on their bikes with the bag on the side containing the money orders from emigrant children all over the world who'd wire it home. Then it would be brought straight down to the post office to cash and a big load of shopping would be bought in. A lot of families in Ireland would not have survived without the money we sent home. In a way, we have a lot to thank England for.

**Interviewed at his home in Ballinafad, County Sligo.
On September 11th, 2007**

MAUREEN & PATRICK HIGGINS

Maureen: We went to Rhodesia in 1963 on our wedding day – the 29th of October. It was as far away from Ian Paisley as we thought we could get. We'd left University – Queen's in Belfast – and there was nothing really for Catholics then in Northern Ireland. So we decided to seek our fortunes elsewhere. My brother had gone to Northern Rhodesia three years before that and I had an uncle who was an ex Naval officer and had retired to Rhodesia. I thought it would be a grand place; as far away from the rain and the cold and the religious tension as we could get.

Pat had actually gone to England looking for work and was passing Rhodesia House in London one day. He'd thought he'd just pop in and they interviewed him straight away. Within a few weeks he was offered the position of Cadet District Officer with the Government of Southern Rhodesia. He contacted me and asked how I felt about that? I said great. Almost immediately we decided to get married and had this romantic idea of spending our honeymoon on the boat going over. Then we'd start this whole new life. Next thing they sent us two air tickets and told us to be there by November 1st. So we got married at Holy Cross Church in the Ardoyne at eleven o'clock in the morning; we had the reception in Belfast Castle at one o'clock; and caught the six o'clock plane that night. Forty-eight hours later we arrived in Salisbury with two suitcases and twelve pounds, ten shillings.

From that very first day I adored Africa with every fibre of my being. My first impression was one of awe. If you can picture leaving Belfast in the rain – grey, Victorian, Belfast, and a couple of days later arriving in this beautiful country bathed in sunshine. Our first sight of Africa was quite scary though. We came down in Khartoum at five o'clock in the morning. It was boiling hot and the flies were out already. It was October, the end of their long, dry, season, and I thought, Oh, My God. We had just been allowed off the plane to walk around; then the plane took off again and our next stop was Nairobi in Kenya. Then we came down in Salisbury.

The sun was shining and the buildings seemed to gleam - so clean and white were they. The Jacarandas, the frangipanis and the flamboyants were all in bloom. There were all these amazing flowers and trees, and bougainvillea everywhere. There was cleanliness and order and sunshine. This chap in a pith helmet came towards us in the airport terminal, saying, "Mr. & Mrs. Higgins?" And we said, "Oh! Yes, that's us!" He held out his hand, "Welcome to Southern Rhodesia." He took us to our hotel. The next morning he collected Pat and took him to the Internal Affairs Head Office. When he came back he said we have a choice; we can stay in Salisbury and he can work in Head Office or we can go to a bush station. We opted for the latter.

We were then sent to the bundu (bush station) at Shamva, a district station about a hundred miles from the capital, which was Salisbury, the second city was Bulawayo. There were several smaller towns, commercial farming areas, and game reserves. The rest of the country comprised of what was called Tribal Trust Land. (TTL). The Department of Internal Affairs, which had recruited Pat, administered much of these areas. They were known as 'a Government within a Government'. A bush station was an administrative centre, sometimes in the midst of a huge tract of TTL. For example, Tjolotjo, which was one of our stations and a wildly beautiful place, was over one million acres. Some of these stations had no electricity or other amenities. We had to send our sons to boarding school from an early age and I taught them for the first few years.

On our arrival at Shamva, however, the District Commissioner showed us around an old colonial-style house which was to become our home. Nobody had lived in the house for years and it was hidden behind eight feet tall elephant grass. The DC was a high ranking administrator for government and had been born in Rhodesia. He and his wife were charming, but battled with our accents. We stayed overnight and the next day where taken back to our house.

Inside, we found men spraying the walls with DDT. We were quite taken aback. The DC told us they were spraying the house against mosquitoes. In the early days, Shamva was among the worst malarial areas in Rhodesia and many deaths had occurred there from black -water fever, an insidious form of malaria. He then asked us when was our furniture arriving and we said, what furniture? Pat said we were told that essential furniture would be provided and they said that meant a stove and a fridge. Here we were in a huge house and no furniture! Anyhow, they were great and they gave us fifty pounds and then another thirty pounds so that we could furnish the house. We did it too on eighty pounds, the furniture being crated to us by rail from Salisbury.

The DC was our nearest neighbour. The 'station' consisted of a small police camp, the DC's office, a Greek store, a post office and a sports club with golf, bowls and tennis facilities, a bar and kitchen. There was always a sports club in Rhodesia no matter where you went. Shamva was in a commercial farming area. A lot of the families living on those farms back then were second and third generation Rhodesian.

We quickly settled in our new home. After a few weeks I wasn't feeling very well. Pat was being initiated into this new administrative world and would be away from home for weeks on end. So here I am all alone, no family, no friends, hardly even any neighbours and I felt quite isolated. I wrote to my mother about my condition and she wrote back that it was probably the climate. I wrote to her again saying how unwell I was feeling; that I was putting on weight and she wrote back yet again that she'd spoken to the family doctor and it was definitely the change in climate. After about five months I went to visit the DC's wife who took one look at me and said, "You're pregnant my dear!" So I wrote back to my Mum with the news and her reply was a large box of baby clothes. When our son, Kevin, was born, we'd been married nine months and four days.

By this time we'd been transferred out of the bush station and into the city of Bulawayo. We were in Bulawayo for three years when I fell pregnant again. When I was seven months pregnant, we were trans-ferred back to the bush again, to a station with no hospital. We drove down to Chiredzi, with our almost three-year old son, an Alsatian dog, a cat, and our suitcases, all in this little VW beetle on a dirt road. At one stage a large buck (a kudu) ran across in front of us and Pat had to brake violently, which caused the car to skid on the heavily corrugated road. The back seat of the VW was held in place by a thick rubber band, which snapped, hurling Kevin, the dog, the cat and suitcases all practically into our laps in the front seats. Fortunately nobody was hurt.

I returned to Bulawayo two weeks before the next baby was due. This time I had to travel over three hundred miles all the way from Chiredzi, close to the Mozambique Border, back to Bulawayo to have the baby. I drove there with friends and I think perhaps all the jolting must have accelerated things, because three or four days after my arrival I unexpectantly went into labour. My aunt dropped me at the Mater Dei Hospital, which was run by Irish nuns. I think they thought I was an unmarried mother because there was no sign of a husband, and that would have been a shocking thing in 1967. Kevin had been staying with my Aunt and Uncle and then I put him into a Nursery School that had boarding facilities. I tried to phone Pat a couple of times, but was told he was out in the bush on patrol, and would be out there for some time, and of course the baby coming early, he wasn't expecting to hear from me. So I had my little baby boy, Sean, all alone. I tried to phone Pat again, but couldn't get through.

Pat: I came back from patrol and we were offloading the trucks when

'TARA' Our home in Bulawayo

one of the office staff congratulated me. I said thanks. Then another colleague congratulated me and I thought, well, I hadn't done that well with the tax and dip fee collections. The stations competed for that sort thing on how close we could get to one hundred percent tax and dip fee collection and mine had gone alright. It wasn't outstanding, so I wondered why they were all congratulating me. Then the DC came up and said, "Congratulations." And whatever way I looked at him, he said, "Don't you know?" I looked at him again. "Your wife's given birth to a second son." I ran into the office and I found the number for Mater Dei and a nun answered the phone and we were cut off. I tried again and we were cut off again. Now I'm chomping at the bit. So I rang again and roared, "What the bloody hell is going on there!"

Maureen: This little Irish nun said to me later, "You're from the North, aren't you?" I said, yes. "Are you a Catholic or a Protestant?" I said, Catholic. "And your husband is he Catholic or Protestant?" I said, Catholic. "Well," she said, "with the sort of language he uses, he ought to be Protestant."

I stayed in the hospital for six days with my baby, and now I had to make my way back to Chiredzi, which was at the other end of the country. A friend picked me up at the Mater Dei; we drove to St. Gabriel's to collect Kevin with his little suitcase and his potty; and then she dropped us off at the airport where we boarded this tiny five-seater plane, which could only take us to the town of Fort Victoria; where we boarded an even smaller plane, which took us the rest of the way to Chiredzi, where Pat met us at Buffalo Range airport.

In time, Pat became a District Commissioner and learned the language and customs of the Matebele people.

Over the years we had this wonderful romantic notion about Ireland always, but I didn't go home for fourteen years. My family were very scattered. A year after I left home my mother, father, and teenage sister went to South Africa where my brother had by then moved. My mother had a very dominant personality and she wanted to be near her cubs so one time when my father was away from home, working on a contract, she packed up the house and announced to him when he came back that they were moving to South Africa. That was my immediate family gone from Belfast. While in Capetown, my mother fell ill with cancer, but fortunately she got to see her one grand-child, Kevin, before she died.

Less than two years after arriving in Rhodesia Pat was called up to do his National Service in the Rhodesian Army. My mother came all the way from Capetown, about 1,500 hundred miles, to Bulawayo and spent four months with us. Shortly after her return to Capetown we managed to have one family Christmas together in 1965 and in 1966 my mother died. My sister met an American man whom she married and she, now a widow, lives in Vermont. So apart from an Uncle and an Aunt in County Down, whom we absolutely loved, I had no immediate family to draw me back to Northern Ireland. We spent a few holidays with them in later years and we ate Irish food, and drank the beer and sang rebel songs and visited the heritage centres and there's that part of being Irish that you never get out of your system. To me Ireland was always home. Not Pat though, to him home was Africa.

Pat: Rhodesia was the best country in the world. Its way of life was unique; its medical services were fantastic; its education system was really First World. It really bowled me over. And we were living most of the time in bush stations, which was a totally different way of life to anything we were used to. Whenever I came back to Ireland, I really just came back to see my family.

Between 1963 and 1980, because of my position as District Commissioner, we were transferred many times; largely living on bush stations, but Bulawayo was always our base. After Independence in 1980, when Rhodesia then became Zimbabwe, I resigned my position as District Commissioner and we moved to Bulawayo permanently where I entered the commercial world. We remained in Bulawayo until the end of 2005, when we finally departed from Zimbabwe and returned to Ireland.

I well recall my last major task as a District Commissioner at Independence in 1980. The country was formally handed over to the new nationalist government. Prince Charles represented the Queen at the symbolic handover ceremony in Salisbury and read the messages from her and the British Prime Minister to the new government and the people of Zimbabwe. District Commissioners performed the same ceremony in each of the fifty or so districts they administered throughout Rhodesia. Consequently, I found myself in the position of reading, to the assembled throng in my district, the same messages from the Queen and the British Prime Minister, as had Prince Charles. The irony of an Irishman from the nationalist area of Ardoyne, representing the Queen and the British Prime Minister, and delivering their messages of 'good will' wasn't lost on me!

Maureen: As Pat pursued his commercial career, I went back to college in 1981 and later took a Degree in English & Drama, and taught for the next twenty-five years. My last position was in St. Patrick's Christian Brothers College, where there was still one Irish Christian Brother left. In 1982 we bought our beloved house, which we called *Tara* after the seat of the kings of Ireland. Ironically, as things progressed, it was to have more parallels with the Tara of 'Gone with the Wind'.

Hwange Game Reserve (left to right – Carol, Maureen, Pat, Kevin)

Pat: So you see, we never had any intentions of leaving Zimbabwe. We loved the country. We'd put our roots down, we thought we could make it work, and we did, really, until the year 2000 – until the Government took over the commercial farms and the economy began to implode. You must remember, we had spent more of our lives there than we had in Ireland and our sons were born and reared to manhood there. And what fine young men Kevin and Sean turned into, with a great love of nature and the outdoors and values way above and beyond the pub and drug culture found elsewhere in the world.

People here seem to think that Africa is a dark continent, but the streets of Bulawayo are certainly no worse probably than the streets of Dublin are now, and they were certainly no worse than the streets of Belfast that we had left behind. We grew up with war really. I remember when we came back to Belfast in the Nineties and went to the Ardoyne, one of the neighbours said to us, "Are you not frightened living over there?" I wanted to laugh at the irony of a man who had survived the Troubles in Northern Ireland asking me if I was afraid in Zimbabwe.

Maureen: Especially when we'd had so much trouble getting through the barricades to go and see family in Brompton Park with barbed wire everywhere.

Pat: From 2000 onwards, things continued to deteriorate in Zimbabwe and with inflation spiralling out of control, surviving economically became increasingly more difficult. We had to take stock of our position, and being close to retirement realized that our meagre pensions could not sustain us. Pensioners there now are really charity cases, so much so that there's an organization now set up called SOAP (Support Old Age Pensioners), which assists with their medical expenses and regularly provides them with supplementary food. So we took the hard decision to leave Africa. After all the years of politics and war, it was economics which drove us out.

We sold our house and all our possessions accumulated over more than forty years, for a pittance, in many cases giving much of it away to charity, schools and the SPCA. Our vehicles had been stolen from our house very early on a Sunday morning in 2002 and because of the dramatic escalation in inflation, our insurance on them had become meaningless so we could not afford to replace them. I don't think we ever fully recovered from that. We left with our suitcases and a one cubic metre crate en route filled with our most treasured possessions – somewhat reminiscent of our arrival forty-three years earlier with two suitcases and a tea chest on the way – filled mainly with books and our wedding presents. At least we had left with a bigger crate than when we arrived, but alas, were that many years older!

Maureen: We came back to Ireland in January 2006. I had been visiting my son Sean who was now living on Vancouver Island, and I envied the Canadian senior citizens their freedom of movement and speech and their obvious security. Suddenly the idea of not living behind six foot high walls, with razor wire and electric gates and being able to speak freely without continually looking over your shoulder flooded my being and I knew that I wanted some of that. I had this life-changing experience while sitting on a park bench with my sister, in Butchart Gardens. I decided there and then that when I went back I'd push Pat into leaving Zimbabwe and going back to Ireland.

I visited my old Aunt in County Down on the way back and contacted an old friend, who had come back to live in Donegal a few years earlier, and she told me about Safe Home. I made contact with them while in Ireland and by the time I arrived back in Zimbabwe, the necessary forms were waiting for us, and the process had begun. That was in June 2005 and we were back the following January.

Pat: As it was, Maureen found me more pliable to moving than she would have expected. My little agency which I had been running alone for the last ten years, had substantially folded. I was then sixty-four years of age and whatever money I had invested in the Money Market had quickly eroded.

Maureen: Leaving Zimbabwe wasn't as hard for me as it was for Pat. Getting rid of the material things wasn't that hard, because in the end they're only that – material things. The hardest part was leaving our son and his wife, our two grand-children and our thirteen year old cat, Roxy. We had to have her put down and that was very hard. We brought her home and buried her under the Mexican Apple tree in our garden, beside her old friend, our little dog Steffi, who had died a year earlier. We then said goodbye to both of them. After that, once we started getting ready to move, it became an end in itself and we hadn't time to look over our shoulders and dwell on the past.

Some of our family and several of our closest friends had left the country already, and others were planning to move. Things were changing quickly!

Because of our background from the last forty years, our preference was to avoid big cities. I love the information breakdown that Safe Home sends. They tell you how far your accommodation is from the nearest Church, post office and pub, and that is your picture of the Ireland you're coming back to. I think it's wonderful. When they offered us a place called Ballyhaunis, we immediately logged onto the Internet to find out more about it. On discovering the prevalence of our name 'Higgins' throughout Mayo, we thought we must be going home, and accepted with alacrity.

Pat: For us Ballyhaunis was a rural Irish town, but a metropolis compared with many of the places we'd lived in.

Maureen: And it was surrounded by lots of historical sites; it's got a library, sixteen pubs …

Pat: And we've only been in about two of them.

Maureen: The main change we have noticed since our return is in how Ireland has moved on and is now among the richest nations in the world while at the time of our leaving, the opposite was the case. Also, how the influence of the Church appears to have waned. There's a tremendous emphasis on the material things. For example, when we were children, you got a new suit or a dress for Holy Communion and you walked to the church with your parents – hail rain or snow – not even a taxi and now, we understand some children are being ferried in stretch limos or even helicopters. And we're intrigued by the sums of money being spent in tanning salons. Back when we were young, you had to lie on freezing beaches one week a year (if the sun shone), or on the damp grass in the Belfast City Hall grounds if you wanted to 'catch a tan.' The standard joke then was if you saw an Irishman with what looked like a tan, it wasn't. It was RUST!!

We were only here a couple of days when I had to make my way to the local supermarket to find some food. Now I'm coming from the Third World and up I go and I see all of these trolleys locked together.

I'm trying and trying, but I can't release one. I see this woman coming along with a trolley and I ask her for it. She says of course you can have it, but can I have a euro. I thought that was strange, as I just wanted to borrow the trolley, not buy it, so I refused. Then I met a man who greeted me. I love that about Mayo people - the way they all greet you. I asked him for his trolley and he also asked for a euro. I said what is wrong with you people; you won't do anything for anyone unless it's for money. He said, let me show you, and proceeded to put a euro into the slot and out came the trolley. I felt so stupid. He then explained how I would get my euro back when I replaced the trolley. "Where did you come from," he asked, and I thought if he only knew. Then I find myself in this huge supermarket with all of these choices. One of the assistants told me recently that she loves watching me shopping because I look like I'm enjoying it so much and I take so long about it. Darned right I do.

Pat: I became a member of the Spring Festival Committee, and all of our meetings were in the pub. One night they were talking about some events they were going to stage. There was a lot of noise with glasses clinking and some 'soap' was on TV and someone mentioned the 'sheep tossing' event. I had this vision of them throwing sheep up into the air and I thought to myself that Maureen would be furious on account of her involvement with the SPCA. How on earth was she going to accept the idea of tossing sheep? She'd had a fireworks display at her school in Bulawayo cancelled because of their adverse affect on animals. Anyhow we were greatly relieved to discover, on later reading the minutes of the meeting, that it was in fact the 'sheaf tossing' event!

Maureen: As you can see communication has been somewhat difficult for us! Nevertheless, since our return we've felt that we must put something back into our community and also that we must learn more about our country, it's history and its beauty. Thus, Pat is on the board of the Community Council, is a member of the Town Development sub-committee, and was a member of the Festival Committee last year. I belong to a hill-walking group, the local Book Club, and have joined the Mayo SPCA where I help out at the kennels and with Fund

Raising. I recently took part in the Dublin Ladies Mini-marathon to raise funds for them. I've also formed a little drama group with a rural woman's club, and we hope to present a play for Christmas. Pat and I have joined the Heritage Society and visited many of their centres all over Ireland in Slane, the Hill of Tara, Trim, Newgrange, and Knock. We have been to places that people who've lived here all of their lives haven't been. We've been cruising on the Shannon River in the rain; we've climbed Croagh Patrick and the Sligo Hills; and we'd love to fit in a visit to the Aran Islands before the end of the year. There are days, though, when you can't help but miss Africa.

Pat: When you've lived there as long as we have; your family has been born and reared there, part of your soul never leaves Africa.

Maureen: When my old Aunt Philomena from County Down came back from her first ever holiday in America, all she had to say was, "The butter was great." If only we could sum up Africa so simply. Our two grandchildren were born there and another was born in Canada. We are indeed the scatterings of Ireland and Africa.

Seán at Lowveld Dam, Zimbabwe

Safe Home has been an absolute lifeline for people like us, and indeed many elderly Irish living abroad, and we honestly don't know where we'd be without them. I wrote to the Minister for Foreign Affairs, Dermot Ahern, telling him how fantastic they are, and encouraging him to continue financing the programme. I had a lovely letter from his office thanking me and telling me how cognizant he is of the great work they do. Long may it continue!!

From an interview at their home in Ballyhaunis, County Mayo, on August 7th, 2007, and a subsequent written account by Pat and Maureen

MAUREEN LEAVY

In November 2005 I came back from England and I'm settling in great. I'm very happy here in Cashel with the Rock right behind me and the hospital just down the road. It's only about eighteen to twenty miles from Clonmel where I grew up. I couldn't get any nearer to home than that, could I? I'm very lucky to have this place here; I know I am.

I was the eldest of six and times were hard, but I was the only one who emigrated. Me brother joined the British Royal Air Force so he would have kind of emigrated, wouldn't he? My father was in the First World War and he lost his left arm, so he could never work after that. He was on a small pension from the British, you know. He met me mother in Dublin where she was working for a family and he had just been discharged from the Army. They lived in Dalkey for a while where he had been billeted as a soldier in blue; a wounded soldier. Me mother was Leitrim so they then went to live there, where I was born in a little place called Carrigallen. Then they moved to Clonmel where Dad was from. He used to talk a little about the Troubles, but not a lot. There were a lot of Black and Tans around Dublin, and I used to hear about them now and again, but not much, you know. So there you go.

We lived in a row of little houses in the town of Clonmel. Dad was at home all day when we were growing up, but he was a man who didn't let it get him down. He had a garden at the back of the house where he grew lettuces and that, tomatoes, strawberries and cabbages and potatoes. Even with the one hand he did it. Anyway them times there wasn't much work. It's only lately Ireland got alright. It was always a poor country, you know, it's a rich country now.

I went to school to the Sisters of Charity in Clonmel until I was fourteen. You see, that time you had to leave at fourteen. Then the Reverend Mother got me a job in the shoe factory. I was fourteen on the Friday and on the Monday I was working for The Munster Boot & Shoe factory, but we always called it the Clonmel shoe factory. I was on the eyelet machine for five years putting the holes in the shoes and the boots. It used to make an awful noise. We used to have great fun there though. We didn't make a lot of money, but we had great fun. We didn't get paid much, you know, maybe something like eighteen shillings a week. I can't really remember now

Clonmel was a quiet town in them days. There was nothing much in it except for a few shops. Nothing much happened there except for the cattle market on a Wednesday when the streets would be full of muck from the cows. It would be full of people too selling their wares and what have you. It was great fun. Oh! There were dances too in Collins's Hall and we used to go outside the town to Twomilebridge and places like that. Mick Delahunty, the bandleader, was a friend of mine. We used to work in the factory together. Funny, I used to bring love letters from him to his wife-to-be who also worked there. I remember when he started up a small band. He played the trombone I think, or the saxophone. I think he played several instruments. It was his band, you know. He played in the country halls first outside the town. And we used to walk out to them, a couple of miles, and walk back at night. A gang of us, you know, women. He was still working in the factory at first and then he got a bit of money, of course, and he got a bigger band and started playing in the Collin's Hall in the town. He had a couple of his brothers with him. There was a good family of them in it, three or four brothers, I think. He used to live over the old bridge, you know, in Clonmel. He was a great band leader. Oh! I could write a book!

The factory then was an English firm. The bosses were all English – four men and four women and they were very nice. They came over with the firm. Then when the War broke out they couldn't get the raw materials from England and had to shut down. There was terrible unemployment in Clonmel after that, terrible. There was terrible poverty too because there was no work for anyone. We used to have to queue up for the dole. Oh! That was dreadful. I had me stamps from the factory, not a lot, so I didn't stay on the dole too long. I thought that was terrible. And you didn't get much anyway. It's such a long time ago. I think the factory may have opened for a little while again, but I'm not sure of that. There's a hotel along the river now where it used to be. There was a meat factory in the town that time too and my brother used to work there, but that was it. Times were hard so there was nothing left for me to do, but head to England.

In 1942 they only wanted people who would do essential work; they wouldn't grant a visa otherwise, because there was a war on. I wanted to work in a munitions factory to get money, but that time you had to get your parents' signature and me father wouldn't sign it for a munitions factory, but after a while he agreed that I could go over and work in a hospital, which I did. I found a job in the catering department of Barnsley Hall Hospital in Worcestershire. I don't think I was quite nineteen years of age so I was very young when I left. I didn't really realize what I was doing in a way, you know, but I always had good courage. I knew nobody there and had no idea where I was going. I travelled by boat and then by train and I when I got off the train in Worcestershire there was a black out. There was no lights on anywhere because it was war time. I didn't know which road to take. I was a bit scared; you would be, wouldn't you? There was a tall young woman coming along and I asked her where the hospital was. She laughed and said, I'm a nurse there and I'm going on night duty. This was about ten o'clock, so I walked along with her, and I was lucky because it was all locked up when we got there. She had the keys to what they called the screen doors, so she brought me into the head girl there, the one in charge, and they made me a cuppa. They were terribly friendly. Then she showed me my bedroom and gave me my uniform for the next morning. The work was alright. I liked it well enough. I was very homesick at first, but I had to put that behind me. I had to forget about that, you know, and then I got to know the girls. There was one English girl and we become pals and she lived in the town there and after a while she used to bring me home at weekends. We were good friends for years, you know. And it's funny she met an Irish man from Limerick and I think they married afterwards.

I liked it well enough. Well you had to like it. There was nothing in Ireland. I lived-in; had me own room and that. I worked at Barnsley Hall for two or three years and then me cousin was working for *Hoover's* in Middlesex and she said she'd get me a job there and that I could share her digs. So that was what I did. It was hard to get out of the hospital; do you know what I mean? The Superintendent there wouldn't let me go at first. It was hard. But, eventually he did. I kept at it. One girl ran away from the hospital. They were very strict them times, you know, because there was a war on.

I don't know if I'd like to have stayed in Ireland or not. It's hard to know. I came home for a holiday after a year. I didn't mind going back again; I had got used to England by then. We used to see Coventry being bombed and all to the ground. England grows on you. When you're young you don't care and it grows on you. If I'd been older it might have been different; I might have cared more. Ah! Everybody was lovely. It was wartime and you know the English were lovely. I can't fault them. We'd be down in the shelters and we'd be having the craic together and they'd be giving us cups of tea. Oh! They were lovely, you know. I can't fault them. The social life was grand too. Oh! We had a great time. The hospital was like the League of Nations. There were soldiers there from every part of the world. We could have had loads of boyfriends if we wanted, but you had to be very careful. The fellows were all in the Army or Navy, you know. The men all had to join up unless they were conscientious objectors. The War ended then in 1945. I was there for a good three years of it. I wasn't frightened or anything; you get used to it. You just said a little prayer. It didn't take too long for England to get back to normal. People were just happy to be alive and for the War to be over. It was a different feeling, you know, a different feeling. They had black bread and that here in Ireland, didn't they? But, they weren't really affected. When I used to come home they'd be talking about it, but they weren't really affected as such, except when Dublin was bombed accidentally or that.

When I went to work in *Hoover's* I met my future husband. He was a Westmeath man, Barney Leavy, a foreman in the building trade. He worked with *Taylor Woodrow's* for about thirty-five years. I was introduced to him by a friend and we went out together for nearly two years and then got married in 1947 in Our Lady of the Visitation

Catholic Church in Greenford, Middlesex. We had a small reception in a friend's house. I had to buy coupons to get me things for the wedding. Everything was on coupons then. I had a ration book, but the coupons didn't go far so you'd buy more on the black market or from friends. We were always scrimping and saving, you know. I bought the hat and dress up the West End in London. I went from Greenford up to Oxford Street on the train. None of my family came to the wedding because I travelled home that night for me honeymoon. I got married at eight o'clock in the morning and then that evening, I think, we caught the boat. We went to Westmeath first, because it was nearest to Dublin, to Barney's mother's place. She was an old lady living on her own, you know, in the country, but she had a nice house there. We stayed there for a week and then we went for a week to Clonmel to me father and mother. It was weird coming home married, even though it had only been a few hours, but it was weird. They'd say, Mrs. Leavy, and at first I took no notice of them. I'd say who's that?

My parents liked my husband. They got on well together. Barney was always laughing and joking. He was that kind of man. He had a lovely silver car and he used to bring me Mum down for her shopping and she was delighted with herself altogether, getting a lift down and back because she used to have to carry all the messages up home herself. Me mother used to call it the silver bird. Not many people would have had a car then. It was all ponies and traps and horses and carts, you know. When he used to leave it outside me Mum and Dad's house the kids in the locality would be all around it. So Barney would have been regarded as a good catch. He done alright, you know. He was four years older than me and had a good job with *Taylor's*. He had joined the British Navy first and then stayed in England when he came out.

We had two children, a boy and a girl, Jimmy and Julia, and when Julia started school I went back working again for the Inner London Education Authority (ILEA) where I stayed for twenty-five years as a Cook/Supervisor until I retired. We used to come home every year; sometimes twice a year and I always took the children every summer for six weeks. As soon as school was finished for the holidays, we were off. I missed Ireland more when I got older and I started thinking about coming back. Me mother and father were always on at me to come home, but then I thought it's not fair to the children, changing schools and that, but Mam and Dad used to beg me. The children used to love coming here too, back to Granny and Granddad, you know. Then Mum died. And then me poor Dad was there on his own and me brother used to look after him and we got a woman to come in for a few hours. Then me Dad died; he pined for her, you know, and he died two years later.

Barney never wanted to come back. London was his thing. He loved London. Then he died of a heart attack twenty-two years ago. Sad, isn't it? He was only sixty-two. That's young, I suppose, isn't it? Well, when you're eighty-four, like me, sixty-two seems young. I was often on to him to come home, but he'd say we'll leave it for another while. So there you go. We were living on Hamden Road in Holloway, North London, and he died in Whittington Hospital on Boxing Day. He had been in all over the Christmas. He had just retired a couple of years from *Taylor Wood*. They've always been very good to me. They used to send a hamper every Christmas and up to a couple of years ago they used to send me a hundred pounds, yeah, every Christmas. But, they stopped that about two years ago. They couldn't keep it up because there was a lot of us pensioners and widows, but all them years they were good to me.

Then me kids were grown up and married. They both have English partners. Me son is in Leighton Buzzard near Bedfordshire. He's married with one daughter. She's a big six footer, blond, and she's in America now playing tennis, in Tennessee, I think. How the years fly. Me daughter is in Gloucester, married with three children, and now they're all married. I have seven great grandchildren. I was on my own then, after Barney died, but had a very good friend, Dorothy, who lived nearby. Then she moved to Hertfordshire when she lost her husband and I was on me own, you know, I was on me own again. I was a widow and I missed her company and I used often go over to see her, you know. So I asked for a transfer from North London to Hertfordshire and I was writing and writing for a while and then they granted me a place in Borehamwood near St. Alban's. It was an alright area.

I met a widower then and I knew him for ten years. We never lived together or anything like that, but we used to go all around together. He was fed up asking me to marry him and I said I've been there and done that. I'm not going to wash any more shirts I said. He accepted it. He used to come and call for me and I met all his family. They were very nice to me. We travelled to Ireland together. To hear him speak you'd think he was English, but he was born in Dublin. Jack Jordan was his name; I always think of the River Jordan when I think of him. He died of a heart attack too. He was four years older than me and he died about five years ago. He was a lovely man, great craic, full of jokes and everything. He was a very happy man.

It was alright in Hertfordshire, you know, but I always had it in me heart to end up here. I'd rather be buried here than over there. Me husband is buried there and I would've been buried with him if I'd stayed, but then I got to thinking I'd rather be near Mam and Dad. I came over when they were building the houses here and the minute I saw this one I thought it was lovely. There was a lot of paperwork to complete, transferring pensions and that, but I was always alright at writing. The house was ready to move into straight away. I brought all of my furniture with me. I have two lovely nephews in Clonmel who came over to help me. I insisted on renting the removal van and on a Friday night, after working all week, they crossed over on the boat having picked up the van in Dublin. On the Saturday morning they drove from Holyhead to Hertfordshire and they loaded all up and were off again the next morning. I followed on the plane to Dublin from where me niece drove me to Clonmel. I've got a good family.

As for social activities in Cashel, there's nothing much happening at the moment. This is only me second year, you know. We have a Care Centre that we go to every Thursday, all of us around here. We do painting and pottery and all different things. I always say it's like being back in kindergarten. But, it's interesting and it's something to do. We made these little ceramic tiles to hang on the wall out of a kind of a clay. And we had to finish it off in an oven or something, you know. I like all the neighbours. Me friend, Kathleen Maher, is just

143

over the road there. I've got a lot of friends around here now. I didn't find it hard to settle in at first; I took to it straight away.

I have a brother and sister living in Clonmel. Me brother comes out and stays with me some weekends. He's a bachelor and I'm a widow so we're both on our own. He never married, but he's as happy as a lark, you know. He's the youngest of the family and I was the eldest. Funny, isn't it? It's nice to have the company because you know you get out of talking when you live on your own, you do. Thanks be to God me health is alright and I can get about. I thank God for that. I walk into town every day and sometimes twice a day. They all complain about the hill coming back, but I don't mind. I got used to it, you know. It would be nice to have a little bus into town. Oh! I watch television. There's not much else to do, is there? There's a hall in Cashel for adult dancing and I have been once or twice. I was there at Christmas. When I get out on the floor they don't believe it's me. I love dancing. Quicksteps, foxtrots, always did. I used to go to the Irish Centre in London. We had a great time there. We danced in *The Garryowen* and *The Hammersmith Palais* too. I've always loved dancing and I still love dancing. I could still go out there and do a quick step. Mick Delahunty was over playing in London a few times. I went once, I think, I forget now where it was. I went up to the stage to see him, but it's so long ago now, so long ago. Sometimes my mind plays tricks with me and I don't remember things.

Me daughter did a bit of Irish dancing, but she gave it up when she was young. My children are both very aware of their Irish heritage, Oh! God yes, they always were. We kept up our religion all the time too; everybody did more or less. Oh! Yes, all during the War and that. I haven't been back to England since I came home. They keep asking me back, me friends, they ring me up and all. I've got a couple of women friends and a man friend I knew over there, Sean. He come to Cashel three weeks ago. He didn't come to Ireland specially to see me, but to a brother married in Dublin. He's not really a boyfriend, just a good friend. He's a bachelor, you know, he's very nice. He took me to dinner in the hotel and I showed him all around the Rock and that.

I do miss the children though. Me daughter was never here, but me son visited me in June. I'm not thinking about a holiday to England just yet; I'm still only getting used to here. I loved it the minute I landed. I love the friendliness and just being back home, just being in Ireland. I liked England, but being back home seeing familiar faces and hearing the Irish lingo is just wonderful. The people are very happy here now, they're wealthy and everything I know, but I always found them like that. All through the years when I'd come home they were always nice to me. They never said anything about working in England or anything, because they knew we had no choice when we were young. They knew that. Everything is different now, but Ireland is a much better place than it used to be. I was home every year so I knew what was going on, but I'm sure an American coming back now after fifty years wouldn't recognize the place. It must hit them, the difference.

There are some even in England who never came back. A lot of men go on the drink over there. And they'd be dying to come home, but they'd never save up, you know. I knew one or two of them that that used to happen to. You'd be talking to them sometimes, passing the time of day, and if you were going on holidays or anything, they'd say, aren't you lucky. They could do it as well, but they chose not to, although their hearts were still in Ireland, that was the funny part about it. Their hearts were in Ireland. All of our hearts were in Ireland. It's funny with us Irish; we can never forget Ireland, can we? Not that we'd want to, but we can never forget it. I don't know why that is. It seems to be deep in our blood, doesn't it, more so than other nationalities? The English are not as passionate about their nationality as we are. I don't know why. It's something that's inside of us, you know.

Even though Ireland is different, I like it. I'm happy that I came back, very happy. You missed out on a lot though, going away. You missed out on all those years with your parents and with your brothers and sisters. That was the worst part of it, but you had to do it, that was life. And it was a long life, wasn't it? So there you go.

Interviewed at her home in Cashel, County Tipperary, on Monday, October 15th, 2007

145

SEAMUS RODDY

I grew up in Ballaghadreen, in County Roscommon, but I am just as well pleased to be here in Castelplunkett, because I'd hardly know anyone down there anymore. I was gone since 1957 and returned in 2005. It would be alright here if the weather got a bit better. I spent most of my time in London in the construction business. I did nothing else for forty-eight years. Oh! It was alright. England was not a bad country. There was nothing here when I left, but there was plenty of work in England after the War.

I was born in September 1938 in Ballaghadreen. I went to school in Derrincarter, a small little village nearby. There were two brothers there, Brother Sean and Brother Anthony and they were the finest. I always went to visit them when I came back; they would insist on everyone doing that. I even came for their funerals. There were six of us in the family and three of us emigrated. Three of us stayed and three of us went. My father had about one hundred acres of land at Cloonlumney, near the Mayo border, and my brother, Sean, got that and his sons have it now. There was only room for one; everybody else had to go. Two of the girls got married here and the rest of us left. That was the way it was back then in the West of Ireland. Sure the old farm wouldn't keep us all.

John Lang came over from England looking for workers for his big construction company and he paid our fares back to London – five shillings I think it was. I was up in Kildare at the time with *Bord na Móna* working on the Bog of Allen cutting turf. They'd give us accommodation in the army barracks on the Curragh, but the money wasn't as good as Lang was offering. We were only getting seven or eight pounds there, and we started at sixteen in England, seven days a week, and it quickly went up to twenty, twenty-five pounds a week. Sure it was as good as a thousand euros now. On a frosty morning then I took the bus from Ballaghaderren to Dublin and that was the most lonesome part of the journey. I sailed on *The Princess Maud* with a whole lot of other young Irish fellows and started work straight away digging trenches for pipes and cables. I stayed in digs at first and they were the finest. I got board and lodgings for three pounds, ten shillings a week and that included breakfast and supper and a packed lunch. The landlady was a good Essex woman. You'd take your clothes off in the evening coming in from work and leave them at the end of the bed. She'd then wash and iron them for you; she was a great woman. She only kept the best too; she'd have no drunks or anything. I took a drink, but I was never a drunk. We went to the Irish pubs surely, but any pub would do. We weren't restricted to the Irish ones. They're all the same aren't they? The work was hard surely, but we were young and well able for it. It got a lot easier after 1965 when they brought the machinery in. The JCB was a doddle to operate and that was the end of the heavy graft. But, we took no notice. We got a week's wages and that's all we wanted. That's what we went for, wasn't it?

Oh! We went dancing surely to all the great dancehalls in London and to *The Banba* in Kilburn. Ah! Sure some of them weren't dancehalls at all, they were only pokey holes. If a fire ever broke out the place would be burnt down. They were real death traps altogether, but nothing ever happened. *The Galtymore* in Cricklewood was a good one though and *The Gresham* on Holloway Road. They were the best. All the Irish bands came over like Big Tom and all that gang. Sure London made them fellows in the Sixties. Before that it was all English bands. Then rock and roll came in and you could get country and western too. It was a great city; you could get anything you wanted in it. Sure there were a few drunken Irish fellows around, but I never took any notice of them.

We used to go to work for half a day on a Saturday. We'd come back and have a bath and get cleaned up and we'd go to a football match. We'd come from that to a dinner in the café and we'd go from there to the cinemas up on Kilburn High Road. We'd leave the cinema and we'd go to the pub, and we'd go from the pub to the dancehall and we'd stroll home then at around one or two o'clock with only six or seven shillings spent on all of that. That was a lot of entertainment in one day for a young man coming out of the countryside in Ireland, wasn't it? We'd have the football, the cinema with all the top pictures of the time, cowboys the whole lot, a good dinner in the café especially when the Italians came in, and then you'd have a pint or two in the pub, the dance, and daddle away home after that, all for seven and sixpence. It was a great life for a lad that was raised in the country. We had nothing here only a dancehall in Carracastle, situated on the Roscommon/Mayo border and that was it for us before we hit London. That's the way it was.

I stayed the first time until the awful winter of 1962 when there was no work in England. I came home then for seven or eight months and worked on the homestead with my father, but there wasn't much happening. So there was nothing for it, but back to England again in October 1963. I was working on the London docks for *Balfour Beatty* the day the word came in that Kennedy had been shot in Dallas. The foreman came in over the radio with the news. I remember it so well, because I was just after going back and little did I know then that I wouldn't return again for forty-three years. Oh! I came home every year on holidays and sometimes three times a year when my parents were still alive. My mother died in 1981 and my father in 1986. Things changed after that, but I was always welcomed home by my brother to the old homestead where he raised his family. Sure he never took any notice of me. I'd come home and help him on the farm for a week and we'd go off then in the tractor to the pub and have a laugh or a joke or a sing song. That was life in the Irish countryside. I don't know whether I missed it or not, sure I didn't know that much about Ireland did I? I was only nineteen when I left.

Sure I miss England more since coming back. A feed of fish and chips is the main thing I miss. I can get them here surely, but not as good as in England. And living in the country here is different than living in a big city like London. I never needed a car over there; there was always public transport. I have to have a car here. I have free transport, but there's no bus around. Where would you get a bus around here? I couldn't stay here without a car; I might as well go back to England if I didn't have a car. Sure the nearest big town, Castlerea, is six miles from here. I drove all my life in England. I got my licence there in Cricklewood for seven and sixpence back in 1960. They took me down the road there and I did a three-point turn and just drove around the corner when the examiner said, "Congratulations, Mr. Roddy, you passed your test." It would cost a fortune to do it now. Sure I always drove the auld tractor at home long ago and I drove with *Bord na Móna* too. Once you learn to drive anything; you can drive a car, that's it. I never had driving lessons or anything, I just went in there to Cricklewood and applied for the licence and I got it. I drove company vans and all in England. Sure it was no bother; there were hardly any cars on the road. There was more than there was here, but there still wasn't many. A car was handy over there for going here and there in your own time. So I would miss the city life mainly, but then London in the latter years got very dangerous and I'm glad to be back here now away from the crime. I couldn't go out at night at all in the end in case I got mugged. Years ago I could walk everywhere and nobody would bother me. They'd kick you to death now for a few bob. I suppose you couldn't go out in Dublin at night either and walk the street, could you?

I didn't always want to come back to Ireland, not really, but then when the opportunity came up two years ago I took advantage of it. I didn't really find it that hard to settle back in; sure I took no notice. I go up and down there to my sisters in Ballaghadreen and Sligo and I go to Mass on Sunday and that's it. I can't drink or drive anyhow so unless I walk down to the pub, that's it. I hardly drink at all really except on a Sunday night when I go down to *Flanagan's* and play a game of twenty-five. It's a typical Irish pub; the crowd I'd meet there are all in their eighties now. I'd be about the youngest. Sometimes the bingo bus will pick us up and take us away for a game. I often visit friends who came back from England. I'll often go see them on the weekends and go out for a few drinks; maybe stay overnight and get Mass the next morning; maybe stay for a bite of dinner and come along home that evening. The people are very nice around here too, very friendly and helpful. I have no problem at all. Oh! sure it's grand. I have a lovely house. The family homes are over there and these ones are for the pensioners. Half of them aren't married at all, but they're not malicious or anything. I don't take any notice.

I'm fairly religious and go to Mass every Sunday. I always did in England except for a few times when work got in the way. Sure it was no problem; there was a Catholic Church on every corner. I always went to the Irish Centres too; they were great places. They were mainly for dancing and drinking. I never mixed with anybody else only Irish, sure I never lost my accent did I? Oh! I knew plenty of English people and the finest you could ever met, decent people too. I had no problem with them or with other nationalities either. I worked with West Indians, Caribbeans and Asians; they were the finest people too; always paid us well and on time and always told the truth. The best thing that ever happened to the Irish man in England was when the Pakistanis came in and took over the shops because they always kept them open late. The others would close at ten to six if they saw you coming down the road, but the Pakistani would make you welcome at eleven o'clock at night even if you were only going in for a box of matches. They were always glad to see you. They kept everyone awake. The Italians did the same with the cafes; kept them open until all hours. It was great when you were working late and you could always get something to eat. The Irish and English men wanted your money, but they didn't want to work long hours for it. I suppose there are rogues in every race. That's to be expected.

The changes here are for the better. When I used to come into that auld Dublin long ago after taking a train and a boat over, there'd be nowhere to get something to eat at eight o'clock in the morning. There wouldn't be a café open or nothing. There was never nothing here, not even in Dublin. They were awful lazy here; they still are. I came back on the bus two years ago and when I got off in that auld Dublin, there was still nowhere around Busáras (bus station) to get a cup of tea early in the morning. I said to myself what in God's name did I come back here for? I was glad to get down the country away from Dublin.

This country will never be as good as England with amenities and facilities and that for the public. I'll give them that. You can always get a cup of tea or a sandwich at any time of the day or night in England, at a bus station or train station, anywhere. Even on the ferry you can get nothing. Flying is the only way to travel now. Knock airport in Mayo was a godsend for the West of Ireland and of course, *Ryanair*. Where would we be without them? I use them all the time now when I go back and forth to see my brother who still lives in London. Another sister died there fifteen years ago. I still like to visit though. It's still the same old thing, England didn't change that much. Sure I'm only out of it two years.

I'm happy enough to be back. I paid all my stamps the whole time I was in England and have a good pension. The auld English pension will go anywhere with me now. I don't know if my sisters here are glad to have me back or not; I never asked them. They're both in their eighties now. One of them got knocked down by a car the other day. Some lunatic ran into her and her sister-in-law when they were out walking. They all have big families now, great-grandchildren and all that. I go to see them all the time. I never got married myself. I could have, but I didn't. It didn't happen and that was it. I suppose I wasn't to be married and that was it. I'm nearly seventy now and I'll hardly bother. I'll be sixty-nine this September. I get a free TV licence here and they give us a bit off on the electric too. The rent isn't too bad, so I have a good living. I light my own fire every evening, even at this time of year, and cook my own dinner when the weather is bad. When the weather is good I drive over to Enniscrone or into Mayo for the day where I would get something to eat in one of the cafés. I also enjoy the horse races in Rocommon and Sligo. I like the old horses, although I suppose they kept me poor. I'd be a rich man only for them. I used to go away for weekends all the time in England to Cheltenham and Aintree and to the dogs. At every corner in London there was a dog track. I never went too mad on them, but it was a pastime more than anything. It was a good day out; where you'd have a few pints afterwards and go away home. There are dog tracks here in Longford and in Mullingar, but I don't bother with them too much anymore. Sure it would cost a fortune now to put a bet on; you'd need to be a millionaire. I saw Irishmen in London backing a horse and hardly a shoe on their foot, and they never learnt. It might be an addiction, but sure it's a pleasure too. You have to have something.

I suppose more people would like to come home, but a lot of them are on the old social security and they can't come back. They can't transfer that. They probably never paid their stamps and so weren't eligible for a pension. They worked for cash in hand and never bothered with stamps. They're alright over there, they get their rent paid for and a hundred pounds to keep them alive. A lot of them will never come home. Sure a lot of them went over and never came back at all; they never even wrote a letter. Maybe they couldn't write. Maybe they weren't able. They didn't have the money to come back. You always had to have money to come back even on a holiday. A lot of them couldn't afford that. They probably drank a lot of it and some of them didn't go to work half the time unless they had to. But they're happy enough over there; it wouldn't have been much different for them here. Then there are people who come back and they can't settle. There's a woman up the road there who came back a few years ago and built a fine house, and now I see it's is up for sale.

I saw the ad for Safe Home in the Irish Forum in Luton. This bloke had told me about it and I just filled in the form and hoped for the best. The whole thing only took about nine months. I came over when the place was ready and had a look. I paid a month's rent in advance and got sorted out, then went back and got ready to leave. When I came home then for good Safe Home were very helpful and Máirín Higgins came to visit and help me with the paperwork. After that I was set. Sure it's a grand, handy little place I have now.

Interviewed at his home in Castleplunkett, County Roscommon, on Wednesday, May 16th, 2007

MARY BARRETT
& PATRICK DYER

Mary: I was in England for fifty-eight years until I came back two years ago. I left Ireland after the big snow of 1947. I am eighty-four since last Saturday so I must have been twenty-four when I left. I grew up in Knockmore, outside Ballina, in County Mayo. There were four sisters in it and we all emigrated. The other three went to Yorkshire and I took Cheshire. You had to have a job before you'd be let into England and I had seen the position for a servant posted in the labour exchange in Ballina, applied and was accepted. I went down to Dublin by train and travelled by boat on my own with the cows underneath me. I'll tell you that much, they were roaring down below, believe me, and I was on top. My employers made arrangements to have me met off the boat and I was taken to Nantwich to work in a University where I waited on the students, tidied, cleaned up and washed the pots. After six months I moved on to Manchester where a friend found me work as a checker in *Coat's* factory in Cheetham Hill. I stayed there for twenty-nine and a half years.

I enjoyed the independence that making your own money brings. *Coat's* manufactured rolls of cotton thread and I loved it there. It was everything you could wish for. I had to check the goods out and I'd be fairly kept going. It was a good life, and if you got sick they'd still pay you. I got a pension out of it and all when I left. It wasn't a great pension, but it was something. You see I never joined the pension scheme; the money I had was scarce enough! My money went on rent and that, about £1.25 a week. They were a lovely company, but when they packed up and went back to Scotland; that was it. I retired and didn't work for about twelve months until I got a job in a picture house part-time and then I worked in a pub. The last job I had was in a University cleaning and hoovering, where I was until about twelve months before me and Packy came home so I was working until I was well into my seventies and over it.

I hated England at first, but then grew to love it when I made loads of friends. We used go to *The Astoria* in Manchester and all the Irish dances. We went to the Irish Centre in Cheetham Hill and we used to have a great time. Now I can't put one foot after the other. I met my Packy about twelve months after I went to Manchester at a dance in *Winifred's* above Burton's shop on Stratford Road. He was a handsome man with a shock of black curly hair. He's as bald as a bat now with no hair at all. We've been together for nearly sixty years and have done well to last that long; we're still happy and we're still alive. We shared a flat the whole time over there and must have been in about twenty of them. Sometimes we had to share with different people. Every six months or a year they'd put up the rent and we'd move on to something cheaper. We were also in about four houses, but kept having to leave because we didn't like the neighbours. We did own one house and we sold it because it was falling down around us. Well, we didn't sell it; the Corporation took it from us in the end. They gave us so much for it, and started building roads on it. I'm glad we never did buy another one. So we had our ups and downs, you see. Yet I liked England; I liked it very much, but Packy wanted to come home; that was his hobby to come back to Ireland. He worked on the buildings and in factories; he worked at different things. He played in a band - *The Four Provinces Céili Band*, but gave that up some years ago. I'm not a musician so I don't follow it up so well. I didn't come home at all for the first fifteen years and then came every year to Sligo and we'd go around all the pubs. I knew them all. We used to lodge with a friend of Packy's for a fortnight and he used to be glad to see us coming. Packy always wanted to come back to Ireland for good though. It was his wish, not mine. It was hard at first, but I'm settled now.

When you get older it's not easy to make new friends. And it's harder to make friends here. Everything is harder; when you move here its different altogether. Everything is different, everything; everything seems different. Even the gas and the electricity, everything is gas over here. I had my heater and all on the electric in England and it's much cleaner, the electric is much cleaner than the gas. The way everything works is different here. All the forms we had to fill in. Oh! My God! I'll never forget them. Every time we looked around, another form had arrived. It was all so different. They talk about coming home for good, I wonder if it's for the bad sometimes. Then Ballina is about forty or fifty miles from Ballyhaunis and that was another thing, it wasn't really like coming home at all. My father had died when he was only forty-seven; I was very young, and then my mother lived until she was ninety-two. She got that disease, you know, where she didn't know where she was going, Alzheimer's, and she had to be put in a home. That was the hardest thing in the world. But that's it; that's life. The home place is sold. I think some Northern Ireland people bought it. So coming back here wasn't really like coming home. When you're parents are gone, you're lost in Ireland. Well, I think you are anyway. It's not the same. It's not really the same as coming home at all. I've no relations left here now. I've no one belonging to me in Ireland anymore so that makes it different too.

Yet this is a nice little complex, nice and quiet and peaceful and

The Four Provinces Céili Band

when you're old that's what you want. When you're younger you don't want that sort of life; well, I wouldn't have had it anyway. But, I've settled down now. It takes a lot to settle here especially when you have a lot of friends in England and then you arrive here and you know no one. But, there are a lot of my friends moving back too, one to Kerry and another to Tipperary. I have no idea why, but it was Packy's wish to get back too. He'd say I'll get back before they bury me. It's a strange thing this wanting to come home especially when it's very hard and so different. I thought people had changed when I came back that first time after fifteen years, but by God they've changed altogether now. They're gone mad here, drinking and swearing. In my day we never swore. And the girls are worse now. They're besting the men at everything.

It wasn't all sunshine in England either at the beginning. If you were Irish they'd say don't apply. They'd write it up and all. Oh! They did, when I went there first. Don't apply, they'd write. And if you were a Catholic, don't come either. Oh! They were very bitter. But, then you got around Irish people; you seemed to cling together and started to enjoy life. We used to all go to the dances together. We had no time on anything else. Dancing and working. That was it. We only mixed with Irish and Northern Ireland people. There were a lot of Northern Ireland people there and do you know I found them very nice. They were very good people and again they had to be quiet and all because they were among us and the Scotch people. There were a lot of Scotch people where I worked.

Look at Ireland now it's a marvellous country, isn't it? They've got everything. They hadn't very much when I was growing up. All we had was the auld donkey. But, I still enjoyed life back then too, going to the dances. I had a good life and then I left it. There was nothing in Ireland then. There wasn't much in England either, but there was a little bit more than in Ireland. We all went. There was hardly anyone around when I left. They went to America a lot of them; they went to different places. A lot of them went to London, and now a lot of them are coming back. As you get older in England and start walking around very slowly you're going to get robbed. It's alright when you're younger and you've got quick feet, but when they see you walking slowly they're going to pounce on you and rob you. That's why Packy wanted to come home.

It's all changed here now, but our social life is very nice. We go to Knock every Tuesday. It's great company there. It takes us a few hours out of the house. There's a big hall and we sit down and have a cup of tea and chat to everyone we know. And then they have a Mass and then we have dinner. After dinner we play bingo and after bingo we have more tea and then we come home at about half past three or four. Today there's one of the gentlemen leaving and they're having a big do so the driver, Seamus, took me home early, but I made sure I had the dinner before I left. There's lovely Sisters there too, nuns. Not all nuns are nice either, don't worry. Maybe it's me, but I think they have a very bad attitude, some of them. My friend went to school with them and she said they were really cruel. They were cruel in them days. Oh! And the teachers! God above! Even in my day they were cruel. I went to Killadashin national school and never liked it from the day I went to it; I never liked the teacher. It was the same one we had all the time. If you were two minutes late you got slapped; if you missed school you got slapped. She hit me one day and broke my little finger. It wasn't with a cane either; you know those things they use to point out the music? Well she hit me with one of them right down on top of my little finger and broke it there. She never said sorry or anything. Oh! I'll remember it until the day I die. They were cruel teachers. You know what I think? They knew nothing themselves and they just got frustrated, but they were the cruellest lot ever. It's a good job they took the cane out of the schools, because they were wicked with that cane. They used knock hell out of the children every day. The children today don't know they're alive; they love going to school the children today.

Since I was about six years old I've been going to Mass and I'm going still. It's something we were brought up with and that's it. I wouldn't push it over onto anybody; it's up to everyone what they want to do. It's the same with coming back to Ireland. I wouldn't push that on anyone either. Its hard going at first and it's not for everyone. But, I like it here now. I've got used to it. We've got two bedrooms and a big back garden. And it's very quiet. When you're getting on in years, that's what you want, quietness. And we have a nice social life. That makes a difference too. You see Packy being a musician takes us out a good bit. He plays the flute and he plays all over the place. He played in Knock now today. He plays with Paddy Joe up the town; they play in bars, at weddings, everything. He's brilliant on the flute. Then he's playing here and he's playing there. God knows where he's playing half the time. He's going tomorrow night now to Tubbercurry. I do know that. You see when you're a musician you get out a lot more and you get to know more people. He plays with different bands. I don't always go with him. I hate going on the long journeys. I had an accident on me leg you see when I came back here first and it's all swelled up and I don't like travelling because of it. Yesterday he was out playing all day. This lad called for him at two o'clock and they were out all day. It's a great interest. He likes it. He likes playing the flute.

Patrick: I learnt to play when I was about ten years of age. Just going  to the auld country house dances. I'd hear the old men playing and it would come into my head. Just picking it up and then when I went home I'd remember the tune and I'd be able to play it. There were no tapes that time. I went on the tin whistle first, I paid fourpence for it in Ballymote and I started learning by listening to the old men. I just picked up the whistle and played, that way. That's how I learnt. I used play at the old country house dances round about Gurteen where I was born. Well it was about quarter of a mile from Gurteen, in Curra, not the Curragh of Kildare. I come from County Sligo, Coleman country. Michael Coleman was a great fiddle player who went to America. Sligo was full of fiddle and flute players. Larry Mullanney, the carpenter, then gave me a fife. He had about thirteen or fourteen of us playing the in a Fife and Drum band. Me mother threw it out on the street one day because she wanted me to do the top dressing in the meadow and the mule was sick. Then I joined Johnny Sherlock's pipe band because I wanted to learn the Highland Pipes and he learnt me them. I still play them. Then I went on the flute. The first flute as far as I know was got in Dublin in a shop across from The Ha'penny Bridge.

I went to England in the 1950's when I was a charming young lad of twenty-five. My mother sold a quart of eggs for the fare. The hen laid the cost. They were good old times. You could leave your door open and nothing would be gone out of the house. Nothing would be stolen. You could go to the bog and stay all day footing turf with just the latch on the door. Our Lady appeared in Knock to three people coming from the bog. They were very religious and very poor that time. God this country was desperate poor then. I used to ask for tuppence for a *Woodbine* and my mother would say she could put it to a loaf; a loaf was four pence. You see we had no money. If you had five shillings you were rich. That's why there was no cancer because there was no smoking Maybe we'd get five *Woodbines* the odd time.

Ireland is different now. It's richer they're getting because there is so much money. We had to work hard cutting turf and we got nothing for it. So we made our escape to England. Some was rich, we'll say those creamery managers and them that sells clothes and shoes, drapers, they were different. We had the land, but we only had three cows, and then me mother got old and we all left her. She went to a place called Boyle, then she died and that was it.

My father died from cancer. He got hit in the jaw in California when he was working on the steelworks and a big lump come on it. So he came home to this country and he married me mother. But, he always had this big lump at the side of his face. Anyway he said it spoiled his complexion, spoiled his good looks, he said. So he decided to get it off. He went into Sligo town and the surgeon said, leave it. He wasn't pleased at all and he went to Dublin to another surgeon who made him sign his name and he removed it. Then he got cancer. He should have left it alone. He had survived the San Francisco earthquake in 1906 and came back to Ireland and died like that. There was six of us in it and we all went. Me grandmother got ten shillings a week pension and that's what my mother brought us up on, the six of us. Well you'd get a bag of flour then, they were great bakers, for ten shillings, and that would last nine or ten months. They'd bake a cake and put it on the fire with coals on the top and coals on the bottom and the cake would rise. One slice of that then and I'll tell you, you'd be made up. And then there was colcannon with a big lump of butter in the middle of it and that would keep you going. We were never hungry like, we had no money, but we'd go to the dances all the same. Everyone was mad for dancing and mad for smoking *Woodbines* back then. You'd see a fellow with a *Woodbine* and you'd say "Will you give us a pull?"

I worked in Northern Ireland for about three years, with a Protestant on the land, a farmer. Northern Ireland was attached to England and it still is. The houses were built in brick just like England. They have nicer houses here. Then the Yanks came in that time during the War. They were mental. They'd say "Give me a ride on your bike." And they couldn't cycle at all. They got plenty of women though. Not one woman either, but two. They'd have one on each arm. I was talking to a man one evening and he said to me, "Look at the soldier coming up the street with two women." Then he looked again and said, "Oh! One is me wife!"

To make a long story short, we emigrated. Thousands and thousands went to America and Canada and all over, and we picked Manchester. I went with the crowd on the boat; they were from every county. We went to Manchester because we were starving and I worked on the building trade with *Wimpy's*. Manchester was better than Birmingham, because I don't like Birmingham people. They'd have signs up there with No Irish Need Apply and no Catholics neither. I lived in Fallowfield, Rusholme, Withington, and Hulme, which is quite nice now. We lived in Chalkner and Midlock. We had a lovely house there and it had to come down to build a school. We lived in flats mostly. I stayed in digs when I went first. We didn't want to go at all. We were having great fun in this country dancing and that, but we got used to England and fifty odd years later we didn't want to leave it.

When I got settled in I started playing the music, not right away, not until I got to know the lads and all. I played in dance halls and worked for *Connor & Finnegan* and there was another one, Kennedy, he owns half of Knock. Sometimes a fellow would go bankrupt and we'd get redundancy. It's a good job that came in because you'd get a good few thousand, the longer you were there you'd get more. At the end then I was working in a slaughter house and the Manager would say, "Do you want to see the piggies dying Paddy?" My mother used to want me to kill a cock at home and I wouldn't. She could tell the minute the chickens were hatched if there was more cocks than pullets and she'd grab them by the neck and cut the head off. Oh! You'll eat the broth alright, she'd say, but you won't help me kill them.

I started playing with this other fellow in the pubs for money. One night he said we can get two more musicians, they're all dead and gone now, so we got two more anyway, and we made a bit of money about twice, three times a week. Sometimes we were very busy. Mickey Rooney was going that time and Matt Molloy; they made a lot of money. Then in England there were sessions in houses. When we'd meet in a pub, we'd have a session and the landlord would give us tickets for a drink, no money. You could come in with a tin whistle and play; anyone could come in and play in a session and they'd get a ticket. That was in a place called Chatham. I'll tell you there were English girls and they could play good. They were traditional players. We played in *The Astoria*; in *Sharks*; in *The Tara*; there was another one that was part of the University; and then we played in *Winifred's*. I made a bit of money. The Paddys would come out fighting and the Biddys would let them out of the police vans. On Paddy's Day they'd all come out fighting. A policeman said one time that there was more blood shed on the shamrock than Holy Water. Then the Black Maria would come and they'd be arrested. The police would have them locked in from the outside, but the girls were able to open the door and let them out. Or the girls would come along and say that's my boyfriend and they'd get them out that way. And those lads could run. The Irish fought over everything, women and all. The Irish were too fond of the drink too. That time it was only a shilling for a pint; it was cheap. And when you were working and getting seven or eight pounds a week in the 50's and 60's it was good money. Good money. Then it climbed up into the hundreds. It's hundreds and hundreds now. They get three and four hundred pounds a week there now.

We used to come on holidays to Westport. And we went to Dublin a few times. That's how we heard about *Slattery's* on Capel Street. I played there about fifteen or twenty years ago. And I came across another place too; I can't remember the name of it. There was a big statue outside of the fellow who helped the Germans, Lord Ha Ha. There was another big monument down there too on O'Connell Street, Nelson's Pillar it was, and I believe someone put a bomb to it. It was near there we used to stop in a bed & breakfast. I wouldn't go back there again though. Dublin is too dangerous now. We come home another time on a coach to Meath and stayed in a chalet. There was music there every night and I used to sometimes play with them. That was a great holiday. I loved coming home for the holidays, but I always wanted to come for good. I wanted to be back before I was buried. I'll tell you a story about the day I went to change my English driver's license. I could drive on that for the first three months, but then I had to change over to the Irish one. Although one fellow from Castlebar told me he's been driving for sixty years on an English one. Ah, I said, but you could be pulled. What would he do if he got pulled, or if he had accident, he'd be caught then? It would be a bit dodgy. He could be fined about five hundred euros. Anyway I went to the Guards to change over to the Irish license and they said, "How long were you away?" About fifty-four years, I told them. "And what brought you back now?" The auld Sergeant asked me. "Well wouldn't I be better off coming back now than coming back in a box? I told him. "Good answer," he said.

Then the forms I had to fill up to change an auld licence. I never seen so many forms in my whole life. I'm still glad to be back though. I'm glad I came back because there's more money. Everyone has money now. We have money, but we're too old to spend it. I have the Irish pension and the English pension and I can't spend it. And everything is fresh here too, isn't it? You get hens here fresh and chickens fresh. But it's getting rough here too. I'll tell you what brought me home though. When you're old in England, they know you're old and they just pounce on you and they rob you. They broke into a ninety-two year olds house near us, and they blackened her eye and robbed her. I was saying to the Guards here that it's getting rough here too and he said you're right; it's getting rough for old people. He said he'd been in Shepherd's Bush and it was getting rough there too. He said I don't blame you for coming home when you're old because they know by the way you're walking and they just pounce on you.

I'm glad I have me music, that's for sure. There's not too much music in Ballyhaunis, but they bring me to a place in County Roscommon to play. They call for me like. It's a big club, but there's no beer in it, more like a Heritage Centre. They come for me here and they take me to it, Joe Byrne and them, the Mid-West man. There's great music on Mid-West radio. There's great music and they call out all the people that died around here too. I got into the music here through Helen who runs this place. She helped us fill in the forms too. She used bring us down to the seaside in Enniscrone; she brought us all over the place. I'm eighty-seven now next

The Pipes are calling

March so I'm getting too old for it. I am playing in *Killoran's* in Tubbercurry tomorrow. They're supposed to be coming for me at two o'clock. There's a festival there. Do you know where we were treated well? In Cloonfad. There's a priest there and he gave us fifty euros, whiskey to drink, and as much as you could eat. We were all playing in this big hall and the priest set it up. Even the priests here have plenty of money.

We saw about Safe Home in *The Irish Post*. We applied about two years before we got here. We just put down our names to say we did it. Then they started sending these pen letters; they still send them here, the newsletters, and so they said come back for an interview. There was a doctor here, a man and a woman interviewed us. They put us up in bed & breakfast and then they brought us up to see these houses.

People ask us all the time here how we got this house. It was furnished and all, teaspoons, towels, everything. They're nice, cheap too. Then Mickey Daly, he used work in the timber yard, he gave us plenty of wood for the fire. And I bought that heater for the summer because I wanted to get rid of some of me money!

I don't miss England at all because you could get mugged and kicked. There were men like me who did. I don't miss it, not with that lark. Even though I was playing music with the céili bands in the halls up to the time I left, all that was dying too. So I chucked it in and started playing in pubs here and there, getting money. Then when I got older and older and older I joined the sessions and got a ticket for the drink. Music is a great pasttime. Sports is another. I followed the boxing, Mohamed Ali and them. I don't follow football at all. I don't like wrestling either. That's all put on. I liked Barry McGuigan, he was a hardy little fellow. But, it's the music that really keeps me going here. I don't know what I'd do if I didn't have that. I'm blinded with all the cameras taking me picture. I was playing in *The Hazel* up the town and a girl from London took this picture and framed it. They presented me with a plaque in the Ballyhaunis International Festi-

RUA STAR 2007

val 2007 – *Rua Star in Our Eyes*. It's made of marble. I thought it was a peat briquette when they handed it to me first. I've won loads of medals in feiseanna in England. I'll play you a tune if you like, an easy one, *Shoe the Donkey*. Anyone can play that. I can play this one with my hands upside down. It's easy. The reels is the hard ones, and the hornpipes.

It's nice here. There's no noise. You know in England there were hooligans up above us and on a Saturday night they'd be lighting bonfires and making noise. And you've have to call the police to get them shifted and they'd have parties over us. I'm happier here now because to tell you the truth I got scared going out. Them come at you in gangs. You can go out here. They're alright. They don't jump on you anyhow, so far. Dublin is worse than anyplace now and Belfast. It does be on about them on Mid-West radio all the time. And it's full of drugs. It's got out of hand. That auld Bertie Aherne is very soft on them. The last time we were there this woman said to Mary, mind your handbag. But, I suppose it's bad everywhere. Even in Knock. There was an apparition there you know. It was pouring down raining that day and it wasn't raining at all where Our Lady appeared. It was bone dry all around her and raining everywhere else. Pity she wouldn't come back now and get rid of the rain we're having this summer! Or maybe she already worked another miracle in getting me and Mary home in one piece!

Interviewed at their home in Ballyhaunis, County Mayo, on Wednesday, August 8th, 2007

ADRIAN O'BRIEN

I came back to Ireland in April 2005 after spending twenty-eight years in Manchester. I always had the inkling to come home where I had very strong links with family and I never really liked living in England. All my family is here in Dublin, in Tallaght, although I was born in Rathmines in January, 1939, and grew up in Crumlin. The family were housed there when I was about six; that was the first movement out from the inner city – to Crumlin and Drimnagh. Although Rathmines wasn't really the city, Crumlin was nonetheless a small village to us at that time. We were surrounded by fields, and the football pitch, Pearse Park, which was owned by Guinness's then and I think the Corporation now, was right across the road from us. That was where we played after school. We also went blackberry picking and fishing.

Crumlin could be rough too, especially at school. We used to get beaten every day at St. Columba's, which was run by the Christian Brothers. They'd hit you for the slightest thing, for putting up your hand, for answering out of turn, for anything. They'd put one hand on the side of your head to hold it steady and then hit you with the other. One time I got dizzy and fell, and hit my head on the side of the desk on my way down. There were three of us in the family – two boys and a girl. My father who was a carpenter originally worked in the North of Ireland where he got hit by shrapnel and it affected his ear. He couldn't get any work in Ireland because of his disability, so he went to England, and shortly afterwards he and my mother separated. That was very unusual for Ireland in the Fifties. He kept in touch, and still came home on holidays for a long time after, but I always felt different because of it. I always missed not having a father when I was growing up.

I stayed at St. Columba's until I was fourteen and then I left to go out and work. At first I had a few temporary positions; then I got a job in *Weir's*, the jewellers, on Grafton Street, where I stayed for nine years. I used to have a handcart to carry the shutters out to open the shop in the morning. Then I'd have to get the furnace going for the heating and clean the windows before going out to deliver the parcels, mostly on foot. If there were any long distance deliveries they'd give us our bus fare and for a really long journey they'd pay for a taxi. I enjoyed it well enough visiting all of the wealthy homes around Dublin, but eventually decided that I needed some adventure and headed off to London to stay with my father for a while. I went over on *The Princess Maud* from Dublin to Liverpool. It was an old cattle boat and everyone was getting sick over the side and then you'd be sliding across the floor on the vomit. Everyone looked despondent; crying, sitting on their suitcases because there were hardly any chairs except for a few in the bar. It was terrible. Another boat, *The Leinster*, came into operation much later and that was more passenger friendly you could say. My father fixed me up in a room in Battersea with four others and found me work on the building sites with *Nine Elms Gasworks*, but I didn't like having to share and only stayed four months. My mother didn't want me to go, but she was very badly off and I sent her a lot of money. I went back to Dublin, but couldn't get any proper work and had to head off again.

A friend of mine was working in Coventry at the time, so I decided to have a go there. I ended up staying for fifteen years where I worked as a bus conductor and eventually became a driver. There was a lot of Irish there especially in the car factories. We would pick them up very early in the morning, sometimes at four o'clock, and take them to work. I went to a lot of the Irish clubs around there. Then I came home on holidays one time and got a job with CIE here as a driver and didn't go back for three years. I worked on the number 18 from Sandymount up to Ballyfermot and on the Dalkey route too. I was also on the 58 route that used go around Dun Laoghaire, up to Sallynoggin, and back down to where the ferry went out; that's where we had our break, on the seafront. I lived in a flat on Royal Terrace. Dun Laoghaire was a bustling town back then and quite enjoyable. But, I got fed up again and sticking a pin in a map one day, I came up with Manchester. Off I went. I had quite a bit of money saved so I stayed in a bed and breakfast until I found a flat. Of course with all my experience I just walked into a job - bus driving again, this time with *First Manchester.*

There wasn't too many Irish where I was on the outskirts of the city in a town called Oldham. There was some Irish clubs in Manchester, but it was too far for me to travel. I wasn't much of a drinker in the early days so I didn't have much of a social life other than the club over the bus garage where we would play billiards and things like that. It was a lonely life really. Everything is so spread out over there and there's too much emphasis on work. The years caught up on me and I never got around to planning on coming home before now although I used to come four or five times a year on holidays. Even when I officially retired *First Manchester* asked me to go back and drive the school buses part-time. Oh! My God, the kids were terrible. They used to pick up the seats and throw them out the back window and the cigarette smoke, you couldn't see out the window with the smoke. They were terrible.

If I had my life all over again though, I would never have left Ireland. I used to be in tears going back after holidays. I don't know why I ever left the second time. But, in the Seventies in Ireland things were still pretty bad. A lot of people were leaving. I had a lot of friends who went before me to different parts of England and I never saw them again. And I just wanted to be one of the boys. It's so great to be home though; it's the best thing that's ever happened to me. In the end it was my family who sort of instigated my return. I'm the only one who emigrated, the black sheep so to say, as my brother and sister stayed here. My sister worked for Iris Kellett, the show jumper. She started as a stable maid, and then worked her way up. She met her husband there; he used to get the horses ready for show jumping; plait the tails and all that. She always wanted me to come home. She was the main instigator of this but, she had no accommodation for me what with looking after me Mum and that, and she had a family of her own. My mother is still alive at ninety-eight. She wrote a short story when she was eighty that was published through her local community centre. A writer had asked them to recount childhood memories. Mum's story is called *My Golden Tresses* and appears in a publication entitled *No Shoes in Summer,* by Eilish Dillon. In it she recalls having her beautiful curls cut off when she was only three years old before she and her sister were put up for adoption after their mother died.

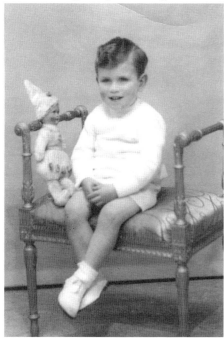

Adrian, aged 4

Mum is still very lively. She can only walk for a little while and then she'd be breathless, but her mind is very active. She reads books and she's got a sense of humour. She still moans a lot too. Every time I go up to see her she'll say I've had a terrible night; you won't have me much longer, but she's defied the whole lot of us.

So that was another reason to come back, for me Mum. My Dad passed away eleven years ago. He was still in London and I used visit him a lot. In the end he contacted Alzheimer 's disease. In a way that was my last tie with England severed. It was time to leave. My aunt knew about Safe Home and my sister sent for the information and I had to sign all the forms and that. That took about six to twelve months. I was getting the newsletter all the time, but I didn't think anything would ever come of it. Even when I got the interview here I thought I had no chance because I thought there'd be about a million people looking for a few places. Then at about nine o'clock one night I got the phone call to say they had a home for me here; to come in my own time and have a look. They asked me to pick a number and I said thirty and that is what I got, Number 30 Willie Bermingham Court. That Willie Birmingham was a great man and thirty turned out to be my lucky number.

169

I didn't find it hard at all to settle in. I went back to Manchester last September for a week's holiday and only stayed two days. I couldn't wait to get back to Dublin. I have made more friends here in two years than I had in the whole twenty-eight in Manchester. I feel that Divine Providence brought me back to Ireland. Life is pointless if you haven't got a faith. I did drift away from my religion at one stage, and had started to take a drink. I knew there was something missing. I have a special affinity to Our Lady and I believe she guided me back here. I've always felt since I first went to Medjugorje that she does all the work, not Jesus. I've gone three times and as soon as you get off the plane you feel a presence. The first time was in the Nineties when I was still in Manchester. I came back to Dublin and flew out with a group, which included some members of my family. That might have been the start of me coming back to religion. I was still going to Mass, but I had an awful lot of things on my mind.

Life has opened up very much for me since I came back to Ireland. I have joined a prayer group where I've met a lot of people. I go twice a week; once to my own parish and on a Wednesday I go to Kimmage to the Medjugorje group. Next week now I'm going to Lourdes for the first time with the Garda A Division. There are social

St. Columba's National School, Crumlin, 1949

groups all over Dublin and this ex-Sergeant, O'Sullivan, co-ordinates them. I got involved through driving an ambulance for a day centre up on the Bulfin Road for ex-CIE workers. It's mostly for men who go there for their dinner. Sergeant O'Sullivan and one of the people here in ALONE asked me if I'd drive the bus. I've been doing it now for eighteen months, six days a week. Sometimes I work with a driver and help the people out of their homes. It is such fulfilling work and so rewarding.

I've also completed a computer course in Inchicore College. There are two computers in the common room here and I use them for communicating with my cousin in London by email; for browsing the Internet and for making posters. I'm into photography as well. I love snapping elderly people; I'll be doing it now on the holiday to Lourdes. Then ALONE are having an open day in Wynne's Hotel in Dublin and they want me to supply the photographs for that. I was always interested in this hobby, but never got the chance to go forward with it in England. I have a digital camera and printer so I am able to develop my own pictures. That's been one of the most rewarding things for me; being able to pursue my pastimes. I go to the bingo on a Monday night in *Murray's* pub down the road there and I have a few drinks afterwards. Tonight at half six I'm being picked up and brought to a pre-departure get together in the Garda Club on Harrington Street. They'll serve sandwiches and tea and that will be that; no alcohol. As you can see the social life here is much better for me.

I thought at first that I wouldn't fit in, but that's not true. I was told that the Irish wouldn't be interested in me because I was away so long, but I haven't found that at all. I feel I've moved on now and I've left the past behind. I'm happy the way I am. Maybe if I'd been part of an Irish community in Manchester it might have been easier. I was never into dancing much so I didn't really frequent the dancehalls. When you're isolated from your own community it's very lonely and it doesn't really get any easier as time goes along. I sometimes went into the Irish Centres and even though they were good fun, there was a lot of crime in the city in latter years and I didn't want to get into all that. The crime here has definitely got worse too I know, but so far I feel very safe. It couldn't have just been me and my family who brought all this about; there must have been Divine intervention. I always felt my calling was back here and I can't believe it to this day that I was fortunate to get a home when the odds against me were so high.

I'm also better off financially than I was in England. I don't pay Poll tax; a community tax introduced by Margaret Thatcher. I was paying £900 a year just for that alone, then water rates on top of that and rent. I didn't have much left out of my pension after all that was paid. Now my money is changed over from sterling so it's worth much more and as I am an EU (European Union) citizen I'm entitled to a medical card and a social welfare package. That's a great help. I don't pay any income tax here whereas I did over there and you don't get any relief from the community tax either.

I would tell people who wanted to come back to be cautious as to where they go to, and it depends on their outlook too. But if they really want to come home I'd say go for it. The pitfalls along the way are mainly to do with red tape; changing everything over. There are a lot of forms to be filled up; then the authorities lose them. One time they cancelled my social welfare because they said my income was over the limit. I explained to them that I was applying as an EU citizen and they asked, "Why didn't you tell us that before?" And I after sending in all the forms? There's no communication between one Department and another. So that can be frustrating when you come home first, but I wouldn't let that stop anyone. However, you have to be the sort of person who gets involved socially. There are a lot of activities for seniors here, as there probably were in England, but I found here that I had to go out and become involved. I had to put myself out there in order to get out of the house. And, of course, I have my family here and that has helped a lot too.

The only negative aspect I've found so far is that I seem to be picking up more colds and I've discovered that I have a form of asthma. I also had to have a skin cancer taken off my eyes; a few things like that have happened. Then I get allergies from the pollen in the plants; hay fever and that. I never experienced that before. I'm on tablets for it now. The last couple of days I've been sneezing and my eyes running. Maybe I'm allergic to the place! But no matter, I'm here to stay.

Interviewed at his home in Kilmainham, Dublin, on Wednesday, May 2nd, 2007

Adrian (left) with brother, Clifford, in Medjugorje

MARIAN & KEVIN MOLONEY

Marian: My husband and I returned to Ireland in January 2005. I had lived in Africa for thirty-five years; Kevin for fifty; and in the end we had to leave without warning with only two suitcases. That is all we had to show for the lifetime we spent there. We had to leave everything else behind, including our money and all of our possessions. When President Mugabwe took over Rhodesia in 1980 he was quite moderate and everybody had great hopes, but then he became very brutal and now it looks like he's going to wreck the country. He has become filled with greed and power and is even driving his own people mad. There is no democracy there like they had hoped; it is a true dictatorship.

When I went to Northern Rhodesia in 1969 it was fabulous. I had trained as a nurse in St. Giles Hospital in London, having left Ireland in 1959 on a boat like the rest of them. I then completed my midwifery in Lambeth in Surrey and after six months night duty in Lewisham, outside London; I secured a job in the Royal Maternity Hospital in Belfast. I found it a very difficult place to live in, as I'd been expecting it to be like England and it wasn't. Belfast was very different. The Northern Ireland accent was hard to understand and the religious divide was very obvious and very difficult to take. The first question they'd ask is what foot did you kick with? It was 1968, the Troubles were about to begin and Bernadette Devlin and Ian Paisley were at loggerheads. After a year a couple of the other girls and I started applying for jobs in *The Nursing Mirror* where the vacancies were listed in alphabetical order by country. We mustn't have gotten any further than 'A' because my friend, Stephanie, went to Australia and I ended up in Africa. Another girl, Adele, went to America. We were trying for ages so it was just whatever we got in the end. Funnily enough, we are all back in Ireland now.

I had applied to Roan Selective Trust (RST), which was a large copper mining outfit in Zambia formerly called Rhodesia Selective Trust, and next thing they had me over in England for an interview; and my ticket booked before I knew where I was. They offered great incentives with a good salary, tax-free; accommodation; the whole lot. They rushed me through the process and I signed a twelve-month contract as a nursing sister in the hospital there. I loved it from the very beginning. I loved the social life; the climate; the wild life; the safaris. There were three other Irish girls nursing there and we had a great time; a great life. We had servants, sunshine and space. There were loads of young people coming out that time from England and South Africa and of course there were loads of single men on the mines so we had our pick. I never missed Ireland at all. I missed my family, but that's it. I grew up on Western Road in Cork city and I attended the Ursuline nuns at St. Angela's Convent. My father didn't want me to go away. He said there's a perfectly good hospital across the road there, the Bons, pointing at the Bons Secours Hospital, but I had already written off and been accepted so there was nothing he could do. There were six of us in the family, but I was the only one who emigrated and I'm glad I did, as it was a great adventure. Then again it was only for twelve months initially.

We got great nursing experience in Africa; the things we had to do in the hospital we would never had the opportunity to do here at the time. Where they do caesarean sections here they did episiotomy there. I learnt a lot about my profession. The hospital I worked in was fee-paying and mainly for white people. There were also non-fee paying hospitals where most of the African locals went. They were also owned by the mines, but were for the workers who didn't want to join the Medical Aid system. All employees had a choice as to whether they wanted to subscribe to Medical Aid or not. The locals were treated very well by RST where they had great hospitals and marvellous amenities. Later on I would work on a Mission hospital where the nuns, both Irish and German, were great and very hard working.

During my first week in Zambia I met this lovely Dublin man at a whist drive. Kevin had spent sixteen years there already, working on the railway. We fell in love straight away and were married three months later on the 26th of July, 1969, at St. Patrick's Church in Mufulira and afterwards we held a reception at the British Ex-Servicemen's Club (B.E.S.L.) for one hundred people. My sister came over from Ireland for the wedding and I asked her what they all thought at home. She said they think you're pregnant. I said well you can go back and tell them that I'm not. She thought we were terrible the way we lived with servants and that, but I explained that we were giving them a job and accommodation that they wouldn't have had otherwise. She was going to University then and was very liberal.

Kevin and I have been very happily married now for thirty-eight years and have one son, Luke. We came back to Ireland shortly after the wedding and it was only his second time home in sixteen years. There had been a split in the Federation and as Kevin worked for the Zambian railway he was regarded as part of the Ian Smith Regime and we were declared prohibited immigrants. We were flown back to Dublin and after a short holiday we sailed back to Capetown on *The Edinburgh Castle,* which took ten days, and spent three days on a train to Bulawayo where we settled, and where Kevin began working with the Rhodesian Railway. After that we came home every two to three years and must have spent all of our money on fares! We also travelled throughout Africa and Luke and I made a very memorable trip through the Chimanimani Mountains with a German priest friend of ours, Fr. Odilo. He even celebrated Mass for us in a cave, which he called the catacombs and we slept under the stars. It was fabulous. Other than that our social life included membership of the Irish Society where we'd have a get together on St. Patrick's Day and at Christmas. Then there was a quiz every week. There was plenty of drink in Rhodesia because alcohol was cheap and we socialized mostly in clubs - The Lions Club, the Rotary Club and the Sports Club. They played polo; cricket and bowls so it was a very English lifestyle. Our friends were of all nationalities so it was also a very multicultural way of life. And, of course, I had my job. Nursing is hard work, but I loved it and have no regrets. I remained nursing until 1980 and then I had a spinal operation and couldn't continue. Instead I went in studying with the youngsters and did bookkeeping and accounts. After qualifying I was employed by a legal firm as an accountant and eventually promoted to run their Deceased Estates department. It was a great position and I felt in a way that it was an extension of my nursing experience in that I was dealing with the bereaved again. I thoroughly enjoyed it and was still working right up to the time we left.

I never thought of coming home; I was there for life. It then started becoming apparent in the last year we were there that we'd have to leave. There are still some Irish and English there, but they're all trying to get out. It's very difficult as you can't take any money out and it's very hard financially to start off somewhere else. If we'd known we could have prepared for this long ago when it was possible to take money out. We decided to leave after I was threatened by Affirmative Action. They wanted one of the estates I was working on, but I refused to give them any

Marion (left) with colleagues at
Guy's Hospital, London

information. The youth brigade member who accosted me said, "We are going to get you" before he left my office. I'll always remember his voice. I wasn't frightened, just uneasy after that. Our good friend and neighbour, Gloria, was shot twenty-three times at the gate to her farm because she refused to give it up. I was talking to her the day before she died. They found twenty-three bullets in her body. Her son had been shot some time before that. She was English by birth, yet the English government did nothing about her death.

Then there was a shortage of petrol and no foreign currency in Zimbabwe. We get the Zimbabwe news every day on the Internet and the people are really struggling there now. They have nothing. There's no oil there and that is why the rest of the world haven't stepped in to help them; there's nothing in it for them. Zimbabwe is a relatively new country and it will be another thirty years before it gets on its feet. Our son had left many years ago to attend University in England where he is now settled. He was very worried about us and encouraged us to leave too. My husband had retired so maybe it was time to go.

We came back and settled in Ballybunion, County Kerry. Well, I don't think you ever settle back, really. Ireland is a totally different country now and Ballybunion is so isolated. There's no bus or train service; it's the end of the world. The road ends here. I love the town, but I feel long-term it is not the right place for us. At first we didn't know anybody and how do you get to know anyone in a new place? There was no community spirit here because it is a holiday resort. In the summer everybody is busy with tourists and in the winter every-one hibernates because of the winds. The first house we got was full of mildew; it was even on our shoes. Kevin got a chest infection so I really had to fight to get out. We got another place after six months and had the stress of moving again, and the expense. I would advise Safe Home to never, ever, send the elderly to Ballybunion. It's not a place for people who've been overseas and used to transport.

Kevin in Matopos National Park

Then there was nothing to be involved in with the parish; the Priest does it all. There's no Church centre and no parish council. The Priest is a one man band. They're lucky they've got such a good man; I don't know what will happen if he leaves.

One day in February, 2006, I put an ad up in the supermarket and asked that anyone over fifty-five please come to a meeting in the local community centre. I had decided to start up an Active Retirement Group. Twenty people turned up. I asked a community worker with the HSE, Caroline Doyle, to speak on the first night and it just went from strength to strength after that. We now have about thirty-five members and meet every week. It's just great. We go on outings; next week now we're off to Glengariff for the day. We practice yoga; I love the breathing techniques taught by Dr. Davey, an Indian lady. There's no way she'd get us down on the floor or we'd never get up again! We do chair exercises with another teacher – he calls it Go for Life. We held art classes and a huge crowd came out to support our Art Exhibition for Bealtaine a few weeks ago. I'd never even held a paint brush in my hand before that. We have a woman who does quilting; she's great at arts and crafts. We have a book club. At the moment we're reading *My Sister's Keeper* by Jodi Picoult, but none of us like it. There's no end to our endeavours. We attend lectures and a self-assertion course; we pray; we argue; we get together and we stretch ourselves and our minds. We'd try anything. It's great for the locals. Many of them told me that they never really knew one another before the group got together. They might have known one another to see, but not by name, and not to speak to, which I think is rather sad.

I wouldn't say it has necessarily helped me to settle in, but it certainly keeps me busy, let's put it like that. There's a tremendous amount of hard work involved. I wouldn't say I've settled in, not at all. But the people here are very nice. The email is great, as it has helped us to keep in touch with people all over the world. When you're away from home your friends are your family and we were surrounded by friends, whereas here we're very far away from family. I have two brothers in Dublin and Kevin has one sister there and that's it, and to get up there is almost impossible. As I said, we have no bus service in Ballybunion and no train service. Kevin has the free pass and I can accompany him, but there's no transport to use it with. I started up a bus service into Tralee every Friday. Kerry Community Transport pays for it, but I had a job to get it going. I had to go around and get names and addresses to show that there was a need. I handed them in and said these people need transport. Then not everyone likes giving out their telephone numbers so it was quite a job. We made a petition. It's free if you have a free pass and only four euros if you don't, which is still very cheap. Anyhow now we have a bus that takes us into Tralee every Friday, so that's something.

It's good to be alive when you think of the alternative. I'm so glad we went away. I am so glad I had the opportunity. I think it's good to get away; it's a great experience. The young people here are very stressed out, not so much in Kerry where they don't have a long commute, but in Dublin people are stressed out. I have two brothers in Howth and they said they never go into the city anymore. They spend their time playing golf. If I was young again I'd head off to Australia for a slower lifestyle, a slower pace. I've met people in Ballybunion who located from Dublin for an easier way of life. Progress is not all for the best. There's massive emphasis on clothes here. In Africa nobody worried about style or keeping up with the fashion. We went over to our granddaughter's First Holy Communion last week in England and there's not the fuss there that's made here. It's disgraceful here; all their money is taken up with make-up and stretch limos and no thought is given to the actual sacrament at all.

Life could change here too. We never foresaw what was about to happen to life in Zimbabwe, as we knew it. And it could happen anywhere. Look at Iraq. Look at Afghanistan. They probably never foresaw it happening there either, and they probably lived normal lives before these wars began. The Americans never foresaw the falling of the Twin Towers on September 11. We were on a caravan tour of South Africa that day and the reaction was unbelievable. Even that far away people were appalled and touched by what happened in New York. A friend of ours had been at the opening of the World Trade Center and she was very distressed to see it collapse. So you never know, your whole life can turn upside down in just one day. Its Kevin I really feel sorry for now. He was out in Africa for fifty years – a lifetime. It's very hard for him to adapt.

Kevin: I never lost my Dublin accent. Maybe I'll have to go away for another while. I grew up on the South Circular Road near the National Stadium, that great venue for Irish boxing. After I left school I was working in a shop on Pearse Street down near Ringsend and decided I needed some adventure. I answered an ad in the newspaper for a job on the railways in Africa and went along for an interview. That was about fifty years ago. I loved it from the start and wished I had gone there earlier. It was the weather brought me out there; it was very hot and I loved it. Rhodesia was a beautiful country, both

North and South. Northern Rhodesia is now Zambia and Southern is Zimbabwe; they're separated by the Zambesi River. There was wild life everywhere. You could go out and shoot for the pot. The animals were never confined. There were huge wild life parks where you'd see the herds of elephants running wild all over the place. The Hwange National Park was about the size of Ireland, North and South. Life was one long safari.

I sailed from Southampton to Cape Town on the *Rhodesia Castle*, part of the Union-Castle line that united England and South Africa. The boat was fabulous, like a hotel. I was hoping it would never land; that I would never have to get off. There were lots of different nationalities and we all had a great time together, dancing and singing. There was a good group of Irish too all recruited at the same time and we were all brought by train up the centre of Africa to Salisbury, the capital of Rhodesia, and from there on to Bulawayo, the second largest city, to the College where we were trained as railway engineers. That took about two months and then we became fully fledged employees of the National Railway. Everything was laid on, accommodation, work, hot women, cold water and whiskey of course. It was a far cry

Marion & Luke (right) at Mass in the catacombs celebrated by Fr. Odilo

The rocks above Tessa's pool.

from the South Circular Road let me tell you; from one extreme to another. I never thought I'd stay fifty years though; I just wanted to go over and see what it was like. Then you get in with a crowd and it's like a home from home; the years go by and you forget to come back. My parents were broken hearted. I wrote once a week and so did they and all they'd say is when are you coming home? I was the only son you see, with three sisters, and the only one who ever emigrated, so it had to be hard for them.

It was hard for me too sometimes. I was very homesick when I went first. There's nothing worse. Homesickness is a terrible thing. You'd be better off sometimes not having any relatives. I was there seven years before I came home on holidays. But, the social life was great; it was a young man's country. You could do what you liked, within reason. I didn't sow all of my wild oats; I still have a few left! Then this young Irish nurse came on the scene and I thought God had sent her. I had many girlfriends before that, all colours, but nobody had tempted me into marriage. Then Marian came along and it was love at first sight. We were married within six months; you couldn't let the grass grow under your feet. After sixteen years away it was time to settle down. I came home on my second visit the year after the wedding.

There were an awful lot of Irish in Africa at that time – working as teachers; on the railways; then of course there were the missions so there were always a lot of Irish priests and nuns. I had attended St. Theresa's National School on Donore Avenue and then the Christian Brothers at Synge Street. The last teacher I had there ended up going out to Africa too. I met him one time and he was teaching in Queque, which means frog sound, which is exactly how it is pronounced. The next time I met him he was in a teacher's training College in Senka. We kept up our religion the whole time and attended the Catholic Church. There were mostly Irish priests and some German too. The Irish were great.

I would never have gone if I hadn't seen the ad in the newspaper. I wanted to see what Africa was like. I didn't see much of it mind you, but a lot more than other people. I suppose I always had a sense of adventure even before I left Ireland when I used to travel around a bit on my motorbike. In 1950 I went to Rome for the Holy Year, the following year I went to Lourdes. It wasn't that I was very holy; it was just somewhere to go. I'd take the bike over on the boat and ride across country. I spent a week or two anyhow in Rome with a Mayo chap whom I'd never met before. I had put an ad in the newspaper for a companion to accompany me and he had answered. A lot of the important events in my life seem to have been triggered by newspaper ads! There's that adventurous streak in me again. Then on our way back, about 40 kilometres outside Paris, one of the tyres had a blow-out and we were both thrown from the bike. That was when you didn't have to wear a helmet and I was left unconscious as a result of the accident. The Mayo man, who had been on the pillion, disappeared and I never saw him again. I was taken to a hospital in the nearby village of San Quentin where I remained for three months. One day I suddenly regained consciousness. I couldn't remember time from before the accident happened. I woke up in my hospital bed and was surrounded by nuns in white habits speaking French. I thought they were angels; I must have died and gone to heaven. My Mayo companion had contacted a cousin of mine who was the Parish Priest in Bromley, Kent, and told him I was in hospital. That's how my family found out where I was. The Red Cross used to send me parcels and after I was discharged they sent my mother the bill. The local Parish Priest was from Ireland, but he'd forgotten all his English so it took us a while to communicate, then it all came back to him. So I suppose it's not surprising that someone like me ended up in Africa; I was always game to try something new. Now I'm in Ballybunion!

It's most unusual for a Dublin man to end up in Kerry but, I'll just treat it as another adventure. I don't mind being back in Ireland because I always loved it here too. We had to leave Africa when everything started going downhill. I spent three days in a petrol station one time trying to get fuel. Then when Marian was threatened, that was enough. What was there to stay for? It became too dangerous to live in Zimbabwe. That's how we ended up in Ballybunion. It's nice enough here and the people are nice, but it's not Dublin. Although I know that town has changed too. The city is too big and as a capital it's commanding the whole country. People who live in Wexford are working in Dublin. I don't know what kind of life that is, commuting so long every day. It's no life. When I lived there I danced in *The Four Provinces* in Harcourt Street opposite the railway station. We travelled by tram back then and by ferry. It cost a penny to cross the Liffey there where *The Point Theatre* is now.

We live in a convent that has been renovated into apartments and also contains the community centre where the Active Retirement classes are held. I participate, but don't take an active part in the organization or anything. I leave all that to Marian. She's doing great work and some of the members have told me how she has brought a whole new dimension to their lives here, so that's good.

We get on alright here; we're not short of anything. It's lovely all the same to be home and I don't think any place else would take me at this stage.

**Interviewed in Tralee, County Kerry,
on Friday, June 8th, 2007**

EDWARD CULLEN

I came home from England with my wife, Jenny, two years ago in January 2005 and I find the changes in Ireland amazing. There are so many cars here; plenty of cars and I don't have one at all. I don't need a car. I can walk up and down the town in five or ten minutes; hop on a train to Dublin or go anywhere I want. The free pass is great. We never had that in England. We never had it in Granard either before I left.

Granard was quiet when I was growing up. We made our own fun. There was a cinema there and a dance hall. I used to run messages after school for a local guesthouse owner beside the convent. I was the gofer; I'd go for milk, bread and whatever else she needed and for that I got a pound a week. That was a lot then. Sometimes the owner wouldn't be able to give it to me when Saturday night came around and I'd have to wait until the next week. But, you know, my father might have been depending on that pound. She used to serve tea to the bands playing in *The Granada* ballroom. I never danced there, but I saw it being built. Maurice Mulcahy was the first band to play there on opening night and they stopped into the guesthouse for tea, all dolled up in their black suits and sat around the big table. I had never seen people so dressed up before. I was never in the dance hall, but my sister was. It used to be packed on a Sunday night. The Quinn brothers ran it; they're dead and gone now. They did great in those days. It was demolished there some years ago and all that's in its place now is houses and apartments, but it did well in its day.

We never had running tap water in the houses that time. I used to carry water from the well up to the schoolmaster on the hill. We'd have to get it that way for the bath on a Saturday night too. The whole night would be taken up with the wash. We'd keep the water in barrels outside the back door and boil it up for the bath. It used to be some colour when it got to my turn, as I was always the last, being the youngest. That was spring water, then in later years we got a pump across the road where we only had to turn on a tap and that was lovely altogether then, wasn't it? I was only eleven when my mother died from tuberculosis. That disease was rampant in Ireland back then. I believe its coming back now too. She died in the house. I remember the day as if it was last week. It was a Saturday morning at eleven o'clock and I was carrying water up to Master Reid's house when I met Cathy Flaherty, our next door neighbour running up the hill to the post office. She was like a mother to us all and took care of everyone in the town when they were sick. "Eddie," she shouted, "you're mother's after dyin' and I'm going to send a telegram to England." That was it. That was how I found out. It happened that quickly; just as I was out drawing the water. It was a lovely sunny morning in March. The sun seemed to be always shining in Ireland then.

We would run around in our bare feet and we'd wash our feet in the gulley of rainwater running out of the side of the hill. I'm convinced that's why I have such good feet today. I can go into a shop and buy a pair of shoes without fitting them on, or I can walk home in them straight away without any bother. Jenny has terrible feet and

Granard in the 1950's

186

always has problems with shoes. I thank the running around in bare feet when we were youngsters for that, and the rainwater. I never looked back. The auld rainwater. When I was confirmed I had to wear my brother's shoes, which were two sizes too big for me. I had to stuff newspaper in the back of them to make them fit. But, funny thing is, we never went hungry; there was always food on the table. We mightn't have had luxuries like the radio, which some people had then, but we always had food. My sister, May, took over the house-keeping when my mother died and she stayed behind to take care of my father when we all went away. She must have missed us, as she was like a mother to us. We still get along great. My brother, Joe, then had the good job and that's why he stayed behind. He never married, poor Joe, although he had plenty of chances. My father would love to have seen him married before he died, but he was spoilt growing up and he had lovely girls who would have married him, but he wasn't interested. He wouldn't admit it in the end that he was lonely, but he must have been. He'd never pretend to be delighted to see us when we came home, but when it was time to go he'd be sorry. He was probably looking forward to seeing us, but he'd never admit it. He had plenty of friends, but in a way they were only gambling friends. They're never your friends when you don't have a penny. He died in the house he was born in, never leaving it, not like me.

There was no work in Granard that time. *Pat the Baker* was only starting off in a little tin shed in the back yard. We could look over the wall and smell the bread. He has branches all over the country now, North and South. Everyone else was leaving. They were going to America and everywhere, even at my age. My brother, Mike, and sister, Julie, had gone before me and when I was only sixteen I went back to England with an uncle who was home on holidays. He worked for *British Rail* for years and had a house over there where he kept Irish lads as lodgers. We travelled from Granard by bus to Dublin. The CIE bus was a regular feature of the Irish landscape in the Fifties, taking people from every town and village in Ireland, with the suitcases piled high on the roof, covered in plastic when it was raining. We took the boat from Dun Laoghaire to Holyhead, then down by train to Euston.

My uncle left me at Waterloo station where I travelled on alone to a place called Wool down in Dorset in the south of England where my sister, Julie, was living with her husband who was stationed there with the British Army. My first job was as a barman with the NAAFI, the Army, Navy & Air Force Institute, in their barracks social club for the troops who were serving in the various forces. It was a job. We weren't fussy that time what we worked at, as long as we were making money. I can't remember how I felt by the time I got there; I know I was lonely leaving Granard though. Everyone was leaving; they were leaving from every town in Ireland. A lot of lads I went to school with went to America; but it never appealed to me to go there. It was too far away. All of my aunts and uncles had gone there and we had never seen them again.

After a while my brother-in-law was transferred with the Army to Africa so I moved on to Eastleigh where my brother, Mike, was working on the railway. I got a job in *Price's* bakery where they made *Mother's Pride* bread, and *Gateaux* cakes. It's closed now. They're putting up a new car showroom instead. Everything is changing, not all for the good, as a lot of people are losing their jobs. There are a lot of jobs gone in Eastleigh. Even the railways jobs are gone. Mike worked all his life with the railway there; it was hard work laying cables and that. There was also a big carriage manufacturer there and that's gone too. But, back in our day it was great. There were a lot of Irish in Eastleigh. There are a lot still there and they wouldn't come back. The social life was very good. There was the Irish clubs with music and dancing every weekend. The drink was a lot cheaper than in the pubs, not that we were alcoholics or anything, but we worked hard all week, shift work and all, so we enjoyed a drink on a Saturday night. I was too young to miss Ireland at first. I got on well in England. I worked hard and sent my money home to my father every week; the same as everyone else did. I was lucky I had family there so I never had to stay with strangers. I did spend some time in digs and by God they were freezing. The ice would be thick on the windows and we used to have to throw our coats over the bed to keep warm. The young people don't know how good they have it now. I worked at all sorts of jobs and wasn't fussy with what I got. I wasn't well educated or trained for anything so I always had to work with my hands. I even did a stint on the building sites. After *Price's* I had several jobs. Julie came back from Africa and was then living in Surrey. She and her husband were like tinkers, always on the move with the Army. They were down near Epson only half an hour on the underground from London so I got a job in a warehouse there. A job was a job. But, I got on well and I never had any trouble in England. I had great friends there always. I still do. We go back and visit them all the time; in fact we're going now in June for a holiday.

Our wedding day

I came home once a year and after we were married we came back twice and three times. My wife, Jenny, loved it here, as did the children. In fact one of my sons moved back before we did and is now living with his wife and family in County Meath. They love it. We used to visit my sister, May, in Carrick for two weeks every summer; the minute we got our holidays we were back. She'd always treat us like lords when we were here; overfeed us and everything. The boats would be full of people who usually looked sad. Some would be on their own, some with children, whatever, on a three or four hour journey on the boat and then an eight hour journey on the train to

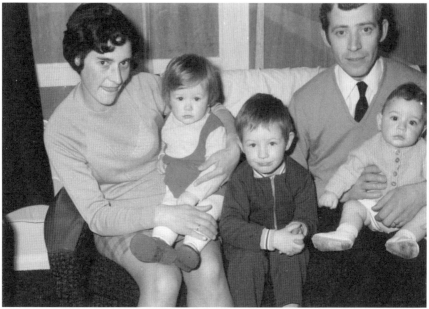

Happy family

London. Coming back I would take *The Irish Mail,* an old steam train from Euston to Holyhead. In North Wales they packed us on the boats like cattle, half of them had no seats. They weren't worried about restricting numbers. And it was rough. Even in the summer the sea would be wild; they had no stabilizers; no wonder everyone got sick. There would be great excitement getting on the buses at Busáras (bus station) to come home. We'd be sorry then going back again.

Irish people always treated me all right. I never felt any resentment from anyone. Jenny was always made welcome too. She was treated royally. Sure everyone knew someone over there; it wasn't a big deal to be living in England. An Irishman wanted to work and he would go anywhere to find it. Now they don't want to work. Ireland wasn't like it is now; sure the country's thriving. I don't know who's going to be elected next, but I think Bertie is doing a great job. Why change things now? It's the same in England, better the devil you know.

I met Jenny in *Price's.* She's from Eastleigh, but hers wasn't a very close knit family. The next sister to her was thirteen years older. So she joined my big Irish clan and they're her family now and Ireland is her home. And wasn't she lucky to get me? I keep telling her that! The wedding reception was in a community hall; a sort of a social club where they would have bingo and things. We went on our honeymoon to Clapton-on-Sea where my brother-in-law's mother had a house. We took it for a week; then went back to their house where we stayed another week while they took the house in Clapton! We were married in Eastleigh in Holy Cross Church, where the children were all baptized. I'm fairly religious, always went to Mass and that in England. All the Irish did; you'd meet them all in the Church on Sunday. Jenny converted before we were married, I didn't ask her, she did it herself. She went to the nuns in London and was confirmed in Southwark Cathedral there. There's a priest from Cork in Eastleigh now, a young man, Father Donaghy. He's very nice. It's much harder for the priests in England because they have huge areas to cover. There used to be two priests in our parish, now there's only one. They've cut back on the number of Masses being said, but Father Donaghy has jurisdiction over about six parishes, and it's beginning to tell on him now. We would have met a lot of people long ago through the Church. There was always a little community hall to go to and have a cup of tea or coffee after Mass; it was a great social gathering. There's not as many Irish coming into Eastleigh now; it's still mainly Polish. As long as I was in Eastleigh there was a Polish Mass every Sunday morning at nine o'clock.

There are a lot of Polish people in this area too and African. There's a man from Ghana up the street; the reason I know is that he had a Ghana scarf on during the World Cup. But, we all get along fine. I cut the grass for them if they want me to. I won't let them borrow the lawn mower or my garden equipment, but I will help them out if they need a hand. I like to see them helping themselves too; God helps those who help themselves. Some of them don't take care of their homes; I can't stand that. In England the landlord or housing association can come around and check the place, once they've given notice. They don't do that here. A lot of people have gone and left their houses full of rubbish and the poor caretaker has to clean it out. That would never happen in England. And a house like this would cost a fortune to rent over there; they don't know how lucky they are here; they don't appreciate it. Maybe it's just me; maybe I'm old-fashioned, but I'm mighty glad to have this place and I will look after it.

In 1978 we returned to Ireland with our three children when I got a job as a caretaker with the Midland Tourism in Mullingar. It was advertised in one of the Irish newspapers and came with a flat so I applied and was offered the position, and we decided to give it a go. The children went to school in the convent there and the Christian Brothers. That's where they were educated really more so than in England. Our eldest son, Anthony, then went to college in Athlone and Dundalk. The people weren't very friendly, but we liked Mullingar well enough. The children all went back to England as soon as they'd left school, so then we followed them and went back to Eastleigh again after a ten year absence. Anthony had fallen in love with Ireland and came back eventually when he was a qualified Quantity Surveyor. He's the gaffer now dressed in a suit and tie. I am glad he did so well and didn't have to dirty his hands the way I did. Our daughter is in company management in Southampton and our other son is a bus driver there.

My sister, May, always wanted me back. And I was only here twelve months when she lost her husband. He died last year, in March. She's got her own family close by and they're very good to her, but she was also glad to have me back. We go down there at weekends. There's only the two of us here so we can get the bus down or the train from Longford. Around the year 2000 we saw the advertisement for Safe Home in *The Irish Post*. I wrote to them and got the application forms. They made sure we realized it wasn't the country we left, but we knew that anyhow because we were always back and forward. We knew it wasn't the country I had left back in the Fifties. We initially wanted to go to Carrick-on-Shannon to be near May, but Safe Home prefers you to go back to your native county so Longford it was for us.

I know one or two in Granard, but since the brother died two years ago all the ties were severed. The home place is gone. The only place I visit there now is the graveyard. My father died thirty-four years ago. It must have troubled him when we left. He'd never say anything, but he must have been upset. He came over to visit a couple of times. In fact that's where Jenny first met him when he was over staying with my sister. She couldn't understand him at first; she found his accent very strange. We used to send him a couple of bob in the letter, which was great wasn't it? Everybody did the same. The money was good at the time; it wouldn't be great now, but you worked and you earned money. You couldn't have stayed at home and done nothing. I had to go. And England was always very good to me. I don't like people running it down. It was there for a lot of people of my age when there was nothing for them here. I know we didn't get anything for nothing; we had to work for everything we got; but that's what we intended. I wouldn't know now if I would have preferred to have stayed at home. The opportunities weren't there; if they were I probably wouldn't have left. But there wasn't even a sign of things improving. I don't know when this country started to get better - the Eighties? The Nineties? That would have been a long time to wait.

Eddie at Wilton Royal Carpets, Romsey, early 70's

We're back two years now last January. I didn't find it hard at all. I thought I would, but I didn't. It was easier than when I went to Mullingar. I couldn't afford to live in England any longer. We were in rented accommodation because we never bought our own house. I was going to buy that time when Maggie Thatcher was in office, when she was encouraging everyone to invest, but then people couldn't keep up the repayments and ended up in foreclosure with the houses boarded up. We didn't want to get into that. We were only making a very modest living and we couldn't afford to lose like that.

Anyhow the job in Mullingar came up so we went for that instead. It's very expensive to live in England now between rent and Council tax. We were paying nearly five hundred a month in rent. The landlady wasn't cooperative with having repairs done and that. Then I had to think about the future. I'm getting older and a time will come when I won't be able to afford all that. My daughter was sorry to see us go, but she understood why. The two of us were working full-time and Jenny was merely working to pay the rent. I was in a doctor's surgery in Eastleigh and Jenny had to cycle late at night to her job, so that wasn't a good situation. We never paid into a pension. I never stayed long enough in a job to do that.

It's funny though, I'm lonelier here than I was in England. We don't see as many people as we did over there; we don't have as much of a laugh or a joke. We know a few of the neighbours. I cut the grass for the girl next door, but we haven't made any friends to socialize with. There's the occasional event in the Community Centre, but they're mostly for the youngsters. There's a crèche there during the week and some sort of a Gospel service on a Sunday. They're up there with their loud music and the windows open, crash bang wallop on their drums, and whatever else. I suppose they're entitled to their ceremonies too. They all speak foreign languages. I don't know how the children get on at school. And they go to bed so late, you'd hear them up at all hours, but they're not too bad, just from a different culture; that's all.

I don't think I'll look for work here. I have the Irish pension and Jenny has the English one, so we're alright, but what I would like to do is some volunteer work. I've finished redecorating the place here; we just had to replace some of the paintwork, as we weren't mad about the colours, and I have more time on my hands now. But we do get about a bit. The week after next we're going to Cork with our daughter and grandson and her second husband. Her first marriage broke down; I don't know why, but you never think it's going to hap-pen until it does. I was dumbfounded. I think I was more upset than they were. But, they're still the best of friends and they have the one son; he's eleven now and will be twelve in January. So she got married again to a man from Portsmouth whose people are from Cork. In fact, his great grandmother was a sister of Michael Collins. To look at him now and look at a picture of Collins they're the absolute image. He's got the dark hair and the height; he's over six foot, exactly the same as Collins. We've all hired a house in Clonakilty for a week, which we will spend together. Then the week after that we'll be going over to her for two weeks. We move about. We don't be here half the time.

We're going to Medjugorje in August; we were in Fatima last year. We saw the ad in the church bulletin and put our names down. May and her friend will come too. We might meet some local people on that. St. Mel's prayer group is running it. I said to the priest that I hoped it wouldn't be all praying and he assured me it wouldn't! We did some praying in Fatima, but there's only so much you can do. We're flying from Knock; from one apparition to another. These places can be so commercialized; stalls everywhere selling mementoes. May bought a wooden crucifix in Fatima; the width of the wall over there. You'd think it was the real thing. So maybe we'll make friends on the pilgrimage. That would be great. Sometimes there's a dinner for the local senior citizens, but they haven't had one in a long time. They look after their elderly here. When we tell our English friends how it is here they don't believe it. They don't appreciate what they have here. I have the pass and Jenny can travel on it only if I'm with her. I tell her if she behaves herself I'll bring her with me! That was Charlie Haughey who got us all that; he wasn't all bad. Now they're trying to get it for the older Irish in England. They should be entitled to it too if they have an Irish passport and an Irish birth certificate. They sent enough money home all through the years when their families had nothing.

I like it back here, but I miss the people over there; I miss the job I had. Shame I couldn't move the job. I'd like to join something here in order to meet people. I'd mix with anyone. I could do a couple of hours a day, a few days a week. I haven't looked into anything yet. The Legion of Mary called around, but I don't think they're my cup of tea. Don't get me wrong, they do great work, but that's not really what I want.

Julie came back too whenever her husband finished his time in the Army. They lived in Dublin for a little while and then in Cork. She's dead now, Lord Have Mercy on Her; she'd have loved to see me back. Not everyone settles. We heard of a woman who came home from America, but she couldn't settle and was going back. If you're away fifty or sixty years, really a lifetime, it is very hard to come back again. We know a lot of people who wouldn't come back, especially those who have families. But, it's so easy to go back and forth to England now. America might be different, it's further away. Everyone wants to come back in the end; everyone wants to go back to their roots. It's an Irish thing.

Interviewed at his home in Longford town
on Wednesday, May 16th, 2007

Eddie & Jenny

VINCENT & BRIDIE COLLINS

Vincent: Every Sunday morning I used to have a drink with a friend of mine in London and one morning he said to me, you know there's an organization now in Ireland that finds housing for people who want to come home. I had never thought of returning before that; I'd never had the inclination. My friend held out this newspaper cutting advertising The 'Safe-Home' Programme in Mulranny. I said this has got to be a wind-up. I rang the office anyhow and Mary Ann Fadian asked me how long I was away because I wouldn't be returning to the same country that I left. I knew that already because we'd been over every year, sometimes twice if there was a wedding. She thought I would qualify and sent out the forms, which we completed and sent back. Next thing we got forms from the County Council because you have to register with them too. They gave me two choices and I said Ballycastle. But, there was nothing being built there that time so they asked me if I'd like Lacken. My sister-in-law who lives in Killala came down, saw this house and rang straight away to tell us it was beautiful. We took it and moved back three years ago, in December 2004. After fifty-three years I was back in Mayo.

In 1951 my brother, Seamus, and I had bussed it from Ballina to Dublin. I believe there were trains, but funny thing is I've never been on a train in Ireland yet. I remember well getting on that boat in Dun Laoghaire. It was a terrible journey with hundreds of people and no place to sit. Some of them were lying on the corridors. There was loads of *craic* though with the music full blast. There were about twenty accordions going at the same time, including yours truly. I didn't drink, but I took two whiskies and they hit me straight away. Seamus and I were travelling with another gentleman who left his family twice a year; in the springtime, to hoe the sugar beet and in the autumn to pull it. We took the train from Holyhead and made a connection at Crewe

With my sister, Betty, Ballina 1946

for Leamington Spa in Warwickshire. I remember sitting on the platform in Crewe at three o'clock in the morning and the two lads full of whiskey snoring on the seat beside me. I was too frightened to sleep in this strange country. I wouldn't have closed my eyes if you put a gun to my head.

We got the bus then to the town of Warwick and it was market day when we arrived. We met the Managing Agent responsible for rounding up employees to pull beet for the local farmers and presented him with a bottle of *Paddy*. He opened it there and then and started to drink. We piled into a car and he was nearly sloshed by the time we arrived at the farm. The farmer was a lovely man and we had plenty to eat despite food being rationed; the work though was something else altogether. From dawn to dusk we worked out in the fields and there were pains in places we didn't even know we had. We'd never even seen beetroot before but I can tell you, after five or six weeks I'd seen enough of it and decided to head for London. Seamus and I parted company and he eventually ended up in Birmingham. However, I'll never forget my first week's wages – twenty four pounds, which was fantastic money then.

In West London I moved into a small flat in Shepherd's Bush, more of a room really. It had no cooker, only one gas ring, but I cooked a fine stew there. I worked in the building trade for the first five years and it was the greatest five years of my life. The *craic* was mighty because it was ninety-nine percent Irish. Then I went into warehousing and made my way up to Manager. I left that and became a cab driver in London for about fourteen years where I met a lot of famous people – Anne Ford who used to read the news on the BBC; Annika Rice, she's on *The Hell's Kitchen* programme at the moment; Sheena Easton, the singer, and John MacEnroe, the tennis player. When I contacted peripheral neuropathy in my lower limbs, I had to give it up.

At a young age I used to play the accordion, having picked it up when I was about eight years old. I grew up on a small farm near Ballycastle in the parish of Kilbride from the age of seven; prior to that is another story altogether. At seven, as far as I'm concerned, my life began. Before that I was institutionalized in a hospital in Castlebar. It was a place where I didn't hear any music; I didn't see an animal; a car, nothing. I'd never been out in the open. When they drove me home to Ballycastle, it was the first time I'd been outside the hospital and it was the first time I'd ever seen a car. My mother was dead. My father was still alive, but he was a bum. I had two brothers and one sister. I was the black sheep; the forgotten one. I went to live with an aunt of mine, who had three or four children of her own. She'd found me when she was in the hospital having a baby. She was told my name was Vincent and that I was part of the furniture. She put her thinking cap on and figured out that I was her nephew. She took me home, but she really couldn't afford to keep me so she handed me on to her aunt, who was my grandaunt. That was when my life story began.

A short while later there was a party in the house and that was the first time I heard music. I had no music in my head. At first I picked up a little tune on the tin whistle – *The Wearing of the Green*. But, this man, Pat Mahon, he's coming up to a hundred now, was playing the melodeon and I stayed beside him all night long. I couldn't be got away from him. I thought if only I could get hold of the instrument, I know I can play it. I knew it. When the night finished he said to me would you like to be able to play? I said I'm sure I would. He came down to the house the next day with a battered old melodeon kept together with paste. I could not wait to get a hold of it. I had *The Wearing of the Green* in my head and I knew I had to transfer that to the keys. Once I found the first note I was able to play the first couple of bars.

O *Paddy dear, an' did ye hear the news that's goin' round? The shamrock is forbid by law to grow on Irish ground; St. Patrick's Day no more we'll keep, his colour can't be seen, For there's a cruel law agin the wearin' o' the Green.*

Pat was dumbfounded; do that again, he said. I had to find that one first note again and then I was off …

199

I met wid Napper Tandy and he took me by the hand, And he said, "How's dear ould Ireland, and how does she stand?" She's the most distressful country that ever yet was seen, For they're hangin' men an' women there for the wearin' o' the Green.

This lad's brilliant, Pat said, he's a natural, he said, brilliant. And that was it.

But, I had no music in me. I had nothing else only that one tune. The night before Pat was playing reels and things, but you couldn't learn them that quickly. Somebody then came down from Dublin with a radiogram, one that you wound up by hand like an old gramophone, and after that I could play anything I heard. I played all over the place. I played in the Sligo feis, but I don't know if I ever won anything; I haven't a clue. I played in country house dances and then later on when I got bigger I played in Ballycastle with a band called *The Seaside Serenaders*. We played waltzes, foxtrots, quick steps, you know, all dance music. There was a couple of accordions, a fiddle player and a drummer. There was no brass instruments; no amplifiers, nothing like that, just four fellows playing on a small stage.

I eventually bought my own brand new button accordion worth thirty-five pounds, which was a lot of money then. I had seen it in Benny Walkin's store in Ballina and thought if only I could get my hands on that. Benny asked me if I played and I said, a little bit. He asked me if I'd like to get hold of that one, and I said I sure would. He handed it down to me and when I'd finished playing he said you can play alright, do you want it? I said I wanted it, but I know I can't have it. I was only earning one pound a week, how could I ever afford it? He said, take it and whenever you have a few shillings, drop it in. We never signed a document or nothing; he just gave me the accordion. He later became Mayor of the town, but to me he was the Lord Mayor that day and I never forgot him.

That was some time in early spring and in August after I turned twenty-one, I headed for the bright lights of London. That time you had to have a permit to get into the country and I remember going up to Ballina to the labour exchange and they wouldn't give me one. They said there was plenty of work on the bog and I thought this is one fellow who won't be cutting turf for Bord na Móna. I had already spent a couple of years in a local flax mill where you couldn't see the boy beside you from the dust and I'm convinced it left a mark on my chest to this day. I hated that sort of work. So I went to the Sergeant in Ballycastle and told him my story. A week later I got my travel permit, but had to sell the accordion to get some money. I had sold a bicycle too and still had about three or four week's wages. All in all I had about sixteen or seventeen pounds in my pocket, and that was a lot of money, but I needed it all to get to England. It cost seven and sixpence on the bus, another seven and sixpence on the ferry, and whatever I was going to need on the other side to set me up, so I was pretty well off anyway. I never told Benny Walkin that I was going; I just didn't have the heart, but decided that whenever I had the money, after I'd got a decent job, I'd send it to him. I had made one or two pound payments before I left and eventually I sent him the remainder with a letter apologising for the delay. About five or six years later when I was home on holidays, I went into the shop and my letter was up there on the wall, so I suppose he never forgot me either.

After getting off that boat in England, I swore I'd never play another accordion. I didn't either for a long time. Then when I came back here to live almost three years ago, the man who was delivering the

Vince & The Western Wildcats

oil, Sean Healy from Ballycastle, came in and shook hands with me. I hadn't seen this man since I left. He asked me if I still played music, as he said he remembered my lovely white accordion. I told him the story about how I had to sell it to a man called Paddy Lane before I went to England. The fellow with him was listening and about a month later he came back with an old cardboard box with this accordion thrown in the bottom of it. He was a friend of a son of this Paddy Lane who had bought it from me fifty-six years earlier. They found it outside in the shed with bits of turf in it. All the keys were still intact. I nearly cried when I saw it because I had been really lonely after it. I had a job to get it repaired, but I eventually found someone in Galway and it cost me four hundred euros. It was worth every penny.

Having promised myself that I would never play again after leaving Ireland, I got into singing instead. I used to sing country songs with different bands and then I formed my own band in the Seventies called *Vince and the Western Wildcats*. It was formed quickly for a charity fundraiser and it was meant to be for only one night you see, and the organizer needed a name to put on the tickets for the dance. First we came up with Vince and the Wildcats and then we changed it to Western Wildcats because we played mainly country and western music. It was a great night, the band went down well, so after that we bought some equipment and went on the road.

We played mainly in Catholic halls, Irish Clubs, weddings, and the Irish festivals. We were very busy every weekend, booked solid, months in advance. During the day I was a cab driver; at night I was a singer. I did that for years and then I got a bit of a heart problem and I had to get that sorted out. I had a triple by-pass about ten years ago and had to give it all up then.

So this is it, from London to Lacken. I wouldn't have believed anyone if they'd told me three years ago that I'd end up here. Across the strand is Kilcummin where Humbert landed, the French General who came to help the Irish. You wouldn't be able to buy a house here now in front of this view. You'd never get planning permission. We're living within walking distance of the beach, but I can't walk very far unfortunately. When your health fails it changes everything. When I was a young lad I was very active. I played football for Ballycastle, which is really my home town. I wouldn't have been that familiar with Lacken, nevertheless, I settled in no bother. I don't miss London at all and was glad to get away from the noise and pollution.

Bridie: I thought I wouldn't settle. I was fifty-six years in London, and to come here was a huge upheaval. We were living in the fast lane all those years and I couldn't have had nicer neighbours over there. I really missed them at first. Of course I don't drive either so that's a big drawback. But, I stuck it out here in Lacken and got used to it, and now I wouldn't want to leave. It was very daunting leaving our home in London, but we had become very unhappy there. We were thirty-seven years in the area and we had moved in when the houses were brand new. There were a lot of Irish there and everybody knew everyone else and we made friends immediately. Then other nationalities started moving in and the Irish moved out. In the end we were nearly the last ones there from the original group, apart from the woman next door, and the whole place had changed. We were going to have to move somewhere anyway, so it might as well have been to Ireland.

I went to England in 1948 when I was nineteen years old. I travelled on my own, but went over to a friend in London, Mary Lonergan, who is ninety-two now and living in America. She was here a month ago. Wasn't she great to make the journey? She was staying in Clonmel and was supposed to call to see us on her way to Knock, but she fell ill, so we went down to see her instead and brought her a bottle of Knock water.

I went working in the hotels; I never worked anywhere else except in the catering business. I spent seven years in *The Grand Hotel* in London; that was the one I got married out of. After my marriage I went into the banqueting business and ended up working in the House of Commons where I retired out of. I met all of the well known politicians over the years and the nicest man I ever served was Ian Paisley. He was a gentleman to the backbone; a generous tipper and a real family man. John Major was Prime Minister when I was there and I knew him well, and Edwina Curry. I waited on the Queen, the Queen Mother, Princess Anne, Princess Margaret, and the Duke of Edinburgh when I worked in The Army and Navy Club down by the River Thames. The Queen Mother used to come there every Wednesday for her lunch and she used to always order the same lunch as the soldiers. She used to love the steak and kidney pie. She was a lovely lady.

I was never lonely for Ireland. Once you had that first holiday at home you were glad to get back. Ireland back then was a Third World country; the only thing is we had lots and lots to eat; we had lots of meat and fresh vegetables, but other than that we had nothing. After that first holiday I wasn't a bit bothered if I never got back again, although I did come home quite often. I grew up in the town of Clonmel in County Tipperary; there were eight of us altogether in the family. But, once I started a family of my own, England was home. Vincent and I met in *The Blarney* dancehall. He came over and said, "Will you dance with me?"

Vincent: Wasn't I the proper gentleman? There's a picture of me there in the suit I was wearing the night I asked her to dance. We danced in every Irish Club in London. The only night we didn't go dancing was Monday. We even went Sunday afternoon and
back again that night. When we went over in the early Fifties the most famous pub for the Irish in London was *The Crown* in Cricklewood.
Bridie: They even made up a song about it ... *The craic was good in Cricklewood, They wouldn't leave The Crown,* Another was *McAlpine's Fusiliers.*

Both: *(singing) As down the glen came McAlpine's men with their shovels slung behind them It was in the pub that they drank their sub or down in the spike you'll find them They sweated blood and they washed down mud with pints and quarts of beer But now we're on the road again with McAlpine's Fusiliers.*

Vincent: *The Crown* was awfully rough though. It was full of big men from the West of Ireland.

Bridie: And you'd know them straight away in their navy suits, brown shoes, white shirts and red ties …

Vincent: And three fountain pens sticking out of their top pockets. That was their trademark. They worked hard and they played hard. I broke away from all of that. I wore charcoal grey suits, maybe a white shirt alright, but I'd have a silvery grey tie and a hankie always folded in the top pocket. The Irish men were known for fighting too. There was always sawdust on the floor of *The Crown* and the lads maintained that it had probably been the furniture the night before! A lot of the Connemara men only spoke Irish. I was the ganger one time and they were all speaking Irish working with me. One day I addressed one of them in Gaelic and he nearly died. His face reddened up and I suppose he'd been talking about me a lot of the time and now thought I had understood him all along, which I didn't because I only knew a few phrases.

Bridie and I were going out on and off for a while, maybe eight years; we didn't rush into it. We got married in 1960 in St. Cecilia's Church in Kingsway. We had the reception in a pub; that was the usual thing in them days. It was a small wedding with about seventy people and some of Bridie's family came, but only one from mine, my brother. My sister was due a baby the same day so she couldn't come. I knew my brothers and sisters growing up even though we were farmed around a lot, and I didn't meet my oldest brother for the first time until 1956. You have to remember at that time that transportation was very limited. Loads of people didn't even have bicycles.

Bridie: I remember coming home one Christmas with Vincent and we went to a dance in Ballycastle on St. Stephen's night. Some of the girls were coming in drenched, soaked to the skin after cycling miles in the rain. How they got into the dance looking like that, I'll never know, but they enjoyed themselves I'm sure.

Vincent: We had hired a car coming home and were delighted with ourselves to be out of the rain, for a change. Ballycastle was so different then; it's like a ghost town now. You won't see a human being on the street. A lot of the houses are boarded up, not a sinner living in them. When I was growing up there were fourteen pubs in the town, not that they were all doing a trade, maybe on a fair day, but they were there. There was four major shops in it that sold everything; they're all gone now. There's none of them left. That's terrible. A lot of small towns in Ireland have decayed. Killala is another one. It's such a pity. Nobody invested any money in Ballycastle and I think that's a shame. They should promote tourism there. I had visions of somebody building a hotel or they could open a nine-hole golf course. It would be perfect. There is a small hotel in what used to be the convent and the food there is absolutely fantastic. They only open from Easter to October, but they could be one of the top ten restaurants in the country. I remember it when it was a convent. There was about four or five nuns teaching in it and there was a priest who used to stay there and say Mass for the nuns. The teachers in our national school were absolutely useless as teachers. They just did not know how to teach.

Bridie: It was the same everywhere. I went to the Mercy Convent outside Clonmel and the nuns were very hard. They were old witches, pure wicked. They ruled the roost along with the Christian Brothers whose cruelty was just dreadful.

Vincent: Children walked three and four miles in from the country in the wind and the rain and had to sit in wet clothes for the day. Now they have a school bus laid on, but the ones around here go in empty. The big bus goes up there with thirty-two seats on it and only two kids inside. Then it's followed by the Jeeps and Mercedes, the mothers want to be seen in their new cars, and that's happening all over Ireland.

Bridie: A friend of mine used to say that the real Irish people were the ones living over there, meaning in London. We always kept up the old values and traditions. It was what bound us together. It's the same in the Irish neighbourhoods in America.

The Shamrock, Elephant & Castle

Vincent: In 1979 I sang a rake of songs in *The Archway Tavern* on Jerome Avenue in the Bronx. The man who ran it at the time was from the next parish up here. We had been Upstate New York, in Rochester, at a wedding and I met some cousins who took me into Manhattan where we stayed in *The Holiday Inn*. A fellow, Jimmy Ruddy, had given me the name and address of this bar. I rang them and they said if you're a friend of Jimmy's you're a friend of ours. Jimmy also played the accordion. When I went in first the bar was empty. They don't start there until ten or eleven at night and then they stay open until four in the morning. There was a big dance floor and a stage. The barman offered me a drink and we got chatting. I asked him if he'd heard of Danny McCoy who was supposed to be playing around there and he said it was only five minutes up the road in *Durty Nelly's* in Yonkers. He took me up there when he clocked off work and McCoy was up on the stage singing when we walked in the door. When he spotted me, he uttered a few expletives over the microphone, came down and swung me around the place. He then took me up on the stage and announced "Now you're going to hear some singing."

We went back to America again in 1988. We based ourselves in New Jersey in Mary Longergan's, the woman Bridie had gone to stay in England with all those years ago. Then we went to Florida, Atlantic City, Philadelphia, Upstate New York to Rochester again, Niagara Falls, and we stayed in *The Sheraton Hotel* in Manhattan. It was there that I contacted this fellow, Joe Mahon, married to a girl from Kilbride, Kathleen Burke. He took us along this strip of bars in the Bronx and in every one of them the staff was Irish.

Bridie: Every Irish person we spoke to who had started off in England said they'd love to be back there again. The money was better in

Our wedding day. St. Cecilia's, Kingsway 1960

America, they said, but they'd be nearer home in England.

Vincent: Most of the people I knew around here went to England because it was cheaper and you didn't need anyone to sponsor you over. Most people who went to America never came back again. At the Famine Memorial near Louisburgh, you wouldn't hear a pin drop, or a bird singing, it would make the hairs stand up on your chest. Someone writing in *The Irish Post* in England said he cycled along there and he didn't think there was a place on this earth that was so still.

We've been there two or three times, and it really brings you back to the times when people were dying on the side of the road. The lucky ones made it to America; only some of them made it back.

An awful lot of people went to England too and never came back. They're looking at the bottom of a glass now. I knew one fellow who was dossing and I asked him what happened. He said he was a farmer's son and a Mammy's boy when he went to London where he worked hard all day and back to an empty room at night time with no one to cook for him, so he went to the bar and that was it. And that happened to a lot of them. They never wrote home and left it too long between visits. Then they became ashamed. This fellow said he wanted to write and he wanted to come home, but he never did. It's a shame really. It's very sad.

Bridie: They should come home. I would recommend it, even to those who've been away a long time, even if life is really different here now, because everyone speaks to you. Everybody speaks on the street, in the shops, even in *Tesco*. Everything is "grand." I love that about the people here.

The only thing I worried about was the medical situation. I thought we'll have to get a new doctor, and everything, but it's been no problem at all. We have a wonderful doctor close by and he's been marvellous to us. I had what was like a slight stroke since I came back. My legs went weak one day and I lost my voice. Vincent rang the doctor straight away and he was here in no time. I told him I had had a real stroke five years ago in London so he sent me in an ambulance to Castlebar, but it turned out that the arteries in my neck had been blocked up. I was a whole month in Castlebar waiting for a bed in Galway. The nurses were delighted with me because I'd get up and make my own bed and go around the ward filling up the patient's glasses with water. In the end they sent me all the way to St. James's hospital in Dublin, in a taxi if you don't mind, just to be told that they couldn't operate on one valve, but would have to do the two of them together. In the meantime, they put me on medication and that was it. I haven't had a complaint since.

Vincent: Another advantage has been that our only child, our daughter, Jackie, and her husband, David, have moved back now since last May and that's been wonderful, having them so near us. They couldn't live away from us so they've moved back to Castlebar, and we see quite a lot of them. They love it here, even David who is English. They had visited lots of times and Jackie always wanted to live in Ireland since her first visit when she was only ten years old.

There's good changes and bad changes in Ireland. Take for example the suicides; there are so many of them now. I lived in Mayo for twenty-one years and I never heard of a single suicide. We had no money, but we were content. Now they got everything and they're still not satisfied. Now a young fellow on the building trade can get five hundred euros a week. They don't know what to do with the money. They go binge drinking; they're blowing their brains out. On top of that there's all this pressure on them to go to college. Years ago if you take the parish of Ballycastle the only people who had money were a couple of shopkeepers or a few farmers and they were the only ones who could send their children to college. There was no pressure on them. Now the kids are under so much pressure to do well in school, I think it builds up on them, they drink too much and they're into drugs. We couldn't afford to drink when we were young, you might get a bottle of stout, but that was it. Drink is a big problem here. That is the downside.

The upside is that they have everything now, they have plenty of money. When I was young if I saw a tractor I thought it was a great thing. If I saw a bicycle I got excited, never mind a tractor. Now everyone has a car. The European Union (EU) is a great thing. I think England should have gone with the euro. They never will as long as the Queen is alive and her face is on the pound note.

Bridie: There's no downside for me except I'm not near *Marks & Spencers*. The nearest one is in Galway. I like the shops, but Ballina really doesn't have many. Sligo town is better. We were there last week and I got a pair of shoes and a couple of tops. The pub is our social life. *Maughan's* up the road here is our local and we've got to know a few people there. The drink driving laws and smoking ban doesn't help the rural bar business so it's nice to have one so near. There aren't really any activities around here for senior citizens.

Vincent: There's a community centre alright where we meet every second Monday for high noon. A bunch of old fogies like us go in there for soup and sandwiches; we play bingo and scratch the cards. You won't get carried away with the prizes. They should open it up more for the likes of us. It's quite a big parish, St. Patrick and St. Cuimin's, but it's very spread out. There's a few tourists around, but we wouldn't

Bridie in the Willows

notice them except for the odd caravan.

Bridie: It's nice to be back here at this stage of our lives and the house is so new, it's easy to keep clean. All of the houses are called after American trees. I don't know why, but ours is *Willows*. The neighbours are lovely too. I'm celebrating my 80th birthday tomorrow and we're going out to dinner. It's a secret so far, but I'm hoping they're taking me to *The Diamond Coast* hotel in Enniscrone. It's beautiful there.

Vincent (aside): (We're having a party for Bridie on Friday night in *Maughan's*, but she doesn't know it yet. There will be a few there from England, although a lot of people have gone back from their holidays already. We'll pretend we're taking her down for a drink and everyone will be in the room we've booked.)

It's great to be alive and well and able to enjoy all of this. When I told you earlier I was institutionalized it was because I was either dropped or fell when I was a baby. It was top secret anyhow. I was never told what happened, but I broke my back and that's why my father put me in the hospital. I was neglected for the first few weeks and I was eventually left there to rot. My father never came to see me or anything and I didn't get out until I was seven years of age. My mother died when I was about two I think. That's why I was institutionalized. There's a big story to my life and you've only heard part of it.

Interviewed at their home in Carrowmore Lacken, County Mayo, on September 12ᵗʰ, 2007

My Ballina button accordion

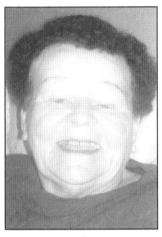

BRIDIE BENNETT

My earliest memory is going to the matinee with Mammy to the cinema there on Pepper's Hill in Kingscourt, County Cavan, where *Supervalu* is now. As we were leaving a very well dressed, respectable looking gentleman approached us, stopped, seemed to hesitate and then walked on. Later Mammy told me he was her father. He had not spoken to her since her marriage, as he didn't approve of Daddy who was twenty-five years her senior and a brickyard labourer.

My father came from Muff and my mother from Turner's Cross. She worked for years in the bank in Kingscourt; for long after I was born. She walked back and forth to work every day and if she had to stay late they gave her a lantern to guide her in the dark. She was very clever and was like a secretary in Turner's Hill, as she wrote all the letters for people from miles around who couldn't read or write. They'd give her fresh eggs as payment and cure a pig to give her lumps of pork, even though she could have done with the money. Unfortunately, my parents were not compatible and I'd say it was mainly due to the fact that my father was not educated. He had been kept home from school as a little lad because he had to work on the farm. They never got on well even though they had seven children, five girls and two boys. Her brother, Tommy, would have kept in touch with her and she was quite friendly with her mother. It seemed to be her father, a schoolteacher, who disapproved.

I was the youngest of the family. I always remember my sister, Katie, who was a few years older than me, washing her lovely long hair from water in the pump. One day I noticed that she had gone and asked Mammy where she was. Oh, you won't see her for a long time I was told. She had entered the Loreto Convent in Balbriggan as a noviciate taking the name Sr. Mary Nativity. A short while later she wrote a very strange letter to my parents. I remember well my mother reading it aloud to Daddy who was home on his lunch break and eating a duck egg. I am very happy here, Katie wrote, and if I get nine years out of the nuns I'll be even happier. I won't mind if God takes me after that. Nine years later she died from leukaemia. Mammy said that it was because of the hard life the nuns led back then; that they probably didn't expect to live long, but it was still a very strange thing to predict from one so young. Katie is buried on the grounds of the convent and I always went to visit her grave every time I came home. The nuns always made such a fuss, making us tea and everything; you'd think we were Royalty. There is still one alive there who remembers Sister Nativity and it always makes me sad to see her, but I won't visit Katie's room, as that would upset me too much. I had another sister, Margaret, who also wanted to be a nun, but her health broke down. She was a receptionist in a residential hotel in Rathmines, Dublin, and one time they sent her home on a very cold bus where she contacted tuberculosis. She was admitted to the hospital at Peamount where she died two years later when she was twenty-three years old. Margaret and Katie were always very close and it's ironic that they both died so young.

Kingscourt Girls N.S. 1914
My sister, Kate (4th from left), middle row

I attended the old National School nearby and the nuns in Carrick-macross. After that I was sent to the Bon Secours hospital in Belfast where I trained as a children's nurse. It was from there that I went to England to my two older sisters, Winnie and Anne, who were living in Manchester. I was seventeen years old and started off as a nanny for business people who lived outside the city. I had no housework to do, but was required to only look after the children. After a while, I went down to my brother who lived in the Wirral outside Liverpool. I started nursing on night duty in the Royal Children's hospital of Liverpool. It's a *Tesco* supermarket now. I liked the work well enough, but was not keen on living-in. If we were out after ten o'clock at night we had to get a late pass and I was always forgetting it when I went to visit my brother and sister-in-law. I stayed there four years and then it closed down. I was getting a bit fed up of nursing by then and next thing I went in behind a bar for *Whitbread's* and even though I never drank or smoked, I loved the work. I loved meeting people, but I had everybody's troubles. All the young men who didn't want to go home after work stopped by the bar first and they would tell me everything. There was one gentleman who came in on a Tuesday when I would do the lounge on my own. He was a poet and he wrote a poem about an Irish colleen and the way I always had a lovely smile for him. I was highly respected there and got a lovely reference when I left, which specified how strictly honest I was.

It was at this stage that I met Ken at a dance. He had been in the British Army and was stationed in India and in Germany. I used to go dancing with my friends; it wasn't strictly Irish but it was the only thing to do when you didn't drink or smoke. I had seen how Mammy suffered because of that. I was only a little girl and didn't know much, but Mammy said Daddy used to drink and she would have to go through his pockets for the price of a loaf of bread. I wasn't impressed with Ken at first because he drank and smoked, which I didn't approve of. He does neither now. Plus his parents didn't approve of me. Mrs. Bennett, I never called her by her first name, didn't like the Irish. Ken was the only son; he had four sisters. It was funny that I had the reverse experience of my mother. Her family didn't approve of her partner and my in-laws didn't approve of me. Nevertheless we got married in a registry office in Liverpool and many years later a priest in Australia blessed the marriage.

We went to Brisbane in 1968 with our two daughters, Lorraine and Debbie, and I never liked it. That time you could go to Australia for ten pounds. We travelled by boat, *The Fair Sky*, from Southampton, and it took six weeks. It rocked the whole way across the sea, as if the ship had no stabilisers. It was a luxury liner all the same with swimming pools and fancy dining halls. The food was good and there were celebrations when we passed the Equator and again when we hit the Indian Ocean. We only stopped twice, at Las Palmas and at Capetown, and I was glad in the end to see the coast of Queensland. We settled in a suburb called Woolloongabba, an early Aborigine site and home of the national cricket ground. The first cricket match between teams from England and Australia was played at the Gabba in 1897. There were nice beaches nearby. Ken would do the cooking for Christmas; usually a barbeque on the beach. I always joke with him that he does the cooking and I pay the rent. We had to be careful with the mosquitoes, though, as our blood was very susceptible to them especially for the first two years. Our blood is thicker seemingly coming from a colder climate. We went to the botanical gardens one day and sat down on a bench. Next thing we were covered with thousands and thousands of mosquitoes.

I worked in the Mater Hospital in Brisbane for four years when Lorraine and Debbie were at school. Ken worked first in a large men's department store called *Lowe's* and later he was in pest control. I had the interview one day and started the following night at eight o'clock. My main responsibilities were washing and feeding little infants, monitoring the incubators and some paperwork. I would get very upset if we lost a patient, as you would get very attached to the babies. We came back to England after eleven years. Ken's father was sick and I hated the heat. I would be pleased to get to the hospital for the air conditioning. Then I had undergone a hysterectomy at Canterbury Hospital in Sidney. I had to have a blood transfusion I was that bad afterwards, but my quick recovery may have been due to the fact that I didn't drink or smoke. I wanted to be back among my own people after that.

We came back to England, back to the Wirral again. Ken got the same job he had left eleven years before that as a caretaker. The job came with a flat so we took it because it was the only way we could get accommodation. I went back to *Whitbread's* to some of their posh branches - The Woodside Hotel and The Central Hotel in Birkenhead. I worked right up the day I left England and I miss that now, not working. I could have got a job in a little newsagent place here in Kingscourt, but I would have to be there at half past six in the morning and I wouldn't mind that part so much except that I go to Church so I wouldn't be available every morning.

We visited Ireland on several coach trips and I used to say to Ken I'd like to move back home because that's where all my memories are. Even now I can go into *Shekelton's* hardware shop there on Main Street, and the owner still remembers me from when I was a little girl

First Band in Kingscourt, 1916
My grandfather, James Woods (4th from left), back row

when he served in the shop. I missed Ireland; the memory was always there. We were always sorry that we didn't come straight here from Australia, but we would have had nowhere to stay, and there wasn't many jobs going. Mammy did have a lovely little bungalow, but there wouldn't have been room for all of us. Then Mammy died; she was found dead in the bathroom by my sister, Mary. My father slipped one day when he was working for a farmer in Nobber and was lying in the bushes for two days before anybody found him. He had worked in the mines in Glasgow for five years and apparently had a fall there and in those days in Scotland they didn't have medical benefits so his leg was never treated properly. This may have contributed to his death in the end. After they had gone I felt very lonely for Ireland. One time I visited the convent in Balbriggan and I sat on a little bridge over a stream and an awful sense of peace came over me. There's a peace in Ireland that we cannot describe. I never got it in Australia or England or any other place I visited.

Ken loved it here too and on one of our trips over we met Clifford Kelly the local Councillor and he gave us forms to fill up for a council house. They were only building forty houses and he couldn't put us on the list. Anything else would have been too costly. Then in the Irish Centre in Birkenhead we met Angie who is in charge of helping people move back to Ireland. She told us about Safe Home and we were blessed we didn't have our own home, as then we wouldn't have qualified. That was strictly forbidden. We had tried to buy a house before we went to Australia, but then decided to move there instead. Birkenhead was getting very rough with drugs and all that sort of thing. Our next door neighbour was the local dealer. We had tried for a place in the Wirral but there were a lot of drugs there too. Then we were offered a place in Monaghan and decided to take it, but found it too isolated. We lived there for a while, but found it too hard to settle so far out from the town with no public transport and at that time we'd no car. That's the one thing we have found about living in Ireland today, you have to be able to drive and you have to have a car. Then Clifford Kelly found us this house in Kingscourt. We've been back three and a half years and we love it. We never found it hard to settle in at all once we bought a car and were able to get about. We don't miss England at all. We've not even gone back on a holiday yet. I'm sure it was an angel who sent us here. Our daughter, Debbie, loves it. She thinks the people are nicer, even the children. I like it for sentimental reasons. There's a lot of people still remember me from when I was a little girl. And I find that my Faith has helped me connect with friends I would not have known before. I praise the Lord for the goodness He has brought me.

For the past twenty years we've been Born Again Christians. We were baptized through water in 1987 and 1988 and have the certificates here to prove it. We have been touched many times since. The Lord got us the house here; we also received tax rebates and other monetary benefits before we left England that we were not expecting. He gave us our good health. We attend meetings in Carrickmacross so that's a great way to connect with people here too, as I think otherwise it would be hard to make new friends in Ireland. It's not the way it used to be with people calling in and out of the houses. You have to go out and meet them now and the Lord has done that for us. The Lord brings a lot of love into the world, just as we try to do in our daily lives. One of our neighbours, Eileen, said to me one day, "Bridie, you've brought a lot of love back to Kingscourt." And I'm glad of that.

Interviewed at her home in Kingscourt, Co. Cavan, May 9th, 2007

With Ken & Debbie at home in Kingscourt

You'd need a jar after a day on the job

We were mad for smoking back then

It was a great job; with a canteen and all

Fr. Paddy Curran (left) with Bishop Edward Ellis of Nottingham, visiting Irish workers, British Steel, Scunthorpe, 1971

SYLVIA O'TOOLE

Nothing has gone right for me since I came home. I've been in hospital three times now in less than three years; all emergency cases. I broke my leg; then I had a fall and they told me I had osteoarthritis. I was rushed off again with an abscess in my mouth; and when I was admitted with a heart problem the doctor said there was nothing wrong with my heart. Despite all that I am finally glad to be back from Belgium where I spent twenty-nine and a half years and even though I loved it when I was still working there; it was always on my mind to come home.

I was born in Swords on July 28, 1941, the second last of eleven children. My mother never went away for the births; she had all of us at home. My father had been with the British Army at some stage and we lived in one of those servicemen's houses. I think he had a very good position with them, but it was never discussed, as my mother was very pro-Irish and she loved DeValera. Both my parents were true Dubliners, being from the North side of the county. My father's family were in Swords for generations; my mother's came from Kinsealy. Most Northsiders are true Dubliners; people from the other counties tended to go to the Southside.

Swords has changed so much, I don't know anybody there now. It was only a little village when I was growing up and I really loved it. I had a lovely childhood. A doctor in Belgium said to me once it must have been dreadful to be around a big family and I said it wasn't. Maybe for the parents it was, but not for the children. She said describe to me how it could have been good. Well, I said you always had a friend and you always had someone to fight with. Oh, I never thought of it like that, she said. Yes, it was great. We lived about ten or fifteen minutes walk outside the village, down by the estuary in a place called Lissenhall. My brother is still living in the house with his wife and family.

When we were growing up my father was a technician with the Department of Posts & Telegraphs. I think it was regarded as a good job at the time. We were by no means wealthy, but I remember the other kids in school would often have holes in their sleeves and that. My mother was good at everything; sewing, knitting, cooking, baking, and we had all our own vegetables, and pigs. The mothers of some of the kids in school would come by our house in the evening and I think looking back they were just hungry and they wanted something to eat. I went to school in St. Colmcille's and after that St.Finian's in Swords, a technical school. That's where I did my secretarial course. I went back for more tutoring afterwards and earned the Royal Society of Arts teaching diploma in typing, but I never used it. I wouldn't have the patience for teaching. My first job after school was in an electrical company called *Hendron Brothers* as a shorthand typist. I had only gone for the interview experience when they offered me the job. I was furious as I'd planned with my friend to have a great summer, to go chasing boys. Then I worked in a garage, it's still there outside Swords, where I had to read the pumps in the mornings. I left that and went to London when I was only sixteen years of age.

I loved London. I went to all the dances, especially *The Hammersmith Palais* where there was loads of Irish. I mixed mainly with Irish people even though I had Greek and Chinese boyfriends. I lived with my sister in Maida Vale. My mother hadn't wanted me to go, but my sister, Maria, got a job in the Aer Lingus office there, and she didn't want to go on her own. My friend and I went with her and while we were there we went job hunting and *Horizon Holidays* recruited us on the spot. They gave us a letter to confirm the position, as my mother wouldn't have let me stay otherwise. At first we lived in a hostel run by nuns because my mother wouldn't let us live in a flat. We would have to be in by eleven so we'd take turns leaving the door open and letting the others in. I don't think girls were drinking at that stage. Then Maria met her future husband in Aer Lingus and he was leaving the job to come back here. She came back with him and I wasn't allowed stay without her. My mother thought we'd never get back.

You'd think she would have had enough children around her.

As teenagers we had a great social life in Ireland. There were céili dances out in Swords and Rush; great dances. All the big bands came there. One of my sisters went out with Brendan Boyer and do you know who danced with me one time, the comedian, Dave Allen. I loved the jiving. Then I spent most of my summer holidays up in Donegal, in Gweedore at the Gaeltacht. I think my mother was glad to get rid of me. I won a scholarship one time and with that you'd get a bit of pocket money so I'd be shipped off. There were lots of boys there too. I learnt how to foot the turf with the husband of the Bean an Ti. He was never called the Fear an Ti, but that's who he was. I'd say I spent at least four summers up there. I think my parents were mainly interested in education to keep us off the roads. They didn't put much emphasis on it. They never checked our homework or anything. My mother only did once and it was my shorthand exercises and she said you're not going back there anymore, all you're doing is scribbling. She wanted me to be a dress designer because it seemed to her that no one in the family could sew, but all my friends were going to be secretaries and I didn't want to be left out. My sisters and I were all great knitters though and I used to cook until Jacques, my partner, took over all of that in Belgium.

After returning from London I landed a lovely job as secretary to the Managing Director of USIT and then I became North American Flight Director, which entailed travelling to the United States. I did my negotiating with the airlines during the winter and then left on the first flight in June and came back in September. I did that for about three or four years. Students would go out there for the summers, medical students in particular would go to work in various hospitals and I would go out with them and arrange visas like the J1 and that from my hotel room, which doubled as an office. I loved America, but I wouldn't have liked to live there permanently. It was the early Sixties and I was very young and not very relaxed in New York City, but I had a fantastic time there. I had to greet the students when they arrived and have a little welcome party for them. Then I'd take them to the theatre or whatever, and on tours around the city. There were flights coming over all the time so I was kept busy. I hadn't got a clue about the city and I'd have the places all written down and if I lost the piece of paper I'd be lost too. At the welcoming party I'd make punch and we'd all get drunk. The highlight of the trip was the Staten Island ferry tour and one time this fellow was so drunk he got sick down on top of some woman's hat. They got to know me going there and they used to say, Oh! Here we go again. I had a right reputation.

Then my mother died. USIT were very kind to me when she was sick giving me lots of time off to take care of her and they told me to only come in if she was suspicious of me being home all the time. Working for them was like a holiday camp. But, when I worked I really did work hard. Then things started getting me down. It took me a long time to get over my mother's death and I decided to give in my notice. The reason I gave was that I wasn't getting any younger and I'd have to be really young and fit to do the job properly. When you think of it, I was only about twenty-four! I then worked down in Tipperary for six months, but I hated the place. I had signed a contract and left on the very day it ended. It was horrific. The lights kept coming on and off because there was no proper electricity. The man I worked for was uneducated and he used to laugh at the way I wrote the letters. When it was raining I had to walk through the muck to get into the so-called office. You name it I've done it. I used to have the wanderlust, but not anymore. I wish I had. I loved anything that was different. Maybe that's what brought me back to Ireland because it certainly is different now.

Meanwhile, I was offered a job in Zimbabwe working for the government. I was delighted and sold my car and everything and went to England to spend Christmas with my sister. Her husband looked at my contract and said I'd be mad to sign up for three years. One year would be alright, he said, but not three so I took his advice and decided not to go. It was very naughty of me, as I had put the people to tremendous expense. They'd sent me for a medical exam and all, but I still turned it down. So there I was in Lancashire with no job. I was going to go to London to make money and buy clothes, but I got landed in Blackpool doing temp secretarial work instead, and I got a job in a bar in the evening. I used to phone into the day job all the time to say I was sick; I loved it so much in the bar. You know back then in England, when you served them a drink, the customer would say have one for yourself and sure of course I was having one every time and by the end of the evening I'd be swaying.

Then my friend, Jude, who was a schoolteacher back in Ireland, wrote and said she was going to Belgium for the summer holidays, as she heard there was plenty of secretarial work there. She asked me to go along with her and I did. We worked for this agency at first and shared the jobs between us. We did well. On one of her assignments with the INA, Insurance of North America, they needed a permanent secretary to the Vice-President. Even though my French was hopeless, absolutely hopeless, I decided to apply and I got the job. I didn't need the French in the end because it was an American company. I had a really well-paid job and a great social life altogether so I decided to stay when Jude went back after the summer. Little did I know that I was signing on for nearly thirty years?

My numerous positions included that of secretary at *Monsanto*, the chemical company, where I was promoted to a more administrative title. I subsequently worked for the European Union (EU) and the Belgian Parliament from where I retired. That was a nice job but I had to work very hard; I had to go to Strasbourg for meetings and things. I was very good at French by then. I could cope, but I don't have a word now. When I'm talking to Jacques, we still keep in touch; I keep using Irish words when I get stuck with the French. To think I'm only back three years and I'm forgetting already.

I attended French classes over there at first, what a beautiful language. The French criticize the Belgians about how they speak French. I don't know much Flemish except how to order two beers! (*Twee biers, als uw blief.*)It's a very guttural language. Brussels is a beautiful city. They have a beautiful square, the Grande Place; it's supposed to be the nicest in Europe. It's carpeted in flowers at a certain time of the year. And then they have what's called Son et Lumiere that's sound and light, when late at night all the buildings are lit up. It's built on the river Skelda. We had a friend who owned an apartment along the coast. Jacques used to do a lot of work for him on the computer and he'd give us his place there in return. It's very expensive, only the very rich would go there. The resort overlooks the North Sea with the most beautiful beaches. Jude and I had taken a day trip there our first summer and we couldn't believe how crowded it was. We'd have to step over the bodies. It was so different from what we'd been used to in Donabate and Malahide where there would be hardly anybody on the beach. We would take the bus out there for picnics when we were kids. There'd be sand in the sandwiches and in the bottles of lemonade. The bus conductor would dread us each week during the summertime.

I cycled all the time in Brussels, as do many people there, not as much as in Holland, but a fair few nevertheless. I had a bicycle that I could fold in two and I used to put it in the back of my car and drive out into the country to cycle. There were some beautiful parts like the Ardenne forest, but still it wasn't as nice as Ireland. I brought my bicycle back with me this time, and actually on my very first day I was talking to a lady on the bus and she said I'd be mad to go out on the main roads here, even on the bicycle paths. So it's down there now in the store room and never used. As for driving here, I wouldn't dream of it. Jude has offered me her car when she goes to India every year, but I have refused every time. I'd be terrified. The traffic is outrageous here.

The Belgian people weren't very friendly. A Belgian girl with whom I worked told me they were much worse altogether before the EU set up there. She said they were very closed altogether then. I think I stayed for the money. I was well paid and I had a certain standard of living. I was filling in a form for my pension here recently and I had to put down what I earned in each job. I don't know why because they have all that information, but I was only earning thirty shillings in my first job in Ireland. I would have to hand it up to my mother and she would give me back the money for my bus fare. I would only pay the children's price and keep the rest for myself. Then I was caught. I was terrified. My mother was very strict. I don't know how I got out of it, but I did. I was an awful terror. They have plenty of money here now. They're all into tipping. When I go out with my relatives I think they're tipping far too much. The taxi drivers are very nice.

Sometimes if it's four something, they'll say leave it at four. I was passing the rank the other day and one of them asked me, how's the leg. When you're away from that kind of friendliness for so long you really appreciate it.

The Belgian food was absolutely wonderful. I took a keen liking to chicory and mussels with chips - *Les mouniers des frites*. The French used to tease them all the time about that. I couldn't find chicory here in the shops and my niece-in-law told me they had it in *Tesco*. I was so delighted when I found it and then all of a sudden they stopped it again. It's a vegetable but it does have some connection with coffee. There was a song, coffee and chicory a hunting we will go. Years ago when we were young we got coffee in a long black bottle called *Irel* and I think it was chicory based. As a vegetable you can boil it and finish it off in the pan; it's gorgeous with pork. Raw chicory and pineapple pieces and apple are lovely in a salad. I really loved the food, but the chocolate was too heavy for me. The only thing I don't like about here is the bread, now I make my own. I have only eaten bread that is toasted since I came home, because there's no taste. It's very bland. I might try *Superquinn* though; the smell of their bread is beautiful. I loved the baguette in Belgium dipped in the coffee. I'm used to the instant coffee here now; I hated it when I came home first.

Do you know if I miss Mass here on a Sunday I won't go out anywhere else. I'd be desperate for a cigarette, but I won't go out. I suppose it's inbred in you. They're supposed to be very Catholic in Belgium but they take the child to the Church to be christened and not again until its First Holy Communion. They're not really bothered other than that. There'd only be a handful of people at Mass on Sundays. One day I went down to this church on the Grand Place to get confession and this woman told me I was too late. I took communion anyhow and felt guilty afterwards so I went to the priest to confess. He said there were only two real sins - if you killed someone or stole a large sum of money. Well I though if you stole a small amount of money from someone who had nothing that would be just as bad. Once I had communion in a Protestant church. After a couple of days I told a friend and she said if you feel that bad go to confession. Well the priest gave me an awful time. He said we are moving forward, but it's not up to you to make the rules. St. Luke's the Evangelist is my parish now. There's a nun attached to it and one day she came down and asked me what happened to my leg. She said she's seen me walking around on the crutch and she'd said to the priest, "I wonder what's the matter with that woman?" Nuns are very nosey. My sister's two boys went to Christian Brothers and the others didn't and the ones who went to the Brothers won't go to Mass at all. Isn't it strange? When we were going to Belgium first a nun down in Connemara asked Jude if we'd visit her sister in an enclosed order in Bruges. So we did and it was surrounded by bars just like a jail. I asked her was it very strict and she said no it had got much better the previous year when she was allowed out to post a letter. What good is that doing anyone? My eldest sister came to visit me here on Ash Wednesday. I never thought about it being Black Wednesday and I had cold meats for lunch and she wouldn't eat them. She said there was only two days in the year when she didn't eat meat and that was one of them. I said sure what good is that doing anyone?

I never got married. I was man mad, but as soon as it started getting serious I'd end it. I don't know why, I just didn't want to get married. I would have liked to have children and I did try to adopt once, but just as we were getting to finalize it I told the people at the agency that I was so looking forward to taking her back to Ireland and they said I couldn't take her out of the country. I don't know why; it was a private organization, so that was it. But, I have enough nieces and nephews who are very kind to me I must say. I have been with Jacques now for twenty eight years. We have absolutely nothing in common, but he is the kindest man I have ever met. I've had a complete change of personality since I met him. I used to be real wild and always out, but he's real serious. I never married though because I couldn't live with anybody and as my niece says nobody would live with me either. Nor would he have moved to Ireland except for a visit. The Belgians are a very quiet race; they keep to themselves a lot. But at the same time he remembers all of my sister's ten children's birthdays, unlike me. I put it straight to them, unless there is an o age they won't get anything. You couldn't keep up with that.

It was always sort of on the cards to come home, before I go completely gaga. It's not that I wasn't happy there. The social life was great, not like here, going out to pubs and everything. I can't stand pubs. We went to dinner parties mainly. Jacques is a great cook and he would cook dinners and then of course we would be invited back. I didn't mix with many Irish. I met a few alright in the EU, but other than that I didn't know many. If my phone bill is any indication I must have missed Ireland because I had huge phone bills and I came home every year, and then twice a year. When *Ryanair* started, there was no stopping me. My family came over to visit too. Oh I had so many relatives and they all came to stay. I used to love that when they came. I travelled a little around Europe, to France and Italy too. A few things contributed to my coming home in the end. I had taken early retirement from the Parliament. A friend talked me into it actually, but I don't think about that too much. If I did I would regret it. Because I've hardly worked at all since then and your mind gets very dull if you don't keep it active. Then my proprietor back in Brussels more than doubled the rent. I wouldn't have been able to pay it. It hadn't been too much up to that and he was a very nice man, a nice proprietor. After an attempted break-in to my apartment, I didn't feel so safe there anymore. It was time to move on once more.

I would have been lost without this place to come home to. I would have had to stay with a relative, which would have been very difficult.

I have one very religious sister, and I said to her recently that I was very lucky; that I'm not usually lucky, but I was lucky to get this apartment. She said it was the answer to a prayer. So she must have been praying for me; she must have wanted me to come home. It was Jude who got in touch with the Safe Home people on my behalf. It was my niece in London who saw the ad in an Irish newspaper. I thought it was only for people who went to England, but I said I'd try anyhow and I couldn't believe it when I got this place. It all happened so fast too. It can't have taken much more than six months. I don't ever regret coming back and I don't miss Belgium one bit. If I had been working I probably would have missed it more, but, no, I don't even think about it now.

Oh! I did find it hard here sometimes. Before I came back people in Belgium would say to me oh it will be marvellous to be home where you'll understand the language. Yet I don't know what they're saying the way they talk around here. When I was having all these complaints and illnesses they'd all be asking me how are you and I thought it was because I must look wretched, but it's just the way they greet you. I asked my nephew what was the reply to "how'ya", and he told me to say "how'ya" back, but that doesn't make sense to me. The man in the cigarette shop always says "how'ya", but I never say it back to him. One time he said, "How are WE today?" I didn't know what he was talking about. But, he's a nice poor fellow. I was in *Dunnes Stores* another time with Jacques and the girl asked me if I had a club card, but it sounded like club car. She said it several times and even shouted it out as if I was stone deaf. I didn't know what she meant. There's a system in Belgium whereby they give out a free car to every certain number of customers. There's a ringing at the till and you win something fantastic and I thought I'd won a car. She directed me over to Customer Services to apply for a Club Card and the girl started filling in the form for me. I said I can manage that myself and then she started explaining to me the various lines to be filled out, the name and address, as if I was stupid. But, she was just being kind. It's a real pleasure to walk along the street here; people are so friendly. They'll always say hello, its great weather for drying. I had lived in the city for so long, in the centre of

Brussels and people there would never say hello. Even with my neighbours in the building, *bonjour* would be your lot.

I joined Irish language classes when I came home first, but then I started having panic attacks and I had to give it up. The same thing happened when I was studying to be a tutor in English. It was very interesting. I learnt that forty percent of Irish people can't read or write. The first night we were asked why we were doing the class. This lady said she worked in the Credit Union and she found that many people couldn't fill up the forms; they'd say they'd forgotten their glasses, but really it was because they couldn't read or write. And I had been doing that in the supermarkets, not able to fill out forms because I had forgotten my glasses or because I didn't know what they were saying. They probably thought I was illiterate too! When I was dealing with the Safe Home people they told me the move back was going to be very traumatic and I said it wouldn't bother me. But, I think the panic attacks might be indirectly related to it. They didn't start immediately and I don't have them anymore and the doctor told me there were people worse off with them. But, he did say they were severe. He prescribed tablets, which I am now easing off gradually. Jude worked for the OECD in Paris for only two years and she said it took her months to get over it when she came back. She found it very hard to settle in, but I didn't at first. I was walking on air, and then the panic attacks started. Oh! The panic attacks were desperate. They were worse than breaking my leg. One day I had to ask a fellow working down in a hole to walk me across the road and I barely held on to a piece of his clothing he was that dirty. Another time I had to go down to the medical centre to pick up a prescription and when I got inside I couldn't move. I thought I was going to fall. This nice lady helped me over to the seat. She then went in and got the prescription for me and offered to go down to pharmacy with it. I thought that was lovely. She came with me to get shopping and let me hold on to her and then walked me back home here. I am really impressed with all of that.

I think the doctor thought the attacks were related to the move too because one day he suggested that I go to Brussels. Take a trip to Brussels with your man there, he said pointing to Jacques. He said you can go for almost nothing, which I thought was very personal. Another time I told him that the hospital said my leg was fine, but he was to look at the swelling. Before I had the leg of my trousers pulled up, he said, you have a good pair of legs. Give us a look. He asked me how many cigarettes I smoked. I quoted a number and he said, sarcastically, I suppose I can add another ten or fifteen to that. I was furious with him. It was after that I started asking for a lady doctor.

I started smoking at home years ago. The first thing my mother knew about it was one day she came into the room where I was smoking out the window and she said, so that's what England did to you. Sure I was smoking long before that. I started smoking on a silent retreat in school. Two girls in my class had a shop and they'd steal the cigarettes and bring them to us and we'd smoke them in the graveyard. I think we were in sixth class. If I could get my hands on them now, they made me inhale until I was green in the face. I was so sick but I kept on smoking. My sister, Maria, never smoked, and we were at a dance in Rush one night and we met these fellows. They offered us a cigarette, that time they'd offer them around, they don't do that now, and she took one to be polite but she never lit it, just kept it between her fingers all the time. One of the fellows said it's the in thing now to light the cigarette.

Smoking is very anti-social now. My sister with ten children was smoking more than me and she stopped three years ago. She told me not to think about it, to just stop, but I don't think I can. I did give them up years ago, but went back on them again. The main thing I noticed was the smell of the flowers in our garden and that the food tasted much better. I didn't put on any weight though. I'm putting on weight now from lack of exercise. The awful thing is I'm still thin on my face, but it's all collecting around my middle. I never had to worry about my weight; I was only seven stone when I went to Belgium. I was always five foot, four and a half inches, and the half was very important. In *Monsanto* they made me do a medical every year and when they measured me the first time I was five foot four inches in height. I said I was always five foot four and

233

half, and the doctor said you must remember you're getting older. So the next year I was ready for him and I stood up straight and he said that's funny most people get shorter as they age, you've just gained half an inch!

I love this apartment, but I didn't realize that the smoke was doing so much damage. I have never enjoyed smoking outside, but I might have to get used to it, or give them up altogether. But, I have nothing else to do. When I was in the wheelchair I couldn't even get out to my mailbox, so all I did was sit here and smoke. And I don't go out in the evenings, but I must say I have marvellous neighbours. There's a young fellow upstairs and he won't go to the shop without asking if I want something. The only thing is everyone knows my business. He'll come in here and I'll tell him what to get and next thing he's shouting outside the window, "Sylvia is it pork chops or lamb you wanted?" Everyone knows what I'm eating. He's really nice. Everybody is. The other day I was in the supermarket looking for mint sauce and I asked this lady if she knew where it was. Next thing another woman came in from the next lane saying did I hear someone looking for mint sauce. It's over here. That would never happen in Brussels.

I even tried to go back to the knitting in order to give up cigarettes, and also because I needed a hobby. At first I tried a matinee coat, they're always turning out babies in our house, and I couldn't get any further than the rib. I couldn't follow the pattern because I couldn't memorize the number of lines. I was writing them down on a piece of paper. Then my neighbour told me they were selling wool and needles down in the pound shop so I went and bought some and knit three scarves, just plain purl, and it really kept me off the cigarettes. Because there's no sense putting down the knitting to light up and I could watch the television at the same time, so I'd love to get back into it again. I was a really good knitter; I used to knit suits and everything. They say if you could do it once it will always come back. I have to get the apartment repainted and the man who is doing the job for me said I'll have to get out because once he washes down the walls I can't smoke anymore or the smoke will come through the paint again. So I'll go and stay with Jude. She lives very near; we see each other quite often. We've been friends now for over forty years. She's the only real friend I have here.

Another thing I love is the computer, even though the one I have has the French keyboard. I don't use it now for letters or anything like that, except when I was applying for my pension, but I play games the whole time, mainly cards. I used to be a dab hand at poker. I did play whist in the afternoon when I retired, but it was all in French and I used to get confused. I knew everyday French, but not for cards where the only word I knew was *coeur* for heart. I used to go for long walks too; that's one thing I miss around here. I'd walk for miles. We used to walk for about three hours at the weekends. Now I can't walk at all. This has been going on since December. They told me I'd be in a wheelchair for three months and after about six weeks I went back and they said you can start back walking as normally as you can so I'm delighted about that.

I would advise anyone to come back without hesitation, but it definitely helps if you have family here and friends; if you have a job; or if you have some sort of hobby. Then again I don't know if I'd say go in the first place. You miss so much when you're away. I was saying to Jude recently that I find I can't get into Irish politics. I've lost touch with all that because we didn't have Irish news in Belgium. I knew all about the American system inside out. I know all about Tony Blair and that Chancellor of the Exchequer looking for his job. That's why I watch *Prime Time* to try and learn something and *Questions and Answers*. Another thing that's impressed me is the way the young people here are able to speak up now. That's fantastic. They're so confident. We weren't like that in my day. Confidence must come with prosperity I suppose.

I never felt poor growing up in Ireland; I think I was so scatter-brained and thinking of having a good time that I never really thought at all, but they're definitely wealthier now and they're more hygienic. At least they're using the plastic gloves when serving food; I don't know how we didn't die before. None of my family emigrated any further than England. Two brothers died there and I have a brother and a sister still there. My eldest sister here is going to be eighty-six soon. I don't go out to see the family so much now since my leg got bad, unless they come in for me. I am starting to manage the bus with the aid of the crutch, but I'm still like a bull in a china shop. So it's nice to be near family again; it's nice to be back on home ground, even though I have had all of this ill-health.

Yet if I'd broken my leg back in Brussels it would have been much worse. I would have had to walk up and down all those flights of stairs to my penthouse place; they wouldn't have let me out of hospital if I'd had stairs here. I should have stayed longer in hospital only Jacques was coming over and I had to go home and tidy up for him. He didn't think I was mad to come back; he thinks it's great that I got this apartment. I was so bored here though at first and I thought I'll have to do something. This was before the accident. I joined a society for caring for people and I got this rich lady to take care of out in Sutton. Her house was fantastic, very luxurious. The first day I wheeled her into the wall, not being used to a wheelchair at the time. Little did I know I'd end up in one myself? I told the agency and the girls burst out laughing. I left anyhow after a few days because I couldn't take how the old lady spoke to me, as if I was a servant. Then I had another man quite near here; I could walk over to him, but I had to call and tell him I couldn't come back after I broke my leg. He rang one day to ask me how I was. He was very nice. The agency sent me on a short initiation course. I met nice people, but I don't know if I'd be cut out for that sort of job.

I feel though you have to do something here in order to fit in, to make some sort of life for yourself. It's the same anywhere really; it's the same as when we went away in the first place, we had to become involved. Just because we're coming home doesn't necessarily mean it's any easier; it's still a strange place, and we are relatively strangers. I might do one of these FÁS courses. I don't want to study computers because they're only for playing with. Maybe I'll do something with drama. I could also get involved with background work for the theatre. I acted one time in Gorey where I won lots of medals. I was on the stage in the Olympia theatre. It was all in Irish. I can't remember the names of the plays, but I had lots of medals, dust collectors my mother said they were. No encouragement whatsoever. I've tried my hand at everything. I used to go horse riding too, back in Malahide. When I was not long in Belgium, I met this Irish fellow at the French class who asked me to go horse riding. It was a beginners' class and they were doing yoga exercises at first to limber up. The instructor said that I looked like I knew what I was doing so he gave the horse a clip on the rear end and sent us off flying. I hadn't been on a horse for ages and couldn't remember how to slow him down; I knew it was a knee movement, but couldn't remember which. I thought I'd never get him to stop. Needless to say I never went back.

Come the end of July I will be sixty-six and I'll get a free TV licence, free travel on the buses, and so much off my electricity bill. Isn't that marvellous? I can't wait. My African friend across the hall said we'll go off somewhere together. Maybe I'll visit my friend in Glenmalure; she has what she calls a log cabin down there. I could take up creative writing too. I've written some poetry. I know I wrote one when I was down there in Tipperary about the conditions of the office. Then I wrote one about how things have changed here; how people don't have time to listen; it's all about nature really. I used to write for the newsletter in one of the companies I worked for. I worry now about all these multi-nationals closing down here and the young people with their big mortgages. What are they going to do? They'll never feel secure during their actual working lives. Not like we did. I still have my references here from every job I held in Belgium and some from Ireland and England too. In every one of them I came highly recommended. Easily fooled weren't they? A man I worked for in the EU thought the Irish were the best workers in the world and he was English, Oxford educated. He still keeps in touch, well on St. Patrick's Day he always sends greetings.

So here I am in Artane. I never thought that this is where I'd end up. My mother used to always threaten my brothers with the reform school in Artane if they misbehaved when we were small. So I must have misbehaved somewhere along my travels from Swords to Strasbourg; Belgium and back. Oh! I'm sure I did!

Interviewed at her home in Artane, Dublin, on Wednesday, April 25th, 2007

PATRICK DUFFY

I am living here in Carrickmacross since October 2003 with my wife, Denise, and our son, Kevin. We couldn't come home to Ireland until I was sixty-seven and could get some money to live on. I was born in Dublin and grew up there, but that's it. I left for Rhodesia in January 1958 when I was only twenty-two years of age and stayed for forty-five years. I wanted a change. I wanted to prove that I could manage by myself because my father didn't think that I could.

We were living in Irishtown at the time on Pembroke Street and I was working with CIE in their office as a clerk at Kingsbridge station. The previous year myself and two other chaps in the office had gone away to Spain on a holiday. We travelled down through Paris seeing all the sights and some of them we shouldn't see; on into San Sebastian and down to Madrid. We were at the European Cup Final in 1957 in the Bernabeu stadium when Real Madrid beat AC Fiorentina two goals to nil. In Paris we were taken by some other chaps in the office, who were on the way back, to see the red light area where the girls pick you up and take off with you. We had been warned to walk on and not get involved in any conversation. At that stage I spoke Irish quite fluently, having learnt it from the Christian Brothers on Westland Row, so we spoke Irish throughout Europe. We didn't understand any other European language.

That same year, 1957, there was an advertisement in the paper, probably *The Irish Press*, looking for people to join the railway in Rhodesia on a five-year contract. I applied and was interviewed in Dublin by an Irish chap actually, Joe Shine. Once they had offered me a job and I accepted, they arranged for me to travel from Dublin on the ferry to Liverpool and onto London by train. There were twenty new recruits from Ireland, ten clerks and ten firemen, and we were met in London and flown out to Africa on a Viscount plane. The first place we landed in was Waddahalfa on the Nile River where we spent one night. We took a trip on the Nile and I signed all of the visitor books in Irish. We went from there to Nairobi and the plane was giving trouble so we had to stay three days. They put us up in a hotel and we visited the Nairobi Game Park. We hired a car, but only one of us had a proper driving license, so he took a group of five out first and then he passed his license on to someone else who took out another group of five. We flew then from Nairobi to Elizabethville, now Lubumbashi, and then carried on to Ndola in Northern Rhodesia on a Dakota plane. One of the chaps had brought a football, which we played on the tarmac, which wasn't really much of a tarmac. We stopped in several other places picking up children coming from the Congo to school in Salisbury. When we took off from Ndola the plane bounced three times. It was absolutely full; people were even standing in the aisles. I had never flown before and was glad to finally land in Salis-bury, which was then the capital of The Federation of Rhodesia and Nyasaland. At that time Rhodesia was part of a federation which included Southern Rhodesia, Northern Rhodesia and Nyasaland, now Malawi.

Paddy (right) & colleagues at Kingsbridge station

That same night we left immediately for Bulawayo where the Rhodesian Railways had their headquarters. It was the second largest city to Salisbury and an important transport hub providing rail links between Botswana, South Africa and Zambia. Bulawayo was very hot. I arrived with practically no money and many of us had to get an advance on our first month's pay in order to manage at all. We lived in railway singles quarters, which contained a bed and a cupboard and a chair. The rent was quite reasonable. We ate in a canteen where we were fed mostly sausage, egg and chips, and then occasionally we'd walk into the town to a place called *The Kingfisher* restaurant where we could get a proper meal, with vegetables and potatoes and that. At first, because we didn't know our way around that well, we'd walk back home pretty early in the evening.

The social life wasn't bad. I'd always been more or less a loner so I wasn't that bothered with it. There was an Irish Society in Bulawayo where I went once or twice, but I had decided pretty early on that I was living now in Africa, not Ireland, and I was determined to adapt to this new country and not harp back to the past. The office where we worked was fine. It was the first time I had come across calculators. They were still using the big ones where

A Bulawayo wedding

we had to crank the handle and there was great excitement when the new ones came in. They were just as big and awkward, but they had buttons we could push and lights that flashed. Our co-workers were from all over the world, but they were mostly English. We came across a few Irish and also Rhodesians and South Africans. The clerical staff were all white at that stage. Up to that I had only ever seen Africa and African people in pictures. I thought they would all look the same, but we found out quickly that they are just the same as us.

I missed Ireland at first, no question about it. I missed my parents and my sister especially. I came back on leave in 1960 for Christmas and of course I had some money and I remember buying them a television and we had a marvellous holiday altogether. But, I can also remember one day in the middle of January, standing outside *Clery's* department store waiting for the Number 2 bus back to Irishtown, and thinking that I didn't mind going back to Bulawayo. Not that there were any problems with the family or anything like that, but Africa had become my home by then and I was quite happy with that. I was making my own life at last.

Upon my return I was assigned to relief duty, which required that I travel all over Southern Rhodesia relieving people who were on sick leave, holiday leave, whatever. I'd be so long in one station and then on again to another one, although I was always based in Bulawayo. One place I stayed in for quite a while was Nyamandhlovu, which means elephant meat. I never managed to pick up the language, but people were very welcoming everywhere I went, especially in the railway offices, as I was usually there to help them out. I didn't go home much after that.

It was during this time that Denise and I got together. I had met her while we were both working in the Bulawayo office. We had been working together, but we didn't have much contact socially. She was a copy clerk and had to Photostat all of the documents going out to the stations. They were still using the old machines with carbon and ink, and the smell of ammonia all over the office was terrible. She had invited all of the staff to her twenty-first birthday party at her home, but after I went on relief duty we lost contact for years. One day when I was stationed in Wankie I bumped into a relative of hers who seemed to think that Denise might like to hear from me. I wrote her a letter and she was quite surprised, but wrote back. We then arranged to meet at her home for dinner and it went from there. Who knows why these things happen? We were married anyhow on September 11th, 1965.

Denise was born in South Africa, but had lived all of her life in Rhodesia. Her grandfather was from Tasmania, and way back in her family tree was a British Admiral of the Fleet, although her maiden name, Morrisbie, a derogation of Morris, is Irish. Her grandfather came from Tasmania to Johannsburg and much later her father left for Rhodesia to work on the gold mines.

For our honeymoon we covered 3,300 miles of Africa. We drove from Bulawayo, down through Johannesburg and on to Capetown, which was just under 2,000 miles and then back again. When we were married first we rented a house for about three years. Then we were going to come here on holiday in 1968, but we decided to use the money instead for a deposit on our own house. We bought a place about four or five miles outside Bulawayo, on two thirds of an acre. It was the same system as here; we got a bond, a mortgage, which we had to pay off and then the house was ours. We had a servant who stayed with us until 1980, and then when Zimbabwe got their Independence we advised him to move on, as we knew that eventually the minimum wage would rise so high that we wouldn't be able to pay him. We gave him as much time off as possible to look for a proper job. He was quite well educated, and we advised him to try and get in before all the rest, as we knew that as soon as the Lancaster House agreement was signed, there would be thousands looking for work. He did get a good job in a shoe manufacturers and went on to get his 'O' levels and did quite well eventually securing a managerial position. He often stopped by to see us and we remained good friends right up to the time we left.

I, meanwhile, progressed through the ranks in Rhodesian Railway, where I ended up as a sub-Accountant. We had two sons, Brendan and Kevin, who were always aware of their Irish heritage. They started off in the local school, which was based on the British style of education and was only within walking distance from where we lived. They had a lot of freedom and mixed with everybody quite easily. We spent a couple of holidays down in South Africa on the coast near Durban on the Indian Ocean. It was lovely and warm and we travelled many miles in our little Austin Cambridge. We would drive from Bulawayo through Bitebridge, the Border Post, down through South Africa to Durban. Denise had a sister in Fort Victoria, which is now Masvingo, and with the children we kept in very good contact with her. They had a farm where the kids could run to their hearts content. Our sons had a very happy childhood in Africa.

Paddy (left) with Colin & Len,
Rhodesian Railways

For Christmas 1973 we came back to Ireland on holiday as a family. We travelled over the cheapest way possible, but the plane got delayed in Johannesburg and they put us up in a luxury hotel, *The Carlton*. There was a big boxing match on that night, a World Championship, and the place was packed so we asked for room service meaning sandwiches or something. Imagine our surprise when they brought up a dining room table complete with white tablecloth and a four-course meal just like they were getting down in the dining room. The airways, UTA, paid for everything; we had never seen anything like that before. Because it was a French airline we also stayed in Nice in *The Negresco Hotel* overlooking the Mediterranean. It is now listed in the top five hotels in the world. The fare had cost £1,200 for the four of us.

I'll tell you something, I had never taken a girlfriend home never mind anyone else, now here I am arriving in with a wife and two kids! My father and mother were still both alive and they were delighted to see us. Unfortunately there was a petrol shortage so we couldn't hire a car and go anywhere, but it was still a wonderful visit. Denise had baked a cake for my mother who had already baked her own cake and had won another one in a raffle in the shop across the road. So we filled up on Christmas cake. My wife and children had never seen a Christmas like they saw in Ireland. At this stage there were sanctions in Rhodesia, which meant for years we couldn't get toys for the children, but there were plenty in Ireland. We even brought a case full back with us. Christmas was hot in Africa, one time we had a temperature of thirty-nine degrees on Christmas Day. It was much cooler and more comfortable in Ireland. We stayed for six weeks and once again I didn't mind going back to Bulawayo, because once again I was going home.

In 1965 the United Nations Security Council had imposed economic sanctions on Rhodesia. It was the best thing really, as Rhodesia was then forced to produce their own goods and nobody thought they could do that before. The Government took steps to counter the sanctions by setting up the Tobacco Corporation to undertake the selling of tobacco to whatever markets were available. Another staple crop was wheat from which breakfast cereals and other products could be manufactured locally. When my parents came in 1976, we went to the Trade Fair in Bulawayo and my father couldn't understand how Rhodesia could produce so much despite the sanctions. He wondered why Ireland couldn't do the same and they had no sanctions? He loved it there; he would stand at the door during rainstorms because he said he'd never seen rain fall straight down before! He thought it was a marvellous place. He would sit at the gate every night and watch the sunset, which of course was just magnificent there. He was also struck by the size of the trees. He was fascinated by the baobab tree in Messina. It is enormous and looks like it's growing upside down, as the branches look like roots sprouting all over the place. It produces cream of tartar. When he was there we crossed the Tropic of Capricorn and he'd never been so far south in his life. We even had a puncture there and he would tell people about that for years. The first day he walked all over the house and he asked Denise who she got in to paint the place and was shocked when she told him that I had done it.

He had worked for a building contractor and would have considered himself an expert on all of that. So he was proud of me eventually, I suppose.

He died in 1979 and I couldn't come home for his funeral because my Irish passport had run out and

My Confirmation Day

they wouldn't renew it because at this stage the railway was considered to be a Government organization, and, as such, the enemy. That was also the year I became a Deacon. I completed a three and half year course for married deacons in the Catholic Church and have a certificate there to prove it. We can do everything except say Mass and hear confessions. There are several thousands of us in America, but we are not recognized in Ireland. I was Chairman of the parish council at the time and some of the parishioners suggested that I take the course. I had to be interviewed by Bishop Karlen, Bishop of Bulawayo. There were a lot of missionaries when we went first, mainly from Spain, and they would have brought Catholicism to the country initially. I remember the year for many reasons because the Pope (Pope John Paul VI) came in 1979 too, and I served on the altar at his open air Mass in Harare, which Salisbury was by then called. It would have been very hot in September, but an engineer friend of ours had been commissioned to build the altar for the Pope. For a whole month before the Mass he had gone out to the place where it would be officiated and measured exactly where the sun would be at any given moment throughout the ceremony. As a result His Holiness was never exposed to the sun at all. After Harare he came to Bulawayo even though President Mugabwe had warned that it might be too dangerous, but he got a magnificent welcome. They came from South Africa and Zambia to see him. They were happier to come to Bulawayo than to Harare. He then visited the Cathedral of the Immaculate Conception where I shook his hand and after that he visited the Anglican Cathedral of St. John the Baptist before leaving for the airport. The people of Bulawayo lined the streets to see him off; he shut down the town. Now I'm talking about the ordinary people; not just Catholics. Bishop Karlen, who later became Archbishop, told us afterwards that he couldn't believe what he was seeing. The Pope is a world leader whether you like him or not and everyone came out to greet him that day in Zimbabwe, all colours, nationalities and creeds.

In 1982 my mother came to visit with my sister and her daughter, Deirdre. My sister thought she'd be able to pick up diamonds off the street! The day before she arrived five British tourists had been abducted on the road from Bullowayo to Victoria Falls. We visited Wankie Game Park and my niece celebrated her eleventh birthday there. We passed through twelve road blocks on the way and eleven coming back, but we were never afraid. We stayed outside Wankie Game Park on a mission station. Deirdre hated getting her clothes dirty and in places like that she had to change three to four times a day. The priests told us to be careful, as the elephants were a bit nervous from the heat. There had been a drought and there were occasional mock charges, so they told us to watch out. We were on the road to Robin's Camp where there was a huge bull elephant in the bush, in off the side of the road. There were five of us in a *Renault 4* so we stopped to take a photograph of him. The elephant turned around a few times and I thought everything was alright until he pulled his ears back, pushed out his trunk, roared, and charged across the road. He missed the back of the car by no more than a foot, probably six inches. We were terrified. My sister to this day says she still wakes up at night and can hear his roar. We never did get the photograph. When we got to Robin's Camp we all had to use the facilities and I'd say some of us had to change our pants! It was absolutely terrifying. The funny thing is we never saw another elephant, all through the park, all the way back, we never saw another elephant until we stopped at Wankie safari lodge where we had supper for Deirdre's birthday. We were sitting outside and the elephants were roaming around quite freely. They gave Deirdre a certificate to say she'd been there for her birthday.

I retired in 1993 and was on pension then. We were fairly comfortable and thought we'd be able to come back to Ireland every other year on holidays, but it didn't work out that way. Prices inflated so much we couldn't afford it. We did come in 1990 to celebrate our Silver Wedding Anniversary while our son, Brendan, looked after Kevin, who suffers from Prader-Willi syndrome. He also paid for us to come in 1998 and when we were leaving I thought I'd probably never see Dublin again. My sister wouldn't even come out of her house to see us off, as she thought we'd never be back. We thought then we were in Zimbabwe for life. We were settled. Then things started to go wrong and Denise's health collapsed and I had no option but to leave. None

Baptizing my granddaughter, Ciara

of us wanted to go but, we couldn't let Denise die. She was suffering from the same symptoms as Alzheimer's disease and senile dementia. She had been diagnosed with diabetes and Parkinson's disease, but it turns out she shouldn't have been taking some of the medication she was prescribed. She has no knowledge of our last twelve months in Zimbabwe and our first six months here. She doesn't remember leaving. The doctor here changed her medication, as the drug she was taking had been taken off the market here six years previously. I even saw a television programme about this drug and one of its side effects was similar to the symptoms of Alzheimer's. She looked like she was dying and I felt that she deserved some hope of living. Even the doctor here didn't think she'd last very long and the local people didn't think she'd see Christmas that year. That was in 2003 and you wouldn't believe the improvement in her now. There's certainly no sign of Alzheimer's or senile dementia. She gets very emotional when I talk of it because she doesn't remember a thing. We've got a DVD of the last Mass I served at as Deacon before we left Zimbabwe and Denise and Kevin were there. Denise couldn't believe it when she saw it. She was just sitting there lifeless. I hadn't a clue what to do or where to go and Ireland was the only place I could think of. I was born here and it was the only place I knew outside of Africa. I had to try. I had to give her some chance of life.

We're grateful to be back in Ireland, as we had nowhere else to go. We have no financial problems now. The only drawback is that I'm overweight because I couldn't get used to the shops being full of food so I bought everything I could see at first. Some of the changes in Ireland are good, but the sad part for me is that where we were born on Essex Quay in Dublin no longer exists. Before we moved to Irishtown we lived in a one-bedroom flat on the third floor of a house there, Number 17, beside St. Michael & St. John's Church. The other changes in Ireland that I worry about are crime, which I think is very bad, and I don't think the Catholic Church means anything to most people anymore. We go to Mass on Sundays and there's very few there. The priests are not too worried; they don't want to upset the apple cart. I've spoken to a few of them, but they seem blasé. They've no interest in opposing anything that is wrong. I'm fairly certain many people are living together; not married; they might even be divorced and remarried, yet they're receiving Holy Communion. Somehow moral standards have dropped. And yet people have their children baptized. They celebrate their First Holy Communion and have them confirmed in the Church. They're

still getting married in the Church, but it's all for the parties. And it's all about how much money they get for these occasions. About twenty percent of the population in Zimbabwe are Christian and only half of them are Catholic, but they have their problems too. Of course the big problem in Africa generally is AIDS. You will have local councils who will deny that it exists; they believe it to be American propaganda to stop them enjoying themselves. The biggest regret I have here is that I am not allowed practice as a Deacon. I am very disappointed about that.

At home in Africa with sons, Kevin & Brendan

The good changes in Ireland are that people are much better off, there's no doubt about it. I sit here at times and think, "I did nothing for Ireland." I was born here and I worked here for a while, and then at twenty-two I left. Yet I have a pension, as has Denise and my son and we are quite reasonably well off. The health services have been very good to us. I arrived here in October with a hernia and had to have an operation the following March, and they were marvellous. Kevin, our son, attends Steadfast House for the handicapped in Carrickmacross, where he is doing really well. The bus fetches him every day and brings him home. He'd been told in Zimbabwe that he was losing the sight in one eye and that a cataract operation wouldn't do any good. Well when he had an eye examination here they decided to operate and now he has forty percent sight back. He can see better now than when we came back first. I can't complain about the HSE; it's been marvellous for us.

We haven't really got involved in anything locally; it's difficult really if you don't have transport, and the public transport around here is not very good. That's a big drawback. We go to the community centre once a month to play bingo and cards and we get a very good meal for six euros. They have recently put on a bus service to bring us into town on a Friday. We've only been back to Dublin a few times when Kevin had to go to Beaumont Hospital for check-ups. We're hoping to go to New Zealand in March and we've saved for that from our pensions. At times I sit here and feel guilty. To come here with almost nothing and now be able to go on holidays in New Zealand! We often sit here and think that somehow this is all wrong. We want to say Thank you God; thank you Ireland. It was an accident of birth; I could have been born anywhere, but I was born in Ireland and now I thank God for that.

I thank God for Africa too and never regret living there. I've seen every single type of game; every single wild animal. I've been to the Kruger Game Park in South Africa, the Nairobi Game Park in Kenya, and our own Wankie Game Park in Zimbabwe. I'm often watching television here and there'll be a programme on about game or wild animals and I'll say to myself, "I've seen them." The best part of the Game Park was going for a walk with a Game Ranger; walking through the park at the same level as them. Every time Brendan came home on leave he had to go to the Game Park. It was the first thing he would want to do. One time we were in the same group as some Americans, all dressed like they were in the movie, *Out of Africa*. Their loud talk was getting on Brendan's nerves. I told him to wait, and sure enough when we got into the bush and they were so near the animals, it was like someone put a cork in them; there wasn't a word. We even came across a big buck that had just been killed by a leopard and his blood was still warm. After a leopard kills he takes out the entrails and leaves them on top of his prey. Brendan told the Americans to watch out; that they might be next.

There's a joke about the married couple who were driving through the African bush and the husband gets out of the car to take a photograph. Next thing there's a charge of lions coming towards them and the wife shouts out the car window, "Shoot. Shoot. Why don't you shoot?" The husband calls back. "Sorry love, but I've run out of film." That's Africa.

Africa is beautiful and Africa is different. Different things happened to us every single day. We found an Egyptian cobra one time wrapped around our outside tap and oftentimes Denise had to shoo away a snake from our veranda. She even plucked a scorpion from one of my white shirts hanging in the cupboard thinking it was a feather. She didn't have her contact lenses in at the time and couldn't see very well, but luckily must have picked him up by the tail, as otherwise she would have been bitten and scorpions are deadly. A friend of ours went into her sitting-room one time and found a baby baboon sitting on her chair eating one of her apples.

Oh! Yes, I'm glad I went away. I'm glad I had all of those experiences. My childhood in Ireland had been very sheltered. I needed to get away to prove somehow that I could manage on my own. And I did.

Interviewed at his home in Carrickmacross, Co. Monaghan, Wednesday, July 25th, 2007

KATHLEEN DOHERTY

I'm still not settled, even though I'm back now since July 2003. I miss the privacy I had in England, you know? The Irish are a different race of people altogether. The town of Shannon then is different too. They're all blow-ins here, you see. This never was a town in the first place. There was only a couple of town houses in Shannon before I went to England. There was a Russian village here once, for the pilots, but that's been all sold off. This was one of the first housing estates to be built in the Sixties so it is a new town. Then they all came down from the North of Ireland because of the Troubles so you had a mix and gathering of them. This is what it was built for really, for the Northern Irish people during the Troubles, in 1969, and the early 1970's. And then they're in from Limerick City where they won't get a house, but they'll get a house here. So when you put it all together then, you have a bit of a problem. But, I wanted to come home so I have to make the best of it.

I went to England in 1955, forty-two years ago. God! Now I'll be showing my age. I went first to Wetherby, in West Yorkshire, where I worked in the golf club for a while. The jobs were advertised in the Irish newspapers that time; that's how all the emigrants got work over there. We did the jobs that nobody else wanted. I travelled by myself. That was a very lonesome journey sitting on boxes on the cattle boat because I couldn't get a seat. I was as sick as a dog. I was met in Leeds off the train. It wasn't too bad when I got there though because the workers were living-in and we were all the one age. The couple that ran the club, the Steward and Stewardess, fought like cats and dogs. She was from Northern Ireland and he was English, an ex-sailor. There'd be saucepans and oranges and everything flying across the kitchen and I'd be ducking and diving. I thought to myself, there's no place like home!

Oh! God! I missed home something terrible at first. I thought I'd never see Feakle in County Clare again. I had no family in Wetherby; I was all by myself. We didn't really have much of a social life, as we had to work hard to pay back for our fare and keep. It was all countryside around the Golf Club. There was a bit of an Irish community there, but not much. There was a hall where they'd have dances on a Sunday night. It was a homely town and they were kind of friendly

Kathleen (right) & sister Eileen

people anyway. Well, Yorkshire people are very nice. I always thought they were. They were real down to earth. The dances weren't that great, but I just went to have a different atmosphere for an hour or two. After about a year I moved on, once I had found my feet. I went into Leeds to do hotel work. That was a live-in job too. It was very handy. You'd meet a lot of Irish in hotel work, waitresses and that. We had a Polish chef who nearly killed us all. How he got away with it, I'll never know. He used to chase us with a cleaver. I met a lot of Irish in the hotel and catering business and we'd go to the Irish Centre and *The Shamrock* in Bridge Street. You felt more at home then when you met up with your own. I came home on holidays every year. Going back was the worst.

I got married eventually, he was from the North of Ireland. There was just four of us at the wedding. It was low-key, but I wasn't pregnant by the way. The ceremony was in St. Augustine's Church and we had the breakfast in a restaurant. It snowed that day so I always say I had a white wedding after all. I was a bit of a wild card you know. We had two children and after they started school I went to work with Social Services in Leeds where I spent eighteen years looking after the elderly. I had to do a small bit of training and took courses in social care and all that sort of thing. And then I worked my way up to be an Officer for a while, you know, before I retired. I loved it. Leeds was a lovely place. There was a good Irish community there with an awful lot of Mayo people. I found them always very nice, the Mayo people, and the Yorkshire people too. Mayo people were always very faithful to their county.

I used to play camogie in me young days, for Bodyke and I always followed the GAA when I was in England, especially when Clare was winning there in the Nineties. They haven't won an All-Ireland now since 1995. I won't be shouting for Limerick on Sunday. They're huge rivals of Clare. I used to go dancing in Limerick to *The Stella* and to *Cruises Hotel* upstairs, and I used to be frightened to death that there'd be fights. We also danced in *Paddy Con's* in Ennis, at the back of the Cathedral; it's a shop now. I liked all the showbands, especially Brendan Boyer; he was my favourite; and *The Cadets*. I didn't like Dickie Rock, he was too smarmy. We'd all pile into a *Morris Minor* and go to Gort too. We weren't fussy how we travelled. We made the most of it, we were glad to get there and we didn't care what we wore. The style was great in England then and having your own money to buy it, although we didn't have that much because we sent most of it home. They have a new outfit every day now, not like when I was young.

I grew up in the country, in Feakle. It was lovely. That's Biddy Early's country. She was an old woman, a healer actually, but she was classed as a witch. She was a bit like another healer, Mother Shipton, who was born in a cave in North Yorkshire. She could predict things too. I didn't grow up on a farm; we were in the country, but we had no land. It was a good life really, and although we hadn't a lot of money, we were able to get around. I'd say it was a lot worse in a town with a big family. There was eight of us. Feakle is only a little village, but it's a very traditional and famous for many reasons. It was a great old IRA meeting place, and well-known for the Fenian meetings. Our house was on the top of a hill and it was a look-out post once. Brian Merriman, a poet in the 1700's, had taught in our school. He used to write all his stuff on the shores of Lough Greine near Feakle. I would like to live around there again, but I would like a little street light. It's very lonesome in the countryside when there's no light.

I was Secretary of the Clare Association in Manchester where I moved when I was kind of half retired. It was Stockport really, but we called it Manchester because it all joined on together, like Ennis and Clarecastle. You'd think you were in the same town. We used to hold dances and charity fundraisers and we'd have festival weekends of Irish music and all that. It was the first County association to have any sort of a festival where they all came to play music. We'd have competitions for the Dr. Bill Loughnan Cup. He was a famous Clare man; well known in Fenian circles. He was a doctor, our doctor at home, and he was a musician. He was also a historian and very interested in Biddy Early. He had her cottage done up and they always said that all his tragedies were because of that. He had a daughter who died in a car crash, a son who died of cancer, and he died very suddenly himself. It was said she put a curse on him for interfering in her home; that he should have left well enough alone. But, that could be all old wives tales too or pisreógs (legends). Maybe there was no truth in it, I don't know. You know the Irish, what they're like anyway, they exaggerate things.

My children were deeply involved in Irish culture when they were growing up. You could take them to the Irish Centres in those days. We could have a dance and listen to music and play bingo and they could have a bit of fun as well. We used to buy chicken in the basket and chips and all that sort of thing. We always came home on holidays as a family. It was a long trek, but the children used to have great fun. My parents never came over to visit; the old Irish people weren't great for travelling, were they? My husband and I separated eventually, but he died a month before I moved here. It was sad really; he was only fifty-nine. He had been a ground worker in Leeds, pipe-laying and that. He drank fairly heavy and was a boxer in his younger days and I think it affected him later on in life, because he'd all kinds of complaints in his latter years.

My sister had a care agency in Stockport that sent helpers into the community to look after the people who couldn't take care of themselves, especially the elderly. I started working with her and was there until I came back home. It was a kind of a part-time, casual, sort of a job that kept me busy, you know. So I did that for a while and then

I read about Safe Home in *The Irish Post* and I thought that was one way of getting over to Ireland, you know, because it was very difficult otherwise. My daughter was living in this estate in Shannon at the time, so she knew when the houses came up empty. I was eventually offered one and when I got the key to this house I nearly died. Well, it was only three years old then, and it looked terrible. I don't know how many coats of paint it took to bring it back to a normal colour. I put this wooden floor in and lino in the kitchen and fresh carpet upstairs. A full skip we took out of here. Only for my son-in-law I don't know what I would have done. But, it was a house. And I thought well I can do something with it. I never had a new house in my life. If I had been given a new one, I'd consider myself so lucky. The authorities here don't check up on the tenants. They don't check up to see if they've got a bin or not, or how people are taking care of their homes. Everyone in England has a bin. If you can't afford one, the Welfare will pay for it, you know. I think that's why there so much rubbish in the streets of

Sharon, *Darling Girl from Clare*, 1989

this country; people have nowhere to put it. At the same time it's up to the tenants to take care of the estate.

Yet no matter how bad things are here, people still want to come home. It's your roots isn't it? My other sister that I worked with, she's come to Corrofin now, she's built a house there, so she's home. My brother from London is home. He's living in a basement flat in my niece's house. So everybody's back like. It's something that hits you when you retire, there's nothing else to stay for. And a lot of the places in England have gone downhill too like. The more money people have, the more insensitive they are. They're getting very greedy here. They've no thought for anyone anymore. You expect it to be like when you left it like, and it's not. I never thought of coming home when the kids were growing up.

There was nothing back then to come to anyhow. And this won't last much longer either. The Celtic Tiger is on his way out. You only have to listen to the radio every day. There's factories closing down all over the place. I don't know what they'll do then. Drugs is another thing. There's a lot of drugs around here. I am frightened here on my own. I'd never live without a dog for a start. Family breakdown is a cause of a lot of the problems here. The same thing happened in England.

Kathleen with grandchildren Joseph and Selena

My daughter, Sharon, lives down the road here; she was once the Darling Girl from Clare and a champion bodhrán player. She always had a grá for Ireland and her husband is of Irish descent too so they decided to come back and live here. My son is still in Leeds with his wife and three children. You'd miss them. But, I was away the whole time they were babies. When I was in Stockport I didn't see that much of them anyway, which is just as well now as I'd miss them more, wouldn't I? I have two grandchildren down the road, eleven and nine years of age. Sharon moved back before me. Then she wanted to do Nurse's training and she needed someone to mind the children so that was another reason for me to come back. It was a four-year course, a Degree course, and very difficult. It's a big responsibility minding children when you get older, but I stuck it out anyway and so did she and now she's graduating this Thursday from the University of Limerick.

Having family here is a big advantage, and Benjy, my dog, helped me settle in too. I got him off the dog warden in Ennis when he was a year old. He's a Corgi mix like the Queen's, and he used to wander at first, but I took him to the Vet and got him fixed up and that put an end to his wandering. I think all the men should be done! Everyone thinks he's called after the boy in *The Riordan's*, but I wasn't here then you see. I was away in England the whole time that programme was on the television here and I never saw it. He's called after the little dog in the film that was looking after the two lion cubs. Look at the ears popped up; he knows we're talking about him. He's a great little house dog. The neighbours around here hate him because he guards the house so well. That's one thing I've found since I came home. No-one here respects boundaries anymore. The children think they can go into anyone's garden and do what they like. And if you've got fences around your home, or you're anyway middling right, you don't fit in and that's it. They set poison in the front garden the other week. They resent Benjy, because he looks after his own little place. If there's anyone around he barks and then he'll run out to see who it is and that doesn't suit them. He was at death's door after eating the poison. If he hadn't been a healthy dog and injected for everything; I think I would have lost him.

People here have changed desperately. The older people aren't too bad, but the younger ones have changed. I don't know, maybe it's my age, but that's what I've found. Parents think that their children have the right to do what they want. As I said before, there's no boundaries. They're out smoking and drinking and they don't know where their kids are. That's why they're getting into trouble then. Certain groups are very bad, and then when the police clamp down on them, they bring in their mates from another estate and let them do the dirty work for them. But, I drive and I have a grand little car that gets me around. I didn't have time for social activities when I came back at first because I was minding the kids for Sharon. And now she'll be going back to work so that'll keep me busy for another while. I've been back to England a few times on holidays and I think if I'd no grand-kids here, I'd probably go back for good. I'd say to anyone coming back to choose their place very carefully. I think you'd be alright in a private estate; I think they'd be a bit more civilized. There's an awful drug element here in Ireland, stealing cars, joyriding and all that. The guards are too soft. The British police are much tougher. Although the old guards now when I was young you'd be frightened to death of them. Sure everybody was frightened by authority in them days, weren't they? It's different now. If I could have stayed in Ireland in the first place, I would have stayed. I don't think anybody goes away on purpose like. The only reason I went away is because I had no job, but when you come back you're classed as an emigrant again. There was a lot of paperwork to take care of on my return, but my daughter helped me with all of that, and I suppose Safe Home did too. I wouldn't like to be coming back all on my own with no one here. It's kind of a bit daunting at first because there's a lot to be done. For instance in order to open a bank account you have to have a utility bill so that takes a while to come through and then you have nowhere to put your money or to get cheques cashed and that. Anyone coming back after fifty years with no family here will get a quare shock.

In a little village like where I came from I'd say not much has changed. We go over to Feakle every now and then. But, there's no-body we know there now either. There's no one in the house we grew up in. My mother died in 1983 and my father in 1992 when he was ninety-three years of age. I think the death of my mother was the hard-est though. My father was a bit of a stickler for rules and regulations. My mother was softer. You always have a soft spot for your mother. I imagine they were heartbroken when we all went off. Can you imag-ine losing all your children like that? There were only three of us that didn't go. None of us went to America. I've been there on holidays, but it was too far to go for good. The whole family took a trip some years ago to Arizona and Las Vegas; to California to Disneyland; that was a fabulous place. We went to Tucson where they made all the cowboy films, to The Grand Canyon, and the Indian reservations. It was great, but very tiring. I got stung by spikes of a cactus. We met

Leeds Irish Centre, early 70's

an Indian there called David O'Donovan. He had a little shop on the side of the road selling trinkets, the turquoise and all that. I told him he was a handsome man.

They don't have any social activities in this estate at all. If I go out it's for a night with my family. I've got myself a fellow now, would you believe? I know I look kind of auld, and I should be over the hill, but we're more friends than anything. He's a nice man, a widower from Ennis. I met him at one of these céili do's, you know. He's a musician, and a few years older, but a gentleman now, old fashioned. They have the adult dances in *The West County Hotel,* but I don't go to them. I prefer the céili dancing and the traditional music sessions that I used go to in England. You'd meet different people and that. They'd have the old Irish sessions in the pubs. They're the nicest kind of nights out, aren't they? You walk in and you meet different people.

I'll do some gardening now for the afternoon. There's marigolds growing up between the stones and I have to weed them out. My boy-friend made the archway for me. I always had a garden, everywhere I went. Believe it or not my uncle was a gardener with *McLysaght's* over in Raheen. They had big nurseries and gardens there. There's a lodge

259

still there in the wilderness, in the middle of the woods, Tom Mullin's lodge, which is my ancestors' name. So it's in the blood. All of my uncles were gardeners. It hasn't been a summer really for gardening. The back garden here was like marshlands when I moved in; the soil is very boggy. I made a rockery down at the end and I covered the walls with greenery because I hate looking out at concrete walls. I have some unusual hydrangea and I'm trying to grow some bamboo. My little granddaughter, Selena, bought me the garden ornament, Archie, in the RSPCA shop in England. I had hanging baskets all over the place, but sure they all died with this weather. It was lovely there for a couple of weeks, but then it got bad again. It's quite noisy here because my garden is facing onto five other gardens. The fences are always being climbed over. People around here are not interested in gardening, only the pensioners, I've noticed. My immediate four neighbours are nice, but the rest of them do nothing. They think you're sort of an odd ball if you're interested in gardening.

I like to read and have a Celia Aherne book there that I'm ready to start. I like Edna O'Brien, the Clare author. She was very outspoken about life back then, but she told the truth. That's why they didn't like her. But, she told how it was back then in Ireland, how we all had to

In the garden with Benjy

go to England and the influence the Catholic Church had on everyone. I practiced my religion for a while and then I gave it up, but I've come back to it again now. I've been to Medjugorje twice and that has influenced me greatly. I had been very lax, but my sisters were going on a holiday and I decided to tag along. There's something special about it. There's definitely a presence there, I can't explain. It is a beautiful place, very barren, hilly, lovely weather, but very poor. My rosary beads were turned to gold there; that's one of the phenomenons. My sister noticed it first and I didn't believe her. It doesn't happen to everybody you know, so there must have been a reason. All of the links between the beads were silver; now they're gold. Our Lady must pick the people that need help. She is still appearing there; there's an apparition every week. It's only the Visionaries that can see anything though. I was sitting beside a man one time who had a vision. He started shouting at me, "Can you see? Can you see?" And I thought I wouldn't be sitting here if I could!

A lot of the things that are happening today, I believe, are because of lack of Faith. People might have turned against religion because of the behaviour of some of our Clergy, but that shouldn't stop them from going to Mass on a Sunday. The man with the hairy legs is working on all of that. He's got a bigger victory now, you see. He has the power over certain priests that caused them to sin, so of course he's gaining more for his side now when everyone turned against them. If people were just strong enough to pray for the priests who have fallen by the wayside, you know, we wouldn't be having all of the drugs that are causing all of the misfortune today. And we wouldn't have people who think they don't have to work for anything anymore; people who think everything should be handed to them.

I'm glad I went away. It broadens your mind, doesn't it? I think that's all made out for you anyway, isn't it? It was in our destiny. And I suppose it was in my destiny to come back too.

Interviewed at her home in Shannon, County Clare, on Tuesday, August 28th, 2007

BETTY HOMER

The first day I set foot on Inishowen on the 1st of June, 2003, I went down to the beach at Culdaff and in the clothes I stood up in, I went in for a swim. I got back into the car, wrapped a rug around me and said, "This is it." We flew into Derry Airport six days later and got a taxi to Malin, where we lived first. I wasn't worried about the fare, I was that excited. I loved it from the very beginning. I loved it even though it was a big, big, change, but it was coming back home. Although I'm from Dublin, any part of Ireland is home. Do you know what I mean? I never left it. I never left Ireland in all them years. I had a good job in *Will's* Tobacco factory on the South Circular Road in Dublin before I left, so I wasn't out of work. I grew up on Bath Avenue in Sandymount, which was a nice area, so I'd say I went to England mainly for adventure.

I went to Leicester in the Fifties where my first job was in *Byford's* where they made men's socks. Leicester was that type of an industrial town. I used to work on the tabulator in the office. Then I married a Leicester man, got pregnant, and like a fool I told the landlady and next day she told me to get out. That was the sort of thing that happened to the Irish. I was only twenty-one years of age and living with my husband in one room for which we paid thirty shillings a week, but he was cruel so I left him. I then left for Birmingham to stay with my sister where my eldest son, Peter, was born. A priest advised me to send him home to my mother and she minded him until I got married to George. In the meantime, I became a bus conductor with Birmingham City Transport and I loved it. I met a lady on the bus, a Polish woman, and I went to lodge with her. I didn't even have a bed to lie on, only a canvass with an orange box at the end to hold it up, and a curtain dividing the room. She was like a mother to me. When I'd come in from work she'd have a hot water bottle in me bed and me clothes ironed and folded over the chair beside it, and the fire lit in the room.

I met George on the buses. He was a mechanic in the garage and went to feel me leg, because he said I had a nice bit of leg. I was waiting to go out on the road and was sitting on the bus marking up me route. He said he'd never speak to me again because I smacked him in the face. You see in those days a lot of Irish people would go away if they were married, separated or divorced. They had a saying then about women who'd been married that you'd never miss a slice off a cut loaf. So I was always on me guard. I would never let anyone touch me. The only way a man could touch me was with a bit of gold. George and I were going out for a while because I had to wait two years for me divorce. And I worked all the hours God gave me to save the money for that. Plus I was sending home every penny to Mammy for looking out for Peter. I used to work eighty-eight hours

UK Idenity Card

some weeks. But, I loved it, and I never got out of the habit of getting up at three o'clock in the morning. We eventually got married and had a second son, Georgie. I left the job when I was six months pregnant, but as soon as Georgie was five, I went back on the buses again. I loved it.

We came back to Dublin in the Sixties and bought a house in Blackrock. George packed up his job in *The Rover (The Land Rover Group)* and we stayed for four years. Then he got made redundant and we had to go back to Birmingham again. I was paying a mortgage on the house in Leopardstown Road and we couldn't afford to keep it up. I didn't like going back because we'd done everything we could to make a good life for ourselves in Dublin. George used to travel way out to Santry to work in *Buckley's* garage, where he used to do vehicle body building and the company closed down. I used to make cakes and go around all the houses selling them. I

Happiest conductor on Coventry Road

had lodgers; I did bed and breakfast, I did everything to pay the six pounds, fifty shillings, a month mortgage, and after all that we still had to go back to England. The house we sold for two thousand, two hundred pounds is selling for two and half million euros now. Sure it's only a house, what you never had you never miss.

I went back on the Birmingham buses again until I got colitis, and I went down to five stone, ten pounds. I felt embarrassed being off work for ten weeks, but I wasn't back a week when it flared up again, so that finished me on the buses. What I should have done is got meself turned down; I should have had meself declared medically unfit for the job, and I would have got a pension for life from them, but I didn't think of that. I loved the buses though and I loved Birmingham. We used to be down in the Irish Centre in Deritend. I used to bring me Red Setter, Christy, down there on St. Patrick's Day all dressed up in his green, white and gold, football jersey.

We lived in Sheldon and Yardley mainly. I bought a house off a bus-driver in Sheldon. I used to have a lodger and when we were coming home in 1960 I sold the house to him. When we came back we moved on to Yardley Road, where they knocked all the houses down beside the cemetery. We spent twenty-six years there. I used to keep six student teachers at one time, and I worked as well. I was supposed to only give them a cup of milk and a bed, but for God's sake, they were the same age as me own kids, so they were treated the same as mine. I would have liked mine to be looked after. Then when I packed up that George's mother came to visit one time and she said, I don't feel well, and I had her then for the last four years of her life. She went blind in the end. When she died we went to live in Blakesley Close, which was a sheltered housing scheme for the elderly. After the buses I went working for *Dollond & Aitchison*, the eye glasses people where I used to answer the telephone all day. The children were grown up, but I had always taken hours that coincided with their schooling anyhow. Peter went to *Archbishop Williams* School in Bordsley and Georgie went to *Archbishop Ilesley* in Acocks Green. I liked the receptionist work. I always liked dealing with people, but nobody knows how rotten the public are until you go working for them. You couldn't even get people to stand up and give someone a seat sometimes on the bus. I used get awful remarks. It was a very bad time for the Irish there when the Rotunda was bombed as well. But, we survived it all.

We came home regularly on holiday. I've done nearly all the *Jury's* hotels in Ireland by now, and was sad to see them close down. Then of course I had been back and forth all the time when Peter lived here and we had lived here for four years. So it was always on the cards to come back for good. I never left it, you know what I mean? I was always going home. Where are you going on your holidays, people would ask. "I'm going home," was always my reply. Now I worked with all nationalities and no matter where they were from in the world it was always home to them too. They never referred to their country by name, just home. Irish people never said, Ireland, they always said, home. My sister used to say, this is your home, meaning Birmingham. And I used to say, no it's not, this is where I'm living. She wouldn't be bothered coming back here because all of her family are still in England. She'll say she got her living out of that country, and I say, well, we worked for it. We never got nothing for nothing. We worked hard for it.

I think I saw the ad for Safe Home in the newspaper or I found it down in the Irish Centre and I went and saw about it. I came over and had a look at Malin, and decided straight away to take it. I left the kids to do the packing over in Birmingham and a fellow from Ballyliffen brought the furniture back for us. I asked this taxi man in Birmingham if he knew anyone who shipped furniture and he told me about this place in Sparkhill. When the bloke told me he was from Ballyliffen I couldn't believe it, as it's only miles from me here in Carndonagh. In fact I go up to the *Ballyliffen Lodge* for the swimming, but I've gone blind in the last few months and I haven't gone into the water in a while because I'm having injections into me eyes. I loved Malin and I was all right there as long as me money lasted. Weren't eligible for rent supplement, because it was already funded by the Government. I would still be there otherwise. We were on the North-West housing list all that time and eventually got this house in Carndonagh. We moved in on the 17th of July this year. I didn't mind all the paperwork, because we had nothing to hide. The only reason people have a problem about that is they're afraid of anyone nosing into their affairs. If you've got nothing to hide, what is there to worry about?

I've never missed Birmingham from that day to this. The only thing I miss is going into *Chilly Billy's* in the Bull Ring because we used to get food cheap there. I knew all the barrow boys, the fellows on the stalls, I'd talk to anybody. I had loads of Irish friends there. Even up to the time we left I'd see people I used to know on the buses and I'd think how old they looked, and they only me own age. I used to have two passengers and they always reminded me of a pair of Betty Boops, with the make-up and all, and every time they saw me they'd stop and they'd say how much they missed me on the road. I had that reputation of being the happiest conductor on Coventry Road, you know. That was me run and me number was 39273; I'll never forget it. They wouldn't have a bus run in Birmingham or a road without the Irish.

They all call me the Dub around here. I haven't got involved in any community activities at all. I like doing me own thing. I might go to the strand at Five Fingers just past Culdaff, or I might go to Ballyliffen or up around Lagg is beautiful. I go to Buncrana or I go into Derry. They're both only twenty-five minutes from here. I've never gone out in the night since I've been here. There's quite a bit of crime up here, there's drugs and crime everywhere you go now. I think they've spoiled Ireland really, especially Dublin. I'd have no interest in going near Dublin now. There's no one I know left there anyhow. My brother moved out to Celbridge where my mother's relatives originated from. They all worked in Castletown House where my Granny was the wet nurse to one of the Guinness ladies. There's nothing down on Bath Avenue for me at all now.

I had one great friend there, Bridie. I only rang her recently to see if she was still alive. We used to have great fun dancing up in the mountains in Kiltiernan and in *The Olympic* and *The Metropole* in the city. We used to be in *Cleary's* on O'Connell Street; in *The Palais* up the top of Parnell Street, up around by *The National Ballroom*; and in *The Lido* in Blackrock. I used to like dancing. I like all music. You'd want to see the boxes of tapes there are in this house, you would not believe it. In Birmingham I went down to *The Emerald* a few times, but I was always working a lot there, so I didn't have much time for dancing. Bridie's husband used to be a chauffeur for the Papal Nuncio and when they'd have a do up in the Phoenix Park he used to bring us up to see them in their long dresses and everything. We used to love going out to Dalkey and Dun Laoghaire on a Sunday and doing that walk down the pier. I've got a bit of a dickie ticker now so I don't walk so much. The only time I don't feel exhausted is when I'm in the water swimming. It seems like you're weightless, but having these injections in my eye, I'm afraid to go in the pool, in case I pick up any infection. That blindness has come all of a sudden on me and I'm finding it very difficult to accept. But, I'm still coping. I'm still getting the food ready and all that. I've to go next Monday to a near-vision eye clinic in Sligo.

We were in a head-on smash in April. How we didn't die, I don't know. That's no lie. It happened down on the Moville by-pass. A seventeen year old learner driver crashed into us, but the police said it was George's fault. There was not a soul about; it was a beautiful morning, and where the witnesses came from I don't know, but everyone knew them, not us, and that was it. They took me away in an ambulance because of me chest and I broke me finger. I was bruised all Technicolor. Sure I could've broken me neck, it could have been worse, couldn't it? I've been in Letterkenny Hospital quite a few times now, and I couldn't find fault with them. The main fault I do have here is with the cost of living; its very high. I mean you wouldn't see a hundred euros go, would you? It's all greed. I'd say they've spoiled Ireland because they've taken away the pace of life that was Ireland. It's a rat race now. Nobody has time to say hello to you. Now the people up in Donegal are lovely, and they're very inoffensive. That's one thing that struck me when I came up here first, was how nice the people were. They keep to themselves, the Donegal people, they don't come to you; you go to them. I found that.

Sometimes there's a dinner for the seniors, but that's not my scene. I wouldn't go for the sake of a free dinner, you know what I mean? I like to be free as the bird. Peter has since followed me home and bought a big ten-roomed house down the road in Malin. He packed up his job two years ago and came back. He loves it, he does. And now the other one wants to come over, but his wife won't. He lives in Willenhall. I have a grandchild here and a great grandchild and I have two grandchildren in England. I went over when Peter took sick two year ago. He had cancer of the kidney, but Thank God he's alright now. It really surprised me him coming here.

Another reason I like Carndonagh is that I'm closer to the hospital. The only thing is, they're very slow with tests and things here, and if you're really sick, you've to go forty miles to Letterkenny. I've been in quite a few hospitals in me day and I find meself going around and filling up water jugs for the other patients and that. It's in me nature. I know a few of the neighbours and quite a few of the locals down in the town. You'd get a lot of the young ones partying around here, and it can be noisy, especially at the weekends. A bloke was supposed to come and paint the place, but I was waiting too long and then I got a woman in to do it instead. Another fellow down the road is going to tile the kitchen for me. You have to wait for everything here.

George and I on our Wedding day

There's only one trade and that's plastering. Everyone's a plasterer. My Granddad Sanders was a plasterer and a master tutor in Bolton Street Technical School. He did the ceiling of the Bank of Ireland in Dublin. He worked out in Ardmore Studio with my Uncle Jack and me Uncle Georgie. Even me Mammy's family, her seven brothers, were all plasterers. My brother in Celbridge done seven years at the plastering trade; now if they do two years, they call themselves plasterers. They used to say the only place you'll find better than the Sanders brothers is in Mount Jerome cemetery. That's where they're all buried. Me mother's buried there too and that's where I'll go when I'm gone. I'll get cremated and go down there. I went into *Wroe's* and picked out the grave and all a fortnight before me Daddy died.

I'm not really religious, but I'm never without my parents' memorial cards in me pocket. My father was a great footballer, Michael Keegan, he played for Shelbourne Rovers. They used to call him Dirty Keegan because he was a dirty player. Their shorts used to be down to their knees and they wore shin guards. They used to put tallow, like lard, on their football boots to keep them supple. He played for Ireland when it became the Free State. My brother, Michael, played for CYMS in the Leinster Senior League and his son, Robert, played for Bohs (Bohemians). My brother, Jimmy played for Hammond Lane; he'd only retired a few months when he died. He was a delegate in the Trade Union up in Liberty Hall. I'm all into politics too. It was hard luck that Dr. Jerry Cowley didn't keep his seat in the last election. I don't like Bertie Aherne; he had a good tutor in Charlie Haughey. I

40th wedding Anniversary

backed Joe McHugh, and he's the only Senator to be elected in Donegal. Last time there was a local election I backed this school teacher because in my opinion they need to do something for the youth. You wouldn't have teenagers becoming fathers if they had something else to occupy their time. Instead of building posh buildings they should build them workshops to teach them mechanical engineering.

Between Lansdowne Road and Connolly DART stations in Dublin, I counted twenty-six giant cranes; that's in the space of three train stops. They're tearing down the most beautiful architecture in Dublin. Is Dublin able for all that they're doing to it? They're wrecking it. This has all only happened now since they joined the EU (European Union). Ireland has prospered, but they've left the gate wide open for companies to start up here, stay a few years and once they've got their foot in the door, they're going to China. It's very scary really if you stop to think about it.

When you emigrate, you don't intend staying forever. We were so young, and innocent, we didn't think about things. I used to smoke, mind you, untipped cigarettes, six and tuppence for two hundred when you worked at *Will's*. They made *Gold Flake, Capstan, Passing Cloud*, and *Woodbines*, but the *Capstan* was the best because the leaves weighed the heaviest. *Woodbine* was the worst, being made from small leaves. George always says I was a stripper, because I used to strip the tobacco leaves. I never liked that job though and was sick since the day I went into it. I don't know whether it was the tobacco or what, but I always had trouble with me stomach. That was probably the real reason I went to England, to get away from *Will's*. I'd been there since the day I left St. Brigid's National School on Haddington Road. I loved school and would have loved to go on to St. Mary's Secondary, but my mother couldn't afford to keep me there and I had to go out and work. My father worked on the coal boats and they didn't have a lot of money. I have a mind like a sponge, though, and can remember all of the teachers. Miss Kelleher was the music teacher; Miss Rogers taught arithmetic, and Sr. Thomasina used to knock hell out of me. Sr. Marie-Celine was the most vicious person I ever came across in my life, and she had the face of a saint. She was beautiful looking. She looked to me as if she was six foot and I remember her poking me on the side of my head when I was going in to do the Primary Cert, but I still got the certificate in anyway. I came second out of fifty-two in the class and the girl that came first was Clare Byrne who ended up being the Lady Mayoress of Dublin once. I was besotted with school though and hated leaving it when I was sixteen.

Now I'm seventy-seven and take every day as a bonus. George does say, what's the programme for tomorrow, and I do say, wake up. As my mother used to say, I wasn't born, I was invented. I've had a lovely life and one of the best parts of it is here, because this is now. What you can do about the past is think wistfully of what was and what might have been, but we can't live on memories, we've got to make the most of the here and now. I love everything about life here; its home. I never found it hard to settle in or nothing. It's home. No matter where you go in the world, Ireland is home.

Interviewed at her home in Carndonagh, County Donegal, on Monday, September, 10th, 2007

Home at last

THOMAS MURPHY

I was in England for forty six or seven years. It was in 1955 or 1956 that I went and I came back in 2002. I was born in Cavan town where there was no work once you left school. All there was then was the bacon factory, *McCarrons*, but you hadn't an earthly chance of getting into it. I went to St. Phelim's De La Salle national school. After that it was hanging around the town with nothing to do. I might help out in the cloakroom in the sports centre and on a Tuesday night I helped pack *The Anglo Celt* newspaper for which I received six pence. That brought me to the céilí in the Town Hall on a Sunday. That was it. So I took the bus to Dublin one day and then the train to Dun Laoghaire. I was only about fifteen or sixteen years of age and I hadn't a clue where I was going, but I was heading for London anyhow.

I went on my own and knew not a soul there, believe me. I got off the train; I think it was Euston it pulled into then, and started walking around and around. I had about five pounds on me to be honest, but I found a bed and breakfast and the next day I walked around and around again until I met this Wicklow lad called Jimmy. He was looking for a room too, so we sort of teamed up together and decided to try a tube to see what it was like, for a bit of *craic*, you know. Anyhow we got off at Shepherd's Bush and found a job on a building site straight away. The sub-contractor told us about rooms in Finsbury Park and right after work, at about half past four, we took the tube again. We thought it was great to be underground; anyhow after about an hour and a half we found Finsbury Park where we ended up living. Imagine we had that long a commute every day going and coming from work and we had to start at seven in the morning, which meant we were up at five. A landlady ran the house; there were other lodgers there too, all Irish. The work was very hard, filling a lorry on your own with a shovel. Sometimes I swear when I think about it. Back then you'd have to lay concrete with a plank of wood, there was no machinery. When I think of it, the hands used to be swollen, believe me.

Jimmy and I would go to the dancehalls but by the time we got around to asking a girl up to dance it would be over so we'd say we'll come back next week and try again. Once they heard your accent they would refuse you anyway. Then we heard about the Irish dancehalls; we went to one in Hammersmith, not *The Palais*, the one next door to it, and to *The Galtymore*. At least the Irish girls would dance with you. In *The Palais* it was mixed and you could always tell the Irish and English girls apart. The Irish would be always well dressed in long dresses; the English would be more revealing. It was all Irish showbands in those days. I never heard of any Irish Centres back at the beginning. There were none of them as far as we were concerned. We were on our own. We had to learn fast because we had to work. The money wasn't that great, but it was better than the dole.

The subbie (sub-contractor) got the contract from the foreman who was hired by the company, so the subbie would have to give the foreman a few bob for the contract. Then he'd pay us say two pounds a day, but he'd dock a few bob for giving you the job in the first place. The bloody subbies never paid our stamps and a lot of people didn't find this out until they went to apply for the pension. Then they were left with nothing after paying these blokes all their lives. It was a good thing to be working with *Fitzpatrick's* or *Wimpy* because they stamped your cards. It was such a fiddle between the foreman, the subbie, and whatever clever bloke was working for him. It was a rat race and we were the innocent victims. You had to be clever, keep you mouth shut and keep your job. It was hard, believe me. It was all Irish on the sites because many of the factories would have signs up 'No Irish Need Apply'. The bed and breakfasts did that too. They just hated us. We were the laughing stock of the world for some reason. And they would never call you by your right name, it was always Mick or Paddy or Seamus. The English loved that. And then there was the drinking. Oh, cor blimey, the drinking on the buildings, now that's hitting a sour note. When I was on the buildings I was a heavy drinker and so was every other Irish man who ended up on the sites. On a Friday evening you had to go to the pub after work and buy drink for the Irish subbie and the English foreman. If you didn't there'd be no work for you on Monday morning. And you had to keep the foreman in cigarettes during the week at tea breaks. It was the only way you could keep a job. Believe me. We just accepted it like. And you couldn't argue with them. That was the problem. You had to keep them happy and you learnt the hard way.

Then you had the landladies who were very cruel. They used to go up and check your room and you'd have to have it tidy. The door was closed at a certain time at night and if you were going to be out late at a dance you'd have to tell her. We'd take that 266 bus up to Chichester and we'd be running to try and get home on time. These women were Irish and they owned big houses and raised their children as English. The husbands would have to have been in a trade to have the kind of money that would buy a big house. They were crying out for tradesmen that time, who would earn more money than a labourer. They'd have a deposit for a house and then they'd make loads of money from the lodgers who were mainly Irish lads. There would be two or three in a room and if it was a double there would be four beds. You'd share a bathroom; you'd put your money in a meter and maybe wait an hour for a bath. That was another reason to go to the pub. You'd need a drink after that, believe you me, you'd need a drink after a day on the buildings. You ate wherever there was a café; there was no such thing as home cooked meals. If not you'd come home to where you were living and bring something with you to eat. I had family there, but didn't stay in touch with them. They were in Birmingham, Manchester, and Preston. We were all spread out and had to make our own way. By the time you paid the subbie and paid for your room you hadn't a lot of money to spend, believe me. And you had to feed yourself because nobody would loan you money in those days. We made loads of friends along the way and most of them would help you out if you were stuck for a room and that. The Irish stuck together; danced together; drank together.

Sometimes you didn't have a job and dole money was terrible. Sometimes you'd have only half a loaf of bread to eat. One place I stayed in had an apple tree outside in the garden and I'd wait until it was dark and rob an apple to make a sandwich. That's how hungry we could be. Or sometimes we'd get pork pies; they were terrible things; three and four to a packet and we'd bring them back to the room, but if you let a crumb drop you'd make sure to clean it up before the landlady saw it. I tell you it was very hard, but it was an education and a toughening. It taught me to keep a few bob when I had it. Sometimes I'd buy me drink and bugger off. It was very hard to save though, no such thing as bank accounts. You'd keep it with you, hide it. It was easier when I was married.

We worked on the buildings for a couple of years until I said to Jimmy I can't do this any longer. It would kill you. That's how I felt anyway, so I went back to Shepherd's Bush and got a room. That's the first thing you had to do is get accommodation and I went walking, walking again until I found a job in this factory where I stayed for a short while. That's where I met Mary, the woman I would marry. She worked on the line with me. After a while she moved onto an ice-cream factory while I went into an engineering firm. She loved it in London because there was great freedom for her. She didn't have her mother watching out for her and giving her a belt when she came home late. She was in a room with other girls in Shepherd's Bush. I think it was harder for girls in a way. Some of them came over on their own and if they met in with the wrong person they could get into trouble. There were so many that ended up pregnant, living in a little room on their own, God love them. I haven't a clue how they supported themselves. They had no chance with some of the landlords. If they were lucky they'd get in with an Irish family, but I met many who weren't that fortunate.

With my beautiful daughter Lisa

I had found a job anyway with *Lucas* in Acton Vale, a big engineering firm where they made parts for cars, buses, coaches, all forms of vehicle. At the interview I said that I had spent three years at Cavan University and luckily they didn't ask me what degree I earned there because I was going to say my CDM – Cadbury's Dairy Milk! Of course they thought they had a clever one here and started me off in the storeroom doing bits and pieces and then I got a promotion with a suit, collar and tie. I didn't have to clock in, clock out, nothing, and earned good enough money. When I put that suit on in *Lucas* I stopped drinking. The IRA was bombing England when I got the promotion to Progress Chaser in charge of two big assembly lines. I'd get a mouthful from the English foremen, "You Irish Mick telling me what to do." The Manager would have to have a word with them, but it was a big insult for them to have an Irish man telling them what to do. After four or five years they accepted me. It was a hard time then; that's why the Irishmen went on the buildings because they'd be with other Irish. It was hard, during the Troubles believe me. You'd go to an Irish pub, but not to an English one or you'd be in serious trouble.

I stayed in that job for fourteen years until they closed down the bloody thing when the Japanese started making cheaper parts. Then I went into security; *Superior Security* they were called. I started off in London, but had to travel to Birmingham, Liverpool, Manchester, Leeds, wherever I was needed. They moved you around wherever the job was. You just found digs wherever you went. I travelled and travelled all over the country, and in the meantime I got married. April Fool's Day it was, in 1967. I went to the Governor, John Fisher, and said I was married now and by this time had a child so I'd have to cut down on the travelling. He lined up a big job for me in Earls' Court, in a massive exhibition centre. I stayed there until I retired.

Nobody ever wanted to leave Ireland, but in our house there were seventeen children, ten boys and seven girls, so really you had to move out to leave room for the next one. I came somewhere in the middle, I always lose count. The eldest brother is still alive, Phildea. Rose is still alive too. Jimmy is buried in Mayo and one day I'm going down to see his grave. Every one of us emigrated bar two. Mamie is buried out in South Africa; the rest went to England. The two that stayed at home are still alive. They were lucky to get into the bacon factory. We grew up in a row of houses a wee bit outside the town. My father was in *McCarrons* and he used to work for solicitors part-time delivering summonses, which we had to deliver and he got the half a crown. He was in the army before that.

We came all the time to Cavan when my parents lived in Tullymongan where they'd moved to a three bedroom house; a step up from the ones on Breffni where I was born, but nevertheless there'd still be three or four to a bed. We'd come by coach and it was an awful journey. After my father died in 1967 and my mother seven years later, we mainly went to Donegal to my wife's people. My children suffered quite a lot from the teasing from other children who were very cruel. They couldn't understand it because they regarded themselves as Irish too, but as they got older they learnt to defend themselves, and it didn't put them off Ireland at all. As far as they're concerned they were born in London, but they're Irish. We lived in a big community in St. Augustine's parish in Shepherd's Bush. They went to school there too. I was always very religious and always went to Mass on Sunday but there was nothing the priests could do for the Irish when times were bad. I have seven children and they were all raised Catholic. I also made sure they attended Irish dancing classes every weekend. We didn't follow the Gaelic games that much. I brought them up to Ruislip one time where the games were played, but they said the boys had to be born in Ireland. I played when I was young for the school. You'd never see the all-Ireland games in England until the early Seventies when they'd show them in cinemas, before that we didn't even know if it was on.

Sixteen years ago I broke up with my wife and ended up in a block of flats all by myself. My children were all grown up and married with their own families so I moved into this flat surrounded by fighting, drugs, drink, and loud music. I couldn't bear the noise; it could go on all night. I would contact the noise control people from the Council but they were afraid to come over, there were so many drugs. I would sleep during the day because it was safest that way.

I had often thought of coming home through the years especially after splitting up with the wife because I was on my own then and I thought I might as well be in Ireland. I missed it all along; it's where you were born sort of thing. I used to get *The Irish Post* and I used to see this advert for Safe Home for Irish people wanting to come back. Eventually I got in touch with them and it was the best move I ever made. They kept me on their books and one Wednesday evening I received a call from Killeshandra Housing Association offering me a place. Here I am today.

It was still very hard settling back in. There were times I was going to pack up and go. It was too quiet around here; it took me eight months to get used to it. There was no fighting; no drinking; no dancing outside the door; just quietness. I just wasn't used to it after nine years in the other place. Even though England was very depressing and I used to get down and lonely there; I suppose it was just familiar. Then I started going up to the Resource Centre here on a Friday and met my neighbours. They're the nicest people in the whole world and there's a great community spirit here. I have made more friends here in the four years I've been back than I had my whole life in England. Back there I didn't know the people either side of me; I'd hear them fighting, but I didn't know who they were. Here I have Helen, George and Joe and anytime I need a lift anywhere I only have to ask them. And look at the house I got. I can leave the door open anytime I go up town, as I know the neighbours all watch out for each other. In that respect Ireland hasn't changed.

I couldn't believe all of the other changes I've seen though: the amount of houses going up around Cavan; the new roads; the lights at night time. There were no lights when I used to play around the town, believe me. And then I got all the help from Safe Home. They put me in touch with the local Welfare Officer who told me my entitlements. The benefits here are fantastic. The pensions in England were good until Maggie Thatcher started the war with the Falklands. They dipped into the pension money to finance that. I have my medical card here; fuel allowance; electricity allowance; free travel; and free TV licence. I was getting confused with all the bits. At Christmas time I get two weeks money and fifteen packets of briquettes; another fifteen in February. You wouldn't get that anywhere else. I had to pay my gas over there, electricity, telephone; and we only got ten pounds extra at Christmas. I have rent allowance here, and living alone allowance. I used to wake up dreaming when I arrived over first. Pat Tierney is the main man here; he's on the housing committee; a great man.

My children were all for me coming home. As long as you're happy they said. One of my daughters has gone off to Spain to start up a new life there and my son is a police officer. They've all been over to visit; they love the place. Of course they would know it from when they were children. It's not for everybody though, the wife would hate it here, she said. I am still in touch with her sometimes; occasionally we'll give each other a ring. She came here to have a look, but she thought Killeshandra was too quiet and there was no dancehall. She loved to dance even after we were married. I would baby sit and she'd go out for a dance with her sister and if I went out to the pub for a drink she'd stay at home. We had a house in Shepherd's Bush with the Notting Hill Housing Co-op where she still lives. I've been over and back to visit, but not now for a year because of my sore leg. I have seven grandchildren, all with Irish names, one of them is called Cavan and they're all very interested in their Irish roots. We used to take them down to the big parades on Paddy's Day and my son's wife loves the Irish music. They all go to Catholic schools and they've all been christened. I do miss them. That's another downside. If you have family back in England it's hard to be away from them. That's another reason Mary couldn't come back, she says, she'd miss the sons and daughters and the grandchildren too much.

To anyone out there who is thinking of coming home to Ireland, I would say please come. Please come, but be aware of the pitfalls. It can be very hard to get used to after living a lifetime somewhere else and no matter how hard things had got in England or elsewhere you will miss it still, because it was home. But if you are prepared to make the effort you will get used to it here eventually and if you are lucky enough to meet the people I've met here, then you have it made. You listen to people over there and they say you can't do this in Ireland and you won't get that and people won't accept you. It's all rubbish. I walk up that street and the horns hoot, everyone that passes says hello, nice day. I used to wonder at first if I must know them, because nobody would speak to you like that in England.

Every Friday in the Centre there's activities between eleven in the morning until two in the afternoon. We might have bingo and then dinner or painting classes with soup and sandwiches. Then once a month we visit another town for a night out dancing. I've gone twice but my dancing days are over now on account of my ankle. I broke it several years ago and had steel brackets and screws put in. They're acting up now, the bones are starting to grind together, but an operation would mean paralysis so I told them in Cavan hospital to forget it. It's not the end of the world if I can't dance, but it would be if I couldn't walk. I was a great auld dancer, I was a rock 'n roller; I could swing them around. That's all over now. But I'm happy to be alive; I have a lovely house; great neighbours; lovely people. I don't go out at night. I have lunch in *The Lough Bawn* pub every day and Martin said if I'm ever stuck for money I'm still to come in for dinner. He and his wife are two lovely people. And the food is perfect. You'd never get anything like that in England. If you ordered a pork chop over there you'd need a chainsaw to cut it and you wouldn't get half the portions you get here. You'd be still hungry, believe me.

Some people did great in England. There are some Irish families over there and the children think they're English, which is fine for them I suppose. I'd say the ones who got on well wouldn't come back, and they'd probably be right. Even for those who didn't do so well it still wouldn't necessarily be the right move. I didn't get on great by some standards. I never had my own house or my own car, but I raised a wonderful family and I'm very proud of that. And I'm lucky that it worked out for me in Ireland so far, because it could easily have been a different story. But, I'll tell you one thing, if I'd stayed in that flat in London I wouldn't be alive today.

Interviewed at his home in Killeshandra, County Cavan, on May 9th, 2007

BRIDIE O'CONNOR

I always wanted to come back to Ireland; sure I never wanted to leave it in the first place. I even have my grave sorted out so that I will be buried with my parents. It's written into my Will. Dead or alive I was coming back. I signed on with Safe Home and was elated when they offered me this house in Clonberne, County Galway, close to where I had grown up. Now I gaze on pastures green and the trees seem to lift their leafy arms every day to greet me. I was like the Pope on my return in 2002 and could have kissed the ground I had to leave behind to suit a man who took me away from it. Ireland was always home to me; it was all I thought about. Yet I did think, "Oh! My God! What have I done?" the first time I drove out here. It was so far out in the country and I thought too isolated. It reminded me of that song, *Country Roads*. Then the housing association held a welcoming party for us and that changed everything. I decided to become more involved in the community and they now involve me. At the beginning some people were resentful. One man asked me why they hadn't given this house to one of their own. "I am one of your own," I told him.

On a cold March day in 1960 I went to Birmingham with my husband and three children. Through my tears I could hear the cows lowing and the curlew calling. I looked at ruts of newly ploughed fields, inhaled the sweet perfume of heather from the bog and said goodbye to the dogs. My toil-worn parents could hardly contain their grief. The parting cast a veil of doubt over every bone in my body. My life had been likened to a daisy chain; which was now being broken. From rural Ireland I found myself in a sooty city with people flitting around like headless chickens. The vast crowds seemed to swallow me up. I felt trapped. This enormous invasion of people was a terrible culture shock to someone from the wilds of the country. I peered at the sky, but somehow could not locate the moon. Back home I had so often gazed at that mysterious ball of light. I couldn't equate England to anything I had found familiar before. I couldn't equate the life of a man working in the fields, stopping every now and then for a puff from his pipe, to a situation where everyone was going mad. At first I somehow thought I could not stay away from the green fields of Ireland; from the paddocks decked with wild flowers; from the silence filled with the sweet music of the lark and the thrush, and the distant voice of the corncrake. That's all my sons had been used to too – solitary fields and fresh air. The only car they had ever seen was the one outside our front door in Gowla, and the nearest house was down at the end of our boreen. On the coach from the airport in Birminghan the boys were fascinated with all the cars on the street and kept calling out, as each one passed by. The other passengers must have thought we were very primitive.

My sister and brother-in-law met us at the airport and they had found a house for us to rent on the same street as them, Springfield Road, which was about five miles outside the city, in the suburbs slightly. That too was dull, but it was a home. My husband bought some second hand furniture and a few bits and pieces and that's all we had. There were lots of Irish in the area. The first day we moved in an Irish neighbour called to offer us help and I'm still friends with her to this day. That's the only thing that kept me going over there, the wonderful friends and neighbours I had, and my boys, of course.

It was not the life I had planned. I had never wanted to leave Ireland and could have done so long before that if it was what I had wanted. But, my husband had let the land go and eventually he sold it. There was nothing for us here. He actually wanted to go to Australia on that ten pound incentive, but I refused because by then I knew that he would probably leave one day and I didn't want to be stuck in Australia all by myself. I reluctantly agreed to England. At first he struggled to get work on the buildings, and he eventually succeeded. If he'd worked on the land half as much, we wouldn't have had any need to go. He started off as a night watchman and quickly moved up to foreman. I couldn't work at all because of the three children and another one on the way. Then my husband saw the city lights and began to ramble. I let it go for a long time until one day I found the courage to stand up to him. I asked him to leave, and he did. When he packed his bags that night, it was the first time he had ever done anything I had asked him. When he walked out and left me with a sick baby in my arms, I broke down.

In order to make a living I got registered as a childminder and kept a lodger or two. I'd love to have come back to Ireland then, but there was no way for me. I had no money, no means, no way at all. My husband eventually divorced me and married again. I didn't go outside the door for fourteen years, but my friends lifted me along. One would bring the tea; the other the biscuits and they'd keep me company. When the boys were grown up a friend brought me to the Irish Centre in Deritend. She was married, but her husband worked away and only came home every fortnight. It was great to get out, to relieve the tension, to enjoy a bit of dancing, but of course, we always fled home before the last dance. I met lots of men who wanted to have a relationship with me. I was still only in my forties, or fifties, and I was still fresh looking, but I told them the truth. I had four children at home, four men in my life and whilst I wouldn't have minded some male company I wasn't interested in getting married again and washing another man's socks. I'd had a bad doing the first time around. Anyhow I didn't want anyone to interfere with my life with the boys. They are wonderful sons. Two of them now live back in Ahascaragh. They always loved Ireland growing up; they loved the freedom of the fields and wanted to raise their own families here.

My parents were bitterly disappointed with how things turned out for me. My father was very upset that a man would treat a woman the way I was treated. I came from such a loving home. When I was nine years old my parents decided to exchange our small farm for a Land Commission holding a few miles away. The Government built us a large house and there were about 60/70 acres of land to go with it. This was most exciting considering we left a small thatched cottage with only a kitchen and two bedrooms. My grandmother also lived with us. The new house had three large bedrooms, a parlour, a large kitchen, scullery and a little dairy. I thought we'd hit the jackpot and had become middle-class. I soon learned to love this home in the middle of nowhere. To me the sky was blue even if it snowed, the birds sang sweetly and the sun shone every day. I felt that God picked my parents from all other beings to be our guardians. We were never slapped or anything; they loved all six of us until they died. We all emigrated except my brother who got the land, even though my father didn't want any of us to go. We weren't the poorest growing up, put it like that, but I went to the poorest when I married.

My mother had spent twelve years in America, in Boston I think. I am not sure

Bridie with Dad and brother, Eugene

what year she went, but it was before the Titanic sank. It was a three week journey by boat then, but she had no fear. She never came home in all that time and had four sisters there too. Her older sister paid for her passage and she paid for the next one. She was probably a maid first and then she graduated upstairs to lady-in-waiting. She'd have to go to the seaside with her mistress, Mrs. Strauss, a German Jew, and rub cream on her back. They kept in touch for years, and when we were growing up she would send us lovely parcels. Mother didn't like coming back to Ireland, as she was engaged and all over there, but her two sisters had died from tuberculosis and her brother here who was for the land also died and she had to come back and look after it and her aged mother. She had made some money and was able to stock up the farm. Then a friend introduced her to my father. She was so lucky to meet a man like him, so lucky because he treated her with love and kindness. She was a petite hard-working woman who made us a currant cake every day. He was a great worker too, never went to the pub, we never saw him drunk, not like the others. There was a lot of drink that time and a lot of women married in order to have a house, a home of their own, and a roof over their heads. A lot of women compromised just to get married; there was no other way. It wasn't for love; there was no such thing as romance. Then men didn't want you to be educated. You'd nearly have been better off stupid.

But, my father was such a gentle soul. Even my daughter-in-law who grew up near us said they used fight over him as kids. They all wanted him to be their Grand-dad. He loved children. He loved life. He loved the world he was given by God. He loved his

Growing up in Gowla

mother who he looked after before his marriage. He loved nature and he died of a heart attack when he was eighty-six, which was lovely. He had been out earlier chugging along in his ass and cart. He was so kind, unlike the neighbour's fathers who were all pretty gruff. We'd hear them shouting and hitting their children with the belt. My father wouldn't touch us. Three of us made our Confirmation on the same day and he cried when he saw us in the Church together. Later he remarked on the innocence of it all and spoke of our lovely faces. "None were nicer than my own fachines! (faces.)" Meaning us like. He always thought his own children were the nicest. Sure when I'd be going out to a dance, I'd ask him how I looked, if my dress was alright. He'd say you look lovely; some fellow will fall for you tonight. He'd ask me the next day if I'd met anyone nice and I'd tell him. He's in Heaven if anyone is. He never raised his voice to my mother, never let her lift anything heavy, and would always say, "I have the best wife in the world." I was so looking forward to that in my marriage, but it was the complete opposite.

I met my husband at a house party. He was very handsome. If he wasn't I might have done better, he might have stayed at home, but he could always get the women. I could always get the fellows myself and waited quite a while before I got married. So I certainly didn't rush into it. Look, I was all over Ireland working. I was always game for new adventures. I worked in shops and offices and that kept me going. We didn't get too much money then. Five pounds was the biggest money I ever got. And I went dancing. There were dances in Mountbellew, Caltra, and Ahascaragh; there were the carnivals in Ballygar, and there were the Maypole dances. A fellow on a melodeon would be playing and we'd all gather to dance, with ribbons in our hair. I had loads and loads of boyfriends, but I only fell for one, so I do know there is such a thing as love. I once loved a lad and I know he felt the same about me, but we couldn't get married because we had nothing. We had no money. He moved to Oslo in Norway to teach English. He married an English girl afterwards, had a couple of kids and died suddenly six or seven years ago. He was lovely and gentle, a gentleman like my father. The one I was looking for.

I did have an idea that my husband was unsuitable, but we got married nevertheless. We had the reception in the Hodson Bay Hotel in Athlone and I paid for it all because I had a job in Gowla bog as a wages clerk where I had three hundred men to pay. That was all done by hand, without a calculator or a computer or anything. I got back to it until I had my first child even though it wasn't usual for married women to work at the time. That gave me the opportunity to stock up the land, but my husband sold it behind my back without saying a word. Then another child came along, and another and he never got any better so we had to pack up and go to England. But, I have four smashing boys, I agree with all their wives and I love the grandchildren. I wouldn't have had any of that without him.

Two of my sons live side by side in Ahascaragh, and I suppose that has helped me a lot in coming home. As much as I wanted to come back to Ireland I don't know if I could have left them all behind in

Birmingham. They come here to visit me all the time. They were delighted to have me home; they couldn't do enough for me, putting up curtains and doing my garden. I have a beautiful garden, front and back. I like my flowers and that and I like to keep the house nice too. I go back to England all the time to see my other two sons and my grandchildren. In fact I'm going in a few weeks time for a First Holy Communion. I have fifteen grandchildren and they're all smashing kids. Two years ago the family treated me to a holiday in Spain for my 80th birthday, which was on May 26th, 2005. Up to that the only countries I had ever been to were Ireland and England. I have an album here with all the photographs under each of which I have written a special caption. It was wonderful. Three of the boys married English girls; the fourth married a girl who lived over the road from my parents. They've known each other all of their lives, from the time they were kids when we would be home on holidays.

I got over the hard feelings I had for my husband when I started to pray for him. I realized he had less than I had; I had the children and was surrounded by so much love. He had nothing. Perhaps he had money, but I got the better part. I had no choice, but I would have chosen the family anyhow. He was a bitter man and I wasn't bitter. Praying for him gave me an awful lot of comfort. That's how my religion took care of me. I know the clergy double-crossed a lot of people long ago and that turned a lot of them against Catholicism. They would declare on the altar how much people had put in the plate. I saw the priests separate couples after dances; they had a very narrow-minded view of sex. We were all virgins until we were married, even the men, that was a given. But, I know that many young girls were raped and nothing was ever said about it.

I liked Birmingham in the end to the point where I knew it, and I got my head around the chaos that I saw when I first arrived. And the friends I had were very faithful. I still hear from them and they all head this direction when they come back to Ireland. They all go back with photographs. Not everyone in England wants to come home. My sister hasn't even visited here since my mother died thirty odd years ago. Not me, I even hated going back after holidays. I would save loose change in a tin and head home whenever I could. The arrival was always overwhelming; the emotion, the hugging, the tears and the stay itself always memorable. The boys would explore the woods, the streams, the fields, and experience the freedom they had not known. Then it would be time for the heartbreaking departure all over again with promises to write, which I did regularly. I would send pictures

Bridie (second left) celebrating 70th birthday

too and describe every detail of my life except for the fact that money was scarce. I hated going back to the soot. My friends were the only thing that saved me. When the boys left I was lonely again. I'd never been lonely when they were with me. We were still in the same house on Springfield Road and after twenty-six years there, I got a flat in Mosley, where I stayed for a further sixteen years until I came home. I had quite a good time there and I do miss the shops and the car boot sales and flitting around. There was much more activity.

But, here in Clonberne, five years on, I can visit my sons and my brother, and people come to visit me all the time. I tend my garden most days in the summer. I drive a car and I go somewhere every day, which also means a lot. If I didn't drive and if I didn't have family here, I would probably be lonelier. I've joined the ICA and am the Chairperson of the local branch. I do apostolic work. I do needlework. I should be at Adoration this evening, but my shift is over now. I was professed into the Third Order of St. Francis last year. The main thing I'd say to people wanting to come home to Ireland is that you have to get involved in the community you are moving to; it's not really like coming home at all, it's like going to a completely different place altogether. If you are outgoing you will survive; other than that you can stare at the same four walls in Ireland just like you did in England. I would also say come back and have a good look around at what's happening here. Some people have a false sense of the past. Ireland is a lot different to what it used to be and living in Ireland is quite different to living in England. The main changes are the attitudes of the people. They're not like the old folk that used go rambling to other houses. When I was young I could walk into the neighbour's house and if they weren't there and there was a griddle cake on the range I could take a chunk out of it and leave. When they'd return and see the lump gone out of the bread, they'd laugh and say, "Bridie must have been here." I don't

My garden in Clonberne

think I could do that now. I find that their principles are not as good. We were very religious back then and I still am. I know it was over-done sometimes, but it was still better than it is now. We were told not to curse; not to tell a lie; it's not like that now. I kept up the religion all through my years in England; my children are all baptized, as are my grandchildren. Yes, it is different here now so don't come into the bleak not knowing where you're going.

My teacher in Castlefrench primary school had always told me I was stupid. She told that to a lot of the pupils, but she set on me in particu-lar, calling me an ass, putting me at the bottom of the class. In Kilglass, where I went next, they weren't like that. I improved no end there and was tops at maths. Only one teacher brought me down and I had an inferiority complex all my life because of it. Imagine then the surprise I got when I won a competition with my poem about the view from the window of my flat in Mosley. It was published in the housing associa-tion magazine. Another one I wrote for my grandson about a wicked witch was displayed in their local bank. He was so proud of me. I wrote another one about the bingo on Bradford Street where we used to go every Thursday, our big night out. I write all the time now and it is great company for me. I have a whole folder here of all of my poems.

Now I'd love to write a book. No, not the story of my life, but for women on how to beware of a bad husband. I'd tell them that if you catch him out on one lie, get away. I'd tell them to beware of selfish-ness; to watch out if he always says 'I' instead of 'we'. I'd warn women to beware of men who don't buy presents. I'd warn them about the con man and the type who is always late for a date. I would advise women to be careful when choosing the man they were going to marry. Then maybe I will write the story of my life.

From an interview at her home in Clonberne, County Galway, on Thursday, May 17ᵗʰ, 2007, and beautifully written accounts by Bridie herself

TOM REARDON

I was born in the Coombe Hospital and grew up in Dublin down by Whitefriar Street Church and *Jacob's* biscuit factory. We lived on Kevin Street across the road from St. Patrick's Protestant Church. It's all changed now, you know. That's why when I had the opportunity to come home to Ireland, I chose Mayo. I've been here since August 2002 after forty-three years in England, and it's the best thing that's ever happened to me.

There are too many changes in Dublin and too many memories there for me. I had a bad experience really when I was a child. My father deserted my mother, you see, and he went to England. What happened was then my mother reared us by herself. There were two of us then, me and my brother. The authorities caught up with my Dad after twelve months and brought him back. That time it was a crime to desert your family. He told the Judge that he had a place for us in England, but my mother wouldn't come. He said she was tied to her mother's apron strings. He told a pack of lies and got off Scotch free. The old Judge told her the children will be put into care if she didn't go with him, so she had no choice. We all had to go back to Birmingham. I was eleven years old then and my brother was nine. We were there a very short time when a knock came to the door. This woman asked my mother, "Are you his wife?" My mother said yes. "Well I have three children by him," the stranger said. My mother came straight back home to Ireland after that and never told anyone. She was pregnant with my younger sister who was born in Dublin shortly after our return. She told the story to this sister just before she died in 1992. I only found out lately because I had lost contact with all of my family since around 1978.

The other woman's two sons were brought to Australia. I was told that's what they done then. The authorities took them in because she wasn't married to my father. They gave them different names so that they could never trace their past. They were put into Christian Brothers' schools on the opposite ends of the continent; one was in Brisbane, the other in Perth, and I must say they got a good education. They were lucky. They found each other eventually and were united. The mother had gone her own way. Their sister had been put into care until she was eighteen and she went her way. No one ever heard from her since. It's a sad story then. One of the boys was with *Quantas* airways and the other one joined the Army. He become a Colonel and when he came out he retired and started looking things up. Then he found us. They paid all their own expenses to come and see my sister and brother in Dublin who told them that they didn't know what had become of me. Shortly afterwards one of them rang my sister and said "Your brother is living in County Mayo."

How did I make my way from inner city Dublin to outer Mayo? How did that happen? Well we come back to Dublin that time from Birmingham; back to the same place, back to the same tenement building where we were living in one room; where my sister was eventually born. I had gone to school to the Christian Brothers in Francis Street, which was great at first, but when we went to England and came back it never seemed the same for some reason. I don't know why. It wasn't as good the second time around. I don't know what happened there. I left school at sixteen and I got a job in a factory across the road called *Held*. It was a German run sheet metal gaff. They made baths and bins and buckets, you know all that? I just carried on. I was young then, I'd only left school, and they were training me and that, but I never liked it so eventually I left. My Mam had a sister married in Birmingham and she said why don't you come over for a year and we'll see how we get on? I went in 1951 and met a man there who wanted me to sign up for the Navy for twenty-one years; that was when conscription was in. I filled in the forms and everything and I came back on holidays and when my mother saw the forms, she tore them up. She said you're not going back to England. So I got another job in Dublin, this time in *Hammond Lane Foundry* taking up the tram tracks. The trams went all the way out as far as Dun Laoghaire and Dalkey. That was the countryside then. Blackrock, DunLaoghaire, Seapoint, they were all little villages then. The tracks were all taken up during the year 1954. I believe they had to put them back again for the *Luas*. They were used to build the hay sheds in the country. We used to cut them a certain length with burners, and then load them on the lorries to be taken away as girders for the hay sheds.

The social life in Dublin was alright like you know. On a Sunday night we used to have a drink. The pubs closed then on a Sunday night from five o'clock until seven I think and then we'd go to a dance. I used to know a lad, he was a butcher, he had his own shop and he used to come into town and I'd meet him then for a drink in *Mooney's* on Bachelors Walk. There used to be an old bookshop right on the corner and on the other side of the road there was the *Corinthian* cinema. There was another branch of *Mooney's* on Abbey Street facing *Wynne's Hotel*. I drank in *Mulligan's* a few times at the back of *The Theatre Royal* where all of the staff of *The Irish Press* used to go. It had the best name for a pint of Guinness.

Eventually I left Hammond Lane and went back to England then in 1959 for good. I was twenty-five years of age and I headed off to Wales first where I stopped for a while. I really liked it there and if I'd found a job I liked I probably would have stayed. Maybe it was in my blood, as that's where my father's people came from. Then I headed on to London. I was on my own and I had nobody there to stay with, but I just got a room and it went from there like you know. I was in one job after the other and then I got a Heavy Goods Licence and it wasn't hard to get a job then. One day this lad told me about a really good job in *The Book Centre*. That was in 1971 and as far as I'm concerned my life changed then and I never looked back. *The Book Centre* was a great place. All the publishers used to send their books to be distributed there, *Houghton & Staunton*; *Penguin*, *Joseph's*, all them people, you know. All of the books that were printed and ready to go out went into *The Book Centre* and we delivered them. Then in 1980 that closed up. If you were in the Print Union you went into Fleet Street, but you only got three or four nights a week. You weren't taken on permanent like. So I stayed there for another eight year and what happened then was, I went with NCR, the *National Cash Register* crowd, and that was where I finished up like. I was taken off the road and put on the loading bank, which was the best job ever. I wished I had been in it from the time I first went to England. It was one of these jobs where if you were sick you got paid, you got holidays, there was a canteen. It was a job for life really and there was a lovely atmosphere. It was like a family really. There were a few Irish in it, but I never had any problems being an Irish man in London. I just got on with it. I never thought about it really. But if it wasn't for *The Book Centre* I never would have ended up in NCR, so that's why I think it changed my luck because it was the first job I ever liked. I just knew it was for me. And that was my life as far as work is concerned.

I came home the odd time on holidays. I was away about thirty years without coming at all. Around 1978 I lost touch with my family and that was it. We just had a bit of a disagreement and the longer it went, it kept going, and that was it. I never made contact with my father again after leaving him in Birmingham that time. He worked all over Wales as a steel erector and his settling point was Llanelli. It's funny that he ended up there, as that is where his people were from. Someone got in touch with my mother to say that he died. I was on terms with her then and she rang me and said will you pick me up in Euston Station? I did and I drove her down to Wales and she brought the body home. There was the only one thing he wanted. It was in his Will like. His mother was buried in Glasnevin and he wanted to be buried with her. So my mother brought him back home to Dublin and buried him there. When we got to Wales they told us that he'd had a woman for many years and she had died a couple of months earlier. That knocked the stuffing out of him altogether, they said.

I lived in a couple of places in England. Then I found John's place in Inacre Road. He was an Irish man like you know from Kerry and he rented me a room and I was there for most of the time and I liked that. I had a social life. We used to go into the Galty sometimes, *The Galtymore* ballroom, a great place on a Saturday night. It was wonderful. I'm not into music that much. I can take it or leave it, but early on I used to live across the road from the Galty and Big Tom used to be there on a Saturday night, and he'd draw a great crowd. The Irish girls mustn't have liked me and I never really met a nice girl I'd like to marry. It was just one of those things. Either I didn't like them or they didn't like me, but I just got on with it. Nothing like that ever got through to me, I don't know why. But, I don't regret it. I definitely don't regret it. A couple of blokes told me on a couple of occasions, you know that girl thinks an awful lot of you, you should go and ask her out or something like that, but I never bothered. It never worked out for me. In later years I drank in *The North London Tavern*; it's very well known. The North London we used to call it. It was an Irish pub, the North London like you know. I become very friendly with the landlord and the landlady. They were a lovely couple and then one day she told me they were retiring and going back to Galway. New people took over and I never went back in. Well I'd stopped drinking; I'd stopped going into pubs. I haven't been in a pub in over twenty years; I stopped doing all that. I just thought they were boring so I lost a lot of friends after I stopped drinking. I still had Alan though who brought me out on a Wednesday afternoon to do the shopping, and I had Larry from Leitrim who bought a house in Sligo and his wife wouldn't go back with him. She wouldn't have it, not a bit of it. But, I've lost touch with all them now.

Then I had Evelyn who was a buyer with NCR so we worked a lot together because I was on deliveries and we became very friendly. It's really because of her that I'm back in Ireland. When I got a heart attack and that sort of thing I couldn't work, and she'd take me out for lunch and that and out for Christmas. One Christmas Day after dinner she said to me, "Have you ever thought of going home, Tom?" And I said I'd love to and that was it. She told her sister that worked for the Irish Centre in London who got me the application for Safe Home and I went from there. I'd had a heart attack at sixty and I never really worked after that. I was living in Willesden, which used to be a lovely area, but it had started to come down and down. There was so much crime. You see I got mugged six times. Well, twice really, and then I was confronted and told to hand over my money four times. I become very vulnerable. I was an easy target. I'm not as fit as I used to be and I had a stick when I had the heart attack, so I felt I was an easy target. The first time was bad enough, but then when it was repeated I became vulnerable and I stopped going out altogether. It was the state that I'd got into. It just got to me. Mugging is a terrible thing. I was getting letters from this local authority. They wanted to visit me, you know, and I didn't answer them. All I wanted to do was come home. When they asked me in the Irish Centre, where would you like to go in Ireland? I said, well I wouldn't go North, and I wouldn't go South and I wouldn't go East; I'll go West. All of the people that I got on with in London were from the West. Most of them were from Galway. I don't know why I said it. I just did. I always liked people from the West of Ireland and I like them even more so now.

Coming home is the best thing that ever happened to me. I couldn't get back quick enough, as I never thought I would, you know. It's uncanny that I ended up in Newport because that was the name of a little town I stayed in when I first went to Wales. Life in this Newport is great, its lovely. Nobody has ever said an unkind word to me. It's so quiet and peaceful after all the noise, noise, noise, in London. Mind you, when I first got back anything that could go wrong, did go wrong. I thought it was never going to end. They all thought in Safe Home that I'd never settle in, that's right. It did take a couple of months alright. Then one of them Australia blokes rang me sister and said, you'd better sit down, we found your brother here in Ireland; he's in County Mayo. She couldn't believe it. She thought I was really for London. She came knocking on that door and that was it. I was delighted. She's on the phone nearly every day now.

Signing my life away

My two Australian half-brothers came back on a second visit and they knocked on that door too. They were fine looking men, over six foot tall, and still so interested in their Irish heritage. Interestingly enough our father's family had all emigrated to Australia in the Thirties, so they probably have lots of cousins there too. If it wasn't for them, however, I'd never have been reunited with my sister. I went to visit her once and I spent a weekend at her home in County Meath. She's got it made in this beautiful place. She told me that my mother died in 1992 from Alzheimer's and she took me out to her grave. We drove around Dublin, but it was nothing like it was when I left. It's all changed like you know with so many new buildings and the atmosphere is completely different. She put me on the train that night and asked me when will we see you again. I said, never, I'll never go to Dublin again.

When I think of the city I grew up in. Although we lived in a tenement, down the road was residential in Harcourt Street and on Stephen's Green. It was all upper class. All the Irish girls from down the country used to work in St. Vincent's Hospital on the Green and in all them beautiful Georgian houses four and five stories high and in the *Shelbourne Hotel* on the other side. I've never forgotten all that. I only lived down the road from Grafton Street, a big shopping street, and you couldn't move in it with all the shoppers. There was *Switzer's* and *Brown Thomas* department stores and of course *Woolworth's* was big in them days. They had a cinema there and *Bewley's* coffee house, although we were never in places like that. It was only for the wealthy. But, we did go to *The Gaiety Theatre* around the corner to see Maureen Potter and Jimmy O'Dea. Me mother used to bring us to the pantomime. The old people in Dublin were great for the theatre. My mother done everything. She scrubbed and she did part-time work and everything. She used to go and serve in the vegetable shop and she'd get all the vegetables free. Oh! She worked hard. The *St. Vincent DePaul Society* was very good to the poor people of Dublin. They handed out vouchers for food and my mother would give them to me to take down to *Pidgeon's* shop to get the groceries. I've never forgotten the *St. Vincent DePaul* for that. It was a great help. I've never eaten bread and jam since then because that was what I got going to bed at night. Go up to your Granny's and get your bread and jam before you go to bed. No wonder I've bad teeth. I remember me Granny well. She was the best person I ever met in my whole life. And I had two uncles who never got married and they used to look after me mother as well, so we never really missed out on not having a father. If we'd no soles on our shoes my uncles would repair them on a last, a steel contraption that he'd fit the shoe into and repair the sole. There was no such thing as getting new ones. We used to play football up the laneways in our bare feet and all that carry on and we'd get run by the policeman, Scarface. He used to be in plain clothes on a bicycle. And he'd have a hat and he never smiled in his life. I'd prefer to have the memories really than go back and see how it is now.

So here I am in my little grey home in the West. I enjoy a bottle of *Newcastle Brown Ale* every now and then. I always have that from the off-licence in Westport. It nearly broke my heart at first when I couldn't get it. I watch the sport on *Sky* television, but not as much as I used to. I used to like the football but I stopped watching it. I always followed whoever had the most Irish players like Arsenal back in the Sixties and Seventies when they had eight Irish players. I watch the snooker sometimes, but I take it or leave it. I don't watch television if I can help it. I switch it off and go upstairs and have a read. I get all the papers. If you buy them on a Saturday or Sunday you have enough reading for the week. The nationals I mean, not the tabloids. If you buy the *Irish Times* on a Saturday and *The Sunday Independent* on a Sunday there's an awful lot of reading in that. I don't go to the pub as I said; not even in Ireland. I just walked away from it all years ago and I'm happy with that. I don't like going into restaurants or cafes either. I don't know why; that's the way I've become. Some people might say I'm a recluse, or a hermit, but I wouldn't change it. I prefer it. I never thought I'd end up like this, but I've thrown in the towel, I suppose.

It's hard to get through to some people that I prefer being on my own. My sister comes down and she says, who's this and who's that. All my neighbours are wonderful people I tell her, and so they are. They seem to have more intelligence in that they seem to know when you don't want to be involved like. In London and in Dublin they'd keep asking you to join them and they'd say Oh! Snap out of it, if you wanted to be on your own. There was all that carry on. You know what I mean like? So coming back to Mayo suited me because I found a place where I could be by myself. Coming home is not for everybody. There was a woman just a few doors away from me in London and her husband died and I said to her I suppose you'll be going back now, and she said what would bring me back there? As if I'd said something out of the ordinary you know. Looking back when I think about it I was glad I went away although I didn't have that good a time of it. If I'd had a job I liked in Dublin I'd never have left. It was just desperation really. I didn't want to hang about. I made the best of it in London for a long time; I always got on with it, but then I withdrew. I stopped drinking. I didn't go out to the pub. I thought it was depressing and I said, this is not for me. I became vulnerable as I got older and I felt I'd be safer back in Ireland. If you put a gun to my head now I wouldn't go back to London, not even on a holiday. I even have a job going into Westport and I'll never go back to Dublin. But, then again, never say never, I suppose.

Interviewed at his home in Newport, County Mayo, on Tuesday, August 14th, 2007

MAUREEN GERAGHTY

My father grew up on the North Strand in Dublin so it is apt that I am back in the county of his birth. While driving over the Knocknarea Mountains one day he saw the whole strip of Sligo, and swore if he ever settled down outside Dublin this would be the place. He could see the lakes and the Ox Mountains, Sligo Bay, and Ben Bulben. He met my mother in Donegal where she was a jubilee nurse and fulfilled his wish by settling in Strandhill where I was born on February 10, 1939. Daddy always said that he found me on the doorstep after I'd been blown in by a gale and I believed him for a long time. He was a Creamery Engineer for the West coast of Ireland and he also had a cold storage business. When the war came you couldn't get petrol so we had to move into Sligo town where I attended the Ursuline Convent.

We were there only a very short time when my mother got ill and took me to Belfast where her people came from. She had great faith in the Mater Hospital there where she had completed her nursing training and after undergoing a gastectomy operation, she died ten days later. It was December 17, a week before Christmas and I was only four years of age. I have fleeting memories of her, but I wouldn't know her now if she walked down the street. Her death created havoc in our home. My father was heartbroken, but luckily my aunt came down from Dublin to look after us. I know it was terrible that our mother was gone, but it wasn't as traumatic having Auntie May there because she just sort of filled in the place where my mother used to be. I wanted her and Daddy to get married and to have a baby, but they only laughed at me. They were still very Victorian back then. One day I asked the girl in the Red Cross, Rose Rigney, to get me a black baby that I would wash white. Little did I know I'd be taking care of the black babies for the best part of my life?

Daddy did eventually remarry a local woman who was home from America and some time later I was packed off to Dublin to a Convent in Cabra where I was a boarder, and where I lived with Auntie May in between times. After a while I became a day pupil and cycled every day from Fairview just to be with Auntie May. She was marvellous and like a second mother to me even though she wouldn't advise me and wouldn't be making any big decisions for me. Daddy always did that. He was a wonderful father and taught us everything through telling us stories. When we went away on holidays he would make us tell a story when we got back. My most vivid childhood memory is sitting around our supper table sharing stories. So I was thrilled to be living in his county and that of my ancestors. My grandfather had been an engineer in the Pigeon House at Ringsend and was the first man to turn the lights on in Dublin. My grandmother, living on a farm in Wicklow, had been given two lambs to rear with the understanding that when they were sold it would pay her passage to America. She made it as far as Dublin, met my grandfather and never left. Even before I had come to live here permanently, my brothers and I had spent all of our holidays here with Auntie May and her brother. When I finished

school I began my children's nursing training in St. Ultan's on Charleville Street. It's smashed to smithereens now, raised to the ground, as they say. Then I went to England to become an RN (Registered Nurse), because over here you had to pay a fee to study nursing and buy your own uniform, all on £3 a month. I said to my father, look I'll get £9 a month in England, free food and accommodation, and my uniform supplied. He was reluctant and would have preferred me to attend Jervis Street hospital in Dublin. In the end I just said, let me go Daddy, and he did.

With mother and brothers, Strandhill

302

I was only eighteen years of age and I had a lovely time in England. I trained in Lewisham in London and then I went to a holiday camp in Cornwall where I was the nurse on duty. I had a great time altogether, but came back home to the Coombe Hospital where I did my mid-wifery and where I met my husband, Michael. He was a medical student and somebody sent him over to me one day to get the tin opener and we started to chat. He had been in Galway University and knew a lot of my brother's friends who had been there so we got to know one another and I helped him with his exams. Then he went back to Galway to finish his final year and I did various jobs in Dublin. When his mother got cancer I went down to take care of her and we decided to get married. It was a very quiet wedding because my mother-in-law had died the month before. We got married in July 1963 in Sligo at the foot of Queen Maeve's grave. When we came out of Carraroe Church after the ceremony my husband turned to me and said, if we ever have a little girl, we'll call her Maeve, and we did.

We lived in Galway when Michael was doing his internship and then in Dublin when he went back to the Coombe where he got into Gynaecology and Obstetrics. He was only earning £45 a month. We had a little boy, Sean, and were staying with relatives so we just had to make a more decent living. In 1965 we decided to head for South Africa. Our fare was paid out there and Michael had a job and a flat waiting. It was very lonely at the beginning and I didn't like Durban at all. I didn't like the apartheid laws and all that sort of thing. I missed Ireland so much. I used to watch the boat go out every Friday and cry. Durban was a real holiday resort and *The Windsor Castle* used to dock close to where we were living. I used to sit on the window sill and cry when it would leave for England again. I used to wonder how anyone could come to South Africa on holiday because it was so lonely. Nobody prepares you for any of the protocol before you go out there. There's so much to be learnt. It's very bad manners for the locals to look up at their superiors, they must always look down. We must always be at eye level when we speak to them; its bad manners to hold your head up. They accept a gift with their two hands to show that they have no weapons. The reason the doors to their *kraals* (huts) are so small is to make visitors bend down and if you're an enemy, they have the chance to kill you. It was very hard to get used to; it's such a different culture. My husband was working all the time at the beginning. I couldn't work because I had a child and I was just heart-broken at first, but then I made friends and started to settle down.

A lot of Irish were recruited at the same time as were Welsh and Scottish. From that point of view we had a little click going. The Af-rikaans were not too friendly, and the Africans in Durban were not allowed to be friendly with us. We got to hear, through the priest, that they were anxious for doctors on the missions, so we headed for a Dominican mission, Montebello, outside a place called Pietersburg. We got a lovely house for very little money and our food was supplied, but it was right in the wilds, in the middle of nowhere. We used to go out in the jeep and have clinics on the side of the road. After our third child was born we moved around to another mission in a place called Harding in East Brickloland. Unfortunately my husband and one of my sons were asthmatic and a very heavy mist hung over the region. It was warm during the day and extremely cold at night. They couldn't bear it with the asthma; they were always getting attacks so we had to move then to a place called Apothella. We were very happy there because the mission was run by all Irish priests, the Franciscans from Merchant's Quay, and there were Irish Franciscan nuns there too so we made a lot of friends. We used to hold clinics and I would help deliver the babies. Michael handled the emergency cases. He would go out and pick up people at the side of the road. I couldn't do that much, as I had three small children, but I did assist him a small bit in the surgery where the locals would bring their sick children. It was a very interesting time.

We came back to Belfast in 1968 just before the Troubles started. We had enough money saved because we had very little expenses in South Africa, so we bought a house and a car and we were set up. I was also happy to be back in my mother's home place. The last time I had been to Belfast was before her death. Now I was back and the Troubles broke out. The foreman of a building site next door to me, a Northern Ireland Protestant, used to come in and have tea with me.

With Auntie May,
on Strandhill beach

One day he told me there was going to be trouble at the weekend; that I should leave and take the children down to Dublin. He assured me it would be all blown over by Monday. I was a long time waiting for that. We lost everything and had to go back to Africa again, where my husband decided this time to go into a rural practice on his own and treat the people as best he could. We used to get the medical supplies sent out to us, particularly from Germany, and we tried to give the best possible treatment in the circumstances. But, if you didn't charge the natives they didn't trust you. Their psychology was that the more you paid the witch doctor the better the medicine was. And although sometimes we wanted to let them off without paying, we found out that we couldn't. I saw a man throwing a bottle of antibiotics down the drain one time because he hadn't been charged for it. He said he was going to take his child to the witch doctor.

We did that for about ten years and then came home to Ireland again where we ended up in Tullamore. My husband couldn't take the national health here at all because all he was doing was writing sick notes, whereas he was used to doing his own operations, his own deliveries, and his own surgery. He was an all rounder. We were about two years there when the IRA came after him. The Price sisters were in prison at the time and they wanted to demonstrate a forced feeding outside the Church one Sunday after Mass, but they couldn't do it without a doctor present. They asked Michael if he would attend, and he refused. He couldn't take it any more and we went back to Africa again, this time to the Marianhill mission between Pietermaritzburg and Durban. At this stage it was like going from one home to another. We stayed there for a quite long time and had a lovely house, but it involved too much travelling to and from schools. The children couldn't go to the local school and we didn't want them to board, so we chose Durban where the Marist Brothers taught the boys and my little girl,

Maeve, went to a convent. Then my husband opened another black practice closer to the city, where he tried to do the same thing as before. He treated people without charging too much; only a pittance. That's why we had no money in the end.

We loved the life there though and always lived in South Africa or at its borders. Everywhere we went we got on great with the locals. When they know you're helping them they're very kind and protective of you. You could go to bed with the door open and they'd never come near you.

I had a good friend, Theodora, who worked with us for fifteen years. Now she was a nun who came out to get married and because she couldn't have children, her husband left her. When she came to us I thought the children would be frightened because she had no teeth, but they absolutely adored her. On the two occasions we came back to Ireland to try and settle, she went to her sister's farm. Both times we came back to Africa she landed at the door without notice. Bush telegraph we called it.

Maureen (left) & friend, Eileen, cycling through Sligo town

Africa was a charismatic place, but also very stricken. You were very close to evil there; it was lurking everywhere. When Theordora died she was replaced by a woman who was the wife of a witch doctor and she put a curse on us. We don't know why, but she obviously took a dislike to us and left suddenly one night. After that we had a string of girls working for us and they'd only stay a day and be gone. We couldn't understand it. One of them had fits when she went into our bedroom and said the *toglosh* was in there. Some of the natives live in perpetual fear of this evil fairy and even prop their beds up with bricks so that he cannot reach them. He's not so much the devil, but more mischievous like a leprechaun. The whole family had got sick except me and I mean seriously sick. We didn't know what was happening so I said to Michael one day maybe we should give the kitchen a good clean. We found all these clumps of muti (medicinal herbs) hanging in the cupboards in strategic places where they couldn't be seen. We burnt it in the garden and went to see Fr. Gregory who was renowned for converting witch doctors to Christianity. He said go down to the kraal where the woman lives and see was there any unusual symbols on the walls. We found lots of paintings of crucifixes and horse shoes upside down and we had to wash them off and have a Mass said to get rid of the curse. The local girls could see these omens and that's why they were too terrified to stay.

Living in Africa was a great upbringing for our children though because it brought them up to see humanity in all its forms. They were regular visitors to the clinics, the local orphanage and the hospital. When my little son was only two he had a terrier dog tied around his waist to protect him from the snakes. He would visit the children's wards and would ask the priest for sweets to bring them. We used to have birthday parties for the sick children with ice cream cake and sweets, things they normally wouldn't have, and then they would dance for us. AIDS hadn't come in yet or if it had it wasn't broadly known. A very good friend of mine who is a Nazareth sister works with AIDS children in Capetown now. She told me the children were so delighted last Christmas because they got new clothes and shoes and new uniforms for school. Can you imagine the children here being delighted with new sandals and new dresses from Santa Claus? These children were so happy they wouldn't even think of a toy. I found the culture shock coming back from there very hard because the children here have so much. I wanted to gather up all the toys and send them back to the children in Africa. My sons send money every month to the AIDS children and Brendan adopted a little six year old boy who is now attending University. They still give back to Africa even though we're no longer there. Maeve spent many years helping the street urchins who had left home because they were being abused. She collected donations of clothes and money and tried to get them into hostels. They were only youngsters who wandered the streets, homeless, and called each other nicknames like Helicopter and Petrol Tank instead of their Zulu names. They were all boys; the girls tended to stay at home or were kept in separate quarters. They often had babies at ten or eleven years of age and they'd leave them lying on the ground while they played skipping or hopscotch. They were only children themselves really.

One time we lived in the Franciscan mission at Lousiskisiki, where there was a famous witchdoctor called Kotoso who had twenty-three sons and twenty-four daughters. His favourite son was the last one by his last wife, Betinja, meaning Betty of the dog, and he was called Four O'Clock because he was born at that time. Kotoso also had a whole load of adopted children because he used to heal people who suffered from depression. He used shave their heads and have them out in the fields working as he believed hard work was the best cure. He was extremely wealthy and lived in a mansion. He drove a Cadillac which he paid for in silver coins. His father was supposed to have been Kruger's batman during the Boer War. Paul Kruger, President of the Transvaal for whom the largest game reserve in South Africa is named, Kruger National Park, buried a vast amount of gold and coins for safe keeping during the war. After he died in 1904, the story is that his batman went back and dug up all this treasure and became the richest man in South Africa. He then left it to his son, our Kosoto. We went to visit him one time when he was sick and we were brought into a room where he was lying on a bed, spitting into this big open fire. The table was set for a banquet and all twenty-eight wives came out and danced for us. I wasn't allowed in at first because I was bareheaded and wearing slacks. I had to borrow a nun's habit, complete with veil and later he told the doctor that a priest and a nun and their three children had been to see him!

He was renowned in that area; he would have been the king of the witch doctors. He was an old man with an evil look about him who used to perform murder rituals. The natives were terrified of him. A meteor

Geraghty family 1971

had fallen beside his house and dented the ground and it would suction anything that came within a certain radius. As a result the bottom of the hole was lined with cars and other articles and Brendan was always afraid it would suck him in too. He went back to visit when he was older because he wanted to see the big hole that had frightened him as a child. He was determined to face his fears. He went into the local police station for directions and the policeman said, "You're the golden haired boy we've been expecting." Kosoto was buried in the grounds of his palace in a glass topped coffin and his spirit had told them to expect Brendan; that he would be a good omen for them. They had a big celebration for him and took him out to see the hole which he said didn't look half as ominous as he had imagined.

My children did have an amazing African experience, but I think they missed out on a lot not being brought up in Ireland. They missed out on their family contacts and even though we brought them home a lot it wasn't the same. Michael loved it there, but he had to work very hard. We came home to try and settle, but he couldn't because he was used to doing everything himself. At my stage in life, you did what your husband wanted. If he wasn't happy, you weren't happy. People told me I should have put my foot down, because I wanted my children to be brought up in Ireland, but it didn't turn out like that. Then three days before his fiftieth birthday, Michael died. We had been home on holiday and I had gone back before him. He called me one day to say he was staying a little longer because he wanted to visit all the graves. I was surprised, but he said he might never be in Ireland again. He was only back three weeks when he died. He's buried in the

With goddaughter, Dudezela

priest's seminary in a place called Sedorra. At his funeral there wasn't enough room for all of the priests on the altar; some of them had to stand in the congregation. We were always very religious; you could never give up your religion after working with these holy people who lived all their lives on the missions. There was one priest and if we had a problem he'd say, "I'll have a chat with Mary on Wednesday." We thought he was praying to her statue or something, but no, he said Our Lady herself used to appear to him every Wednesday night at a certain time. They were so close to God and working with people who didn't understand them, whom they were trying desperately to understand. There was one priest who used take pens out of their pockets if they didn't put anything in the collection plate. They worked so hard. One of the nuns was a Trojan for work and a real dictator as well. Michael used to maintain if she had been married to Hitler, he'd have won the war! He had such a sense of humour; I missed him so much.

My father died the year before my husband, so I lost the two most important men in my life at the same time, which was very cruel. I was devastated, but stayed on in Africa for two more years after

Michael's death working in one of the hospitals. The children were in their late teens at this stage and two of them at University level. Sean stayed on, while Brendan, Maeve and I went to stay with a good friend in Bournemouth. I got a very good job as a Matron in a nearby girls' boarding school where Maeve was able to stay with me, while Brendan attended London University. After about a year I started working with the National Health and we got our own little flat that could accommodate us all, even Sean when he was home. We were very happy there and stayed for about ten years. During that time I held two jobs: in the hospital seven nights on and seven nights off; and in nursing homes on my nights off, which was quite lucrative, but there was a lot of travelling in the freezing cold and the wind and the rain. That was quite a culture shock after the sunshine of Africa, let me tell you. Then I got into bad health and had to retire in 1988.

Bournemouth is a beautiful part of England opposite the Isle of Wight and I met very nice people there. I did a course with Marriage Encounter for people who were divorced or widowed. It was more Christian really than Catholic and was for people who lost someone through death; it brought them together. There were a lot of women there, as I don't think men like to deal with their feelings. I was asked to join the team and I used do groups and go back for weekends so that helped me a lot to get over the death of my husband. I had a friend for about nine years there; we were only friends – it wasn't a romantic relationship. He was very ill towards the end and I didn't want to leave him, as I was very fond of him in my own way. When he died I decided to come back to Ireland. But, the real reason I came back was that Maeve was here. While we

Sean (left) & friend, Christopher going to school

were in Bournemouth she got a bursary from the British Medical Association to attend the University there. She got her degree and came back here to Ireland where she works for Streetline. She got married and had two children, but had no immediate family support. Brendan was by then married in England and his wife had her family there. Sean had gone back to England from South Africa where he had been a Barrister; now he's a Maritime Lawyer, and he didn't need me either so I felt my place was with Maeve in Dublin.

The only thing is I didn't know where to start because I had no money and no means of returning. Most of my income had gone into the children's education. They worked all through their holidays too; all through Christmases until we got on our feet again. We all worked hard and we worked as a team; as a family, but it was never enough. Then a friend of Maeve's was at a meeting and she met Pat Lane who is the Administrator of ALONE, an organization founded in 1977 by Dublin fireman, Willie Bermingham, to help those needing a home. They were just building these houses and this girl told Pat that her best friend's mother was dying to come back to Ireland. Next thing I had an invitation from him to come over for an interview. He paid my fare and everything. It was very nice, and I was interviewed by the Board and next thing I was awarded a flat. I was over in record time. Safe Home were a great help with the transition, giving me advice, helping me with pensions and their people came to see me and put me right filling in the forms and all sorts of things, which were alien to me at the time. They were magic.

My children wish we had stayed in Ireland and in a lot of ways maybe they're right because you lose track of family and you lose track of a lot of their milestones growing up. Although you keep in touch at birthdays and come home every few years you're still not there for the everyday things so you lose that special contact and you expect it to be similar when you come back, but it's not. They put on a big show for you when you come home on holidays and you expect it to be always like that, but its not and it takes a long time to knuckle in. Having Maeve and her children here helped me to slot in and I am glad to be able to help her with them. I had her little boy now yesterday and I'll have her daughter, Aisling, again tomorrow. It's quite a performance taking care of them so I have to have a day's break. Aisling loves coming here. She gets herself all packed up and picks out her clothes and every morning she wants to come over. But, I wouldn't be able for her every day. She needs my full attention when she's here, but I love her to bits. I miss my grandchildren in England though. I used to go over there every six weeks, but since I got sick I can't travel. I have all this pain now, but I'm going to see the specialist soon so hopefully he'll give me something and I'll soon be back to normal.

It's ironic that I've ended up here, as my father spent six months in Kilmainham gaol during the Irish War of Independence. It was the time British officers had been killed in their beds by the IRA, before Bloody Sunday in Croke Park. Daddy was involved with the old IRA at the time and all suspects were lifted by the Black and Tans and imprisoned. One day they had to march around a residential square where most of the officers had lived and the maids had to look out through the letterboxes and identify anyone they recognized from the night of the murders. The accused was taken out and executed on the spot. I used to have nightmares about that, about Daddy being shot. It's a very different Ireland now from what it was in 1920, even from what it was in 1965 when I left. There's good and bad in it. There are an aw-

With Mother Teresa, Nazareth House, 1989

ful lot of foreign people. You stop someone in the street now and ask them where somewhere is and they look at you. They don't know what you're talking about. I was home on holidays once and asked where *Woolworth's* was! It had been closed for years seemingly. The Irish people are basically the same though; they haven't changed a bit. My two brothers are both in Sligo. I haven't been able to go back to see them in a while, even though I have the free travel pass and everything. One of them comes up very regularly; the other one is tied up in business so I don't see him as often, but we're in contact all the time. Leaving Africa for England was more of a transition for me than moving back to Ireland. There were several times in the first few years when I threatened to go back. Coming home to Ireland was no bother at all. It definitely helps having family here. If all of my grandchildren were still in England, I don't think I'd be able to live this far away from them. And I will be very disappointed if I can no longer travel back and forth to see the ones that are still there.

With my good friend, Anne

It is also important to make new friends here, which can be hard at first. I've made a very good friend in Anne Kelly who lives two doors up from me. She was in England for a while too so we have a lot in common. She takes care of her father most days; he is ninety-six and she goes up to him every day. That suits us both fine because I'm not available during the day anyhow. If I'm not recovering from one of the children; I have one of them. But, the company is great. Another friend comes up from Sligo occasionally and we relive old times. I have great allegiance to that county because of Daddy's love for it and for the great memories I have of my early childhood there, before Mammy died. I still remember the house in Strandhill and our Sunday drives to Glencar where we would have afternoon tea for two and sixpence served by two old English ladies in their quaint little cottage. The great Irish poet, William Butler Yeats, loved it there too and I think that's where he wrote *To a child crying in the wind*. I remember his funeral in 1947 when we got a day off school to line the streets and wave at the cortege. My step-grandmother led the procession, as she was Mayoress of the town then. I hope I can get back there soon. In the meantime, I pray for another William every night - Willie Bermingham, who provided me with this home, and I am so grateful to him for that. Thank you, Willie.

Interviewed at her home in Kilmainham, Dublin, Wednesday, May 2nd, 2007

PATRICK GALLAGHER

I came home to Mayo in 2002 after spending over sixty years in Scotland and England and it is a joy to be looking out onto my beloved Clew Bay once again. I was born down the road on Achill, not far from the post office in Currane. My father was Thomas Gallagher and my mother was Catherine Gallagher; she didn't need to change her name when she got married. They used to have eight children, five boys and three girls, but the second son died when he was only a month old. My mother used to always say that he never cried, the baby. I attended Currane National School where Master Gallagher was my teacher. We were a poor family, and because there was no earning in Achill, I left home in 1940 when I was fifteen years of age. I went to Scotland to my sister, Mary, who was seven years older than me and she looked after me well. We went working as 'tatie-hokers' (potato pickers) and we lived in the Scottish bothys. To give you an example of what that was like, Anna Kenny wrote in the Irish Press in 1945 that, "life in Achill is no bed of roses, but life in the Scottish bothy is life without humanity."

In 1937, our neighbours, the two Kilbane brothers had been burnt to death in Kirkintilloch, Glasgow. Their bothy went on fire one night and as the windows were barred and the door locked with chains and padlocks, they couldn't get out. It is known as the 'Kirkintilloch disaster' or the 'Achill burning', as the ten lads that perished in that fire were all from Achill. There were three sets of brothers lost, the Mangans, Kilbanes and McLoughlins. You could hear the cries of the women all over the island and when their remains were brought home 6,000 people gathered at the North Wall in Dublin to meet them. The roads were lined with mourners all the way from Dublin to Achill and the grief at their funeral Mass at the Church of the Immaculate Conception was reported in the *Irish Independent* as being "too sacred to describe."

I'll sing you a song about it written by Roise Ni Mhaille (nee Gion-ntaigh), also from Currane:

Ar maidin Déardaoin imbothaí an Gramaidh igKirkintilloch,
sé d'ardaigh an gáir.
D'eirigh tine amach san oíche agus ar maidin, ní raibh fear le fáil.
Nar bocht an scéal ar fud oiléan Acla nuair a tháinig an nuacht
chucu anal go raibh deichniúr fir óga bruite dóite a bhí glaoch
ar cuidiú nár tháinig in am.

(On a Thursday morning in Graham's bothy in Kirkintilloch – the alarm was raised. A fire broke out in the night, and in the morning there wasn't a man left. What a sorry story around Achill Island when the news came back that ten young working men, who had been calling for help that didn't come in time, were burned to death.)

It was a terrible tragedy and one that the people of Achill will never forget. In fact the 70th Anniversary of the fire will be honoured next month both in Ireland and Scotland. There had been another accident in 1894 when thirty-two workers on their way to Scotland were drowned when the hooker they were sailing on from Achill to Westport capsized. Their bodies were brought back on the first West-port-Achill train fulfilling part of a 17th Century prophecy by Brian Rua UíCearabháin from Erris who had described "Carriages on iron wheels, blowing smoke and fire, which on their first and last journeys would carry corpses." In September 1937 the last train to Achill carried the corpses from Kirkintilloch. Nonetheless, we still had to earn a living back then and three years later I travelled to Scotland with Katie Cattigan, the sister of one of the victim's, Thomas Cattigan. We visited the site of the disaster not long after our arrival and Katie nearly lost her reason when she saw where her brother had been burnt. She was the life and soul of the squad until you mentioned the fire.

At that time, the Free State was regarded as an alien country in England and we were regarded as aliens. You know we even had to have passports. Germany had taken over France, but was being attacked by Russia, and Britain was threatened with invasion. We were allowed into Britain on certain conditions and we were directed into certain employment. For instance, those from the land in Ireland were directed into working on the land in Britain. We had to report to the police of the district in which we were working and furnish him with our photographs. We were hired on a three-month basis granted by the Chief Constable of the district, and we had to leave the country when we were requested to do so by the Secretary of State.

Before the War Britain was getting potatoes from Jersey and Guernsey, then they were desperate to get more because there was a lot of pressure on Britain at that time from the U boats. Thus they needed extra labour and we were brought into the bothys. Potato picking in Scotland that time was the nearest thing to slavery. The gaffers were the slave drivers and we'd be punished if we were not picking fast enough. Some of them assaulted the women, kicking them in the backside, and I got a kick straight across the back one day. We'd start at five o'clock in the morning and we would have seven tons of potatoes picked before seven. They were sold in the Glasgow market for sixpence a pound, that was some money, and we were getting something like £1.15 shillings a week. We would work in pairs, one digging, and one kneeling. You'd have to kneel on these potato bags that were sewn together, to pick the potatoes. After a shower of rain we would be drenched.

Some of the workers were right cheery though. They used to sing that Bing Crosby song, Pistol Packin' Mama, as we worked. It went: *Lay that pistol down Babe, Lay that pistol down; Pistol packing Mama, Lay that pistol down.* There was one verse, *Drinking beer in a cabaret, was I having fun, Until one night she caught me right, And now I'm on the run.* Our girls would sing: *Drinking beer with Paul & Weir and having lots of fun, Until one night we made them tight and now they're on the run.* They would be having a go at the agents, Paul & Weir, whom we worked for.

The bothys were really cow sheds that were whitewashed, with straws beds thrown on the floor. Straw would be packed into these bags, you see, and we'd sleep on them. We'd get two blankets from the merchants; that was all, and we'd double up. During the War then we were issued with ration books, you see, and we were allowed two ounces of butter, two ounces of bacon, four ounces of margarine, a shillings worth of butcher's meat, one pound of sugar, and two ounces of tea. There was plenty of bread and fish. The Scottish were very patriotic; they wouldn't take any more than they were rationed, so the grocers used give the surplus to the Irish. The butchers would give us extra meat and of course we had plenty of potatoes. We were in one place one time that was over-run with rats. We were sleeping on the floor, with rats jumping over the bed. The girls were on one end; the lads on the other. The girls wanted to be near the lads for safety's sake. The merchants didn't give a hoot. There were no toilet facilities, no such thing as flushed lavatories. It was marvellous how the girls coped in these conditions. It would amaze you. They would go one way to relieve themselves; the lads would go the other. It certainly was life without humanity.

When the day's work was over the girls would dress up and wash in cold water from an outside tap. There'd be a sing-song and dancing. Someone would play the melodeon and we were very cheery, sing-

ing and dancing. They were all great dancers. I made an awful mistake by not learning to dance. I missed out on a lot. I was a wall flower most of the time, even though the girls wanted to take me out dancing, but I was always two steps behind them, and of course I was tired too after all the work. The Donegal ones especially were great musicians. They were very cheery.

I didn't drink until I was nineteen years of age. When I retired in the evenings I had too much time so of course the first thing I'd do is take a drink. Scotland was an awful place for drink. It was a magical place for young men who wanted to be

Patrick (left) & brother Tom, Regent's Park, London. 1955

drinking whiskey, but you could become an alcoholic very easily. In fact, the idea that time was the more you drank, the better you were. But, I always remembered my father's advice. He warned me and my three brothers, Lord Have Mercy on them all since, not to drink and to be very, very careful; that if we saw a row brewing we should leave the company even if it meant calling a drink for them before we left.

The first year we were called greesheens – greenhorns. The only time we went into the town was to get our hair cut and to go to Mass. We'd look forward to going to Mass on Sundays because we were working fifty-one hours a week – nine hours a day and six on a Saturday. When it would rain there was no pay. I was always looking forward to November to when we'd be going home. I did that for eight years back and forth; that was my life without humanity.

My sister, Mary, Ladybank, Scotland

When I was older I'd be asked to stay for the winter. This is when we'd put the potatoes in pits about five hundred yards long. This was the seed, you see. The seed potatoes only were sent to England. The English farmers were relying on the Scottish seeds – they were the best. They were top quality, you see, and sold to the farmers in Lincoln for £44 a ton. The big potatoes were sent to the greengrocers and the chip shops; there was no waste. The very small ones were scattered in the spring time for seed potatoes. The merchants didn't give two hoots about the squads, but were more concerned with profit. The main ones were W.A. Graham and Paul & Weir. The farmers provided the accommodation and the farmers in Ayrshire would shoot the Irish if they could; they hated them that much. We were classed the same as tinkers. I worked in Ayrshire, Perthshire, Darwinshire, and East Lothian, before I eventually went to England.

You weren't classed a man unless you went to England to dig the potatoes or make hay in piece work. We enjoyed it really as the English people were very, very nice. You'd only meet the very odd one that wasn't. The farm that I went to was between Preston and Lancashire. We were registered as agricultural workers and we could not leave the agricultural sector. Even when we came back to Ireland we travelled on agricultural passports. We always had to work at that even though there was more money working on the aerodromes in England. It was the Irish that won the war for England, you know. They built the aerodromes that the American bombers used. There was even a time in 1939, the year Hitler attacked Poland, when the boys were leaving England and coming to Ireland to avoid conscription –

In days of old as we were told, when the sky was full of lead,
Hitler went for Poland and Jock for Holyhead...

I started in England anyhow in 1944 and then in winter time I went to Scotland to go sorting out the potatoes. I knew the gaffers by then, and the old timers who knew the ropes would always be taken back. The haymaking in England was very hard work. We had to make hay when the weather was fine and you might have to work until twelve o'clock at night, but it was great money. You might get twenty pounds a month and that was a lot at that time. But, you worked hard for it, you see. We'd look forward to the rain for a break. There were two brothers that were working with us one time, and of course it was a fine morning to start off with until there came a right shower. One brother said to the other, *Ba mhaith an buntáiste an cith sín* (that shower was a great bonus), and the other one replied, *Cén mhaithais cith nuair nach dtiocfadh túile?* (What good is a shower when there wasn't a flood?)

I was brought up with Irish you know. The schoolmaster who taught us knocked hell out of us, but he was a great man for the Irish, Master Gallagher. He was a very comical man too and died when he was ninety-five sitting on the chair. He used always tell us to take notice of what was going on around us; not to rob bird's nests; to let the birds alone. They used to throw dead animals along the shore at

Currane long ago so that they'd be swept away with the tide. This lad was late for school one morning and the master said, "What kept you. Why are you late?" The lad replied that the clock was slow. "Throw it down on the shore then," said the Master, "along with the dead animals." He was very comical.

In 1951, then I settled in England for many years. I was working with London Transport from 1951 to 1953. I worked on all the stations from Wembley down to Windhover in Buckinghamshire. Some of the characters that were there were really comical. I worked with *British Rail* beyond and with *Wimpy's* on the building sites. I was a rolling stone, you see; I had an awful lot of jobs. I left London for a while in 1957 and went to Wales to work with *Wimpy* marking out a pipeline that was fifty-nine and a half miles long. After Wales I went back to London in 1960 and went working with *Taylor Woodrow's* on the first underground car park that was built in London. They didn't care about anyone. The ganger got killed on that job, a man from Galway. I was talking to him about half an hour before he died. He got hit on the head by an eight foot long and eight inch square piece of timber. It was a very sad case because his wife was blind and they had two children. The building sites were tough enough places. I knew another man that got killed on the job in 1961 the time Princess Margaret got married. We were next door to Westminster Abbey, and we saw her on her wedding day. Next, I went to Scunthorpe where I was working on a steelworks. Then I went from there onto the railway. There was eight of us travelling around the country. It was dangerous work, but it was a great advantage because every six weeks we'd get a travel voucher and I could go to see my sister, Mary, in Scotland. And of course there was no clocking on or clocking off. We used to finish at twelve o'clock on a Saturday and we'd get paid at four. Then of course we'd get the voucher and this was the perk that was keeping us there. I worked twelve years with them and I was hurted three times, but I got no compensation. That's the truth.

I stopped in digs all the time. Oh! God save us, I could write a book about digs. There was one landlady, the Lord save us; I can't eat pork after her! And I could eat anything that time because I was young.

But, when I think about it, she'd give us pork chops and they'd turn your stomach. They were never fried properly. She told us she buried two husbands and I said it was no wonder! I never got married. I could have several times, but I was afraid that I would not give the life to a wife that I'd like to. In other words, I thought I was not qualified to be a husband.

I was made redundant from *Wimpy* in November 1981 and there was no chance of getting any work in Nottingham where I was stopping at the time, so I went to my brother, Terry, in Scotland. He was Chairman of the Union and he was working for the Kilcoy District Council. (KDC) There was no work going at first, so I went on the dole. It was the awfullest sensation ever I had. I hated the dole because it was shocking, you know, standing in the queue in a country where one time you'd get some job, but there was no chance then. I did get a few weeks cleaning the streets. This man who was in the depot, who had lodged with Terry, told him that he would hire me for twelve weeks. I was fifty-eight that time and jumping the gun altogether. There was twelve of us who started that February and we had to sweep the grit from the streets. Sand and salt had turned to grit especially around the roundabouts. The second day I was sweeping; it was great to be working; the second in command said, "How would you like a job for life?" A job for life? Well, he said you can start tomorrow morning. You'll be looking after five skips, he says, where they're coming and they're throwing in their rubbish. There'll be people coming and searching through the skips and your job is to stop them, and if they don't, ring the police. At least you'll have police back up. He said you can have that job until you're pension age and after you have your pension as well. It's a lot better than the dole, he said, and I said, it sure is. Terry, who was on the bin run with the wagons, wouldn't believe me. He was the Chairman of the Union and he said there wasn't a job in the whole town. Not in Kilcoy, Kilcawley, or any place else. I said you're not with it. I asked him if he'd ever heard tell of the Dino Plant. That was where the people were out pitching tents beside the dump and recycle area and he said you won't get in there because there's a waiting list. I said there's five skips and they want me to watch them. He said you'll get kicked to death and I said I might. There's a crowd there that fights among themselves, he said, and they go through the skips and you'll be tortured. I said I don't care about the torture; I'll have the police backing me up. That's how desperate I was for a job. He said you'll be dead before you get the pension, but I didn't care. Now that was the toughest job ever I had. I had three police cars one night there and do you know I was threatened. The policeman said I was too blooming keen. They were dumping their furniture everywhere and trying to steal the machinery belonging to the KDC across the road from where I was. I was reminded of the story Master Gallagher used to tell us about the man who went to the priest and confessed that he stole a length of rope, but never mentioned the pig at the end of it!

Then I got hurted on the job. I went on the sick and was getting the full pay, so I went to live with Mary who was on her own, Lord Have Mercy on her. She was working at the potatoes as well one time. Then she went into a hotel, you know, in the kitchen. Oh! That was slavery. She said she used to go in first thing in the morning and the sink would be packed up high, choc-a-block with dishes and she'd have to wash every one of them by hand. In those days there was no washing machines or dishwashers, or whatever. But, she was always a great worker. When she packed up the job eventually, the chef packed up along with her! She had been married to a Scotsman, a painter on the railway, who died in 1981. I went to stay with her in Ladybank, Perthshire, fifteen miles from St. Andrew's in Fife. We were on the ground floor flat and had the toilet to ourselves. There was two young fellows upstairs with their unmarried mother, and they had two different fathers and they were the living devils. They made our lives a misery with all the noise. They even put glue in the Yale lock in the front door, and we couldn't figure out how to open it. It was terrifying. Mary lived in a Council house, and I wasn't supposed to be staying with her, so we had to get out somehow.

It was my sister, Catherine, who got us the house here in Mulranny. She died from cancer in 2001; I think it was the 17th of July. She was married in Currane, and had six of a family. She knew when this house became available and she asked Dr. Cowley could we come here, Mary and I. She told him the situation we were in. He said to bring us over straight away, we would get priority. I have a lot to thank Dr. Cowley for; I'd be dead but for him. He's a wonderful man and should be canonised. But for Dr. Cowley I'd be in my grave. He prescribed tablets for me, three different tablets, and I'm jumping out of my skin since I came here. Oh! Yes it was like coming home. Sure I was born and raised only a half mile up the road there. It's wonderful to be back again. I

My mother back in Currane

was interviewed on television one time and I told them everything I'm telling you now.

I'll tell you the changes in Ireland are wonderful for old people. It's a paradise for us. I never worked a day in Ireland for wages; therefore, I am not getting a full Irish pension because I had no stamps. I get the English pension from Newcastle though and I get paid once a month. I have the free travel here and I was on the *Luas* in Dublin one day and the young ones got up to give me their seats. I know a lot of people are against the pipeline here in Mayo, "Shell to Sea" they call it, but some of them are just too old for change. I'm in my 84th year and I went back to Lancashire for a holiday just to see the place again, you know. I visited the farm where I used to work and I went to see my brother, Terry in Scotland, and then came back again to the farm in Lancashire for the weekends, just the same as when I was working. I was glad to come home to Mulranny again, even though I'm on my own now since Mary died on the 26th September, 2005. She had cancer and then suffered a stroke, and to think that she was looking after me. There wasn't a lazy bone in her body. I miss her terrible.

I have the life of O'Reilly now. I can jump on a bus and go to Cork,

Dublin, and Galway, any time I want. My mother used to say throw your tail on your shoulder and off with you. That's what I'm doing now. I have my dinner over here in the nursing home every day. Oh! The nurses are wonderful. There's always something coming up. I read a lot. The book I'm reading now is *Farewell to Mayo,* by Sean O'Ciarain, about the Mayo people who went working with the Scots, like I did. Now when I look at the sun shining on Clew Bay, it is, it is Clew Bay I see ... *Brightly glancing, brightly glancing! See, oh see the ruddy beam Upon its waters dancing* ... That's a poem by Gerald Griffin about the River Shannon, but I recite it now about my beloved Clew Bay.

Interviewed at his home in Mulranny, County Mayo, on Tuesday, August 14th, 2007

Patrick (right) with John Michael McNulty, Doontrusk, at Oghilly Mass Rock, Nephin Mountains, Co. Mayo, June 8th, 2008 *(Courtesy Teresa Cowley)*

JOSEPH MULLARKEY

I came back to Ireland in February 2002, for the second time. The first time I was only five years old. I was born in Bolton in Lancashire in 1942 and after my mother died I came to live with an aunt and uncle in East Mayo. My three older siblings had already been to school in Ireland the two older ones had returned to Bolton by then. It was not uncommon in Ireland for children to be separated from their parents. Many Irish fathers lived away from their families for long periods of time while they worked on farms and building sites in England and Scotland. The poor post-war economy of the Forties and Fifties was the cause of this migration and the reason why I had to leave in 1959 when I was only seventeen years of age. The Ireland I returned to five years ago was a completely different country altogether.

I grew up on the Roscommon side of Ballyhaunis in County Mayo and attended school in the Franciscan monastery in Granlahan, which wasn't a very happy place. The monks were totally unsuited to teach young children and believed in corporal punishment, practising it daily for any minor misdemeanour. At ten years of age and unaware of the ban imposed by the Gaelic Athletics Association (GAA), I was punished for playing the foreign game of soccer. Most of the young boys in the area went to the monastery; they had no other choice. Everyone in the parish knew what was going on and you had the extraordinary situation where people sent their own children back to the same teachers, even though they had been brutalized themselves. Of course, there were some children they didn't touch – the sons of farmers and local professionals were usually left alone. Thinking they were better educated, the Brothers may have feared repercussions. My brother objected once to their treatment of me and the Head Monk didn't speak to me for six months. After I left there was a petition from concerned parents to have him removed, but interestingly enough there was a counter-petition set up to keep him there. Those who voted for him had no children of their own or feared ramification from the altar – such was the power of the Catholic Church.

I walked out one day after a severe beating. I packed my bag, said goodbye and walked out the door six months before I was due to finish school. Nobody ever asked where I was after that. My father was living in Bolton and my aunt and uncle were elderly so there was nobody to face down the monks. My father wanted me to continue my education in St. Mary's in Galway, but this was before 1966 when free secondary education was introduced into Ireland and we just couldn't afford to pay. It's not that I didn't want an education; I just couldn't bear the abuse. When I wrote an article for a school reunion ten years ago it was the first time I had thought about this event as an adult. I realized that the school manager was the Parish Priest who lived across the road and would have known right well what was going on. My name was still on the register and they were still getting paid for me so nobody ever knocked on my door and asked why I was not at school. I have since tried to get a copy of the register from the Department of Education through the Freedom of Information Act, but, surprisingly, it is no longer available.

I went working for small farmers in the area. If you were lucky you might get ten shillings a day spreading turf, making hay or digging potatoes. As I had no skills, the only thing to do was eventually go to England. The whole generation before us had gone – there was something like 50,000 people leaving the West of Ireland every year – a huge exodus. Indeed whole villages were decimated while local politicians, church leaders, local and national media acquiesced and turned a blind eye to this mass exportation of young people. Many were badly prepared for life in an urban environment without family support. I went to Bolton because I had a sister living there; all four of us eventually went back. I did have the chance to go to America where my mother's sisters in Boston would have sponsored me, but when I heard that joining the American Army was a condition of entry, I thought, no way. One of my school mates since died in Dá Nang during the Vietman War and is now buried in Ballyhaunis. That might have been my fate too. Instead I headed for England and like everyone else with me, I thought I would be home in two years.

My passion at the time was for Gaelic football and I had played football and hurling for Ballyhaunis, which I missed desperately at first. My last competitive game in Ireland had been for East Mayo seniors against West Mayo in Westport in 1961. The GAA was quite prominent in England, but it wasn't the same. I played for Shannon Rangers in Bolton, and there were clubs throughout Lancashire to which we travelled, playing in the Lancashire League and Championships. There was a great social life attached to the GAA, especially after a match. It was a saviour for many Irish people. Some of the clubs would meet people coming off the trains and they did tremendous work finding them accommodation and jobs; it was a great point of contact. In fact, I've just written an obituary for the first Irish fellow I met when I went to Bolton. He was the secretary of Shannon Rangers and I knew the pub where they used to meet, *The King's Head*, in Deansgate, so I went along and signed up for the team. The GAA brought a lot of people together in England.

I found work on a small farm on the outskirts of Bolton and had to take the first bus at six thirty each morning. I then moved onto a factory that manufactured film while I waited for a place in Bolton Corporation Transport. I had applied for a job as a bus conductor, but my intention was to enter their driving training school to obtain a PSV (Passenger Service Vehicles) driving licence, which I hoped might be the passport to coming home. Irish Tourism was gaining momentum and I thought I might get a job driving a coach here. I was trying to pick up some recognizable skill, as I still intended to come back to take care of my Dad and my aunt in their old age. Working on the buses was in many respects enjoyable, but it had one drawback in that we had to work alternate Sundays. Football was always played that day and trying to get the shift finished in time to get to the venue posed difficulties. On occasions I would pay somebody to work my shift and then I'd work theirs at a later date.

My life changed dramatically one night when I was travelling home late from work. I decided to take a short cut across a railway line and was hit by a passing train, losing both limbs above the knee. I had just turned twenty-three and all of my dreams were dashed. There was no more playing football and no hope of returning to Mayo. I wouldn't have been able to find work here. Being physically challenged, I couldn't have coped in a farming situation out in the country in the West of Ireland. It just wouldn't work. I had to change my plans and re-train. After a period of hospitalisation and rehabilitation lasting about eighteen months, I managed to find employment with an engineering company assembling counting instruments. In hospital I completed some correspondence courses and the Occupational Therapist wanted me to continue, but when you're living in a strange country with very little family backing you have to make your own living. There were many jobs available for me in England so it was better to take that route.

The most harrowing result of the accident was not being able to play football. I still remained involved on the committee side of the GAA, but I found it very frustrating. However, there was a huge melting pot of ideas and attitudes floating around and a great social life attached to the GAA and the Céilí on a Sunday night. In some ways it was very enjoyable living in England in the Sixties; it was a fairly lively place. I became involved in the Trade Union and Labour Movement and was a Shop Steward for thirty years. Like many before me I availed of the Union's education courses. Out of that a whole other world opened up to us, but after a while we started to wonder how we fit it in. What was our identity in this other land?

In Bolton we were always organizing multicultural events with other ethnic groups, so there was a lot of interaction with other nationalities. There was an estimated Irish population of 12,000 in the town back then and a core group of them would have pretty much stuck together. There wasn't an Irish Centre in Bolton, but we had Church halls and there were lots of Irish Centres in Manchester, which was only twelve miles away. We held classes in Irish dancing and the Irish language and céilí on a Sunday night. Yet, when we came home on holidays, it was always very emotional going back again. Ireland was always home to us and the way of life and atmosphere here would have appealed to us more. We would remember when we were young and our parents were still alive. Eventually I married an English girl, of Irish descent, and we had four children so there was some sense of settling and becoming part of the wider community. We were unprepared, however, for the events that flowed from the Civil Rights Campaigns in Northern Ireland that started in 1969.

The Irish living in Britain had no community structures that could cope with the 1974 Birmingham and Guilford pub bombings and the subsequent introduction of the Prevention of Terrorism Act (PTA)*. This Act led to the conviction of the Birmingham Six (B6) and the Guilford Four (G4) and many other innocent people. Detainees could be held for up to seven days back then without human contact; now it is twenty-eight. As a result, a lot of us got dragged into the campaigns and lots of Irish people like me joined left-wing British groups in an attempt to oppose legislation only to find that some of those organisations were primarily interested in using Irish issues to attack the establishment. Following the death of the ten hunger strikers in the early Eighties, Irish activists in Britain established the Irish in Britain Representation Group (IBRG) to campaign; to represent the interests of the community in culture, education, and welfare; to repeal the PTA, anti–Irish racism and political issues. The Bolton branch had a large membership of over one hundred people with about thirty of them actively involved. The branch organised Irish language courses; céilí and set dancing classes; an Irish festival; Irish input into multicultural festivals; an Irish Radio programme; and Irish representation on the Bolton Race Equality Council (BREC) and on the Minorities Joint Consultative Council (MJCC). I had the honour of being branch Chairman for a number of years and represented the community on the MJCC and on the executive of the BREC. I was also Chairman of the Bolton branch of Comhaltas Ceoltóirí Éireann (CCE) for ten years and PRO for eight years. I served as CCE Northern Regional PRO for three years, was Press Officer for Comhaltas na Breataine, and wrote the Comhaltas column in *The Irish Post*.

They were very difficult times and we didn't necessarily have the full support of the Irish community. Certainly in the Eighties when we were involved in the B6 and G4 campaigns it did cause problems and sometimes the resentment came from Irish people. The Bolton Evening News ran a headline one time, "Irish festival fundraising for the IRA" following an event where we distributed information about the campaigns. A local Irish woman, then secretary of the Bolton Irish Community Association, had made this claim to the newspaper. Considering the venue was a hundred yards from the central police station, and the Town Hall had security staff, we would have been stupid to do so. A reporter later confirmed that he knew the allegations were untrue, but had to submit copy to the Editor who decided to publish and because he gave us the right to reply, there was nothing we could do. Prior to our next meeting I was advised to resign from the Bolton Irish Community Association and several members were expelled. The woman, who had complained, later apologised, but nobody else showed any remorse for the abuse we suffered that night. The English didn't understand what was going on either and I had to explain the situation to my Personnel Officer when I wanted to secure a telephone to counter the allegations. Similarly, the Chairman of the Counties Associations in Manchester used *The Manchester Evening News* (10 March 1988) to attack members of the IBRG who were trying to campaign against the B6 and G4 convictions as part of the Manchester Irish Festival. He accused us of "having covert support for Sinn Fein" and trying to taint the festival with information on the convictions. Interesting how the smear against those campaigning for justice was always linked to paramilitary groups. We were frequently told when trying to lobby support that the Irish community was divided on the issue, but, ironically such divisions prolonged their incarceration. Then again they were probably just afraid. When you think of how easy it was for the authorities to lift the Birmingham Six, it could have happened to anybody.

Under the Prevention against Terrorism Act, 80,000 Irish people were being picked up every year throughout the Eighties, creating an atmosphere of fear. If you were flying between Britain and Ireland you had to fill out a PTA Card. They wanted to know where you were going and other details. Similarly on the ferry you knew you were under surveillance. One of the parents of an Irish dancing pupil who worked on the technical side of the Manchester police force warned us not to book tickets for Irish concerts in the Free Trade Hall in Manchester over the phone; not to use a credit card; and not to send a cheque, because the police were doing background checks on us based on information supplied by the Hall. If possible we were to go directly to the booking office and pay by cash. We knew what was going on because the Government published figures every year. If you were stopped at the ports for more than twenty minutes, the police had to record it. Certain sections of the media regularly classed Irish cultural events as fundraising for the IRA and referred to the Irish in Britain as 'the enemy within.'

Because of this we organized speaking groups and would go around to all the Labour Party and Trade Union branches talking about Ireland, the B6, G4 or the PTA. We would take questions from people who were politically involved, yet they wouldn't know much about the Northern Ireland situation. There was a war taking place on their doorstep and they hadn't a clue about it. Margaret Thatcher would talk to the media about Northern Ireland being as English as Finchley. There would be respected journalists present and nobody would challenge her. Many TV programmes that dealt with the Troubles were cut or censored and the one station that broadcast the film about the killings in Gibraltar, *Death on the Rock,* lost its license. From the media English people would have learnt that conflict was a way of life for the Irish; that we were so primitive and bloody minded we wouldn't have known any difference, following the old maxim that the first casualty in war is the truth. The British have had years of experience in controlling the media and they do it very well. They still have to publish the Saville report on Bloody Sunday in Derry. One of our members did an item on strip searching for an Irish programme on BBC radio Manchester. It included a ten minute interview with a woman who had been on a protest march and the BBC objected to it. They cut out the segment and eventually suspended the programme. What they indicated was that we could play our music and songs on air, but leave the politics to them. They're treating the Muslim people like that now. If they're carrying a plastic bag, they're immediately suspected of having a bomb and it's harder for them because they're more visible. Shortly after the M62 bombing I went into the butcher's for some meat and then decided to have a pint in the pub. Luckily I left my bag in the car because later I heard the barmaid saying if she saw an Irish man carrying a plastic bag, she'd call the police. I knew people involved in Irish dancing and they snuck the costumes out in bin bags. It was acceptable to be Irish, but not actively Irish. That was a different kettle of fish.

Atrocious acts were carried out, but every Irish person in England should not have been discriminated against because of the few who were involved. The Irish community in England never supported these terrorist acts just like the Muslim community today do not condone crimes committed in their name. The whole community should not be punished for the faults of a few. There were lots of Irish people in Birmingham who couldn't go into work for weeks after the bombings there. The police knew who had planted the bombs and not a single policeman lost a day's pay or pension entitlement. The judge who convicted them was made Lord Chief Justice, the highest judicial position in Great Britain. What message was that sending to us? Don't forget that many Irish people were killed that day in Birmingham. The media of course had a lot to do with the resentment. One of the tabloids printed a picture of Fr. Joe Taaffe, OMI, from Knock, who was the Chair of the Birmingham Six Campaign, under the caption – The most evil man in Britain. Of course the Irish themselves were divided too. There were twenty-eight county associations in the Manchester area and I couldn't think of anything more ridiculous. It was extremely parochial and I refused to get involved. Some of these associations included building contractors who exploited their own people. Some of them are quite big names today and they got there by having poor safety records, by paying people on the lump, and not providing insurance and pension benefits to employees who were working under very poor conditions. They were also very much into Irish country & western music, whereas I would have been more traditional.

If I could have found a job in Ireland, I would never have left. I would have stayed mainly for the football. My father came back when I was about fifteen. I only knew him for a very brief time. I'd see him every year for two weeks and he wrote every fortnight and sent me sixpence. He had been a yardman in the nearby town of Ballinlough and some men got shot there when they tried to burn down the RIC (Royal Irish Constabulary) Barracks in 1921. The Black and Tans had pretended to vacate the Barracks, but they were hiding in the fields and came back and shot the men who were trying to burn it. My father was essentially forced to leave after that because he was being harassed and he feared for his mother who was a widow. I wish I knew more about him, but parents didn't communicate very much with children back then. You were very rarely told things directly, but picked up a lot listening to adults talking. I suppose when you only see your father once a year you wouldn't feel like asking too many close questions either. Back then we'd ramble into people's houses; we'd lift the latch. If there was nobody home we'd turn on the radio. Neighbours of ours who lived across the fields in County Roscommon had a grandfather who lived until he was ninety-eight. He used to walk ten miles from Ballinlough to Castlerea to work every day. Now he is someone I should have listened to more; if I'd only had a tape recorder. My major regret though is that I didn't keep a diary during the Seventies and Eighties because they were very challenging times for the Irish community in Britain. Very little research has been carried out on the effects of the PTA on that community. Those arrested had their homes and places of employment searched by the police. Many of them would have lost their jobs and been denied entry into their homes, which were cordoned off from the outside world. I knew of one couple who committed suicide after being detained.

The Irish have always had a problem with identity in England. My aunt who died recently aged ninety-one was recruited to work there in the factories. They paid her fare and she had to stay in nominated accommodation and couldn't change her job. Things were bad in the Fifties and Sixties in Ireland, but were even worse in the Thirties and Forties. She saw the signs everywhere - No Irish - and told me about going to a social event that had the sign: No Irish Men. The agents

who operated this scheme were licensed by the
Irish Government. A lot of the Irish in England
lost their identities altogether during the Troubles. We met many middle-aged Irish women
suddenly coming to events whom we'd never
seen before, yet they lived in the area. They had
been married to Englishmen before 1969 when it
wouldn't have been a problem. The men would
have gone to Irish dances and pubs and come
home on holidays with their Irish wives. After
the Troubles erupted everything changed and
they faded into the background. After they died
their Irish wives came out into the community
again. Back in the early Eighties we invited a
very powerful local Councillor who was Irish to
a meeting to enlist support for the community.
He told us that when he chose politics as a career he had decided to leave Irish issues out of it.
Some English people did make an effort to educate themselves on the situation, but it was difficult to get information in the local newspaper;

Aged 17 – the year
I left Mayo

they wouldn't publish anything positive about Ireland. Readers would
be getting a one-sided view of the situation. The only other option
open to the media was to explain what the Troubles were all about,
and they weren't prepared to do that. The reason the war in Northern
Ireland lasted so long was there was no pressure from the electorate
put on politicians to find a political solution. They were allowed to
claim it was a sectarian/criminal problem. Tony Blair did apply his
mind over a considerable time to find a compromise. The IBRG had
a section that managed the English media so that we could reply to
any allegations made by the newspapers. You become very adept at
recognizing how certain events are covered and what perspectives are
taken, in what context and how they are presented. Between the two
countries there is a very complex history.

The Irish Government were very negligent about the situation at first. We were a community under siege and they didn't want to know. If you were picked up under the PTA legislation you were supposed to contact the Irish Embassy, but they were closed for the weekend. If you were picked up on a Saturday or Sunday they couldn't do anything for you. We also had a group who kept a list of the people who had been picked up and held, and we would telephone the respective police stations to remind the police that they must inform the Irish Embassy of the situation, and that suspects couldn't be kept longer than seven days. We just wanted them to know that we were aware of what was going on and what our rights were. We had to give our name and address when we logged a complaint, but the Irish Government didn't give us any support. Unless you were involved with some of the cases, you really wouldn't have any idea of what went on. We knew a girl from Birmingham who was a student at Queen's University in Belfast and had been held in Liverpool one time and interrogated on student union activities at the College. Irish students doing an Electronics Degree at Manchester University and travelling back via Manchester airport were frequently held. The Director General of Comhaltais, Labhras Ó'Murchú, was picked up in Birmingham Airport one time because he didn't sign his name in English, preferring instead the Irish version. The Minister for Foreign Affairs, Michael Kennedy, was even detained. One interesting person, Chris Halliday, a Church of England vicar whose father was from Westport, refused to fill in the PTA boarding card and because of his collar he got away with it.

A lot of the Irish remained in their own communities, lived and worked only alongside fellow countrymen and closed their eyes and ears to what was going on. It had enormous effects on families. You had parents who couldn't talk to their children. Most of them who had only a rudimentary education didn't understand what was going on and even if they did, they didn't know how to counter it, nor did they know how to explain it to their children. That must have been hard. It was hard too for the children to have their parents portrayed as primitive and ignorant. My children went to a convent school where I went to a parent-teacher evening once and I seen some posters about a student concert. My two daughters played Irish music as did many of their companions attending the school. I remarked on this and asked the Principal why they weren't included in the concert and was told that she hadn't known. They hadn't publicised this to their teachers or their peers, but the Music Department made enquiries and some of them did perform and received a very good reception. Nowadays GAA is played in the English schools and Irish language and music classes are available. But, you have to ask yourself why there isn't more done when they have so many Irish teachers.

I suppose my Trade Union involvement sucked me into the writing although I was always an avid reader. They were heavily interested in education and taught people like me how to write Reports, take Minutes at meetings, write Press Releases and that came in handy when we had to handle some very extensive press coverage around some very sensitive issues. The writing just sort of developed from all of that. I went to night classes and some day release courses, but I didn't feel any need to go back to formal schooling other than an Irish language class. It was very difficult back then for Irish men to try and educate themselves because they were often working ten, eleven hour shifts, sometimes six, seven days a week. I was offered a fast track media degree course at Edge Hill in 2002, but it was too late. I did not want to postpone my return to Ireland any longer.

It was always on the cards that when I got to retirement age, I was coming home and I had to take early retirement because of my hands. I use them for driving with hand controls; for working; for using the walking stick, so my hands and arms have been quite overworked over the years. I was getting a touch of RSI from the constant repetitive movements, so I had to retire. My wife and I had always thought we would buy a house in Ireland, but then when prices zoomed beyond the reach of the average buyer, I got in touch with the voluntary housing association here to discuss the possibility of renting. We did consider coming in 1976 when the economy here was beginning to move slightly. We had a look around and my wife probably would have had a good chance of getting work, but I had to think, would I just vegetate? Apart from the body, the mind just flies and I have to keep it active, reading and learning all the time. Would I be able to do that here? We decided that I wouldn't so we stayed put. We had to tolerate living there in the end. The IBRG group in Bolton ran a Sean Chairde (old friends) over 60's group and my wife, as a volunteer, took a party back to Ireland most years. On one occasion they went to Mulranny and got a very good reception from Dr. Jerry Cowley and the Safe Home staff who were also very helpful to us when we came home for good.

Five years ago then we finally got the opportunity we had waited for all those years. We shipped everything back and were able to move straight into this house in Aughamore, which was brand new at the time. We didn't mind that there were no pavements in the area; that the houses hadn't been painted or that there was no grass. I had a dog as well, but unfortunately now he's dead. He used to come home every year on holidays with us and loved it. The children loved to come too. Living in Ireland would be a very normal thing for them. Of course there's been a mass exodus of the Irish born out of England recently and they're all coming back, as are the children of Irish immigrants. Around this area alone I know of at least six second generation Irish who have come back here from England. They grew up as Irish so they feel very much at home here. People who have never been away are confused about all of that.

I love living here with the mountains outside my front door and Croagh Patrick visible in the distance; it's brilliant. The music and football have always been important to me. The GAA coverage on TV is fantastic here and there's a local pitch down the road. I can easily get to Castlebar and Charlestown and all other venues where games are played. Probably the highlight of my return was being able to attend the 2006 Connacht final between Mayo and Galway in Castlebar, only my second Connacht final in all those years. The atmosphere; the colours; people of all ages, male and female supporters all mixed together made it an amazing day. The sun was shining and Mayo won. It's also nice being out in the country again. I lived in Farnworth, a built up area outside Bolton, in the midst of red bricked houses and passing traffic. Even if you put your car in the garage, it wouldn't necessarily be safe.

Coming home for good is something lots of Irish people consider, but if they have children and grandchildren in their adoptive countries, they never get around to it. Others are worried that they won't have the same lifestyle here that they enjoy in England. It is much more expensive here, but does it really matter? I lead a very simple life. I don't drink to any extent except the odd glass of wine; I don't smoke; I use a few gallons of petrol; I drive a small car, so I can manage well enough. Older people are more cautious too and worry that things might not turn out well for them.

I think the changes in Ireland are fantastic. The prosperity and the availability of jobs is great, the access to education, and the impact of other nationalities. It is reputed that forty nationalities live in Ballyhaunis today, which should be seen as a positive resource when you consider all the different ideas and skills that people bring with them. I think it's great to see young Irish children going to school with lots of different cultures and languages and being exposed to different backgrounds. Hopefully, it will inspire them to become more interested in their own culture and language. Ballyhaunis GAA had posters in six different languages last year inviting members of the various communities to participate in club activities. Obviously there's a downside to living here. The infrastructure isn't great. I can't get *Broadband* and have to wait hours for attachments to come through on the email. Hopefully wireless is on the way. If the Government hadn't sold Eircom all those years ago, we wouldn't be having these problems now. Lots of things seem to get started and then seem to stagnate. There's only one bus a week from this village, so you have to drive. I spend most of the summer down in Cork where my daughter and her family now live, and where there is much better infrastructure. The West is neglected and I'm surprised really that the people are so accepting, as they used to be great campaigners. The Celtic Tiger people have worked so hard to make money, yet they seem to have lost the will to campaign. Only the hospital issue is bringing them out on the streets. In the West especially, everyone should super glue the locks of the Fianna Fail offices. Their representatives have done nothing for them so they should lock them up instead of voting for them.

Another area of concern is the senior Civil Servants, some of them in key positions, who can't be sacked no matter what they do. They can be totally incompetent; they can make a complete mess of things, yet they can't be sacked. Government Ministers here never have to walk the line, but I'm glad the Clergy did. I didn't keep up my religion in England. There are certain basic things that didn't stock up; that I couldn't believe in; and there were certain Christian people whose care I was left in and they didn't show much care. You begin to question and you try and work it out. I've no problem with people going to Mass, my wife does, and my daughter teaches Religious Education, but I do get annoyed if someone tries to talk me into believing. I did have to consider my wife's beliefs when my children came along and they were all baptized and attended Catholic schools. I wanted to give them some sort of structure and if they wanted to reject it later on that was fine. Most people follow whatever Faith their parents had; people rarely make their own decisions on that. I worked with a lot of Muslims and even though I had didn't share their beliefs; I certainly respected their right to them.

We go back to England every year for Christmas, as we still have a son and two daughters there and six of our eight grandchildren. There isn't a great deal that I miss about England after over forty years there. Most of the English people I knew there were fine, but many of them didn't have any respect for the Irish. Following the ceasefire and the various political changes, things did sort of ease for the Irish community, but I never felt that I belonged there. I worked with English people, lived with them, was involved with them on a Trade Union level, but I never felt part of them. Some Irish people do adapt into the community and a very well known one would be Terry Wogan. Apart from his accent, he is your quintessential English man. Because of our colonial past Irish people tend to look at things differently. They had collections for the Falkland's War effort where I worked and I refused to contribute. I got abuse for that. Some English people think it's great to go off to war. What on earth is great about it? And I would have thought I had something in common with these people.

We would have agreed on some things, but then when the British flag was flying it was an entirely different kettle of fish. Irish individuals supported and fought with the British Army in the two World Wars, but as a people we are not traditionally warmongers; we prefer singing and storytelling.

Things that would not be that important to you when you're at home suddenly become very important when you're away, like music and songs. When times are bad you turn to music and it's a way of expressing yourself as well. A lot of the Irish songs are about going away. Traditional music in Ireland often filled a vacuum left by our inability to speak our native language. We held a cultural exchange with the Ukrainian community in Bolton and all of their second and third generations could speak Ukrainian. They had passed their language along, whereas we couldn't. We passed our music along instead. There are about forty branches of Comhaltais in England and very few of their music teachers are Irish born. They're mainly second and third generation. Even here in Aughamore there's music lessons in the local pub and the teachers are both English. It's the same with the GAA. Most of the people playing Gaelic games in England now are not Irish born, but are of Irish descent. Who knows, my English born grandson might play for Cork one day!

Irish people in England constantly encountered racism either through the media or dressed up as humour in the latest Irish joke. At a fundraising event in the local Catholic Club a singer opened his act by telling a joke about Irish famine victims who died because they'd forgotten where they planted the potatoes. I complained to the Secretary who referred me to the Chairman, the Parish Priest, who would not accept that the joke was offensive. When we used the annex of Bolton College for Irish dancing classes a staff member was overheard saying, "the Irish are dancing in one room and probably making bombs in another." We received an apology from the College, but the employee was never identified, nor were we aware of any disciplinary action. I have been barred from an English pub for sitting down during *Faith of our Fathers*, which the band had decided to play instead of our National Anthem. They were afraid to play *The Soldiers Song* in case they were regarded as republicans. A couple of friends and I refused to accept this substitution and continued chatting. The landlady was livid and ordered us out – the only time I've ever been barred from a pub! We were subjected to this sort of treatment every day.

Ireland lost a whole generation of very intelligent people who made a massive contribution to another country and in lots of cases got no respect, only denigration, for it. We were ignored by the Irish Government who continues to neglect its emigrant community in England by denying them access to RTE television and not allowing them to vote in Irish elections. Among the Irish people who stood out in my time were Brendan McClure, editor of *The Irish Post*; Pat Reynolds, PRO, IBRG; Tommy Walsh, Liverpool, whose support for Irish people held under the PTA was legendary; and the late Sean Dempsey who did so much to promote music and dance around the Greater Manchester area. I would also like to acknowledge the medical care I received in St. James Hospital, Leeds, following the accident and the help and support of artificial limb fitters at the various centres, particularly in Withington (ALAC) in Manchester. Many of them went the extra mile to repair the many breakages I had over the years. Finally, enormous respect is due to the ordinary Irish person who prospered, brought up and educated their families in foreign lands all over the world, while still managing to hang on to their identity, and to pass on their values to their children.

From an interview at his home in Aughamore, Co. Mayo, on Tuesday, November 6[th,] 2007, and comprehensive written accounts by Joe himself.

*Prevention of terrorism Act (PTA)

The Prevention of terrorism (Temporary provisions) Act came into force on 29th November 1974 following the Birmingham and Woolwich bombings. The first people to be arrested under the terms of this 'new' legislation were the (convicted but innocent) Guilford Four.

Persons arrested under the PTA have no right of habeas corpus, are not informed of the charges against them, and have no right to remain silent or to appeal decisions. Abridging the standard right to freedom of movement within one's country, exclusion orders banish suspected terrorists from one part of the United Kingdom to another (most exclusions are from mainland Britain to Northern Ireland). On the basis of 'reasonable' suspicion anyone can be arrested for being involved in or supportive of Irish Republicanism. There is no provision for challenge and nor does any rationale need for arrest need to be given.

In Britain from November 1974 to December 1992 some 7,052 people were detained. Of these 6,097 (86%) were subsequently released without charge. Criminal charges faced by most of the remaining 14% could have been quite adequately dealt with under existing legislation.

Recording the experiences of people detained under the PTA it quickly became evident that the arbitrary detention of (mainly though not exclusively) Irish people (allowed for in the Act) was being used as a trawling exercise by police to collect information on the wider Irish community living in Britain who (for no other reason than being Irish) became a suspect community.

It, largely, silenced Irish opinion and involvement whether on Irish issues, Trades Union activities or general political participation as people 'kept the head down' fearful of drawing attention to themselves. It divided the Irish community as nothing that went before it, as individuals acted to look after themselves at the expense of their fellow Irish nationals. It's longest lasting effect has been the loss to Ireland of huge numbers of second and third generation Irish in denial of their culture and heritage.

Renewed and extended annually before becoming a fixture the PTA is now used, largely, to target Muslim's.

Funeral procession, Achill, for victims of Kirkintilloch fire disaster, September 1937

Funeral of Achill fire victims

MARGARET CONDON

I came back to Ireland in November 2001 after spending fifty years in England. Most exiles never forget; everyone wants to go back to their roots. But, it's a bit of a shock to the system all the same, as nothing prepares you for coming home for good. Living here is not the same as coming on holidays. It's not the Ireland we left behind, but you have to give yourself time to adjust. I knew people in England who came home and couldn't settle and went back again, but they didn't give themselves enough time. I would say to anyone who has their health to come back and try it. It's not the end of the world if it doesn't work out. The first year is the hardest and after that it will be fine.

I was born three miles outside of here in a place called Dohyle on the 29th of July, 1935. I might not look seventy-two, but can I tell you I feel it sometimes. I come from a family of nine, two boys and seven girls and we grew up on a small farm. As you can imagine things were bad at that time and it was hard really to survive. From a very young age we had to help out on the farm milking cows and all the things that go with trying to make ends meet. In those days you couldn't afford help; you couldn't afford to hire anyone. What my father would do is have a man come in from another farm to help out, and then he would give his day back, you know what I mean? They had no money, and they couldn't sell the land because that was their livelihood and they had to work it out somehow. So from an early age we learnt how to help Dad. We all had our own jobs, and of course in those days we had open fires so we had to collect firewood and draw water from the well. In winter time we had to clean out from the cows; we had to do all those jobs that people wouldn't recognize now. Our younger days were happy and busy and I don't have any regrets. I was born in a lovely spot out in the heart of the country and I don't think we lost anything or missed out on anything. When

I think of the life we had compared with the life they have today. We had everything, and we had nothing.

Hence I had to go to England in 1952 just before my seventeenth birthday. There was no work around and my parents couldn't afford to keep nine of us. Two of the girls were still at school as was my younger brother. My older sister, Josie, she's not with us anymore, was the first to go. She went to Sheffield, into a private house, doing domestic work I suppose, and was earning quite a lot there. She went over with cousins and as she came home each year on a holiday she brought another one of us back with her and got us installed. That is how we all got to England. One year she brought me and another sister, Elizabeth, over to our brother who was married in Derby. We found work in The General Hospital in Nottingham where another sister already worked. At one time there were three of us, all sisters, sharing a room. There were a lot of sisters in that hospital; two Italian girls, two girls from Mayo, and two from Sligo. We all went around together and I still have friends from back then. Our accommodation was provided for and the employers were responsible for us until we were twenty-one. We were maids really, but we had a roof over our heads. Our uniforms were washed for us and all we had to do was look after our own bits and bobs. We were fed and found, and we had a bit of pocket money to spend so we thought we were in heaven. It was after the war and England was building itself back up. There were thousands of Irish going over every week. There was no shortage of work, it was boom time.

It was the freedom that I enjoyed most. I did my growing up in England. I'd say the first five or six years I was in Nottingham, I grew up. Because we were really virtually kids leaving Ireland. Up to that we had done nothing except come home from school and do our jobs. The only entertainment we had was going to the hurling matches here in Rathkeale and to the circus once a year. That was it. That was our entertainment. We were a big family so we made our own fun out on the land and on other people's land. People wouldn't recognize that now. But, wherever you went in England back then there was an Irish club and dancing was my forte. I went dancing about four or five times a week. I loved it. I think I was about twenty-seven before I set foot in a pub. All the Irish lads used to drink because they were living in digs, those of them that weren't married, and landladies didn't like them hanging around, so where were they to go?

Then we had a lovely church hall in Nottingham and they always had dances for the Irish people and of course there were loads of fellows around. Indeed you could have had a different fellow every week if you wanted, you know what I mean? But when you're young and free, you don't want to be tied down. I never wanted to be tied down anyhow. I don't know why. I can't explain it, but I never wanted to be tied down. Not that I didn't have opportunities, I did. Hence, I never got married. I just did not want to get married. Isn't that weird? And yet now when I think about it, I would love to have had a son. I have a favourite nephew in England, he's my godson and he's twenty-six or twenty-seven now and I love him to bits. He could be my own son. If it was now I could have a child without being married. I never knew any girls that got pregnant back then. In those days we went around in a gang; we'd come home from a dance at maybe one o'clock in the morning and we'd walk through the streets and wouldn't be afraid or anything. The fellows would be like that too. But you see in those days, most of the girls were living-in and you'd have to get a late pass if you were going out. When we went to a dance if we were going to be out until any time after eleven o'clock we'd have to have a late pass. Then they'd check you in when you came home so they'd know if anybody was missing. And that went on until we were twenty-one. So maybe the girls didn't have the opportunity to get pregnant because the relationship was a kiss at the gate and that sort of thing.

The clothes were lovely to me because we didn't have them here and then you had some money in your pocket and you could buy a lot. We might only get two pounds a week after we were fed and found and that money would burn a hole in your pocket if you saw a nice frock and then of course you'd send some home to your parents. But, once the novelty wore off and you had a bit of money each week and you could buy whatever you wanted, you didn't hanker after it as much. In hindsight I would have educated myself a little bit more. Whilst I

Mam & Dad in Dohyle

have a lot of experience from the jobs that I worked in I should have strived more to better my situation. I have no regrets in the respect that I was happy in every job that I had, but I feel cheated that I didn't have a bit more education. When you leave school at fourteen you really only have a basic education, but I got through life alright. After five or six years in the hospital I moved onto *The Midland Hotel*, one of the British Railway chains, where I took up reception work. By this time I had moved out of live-in accommodation and was sharing a flat with another girl. After about fifteen or sixteen years in the hotel, I went to work for the buyer in a pharmaceutical company, *Richard Daniel & Son*. They manufactured all sorts of pharmaceuticals and drugs and I was there for about ten years until I decided to change careers again.

My first love was nursing, it always had been, but by this time I was too old to enrol for it so I did the next best thing and I went for a Nurse's assistant's job in a private hospital in Derby. I worked in The Nuffield for over twenty years until I retired and I loved it. I absolutely adored it. I loved taking care of the elderly. I loved to get them out of bed and get them into the bathroom and shower and make them look nice and clean and tidy and sit them in their chair. I just loved to see them getting on their feet and what have you. It should have been my job for life. That's where I missed out. But anyway, nevertheless, I did it for about twenty years so I had no regrets in that respect except that if I'd had the education I'd have gone in sooner. The other good thing about this job was that I was in there from the start. They had just built that branch of the hospital in Derby and I was one of their first girls and had to learn everything from scratch. It was hard actually getting a hospital off the ground. It had only twenty-four beds at first, but they had two day wards as well so it was a wonderful experience of how things work. And in a small hospital it's very intimate. Once it enlarged it wasn't the same and then they put new management in. Nevertheless, I will say that was the happiest job I had.

For the last thirty years of my life in England I was living in a maisonette that I had previously shared with another girl, but after she left to get married I kept it on. I would sit out on the balcony and I'd look at the moon and I'd think, well, that same moon is over Ireland. And I was wishing and wishing and wishing I was there. Whilst I enjoyed England and I had many friends there, many of whom I'd known for over forty years, as I started to get older I had a hankering to go back to my own country. Any immigrant will tell you that. We all have a hankering to come home.

I thought then about my retirement and I thought, no, I couldn't stay in England. I wouldn't have the same space I'd have at home. I'd have the same friends, but somehow I knew that life would be different once I retired and that I'd have to find another place to live. Thank God I was in very good health, but England was getting too built up and noisy. I lived on the main road in Derby and I couldn't see myself retiring there. My hankering was for Ireland. I thought about it for quite a while. Then when I turned sixty I cut down on my hours and went working part-time and what I used to do was come home at Christmas for two or three months and stay out

Queen's Hall,
Nottingham, late 50's

350

in the home place and I got used to everything around here again. So that when I came back for good there was no upheaval or no wishing I was back in England or anything like that. One day I saw an ad in *The Irish Post* for repatriation to Ireland and I wrote to them and they gave me the address in Mulranny. I wrote to Safe Home and they replied and asked me if I wanted to put my name down and where I wanted to go and they gave me all the information on what was available. I wanted to be in the Rathkeale area, to be close to the town so that I'd be near all of the amenities.

Not to this day have I any regrets, none. I came back on a Saturday night and the removals came on Monday and I settled in here and I had no problem whatsoever. Hand on heart, there is not one day that I've said to myself that I made a mistake. Not one. I think coming over for a couple of months in the winter like that for a few years got me acclimatised to how everything was here and I'd never missed a year coming over to see the parents and what have you. That was our holiday back then. Now it's like England never existed. I've settled in here in Rathkeale although not for the amenities I thought I'd have, because there aren't any. The town is dead, completely dead. We have a travelling population that are resident here and they're buying out everything. If a shop closes, they buy it. I don't know where they're getting all the money from, but they're buying everything. The only thing left now is the *Spar* supermarket up the street there and then there's a shop around the corner for general things like milk and bread and papers and that. There's a butcher's, two banks, a vegetable shop, a betting office, post office, a ladies shop for the older generation like myself, a couple of pubs around and that's it. We've only the one supermarket. That's all we have and I think it has something to do with the travelling community because they come in here at Christmas and it's an absolute nightmare.

They come from abroad in the summer time and any property that comes vacant they buy it, and no one knows about it until they see them renovating. It's all done secretly. I heard my late parents say long ago that the travellers had prophesized even long before that again that they'd own Rathkeale one day and I'd say now they have seventy percent of it. At the back of the Church there is a settled community and they have the houses beautiful. There's no doubt about it. They buy a place, I don't know where they get all the money from, but they do it up and the work is beautiful, but when the others come for Christmas or a wedding they disrupt the settled community here. It causes friction among them, but it also causes friction with the townspeople. They all drive those four-wheeled monsters and are indifferent to parking and traffic laws and that and nobody seems to be able to do anything about it. Christmas here is a nightmare, an absolute nightmare. Yet it is the quietest town in Ireland. Nothing happens in Rathkeale because nobody will come into it. We never have trouble here; we never have a problem. There's no crime at all. Newcastlewest, which is about ten kilometres away, is a thriving town, but they have enormous problems with the emigrants that are in there, enormous problems. And they're not all working either from what I hear. They've big problems with rows and stealing and all that sort of thing. There's nothing like that in Rathkeale. It is the quietest town in Ireland.

We have nothing and we have everything because we have peace and quiet, but we have to go back to Newcastle or to Limerick for our shopping and that's because there isn't a decent shop here. There's a hotel over here, *The Rathkeale House Hotel* and we have dancing for our generation on a Sunday night and it's fabulous. I didn't go last night now because I was suffering from a hangover after a barbeque Saturday night. I wasn't up for it last night, but I've made a lot of friends over there as well. It's a lovely place to go too for Sunday lunch or if you want to take somebody out for a meal it's lovely. Or you can go over there and have a drink and what have you.

I have a friend now that I met about four years ago when he was over visiting. He's living in London and he's widowed, and he was here on holiday when I met him over in the hotel one night at the dance and we've become firm friends. He comes over every four or five months or something like that and stays here for a while and it's lovely. It's a lovely relationship. I miss him when he goes. I do because I like having the company, you know, even though I have some very nice neighbours but it's nice to have someone to go out with too. Then

I was only here a few months and I found my pal, Lucky, there. She was picked up over on the Croagh by-pass where she had been abandoned, the poor thing. This man who has a house on the same land as my nephew saw her and brought her home and fed her. My nephew knew I wanted a dog, but my idea had been to have a little one that I could hold in my arms. But when I took her to the vet he said she was only about eighteen months. She was a young dog and she was carrying pups. So I had her sorted out anyhow and took her home and she's been an absolutely marvellous pal. Money wouldn't buy her. When I go to bed at night, she lies down on the mat by my bed and she sleeps there and then calls me in the morning. What more would I want?

I didn't bother joining any clubs or taking up any hobbies. I have Lucky and the TV and I'm an avid newspaper reader. I'm a newshound; I must know what's going on in the world. You know what I mean? I don't drive anymore, not here in Ireland anyhow. I wouldn't drive here for a fortune. They're pure mad on the roads. I'm terrified. My friend who comes over to see me bought a car and he leaves it here

Margaret (right) & colleagues at *The Midland Hotel*, Derby

Margaret (left) and sister, Christine, *York Hotel*, Derby

and he takes me around. And I have a very good nephew out at the home place and anywhere I want to go he takes me. I walk into town no problem for shopping and that. Lucky also keeps me fit. She has to be brought out twice a day. We have a lot of fields around here and I take her down to them. I stand on the road and she runs around. She comes back when she's finished. I have a sister out at the home place whom I visit quite a lot, but unfortunately my brother died last year. He died suddenly last October and I miss him terribly. I feel that loss more than leaving England because he was only up at the top of the town and if I had problems he was here every week. It's nice to have family nearby. I've made a lot of friends around here, but Lucky confirmed everything for me as regards settling in. When I got her that was it.

There were a lot of forms to fill out at the beginning, but that didn't bother me at all. I got myself sorted out fairly quickly and I got to know how things worked and to know my way around. There isn't much difference between Ireland and England anyway. The euro came in a short time after I moved over, but that didn't bother me either. The people over the housing scheme here are very helpful. President McAleese performed the opening ceremony and she came in especially to see me, as she is the Patron of Safe Home. She's lovely, absolutely lovely and her husband is lovely as well. Oh! He's gorgeous. Sometimes the housing association organize outings and they are very enjoyable. We go to Knock twice a year in a coach. We attend Mass in the Basilica and get the blessing and all that and they organize lunch and everything for us. Then we walk around the shops and look at the trinkets and visit the Apparition Chapel. We have our tea then and make our way home. It's a lovely trip. I love it. I love being in Knock.

The only thing I don't like is how Ireland has changed. I have found that people today, not my generation, but maybe the one next to us, are very selfish. There isn't the caring there used to be. There isn't the caring there was when my parents were alive and people would care about their neighbours; they'd worry about them. Today you could be well and truly left to your own devices. There isn't the same feeling for people that we were brought up with and I find that very very hard to cope with. I know that Ireland has moved on and that there is a different values system here that we weren't brought up with. They don't have the same values at all. A lot of people have everything, but they have nothing. Money wise they have everything, but they have no compassion. I do have to switch off sometimes when I think about the changes in Ireland and how the Irish people have changed so much. I'm not saying that my generation was any better or any worse. We had very little, but we appreciated what we had. Today they have way too much and they know the price of everything and the value of nothing. Because it's easy come for a lot of people today. And I think if you were brought up in the years that we were brought up in you'd value very much what you have. Also we were more contented. We were not searching. Today I find that the younger generation are searching for something and they think they'll find it in material things, but they won't. I'm also very concerned with the violence there is in the country. The Irish were respected all over the world. I don't know how we're going to be thought of now with all the murders and robberies. I don't feel it's a safe country anymore. If I go into Limerick city I don't take my handbag; I take my coat with a pocket inside for my money because you don't know whose standing behind you. I love my home very much and my country, but I don't think it's safe. I wouldn't go out at night. I'm frightened. I think we were brought up in a different generation, in totally different times. It's the time that has changed really and the people.

I would say to anyone thinking of coming back do so by all means, but if there's any uncertainty don't burn your boats in England. Come over, spend a bit of time here, look around for yourself, and don't imagine you'll ever find here what you had when you were young. That will never be here again. When I think of what we had when we were young. For the past twenty years Ireland is not recognizable. There are still a lot of lovely people in Ireland, but what I'm sad about too is that there are so many people who have died around here since I came back. I couldn't believe it. The list of people that die every year is unbelievable. But of course we're all from the same age group, and I think it will be very very sad when they're gone, because they were the generation that had hard times and cared. Another thing that would worry me is the health care system. I'd be worried because I don't have private insurance. But I can't let that take over my life. I'm very lucky that I'm healthy. Thank God.

I know it wasn't all perfect long ago. Abuses took place in the Church and it's an awful scandal and it makes me very cross at times and I could get very worked up about it. When we were young, we weren't ruled by our parents, we were ruled by Church and State. We were. They controlled us; they kept us down. They were hard times for parents. You had to have a house full of children, otherwise they were questioned. In that respect I suppose people would say good luck to old Ireland; good riddance to it. But that wasn't my experience of it at all. I had a wonderful family life growing up and I missed Ireland terribly when I left. The time we spent away from our parents; the time lost; we'll never get it back. And that's my only regret about emigration. Before you know where you are they're old and they're gone and then you have too much time for regretting. But, we couldn't do anything about it and I'm sure there is thousands in my shoes as well who would feel that way. I mean today they don't know how lucky they are to be with their parents all year around, you know what I mean, instead of seeing them for two weeks out of fifty-two. It's not easy to cope with and the regrets are always there. You lost out on all those precious years if you left when you were young.

I always knew I'd end my days in Ireland because I think if people are honest they'll say that. You never ever forget your homeland no matter how many years you've been away, you never forget it. It didn't

Margaret (3rd from left) celebrating 50th birthday

bother me at all moving house, maybe it's the fact that I'm on my own and I had time to pack up and do everything by degrees. I know there's a bit of paperwork finishing up in England, and things like that, but it wasn't any problem at all. And I had nobody else to look after so I could do things in my own time. It's also important to move to a place where you'll be near family or where there'll be neighbours. Living in isolation in Ireland is not on. I've said it before and I'll repeat myself again, Ireland is not the same. And it never will be. All that *comm-alya's* (old songs) and open doors is gone. It's locked gates now.

The English people were very welcoming to us long ago. Well, I

357

suppose because there were so many of us Irish there together and the girls we worked with were all Irish so they couldn't really gang up on us! But I had lovely friends, lovely friends. That's another thing people might miss coming back here, the friends they're leaving behind. I mean I have one now over forty years and she comes over all the time to see me. My true friends are in England, but I've made some nice friends since I came here, some lovely friends. I have no regrets about friendships and that. It was easier for me to come back because I wasn't leaving any children behind. Now my sisters in England, they have children, and it's very hard for the women to break away. The men will come, but it's very hard for the women to leave their children and grandchildren although I always say, you won't lose them; they're only an hour away. I've been back a couple of times and it doesn't do anything for me. England is my past now. I enjoyed it; I made lovely friends, but this is my new life here and this is where I want to be. I was one hundred percent sure I wanted to come back. And I have no doubts, nothing whatsoever, thank God, I haven't.

On my 70th birthday my friend from London threw a party for me in *The Thatch* and dressed me up in a nurse's uniform and he wore a white coat pretending to be a doctor! A young girl who was celebrating her 40th birthday on the same night remarked on how young I looked. She said to me you must have had lots of money and been waited on hand and foot all your life by a nice husband. If she only knew!

Interviewed at her home in Rathkeale, County Limerick
on Monday, August 27th, 2007

JOHN COYNE

I came home on the 28th of April, 2001. God! The years are flying. I'm very settled now and wouldn't leave, but found it very hard at first. It was very lonely. And I was gone for forty years so I didn't know any of the young crowd here. It was only the odd one that I went to school with that was still around. I was born about five miles back the road there, in Killeen, out the road there beyond Carrig. That's where I was raised until I was nineteen, when I left. There was nothing here at the time, nothing. I worked for a while on a small farm draining the land, and then I signed on the dole for another short while and got eight shillings a week until I was cut off. Sure I was a young fellow at the time, smoking and everything; eight shillings was nothing. If we had ten shillings we could cycle in here to Louisburgh to dances or over to Lecanvey Parochial Hall where they held dances and plays.

I travelled to England by train and by boat; sure we didn't know where we were going, me and another fellow; it was our first time. There was a fellow home here on holidays and we went back with him. When we got to Manchester, to some station, he said he had to change there, as he was going on to Grantham. We were heading to a farmer out near Southport, where we could lift potatoes and that. We got off the train and it was raining; there was a heavy mist. We were walking up the street when we met these two women from only a few miles from here. They said the best thing to do was get a taxi out to the farm, but the farmer couldn't employ us straight away, as he'd just started two other fellows. We then took the train to Burnley, where me mate had a brother who got us work there and digs. The other fella came back after two or three months, he didn't like it at all, but I stayed. I liked it and I thought, I'll hang on and hang on. But, it was very hard. Work was very hard that time and digs were very bad. God Almighty the digs were very bad. You'd come in there in the evening and there'd be six or seven with you and the landlady would put things out in a bowl, you know maybe there'd be two fish fingers each and a scoop of spuds. The first couple of fellows would get the lot and maybe by the time you'd come down there'd be no fish fingers left. You'd have to go down to the café for something to eat.

We started with *Wimpy's* with a seven o'clock start in the morning until half past five in the evening and one o'clock on a Saturday. I'll never forget my first pay packet; it was sixteen pounds. Sixteen pounds! What I was getting here was ten shillings a day, three pounds a week, and that was working hard for farmers, draining land. I think it was about three pounds we were paying the landlady for digs over there, but that time like you could go out for a pound. Money would go a long way. I liked the life in Burnley. The coach would take us into Manchester every Saturday night to the dances and we'd meet up with all the Irish. So I hung on there for a couple of years and then there was a crowd going up to Scotland. This big job was in Scotland, and there was supposed to be great money.

It was away out in the mountains; the nearest town was Bigger, a small little town, and we had to go then fifteen miles up into the mountains. You had to get a taxi or a mini bus up to work where you also had your living quarters. Four would sleep to a caravan. There was a little kitchen and then a sort of a bedroom on each end. You had to wait until one fellow got into the bed before you got in yourself; the beds were that near one another. The windows were broken and in the morning the sheep would be bleating outside. Oh! 'Twas terrible. An old fellow and his wife were running the canteen and you got soup or whatever to eat and then you went to bed. You could sit in the canteen if you wanted to watch television. I went up there because there was supposed to be great money in it. And there was. Some of the lads had been there for eight or nine months, and when they started off the foreman would give them the van every month to come down to Manchester. Then one weekend they didn't go back up until the Monday or Tuesday, you see, and he stopped all that then. We were there for St. Patrick's Day and we took two vans up to Bigger; two lots of us, and of course the town had never seen the like of it; we nearly drank them dry.

One time it started to snow, down off the hill, and you couldn't stick it. It would cut the face off you. Sixty of us went into this big fitting shed behind the mountain where they kept the coaches for taking us to work, but we had decided it was too bad to go out that day, and we stayed put. The foreman, a Ukrainian man, came down off the hills, walked into the hut, and started shouting at us that if we didn't go out to work that day we'd work there no more. Grady from Roscommon stood up to him and declared that we would not work in them conditions. The next day the coaches went back up the mountains again, but there was no one on them. None of us went back up. The next day the foreman came into the canteen and apologised for the misunderstanding, as he knew he'd have no workers otherwise. Three Donegal men sharing the caravan with me nearly brought the tables with them out of the canteen they were in such a rush to get to the coach, but about thirty-five of us jacked up. We wouldn't go back out again to work after what he said to us the day before. Some of us came back to Manchester, but I got off the train in Wigan because I had a sister there. I went into the pub that night and this Castlebar man told me about a *Wimpy* site that needed men to operate tractors. He told me they mightn't start me straight away, but they'd pay me so much for going out. He said, tell them I sent you, and I did. They took me on nights then, twelve-hour shifts, five days a week. I only did it for six months because it interfered with my social life. Sure I was only young, about twenty-two or twenty-three at the time, so I jacked it up. It was great money, but there was loads of work that time in the Sixties.

Oh! There was great craic too. God Almighty! All them little towns that time; they were only small towns, Wigan and Burnley and them, but they were still crowded with Irish. There was an awful lot of Irish in Wigan even from back here in Mayo. In any of them towns in Lancashire you'd find the Irish. You wouldn't miss home that time, because you'd meet lads from everywhere. Sure everyone was going to England that time and America too, but it was mostly England. And if you didn't meet them in the town where you worked, you'd meet them on a Saturday night in *The Astoria*, lads and girls from all around Ireland, so there was always good craic. Ah! We used to drink a good bit at the beginning too, when we were young and messing about. It was the downfall of a lot of the Irish men over there and there is still the odd one who's gone that rough, they don't care. I used to go see this fella in this big house that was let into eight or nine bed-sits, you know, and maybe there was only the one bathroom in it. There were all using the one toilet. He had just one room and a cooker in the corner, and the bed. He was doing everything in the one small room. Now he never married and he just got into that way. He was working and he'd go out for a few drinks at the weekend and I'd say he'd only be around sixty years of age when he died. I enquired after him last Christmas and they said he got bad at work and he was taken into hospital, a big strong man he was. So there are still people living very rough over there. Some of them brought it on themselves, you know, drinking cans there sitting out in the park. About twelve or thirteen years ago they were putting down this metro link in Manchester, the tram, and we were working in the centre of the city and you'd be ashamed sometimes below in Piccadilly where there was a little park and they'd be there, you know, shouting and drinking cider and drinking cans and singing Irish songs. We had a little cabin for the workmen and they'd be watching you in the morning and as soon as the kettle would be on they'd be around the door, about four or five of them shouting, is there any spare cups? Is there anything for us in that kettle? You know and you'd be ashamed. Oh! Stop. But, the likes of them will probably be found dead somewhere. Some of them would never have seen the sky over Ireland since they left.

It was the money that got to them too. They were used to nothing in Ireland and then they started working in England and making money and it went to their heads. And some of them were only kids. They left home when they were fifteen years of age. It's no wonder they went rough. Going away to a strange place when all you were used to was a small farm, sure you were bound to go mad in a big town with a few pound in your pocket. I don't think there's as many of them now because a lot of them have died off and the young crowd have more cop on in them.

A lot of the Irish weren't treated very well and a lot of it was by their own country people. I seen it myself with some of the old companies like *Murphy's* and *Leydon's*. A lot of them were trying to fiddle tax and that sort of thing. The van would come along to pick up all the workers in the morning; there'd be a trailer behind it with a canopy and they'd be packed in there like cattle. They might travel for an hour or an hour and a half in the freezing cold; with the frost on the ground. There were no facilities for cooking or nothing and you might get to the café and you might not. I seen a lad get sacked one day for being five minutes late. The agent, a Mayo man, told the timekeeper to give him a pound for coming in. I seen them running men in the middle of the day if they thought they weren't working. I seen a lot of different things done by our own countrymen. They have an awful lot to answer for.

I eventually settled in Manchester and I spent the rest of my time there. My sister was always on to me to settle down somewhere. I lived in every town in Lancashire and some in Yorkshire too. My brother-in-law got me the job with the Gas Board laying gas mains like they're doing now between Westport and Castlebar and I stayed at that for about thirty five years. It was rough work and hard work, but I enjoyed it. I was in digs first, then I got a flat, and then I got married and me and the wife got a house. Twenty odd years later we separated and I was in a flat again for about five years before I came home. I had a bad back and the doctor told me if I continued working I'd end up on crutches so she put me off work.

There was no point in England if you weren't working and I'd always said when I retired I'd come back to Ireland. I was on holidays in Louisburgh about five years ago with my son when I seen these houses being built and I thought, God, this would be lovely. The secretary gave me forms to fill up. God! There was a lot of questions to answer, and me sister kept saying, you haven't a hope because there'll be a list the length of your arm. That was September. The following March she rang me and said that the parish priest wants to know if I was still interested and that if I was I'd have to come back and live

John (right) with brothers Padraig & Tommy

in it permanently. I could not use it as a holiday home. I assured him that I intended coming home for good and about ten days later I had a letter from the secretary telling me that they had allotted me Number four. I couldn't believe it. I came back and I signed up for it and then I had to return to England to straighten out my affairs. A month later I came home.

My family was a great help. I have a brother in the home place back there and I go back there all the time to visit him and me sister lives over the road here, about three miles away. She had the whole house here set up for me when I arrived back and had bought storage heaters and everything. She has made a big difference to me settling in. Then my neighbours were very friendly too. Three of the women were from back Killeen way, and a man, he's dead now, was from Louisburgh here, but I knew them all sort of thing, and I think that helped too. We used to call in and out to one another. As I say the first winter was hard. In England there's more to do; there's more places to go, you know and that, but even in England the Irish were all leaving. An awful lot was coming back. Mayo was a big change from Manchester, you know, even though I was born and reared here. I was still a

364

stranger. Even now, you know when I go up the town there they all call out, "How ya John", or "how ya Johnny," and I cannot put a name to them. I hate admitting I don't know them. I used to come to see my parents nearly every year, but you wouldn't meet that many or get to know them that well. There's not that much social activity around Louisburgh, not here in this little town. This time of year now you'd get a lot of visitors and there's music in the pubs and that, but in winter time it's very quiet, very quiet. I was in Castlebar there yesterday just doing a bit of shopping. It's a good shopping place. I do just go up the odd time. Just to get out, you know.

The last few Christmases I've spent in England. I have a son and a daughter there in Manchester. He's a Chartered Accountant and a graduate of Leeds Metropolitan University and my daughter is a Legal Advisor in a big firm of solicitors. I've no grandchildren, no, there's none of them married yet. They come to stay with me. They were home there in March, the two of them, for a long weekend. The lad was home there about a month ago for a week and now the daughter is coming again in September for a week. They didn't like the idea of me coming home at first, no they didn't. I remember when I told the lad I was going back; that I had a house got in Louisburgh, he said, "But you left there. You left your parents and now you're leaving us as well." I explained to him that there was no point in me staying in Manchester, walking around the city. Here I have Carramore Strand and Old Head about a mile over the road and all the way back to Killeen you have beaches on either side. If you get fine weather in summer, it's lovely. You'll meet all different people from different places. There's an awful lot of people from Dublin down here. In fact, an awful lot of people have houses bought here, you know, summer homes.

My children would have been familiar with the area. Each year I used to come on holidays when my parents were alive. The children loved it. Even now when the lad was here for a week we went to Clare Island one day and we were down in Achill at the races. I think he hated going back you know. I said to him, would you live here? And he said no, I don't think I'd live here, but I love to come on a visit. In fact, now he was on the phone to me last night and he said he was on the Internet or whatever and there's cheap flights going again in October and he might have a long weekend with me then. So they like to come and they like me to spend Christmas over there with them. It's alright going back, as I still meet some of the old lads that I used to know there, even though it's changed there too. Funnily enough now, one of the lads does ring me often and he said one of the pubs, *The Derby Inn*, is let now in flats. There's students in it. The pubs scene and everything has gone down and a lot of the Irish have died off and some of them have come back here to Ireland, so it's not the same around there. But, I knew that before I left you know. Six or seven year ago it was going down then. It wasn't the same as it was say fifteen or twenty year ago.

My sister up the road was in England too, and she and her husband came back. I think the majority of people over there would like to come back. I don't know why, it's in our nature. It must have been heartbreaking for our parents to lose all their children to immigration, but that was the thing that was going then. It was happening in every house in Ireland. Everyone was going you know. Oh! It was sad times and you know by the time you'd send a letter or that you'd be gone a couple of weeks. I didn't write until I had work and an address. Now you can pick up the phone when you're on the train, you can ring them from Dublin. They're not even going from Dublin now; they're flying out from Knock. I went up with me son there when he was going back. His flight was at half past four and he arrived home before me. I wasn't in here ten minutes when he rang me and said he was home about half an hour. Long ago we'd have to take the train from Westport. Oh! Christ stop! Three or four of us would get a car or a taxi into Westport. We'd take the train to Dublin, out to Dun-Laoghaire and then the boat to Holyhead and then from Holyhead it was about four hours on the train on the other side again. I remember the first or second time I came home and me cousin was with me and for some reason we come through Liverpool where we got on the boat at eight o'clock. You couldn't stand up, there was that much shoving and pushing. This fella told us to go downstairs where the cattle were tied with chains. There were a couple of women from out

West and they put a few *forms* (wooden benches) down for them to sit on and we lay down on the floor on the straw that was for the cattle. We landed in Dublin at seven o'clock the next morning. That was seven hours on the boat and another four, four and a half on the train home. Oh! It was killing. It was cruel that time, compared to now. Even when I brought the car I'd work up until five o'clock and then I'd come home and my wife would have the kids ready and we'd leave straight away. It was three and half hours drive to Holyhead and

then another four or five hours on the boat and then drive down from Dublin with no sleep. God Almighty! It would kill a horse. It was the same coming back. It would take the good out of the holiday. I used to hate that bloody drive back to Dublin. And the roads were bad that time; you had no by-passes like you have now. You had to go through Kinnegad and all those small towns. The road to Frenchpark was the

My parents back in Aillenmore

worst and if you got behind a tractor, God help you!

Most of the changes in Ireland are good; it's just that it changed too quickly. When you see kids going to school there now and the mobile phone up to their ears, I don't like that. There's a secondary school across the road, and you'll see them pulling up in cars at seventeen years of age. There's coaches there to bring them as far as from Westport, but still some of them drive. I seen one fellow last summer in a jeep, a red jeep! I think that's ridiculous. To pay tax and insurance for a young fella like that is going over the top. And of course these drugs, they're taken over now, sure it's ridiculous. There's discos up the town, but the drugs are in it. Sure any of the big towns, Ballina and that, all have them. So I don't like that about living in Ireland. The children here are spoilt; they've gone completely over the top. It's the complete opposite to what it was like in our day. I went to a little school back in Killeen, a National School. I left when I was fourteen, but even before that I took the odd day off to help me father on the farm. I didn't like it that much. I learnt how to read and write and that was all you wanted that time. A lot of time was spent learning Irish and sure what good was that to me in Manchester? You'd spend an hour a day at bloody Irish, but what good was it to me when I went to England? What good was it to anyone? That time they had to emigrate. There was nothing here. They had to go away. Now they're bringing them back, it's come the full circle. I never foreseen that. I never thought you'd see that day. I would have preferred to stay if I could have got a job here. Oh! I think I would. I would never have bothered leaving. I'd say most people would have stayed if they'd had work, but as I say here was nothing that time.

I always sent money home to me mother and father, because they had nothing, well they had a few cattle on the land, but as I say that time there wasn't much. There was no money. No one had money except the rare odd one that had a shop or a pub or something, but there was nothing. Ireland was poor that time. It was poor all over. In England at least you could get work. You could go from job to job that time if you wanted. Even with all of us going over from Ireland you could still get plenty of work. People were better dressed and everything. God Almighty! I remember going into *The Astoria* and there were some of the finest Irish men and women with dark curly hair and healthy men six foot tall and girls the same. I've said that now to different people. Sure you'd see girls going around now in auld track suits and I don't know. I think they're a different breed now. God that time there were some fine women and men, you know, that had come over from Ireland. And as I say they were brought up with not half enough to eat probably, from big families. There was one family back beside me and there was twenty-one in it. Twenty-one and they living in a little thatched house with just two rooms. When I said it to a woman one time she said sure what else was there for amusement, there was no television or nothing! Sure fourteen was an average family back there in Killeen and I don't know how they reared them because they had nothing.

There always seemed to be food though; they were self-sufficient that time. Even back on the farms I remember me own mother she'd have her churn and she'd make her own butter and she'd bake her own bread, you know, they'd buy a bag of flour. There was no such thing as going to the shop and buying groceries. You had your own geese and hens. You had your own milk and your own butter. So they were self-sufficient. They were never hungry. You had your own potatoes. Every one had a field of potatoes that time. So really all you had to buy was the flour and the sugar and tea. It was all healthy food fresh off the farm. Now you won't see a hen or a duck or a goose, a very odd one. You have to go in and buy milk. For meat we ate mostly bacon. Most farmers that time, they'd rear pigs and kill them for food. We'd always kill a pig in November. And then salt it in a barrel. You'd leave it salted for about three weeks and then they'd take it out and hang it up and you'd have bacon until about March or April. Most farmers did it. And they might kill their own sheep now and again. I don't know if it was a nice life, but it was a healthy one.

Its lovely here if you get the fine weather. But, this summer was terrible; it really affected tourism. These past two weeks were alright, but it's really been a quiet summer. There was quite a bit of building around here, but I think it's slowed down now. I think there's a bit of a slump. I go for a drink the odd time up the town, but I don't bother too much with alcohol anymore. When the lad was here we used go up every night. He likes a few pints of lager, so we used go up during the week. It was very quiet. You might see five or six in each pub and there's about six or seven pubs. I remember when there were thirteen in it. I still go to Church, always did when I was in England. An awful lot of the Irish did. The odd one fell away. It was what they were brought up with. My children were raised Catholic, baptized and con-firmed and I brought them to Church until they were seventeen or eighteen and after that I said, go ye're own way now. I listen to *Faith Alive* there every Sunday morning on the Mid-West radio. Some of their views might be different to mine and you'd wonder why they keep changing the rules to suit the times.

I'm back anyway where I belong in Kilgeever Parish across the road from St. Patrick's Church, even though I spent a lifetime away from it. Last year I was in the garage getting me car serviced and the bloke asked me how long I was in England. "Forty years," I told him. "Forty years," he said, "sure God Almighty that was a lifetime." And it was.

Interviewed at his home in Louisburgh, County Mayo, on Wednesday, August 15th, 2007

At home in Louisburgh

MARY CAFFREY

I came home to Ireland, to St. Brendan's Village in Mulranny, County Mayo, exactly ten years ago, on the 10th of December, 1997, but to me it's only like five minutes ago. It's absolutely beautiful here after spending sixty-three years in Scotland and England. I don't have to die to go to heaven, because this is heaven, where I am now. I came from Achill Island; you're bound to have heard of it, in a little village called Dooniver, down by the sea. Talk about nightmares! It was bad there in the Twenties, because we were very poor. My poor father was sent home from England when he was sick with pleurisy and there was nothing in the line of work for him in those days. We had to plant our own little plots of potatoes and things like that. They gave him two shillings and six pence dole money and rather than let him have that for nothing, they would put the poor old man out on the roads breaking stones and things like that, even though they knew he might have bronchitis or pneumonia. They were very, very cruel. Oh! I could write a few stories about this country. Growing up as a little girl, I seen my parents suffer from poverty. There were the haves and the have-nots. The haves kept what they had to themselves and the have-nots were treated like dirt. It was a bad country in those days; thank God it is different now.

Of course we had to go away as kids. I went to London at thirteen, with a cousin, on service. It was like the television programme, *Upstairs Downstairs*. People don't know they're alive nowadays. It's very hard to understand, but in those days there was only two jobs for young children growing up in Achill. You either had to go to Scotland tatie-picking out in the fields, or you had to go into service in London. My cousins wrote to my father to know if any of the girls could come over to work with them. There were six of us, three boys and three girls and the eldest one, Betty, I think she was seventeen at the time, had found herself a boyfriend back in the next village so she wouldn't go. I still had another year at school. You know in those days you got off at fourteen and we hated school because we used to get murdered. The teachers had a big cane and they'd leather into us in the morning and we in our bare feet. If a teacher was in bad mood he'd have this cane and he'd be battering you out at the blackboard if you weren't able to do your sums or something like that. Oh! God it was a hard life. If there was a film made about the life we had in those days, it would be like a horror movie. The younger generation today can't even visualize what it was like. But, the likes of me who's lived through it has never forgot.

Anyhow me parents spoke to the teacher and he probably spoke to the priest; it was the priest who ruled all. One day me mother says, "Come here *a leanbh* (alanna -child), would you like to go to London?" They were real Irish speakers, the old people back then in their black shawls. Oh! When I heard London, to me it sounded like paradise. As soon as I put that in my mind, my mother couldn't get a minute's peace. She said maybe the poor Master would take pity on us. He knew we were all steps of stairs, and we had nobody abroad to send money home like a lot of families. I finally got permission anyhow and talk about Judy Garland going over the rainbow! London was like a fairyland to us in those days. The lady I was going to work for sent money for my passage, a lovely little pair of shoes and two lovely little dresses, but she didn't realize how small I was. When she seen me, she nearly fainted.

My mother said then we'll have to get someone for Mary to travel with. She went back to the next village, to a place called Dugort where there was two girls home on holidays, the Lavelles who were on service in London as well. All the girls from roundabout were on service; they all knew each other. They'd all meet at Mass on a Sunday, you know. Anyway, Mabel and Ethel Lavelle was going away the following week and me Mum asked them if they'd take me with them and that my cousins would meet me at Euston station. A bus came back from Slieve Mor; the road is all tarred now, they were sandy in those days, at six o'clock. And my poor Mum had to walk the three and a half miles to the bus stop with me and stay until the bus came and then she handed me over to the Lavelle girls. I'd never been outside Dooniver, and in those days you were still a baby at thirteen. We got the bus to Westport and the train to Dublin and then the boat. That was it. There were no planes I don't think in those days. My cousins met me off the train in Euston Station and brought me home to Hampstead, a nice residential area. Oh! I thought I was in another world, it was absolutely beautiful.

It was 1935 when I went to work for the Landours. They were lovely people. I was a servant washing pots and pans that were so big I could have taken a bath in them. They had a butler and a chauffeur and my cousin was the cook. Oh! God, my cousin was a great cook. There was no frozen food; it was the real thing. Her speciality was a big leg of ham with breadcrumbs all over the top. At Christmas time then the family attended to us. They made a lot of Christmas and would come downstairs with presents and cook dinner for us on Christmas Day. Wasn't I glad to get away from Achill, I can tell you. London was beautiful in those days, not like it is now. You wouldn't put a dog in it now. My cousins would bring me to Buckingham Palace, Hyde Park Corner, Marble Arch, and *Selfridges's*, on our day off, and when the Lady's daughter would come home from boarding school, she would get on her phone for the chauffeur to come with the car, a big limousine, and take us shopping. The little girl took a shine to me because I was around the same age as her, you know, and she'd want to be down in the kitchen with me. Her Mum being gentry didn't want her down mixing with the domestic staff, however, she'd sneak down if I was making ice cream. We'd put strawberries and a couple of pints of cream into a big cylinder and there was an organ grinder thing with a handle to twist, and this other thing like the old fashioned washing machine would go around and round mixing the strawberries and cream. The two of us would be stealing spoonfuls of it. When she was due to go back to school her mother would order the chauffeur to take them shopping and of course Mary would have to come too. Everything she bought for the little girl, she bought for me as well. I was absolutely ruined. We would play on her swing in the garden and we went to see the pantomimes at this time of the year, *Mother Goose*, and *Ali Baba and the Forty Thieves*, because there was no television in those days. There was no radios either, as far as I can remember; it was all circuses and that type of thing. It was a lovely time, really. However, I left after two years when my cousin came home to marry a man from Tonragee, and I didn't want to stay there without her. I was fifteen years of age when my uncle who worked in Victoria station came for me and brought me home to Achill. I wasn't long there when I was poisoned and they sent me to the hospital in Castlebar because the poison was going through my blood. I was very ill for about a year.

When I was sixteen I went to Scotland tatie-hoking, where we'd be out in the fields digging for potatoes. My mother came with me because at sixteen you were still a kid. There's no kids nowadays at that age. The world is a different place altogether. My mother had to ask Dr. Donnelly if I was fit to go because I was just recovering from my illness and I was run down and everything. He said that was the very thing for me because I'd been confined for so long. I hadn't had any fresh air for years between working in service, and being in hospital. So me Mum took me to Scotland and that was the start of my travelling. The farmers in Scotland used send the gaffers over to Ireland to find workers. They'd come knocking on our doors and ask us if we wanted work. It was only a seasonal job. We went out in the month of June and stayed until November, but by the end of that first summer I liked it so much I didn't want to go home. Mum left in November and I stayed all winter. We were out in the fields at three o'clock in the morning. As soon as the daylight broke, the gaffer would be shouting at us to get up and out. Our sleeping quarters was sheds where there used to be cattle and that, like stables that were all cleaned out and everything. Bothys they were called. One part was for the girls and the other half for the lads. Our bedding, they'd call it a duvet nowadays, was a big coarse bag filled up with hay or straw. We'd be there at half three in the morning and we'd finish at twelve. Then we'd make a bit of lunch for ourselves. Back out again until five o'clock and then sometimes the foreman would come and say that the farmer had another big order in for more potatoes and then we'd have to work until nine o'clock. Writing letters was the only means of communication we had and of course we had to write regular. I would get paid perhaps two pounds for a whole week and that was maybe for forty-eight or fifty hours work. We did our bit of shopping for the week and whatever we had left went into the letter home to our parents. All the Irish people done that. That's why we were all away in the first place. There was nothing here to eat only the blinking grass. If you were a poor family, you had nothing except if a neighbour had a few sons away in England. The ones who had something helped the poor ones; just your own class though. The higher-ups never helped us, not even during the War.

Scotland during the Second World War was the worst place of the lot. They were after the Clyde because it is a shipping area, the Glasgow Clyde. We were lucky because we were near the fields and could hide. The bombers weren't interested in the farms anyhow. They say that bombs don't explode; they just sink into the ground so we had plenty of hiding places. We would hide under maybe a clump of trees, and they had the odd shelter dug out, with little bits of beams over the top. They say that bombs don't go through the ground, but I wouldn't like to have taken the chance. Thank God we were always very lucky. Your nerves were in such a state sometimes. You'd hear the bombs whistling down and you'd just pray to Almighty God that it wouldn't come anywhere near you and thanks be to Almighty God, it never did. Say we were in Edinburgh working on a farm and there was a raid in Glasgow, we'd see them crossing over, the German planes, and we'd hear the bombs coming down and even at a distance like that we'd see the lights when the place was being blown up. Like the blitz in London. There were thousands of people killed there. And they're still at it in Iraq. People are sick and tired of that kind of thing. I wonder if war will ever end. I don't think it will really.

I stayed out all that first year with the potato-hoking and then the following year a nice little girl from Glasgow started, about the same age as me. She said never mind spending another winter up there, to come to Glasgow with her. Her Mum and Dad was Irish, Crawford was their name, and she said I could stay with them. I didn't feel like staying out another winter, for it was awful cold. It was alright in the summer picking the potatoes, but in the winter it was a different kind of job. You had to pit them, you had to put them in a big place and put the earth and everything on the top of them, you know, to keep them dry. So, she told her parents that I was Irish and they said, yes, to come to Glasgow. I got a job as a nanny with a solicitor and his wife in Bearsden, the posh part. They were out all day working and I'd have to take the children for walks and wash their clothes and iron them. I never got any time off and my friend used to say, you need to get another job where you're not working at night.

Chldhood home in Dooniver

I was a stranger in Glasgow and I didn't know many people. But, I gave my notice in and said I was leaving, and I got a job as a machinist in a biscuit factory called *Grey and Dunn*. It's still there to this day as a matter of fact. They were the first people to make the *Blue Ribbon* biscuits. That was shift work, six to two in the morning, and the next week you'd go on at two until ten at night. The War was still on and we were making Army biscuits for the troops. The machinists all dressed up in white; white aprons, white overalls, and white shoes.

They were so hygienic in those days, you know. There were seven machines for making biscuits and there was numbers on each one. They'd give you a week with another girl to learn how to pick up the machines so I was put on machine number three with a little girl with dark curly hair called Ellen. She shook hands with me and says; just watch what I do now. As soon as I opened my mouth, she knew I was Irish. Well, my God, she says, put it here, my Dad is Irish, and won't he be glad to meet you. His name is Caffrey. You'd be about the first Irish person he's met, she says, since he came over here forty odd years ago. You'll have to come home with me at two o'clock. So I went home with her and to look at the poor old man with his cap on, you'd know right away he was Irish. Dad, she says, I've got an Irish lass here to meet you. Ah! Be the holy, he cried, and as soon as I went in I felt right at home, just like that. There was a fiddle hanging on the wall just like I used to see at home in the cottages years ago. He started talking to me. Oh! He was in his glory. He came from outside Castlebar, from a place called Boholla. Now could you get any nearer to my home place than that? His wife came from there as well, but when they got married in the late 1800's they left for Scotland about five weeks after the wedding and had never been back.

Ellen had two brothers. One was working as a baker and the other, Matthew, was working on the docks loading ships and things like that and of course he asked me would I go out with him. I was about eighteen then. I went out with him for quite a while and when I was coming up for twenty-one we got married in St. Margaret's Church in Glasgow. The priest had an awful job. He wasn't going to marry me because I didn't have any birth lines. He said it's not a case of having to, is it? I said, no Father, its nothing like that. He married us then on condition that I sent away for my birth lines. It was years after before I got them; I think my son went to Castlebar for them in the end. I got married anyhow on the 1st of May 1943, and my aunt said I'd have luck because it was Our Lady's Day. She couldn't have been any more wrong. The Queen was sixty-three years married this year and I would have been sixty-five. Only her life wasn't like mine! I married Matthew because he was nice and quiet and I thought he was decent.

He was a good bit older than me as well, but it was hard to get decent blokes in those days and you couldn't afford to be foolish because if anything happened there was no social security like there is now. Girls used to get deported out of this country for having babies, and look at it now. Thank God things has changed like that. Anyhow Matthew turned alcoholic as soon as we were married and I had a terrible life with him, but bore a beautiful family. My first little girl, Maureen, was born on the 29th of February 1944, so the nurses were saying she'd only have a birthday every four years. I got caught kind of quick because I was just married the bare ten months. The War was still on and gastroenteritis was raging in those days, and all the doctors was away to the Army and things like that. So she died from convulsions and was buried the day she turned two. It didn't do my husband any good, to be honest, he used always be on about that. Then I had Anne in 1947 in the month of February again, the 24th, and I had Matthew in 1948. He's got the same birthday as Olivia Newton-John and Anne has the same birthday as Elizabeth Taylor. There's a year and seven months between those two. I had two good kids and they've given me five grandchildren and three little great grandchildren.

After I was married I had all different jobs. I worked all my life really. Only when I was carrying the children did I give it up. I used to clean offices, dusting the typewriters and that, down on me knees polishing the linoleum floor. I worked in *Stewarts & Lloyd's* the shipping firm. I don't know if they still exist or not, but they had hundreds of offices and hundreds of people working for them. I had another little job in a factory that made firelighters. We had to pack one hundred and forty-four firelighters to get one shilling and sixpence. That was called casual work where the man paid you on the boxes you had filled and you got your money at the end of the day, which was handy for me because Matthew was gone off drinking with his mates. Me and the kids would be left for weeks and weeks at a time and then he'd come back and walk in as if he owned the place. There was no social security or nothing. God they don't know they're alive now. That was sixteen hours a day that I worked for about a full year, and I went down to five stone. The doctor said if you don't take things a bit easier, your

St. Mary's Hospital, Manchester
(holding Gary Lineker's son)

children won't have you much longer. So I had to give up the cleaning job. I went into the firelighter place earlier in the morning and worked later at night and tried to balance it up that way. My hands would be crippled and dirty from the firewood and firelighters, and of course we didn't make much money either. So I had to be father and mother to my children and they appreciate it today and they respect me for it. They always say to me, "You were a good Mum."

I always kept in touch with my parents, and whenever I could get the money together I'd come home on holidays down to Achill. My husband never came with me; he was never in Ireland. You must be joking, he was too busy drinking. He was alright Monday, Tuesday, Wednesday and Thursday, but on Friday they got paid in Glasgow and if you knew what was good for you, you'd clear out. I used get the kids ready after school, after working all week, because he never gave me any money, and I'd run away to Brigid's, my sister-in-law, because you'd hear him coming down the street shouting about what he was going to do to me. He was violent, you know towards me. I would have to run for my life and I had no parents over there or anything like that. Just my husband's people and they were good to me; you know helping me with the kids and that. I got four nights of peace every week but once the weekend came, the house was full of wine bottles. I'd have to come back from wherever we'd been and clean up. When he was sober, he'd be all apologies, but what's the good of that? Most of those people are like that, funnily enough. He'd not a word to say when he was sober, not a word, but the Lord save us, as soon as he got drunk, it was a different story.

In 1970 then, on the 20th of June, he died. Glasgow started to get a little bit rough then in the Seventies and my brother, John, wrote and

379

asked me to come to Manchester. The kids were all for it; there was nothing much left for us in Glasgow, so we moved to Manchester. I worked at the University there for a little while, where my grand-daughter is now a teacher, and then I got a job in St. Mary's Hospital, as an Auxiliary Nurse because I only had the basic training. The Sister used to say what a waste because I had the qualities of a nurse and the dedication. The patients loved me. Is that little Scotch lady here, they used to ask. I worked for eleven and half years there. Then it came up that if you're over sixty, you had to retire, and I was sixty-one. Now they're looking for you to work at that age.

I'll be quite honest, in those days I didn't miss Ireland at all. When you're in any country or any city you just mix in with the people, don't you? Your home is there, your children is born there, and things like that. I'll tell you when I began to miss Ireland is when I got older. When your children are gone, you've got no more interest in life. It wasn't until the Nineties then that I started getting very homesick. I was living on my own at the time in a high-rise block of flats in Man-chester. I'd sit out on my veranda and I'd say to myself, God, on a day like this in Ireland we'd be going to the well for water with a little can and all those memories would come back. I think it's something that comes with old age maybe. You know you start to roam down memory lane sort of thing. You try to grasp what's in the past, you know. Plus when you've been away all your life, since you were a kid, you like to get back to your roots. It's where you were born; it's where all your memories were as a little girl. Then when my brother had Alzheimer's disease and I saw the way those poor people were treated in the Nursing Home, it made me think. I knew I didn't want to end up in a place like that.

I started coming to Mulranny on holidays because my parents had died and we had no place to visit out on Achill. It's not the same once your parents go. But, I used to always try and make it to my own village to see the couple of old mates that I had left. Coming home here and then going back to England again, where some of my old friends were dead, began to get very lonesome. This old girl, Julia, from Achill told me one time that a Dr. Cowley was building houses in Mulranny. I thought I haven't got a snowball in July's chance of ever getting home here. Anyhow I met Dr. Cowley in the village one day and I asked him if there was a house here for me. Absolutely, he said. You are the kind of people that I want to help and bring home, he says, because you are the kind of people that has made Ireland what it is today. So he says, it might be a year, it might be two years, but I can tell you, the first little house that comes empty, you'll get it. A year passed and I thought it was just in one ear and out the other, the way it is with some people, out of sight out of mind sort of thing. Then I was getting ready for Mass one night and waiting on the Ring-a-Ride bus that used come around and take us places. I was on the twelfth floor waiting for the lift down when the buzzer goes with the Ring-a-Ride man and at the same time the phone rings. I'm trying to shout over the veranda at the Ring-a-Ride man to hold on a minute. The phone is ringing, the buzzer is going, and I said, what am I going to do? Because if the kids are phoning and they don't get an answer, it being Manchester, they'll think there's something wrong and they'll start panicking. So I answered the phone. Well lo and behold who should it be, but himself, Dr. Cowley, to say he'd got a little house for me. Well if I could have jumped down that phone I would have done it. I was crying and I was laughing, and blessing God. I didn't know whether I was coming or going. "I'm going to Ireland," I told the Ring-a-Ride man. If I had won the lottery I couldn't have been happier. At Saturday night Mass in St. Francis Church in Garton, all the Irish women would sit in the back row. "I'm going to Ireland," I told them and they said they already knew by the smile on my face.

To tell you the God's truth, it's just like a miracle has happened since I came home. I've settled into this little house and I'm surrounded by Irish people. You don't have to make friends; in Ireland they're already your friends. And to tell you the God's honest truth, I was never one for socializing. I never drank or smoked in my life, never put a cigarette in my mouth. I don't like drink because seeing my own husband; I'd had enough of it, but I have a marvellous social life here. In 1999 Dr. Cowley and his wife, Theresa, put me in for a Glamorous Granny competition. Ah! What chance had an old woman like me, I said, sure they're grannies in their fifties now. You're up with the best of them said the Cowleys. An older woman than me won it, I think she was in her nineties, but we all got lovely prizes. Apart from that, we got money for St. Brendan's Village. A couple of days afterwards we had a big party here and they gave me a plaque to thank me. Oh! We had a great night out.

I've been on the television a couple of times, on *Open House* with Mary Kennedy and Marty Whelan and *An Bóthar Fada*. I've been interviewed by several newspapers and I was in two magazines. As a matter of fact, I'm out in Poland this week. I've phoned into Mid-West radio a few times, so I'm well-known around here. People used to come up to me on the streets as if they knew me. I can't go many places now, as my knees are very bad with arthritis and on those blasted buses the steps are very high. In England the buses are level with the curb, but here you'd need a blinking ladder at times so I can't go to Westport as often as I used. They've come from all over Ireland up here asking me what I thought of St. Brendan's because they were thinking of starting up the same project in other counties. Houses are like diamonds, I said, they're forever. They're not going to get up and run away, are they? They're never going to be empty because the young ones of today will be the old ones of tomorrow. There are always people ready to go into them, so it's never a waste building a house. And the people that were brought home from England by Safe Home; that were lonely and forgotten about and depressed over there, and are now settled in Ireland, I can tell you, they have something to be thankful for. Every community should do that for their elderly people. The only thing is they left it seventy years too late. The point is that what they're giving us now they owed to our poor parents that had to walk to Mass without a shoe on their foot sometimes.

In our church on Achill there were eleven posh seats made from leather. These were for school teachers, shopkeepers, business people; for those who could buy them. Where did we go but down on the bare boards on our knees. There was the harvest collection for the priest and you didn't put it in a little envelope the way they do now, a kid came around the houses collecting the money. If you were well off you gave five shillings or maybe ten shillings, but when it came down to the poor families that maybe didn't have a loaf inside their door, they would take their last shilling. And they were supposed to be charitable people who were supposed to make sure you weren't hungry? If they came to our house my mother might only have two shillings, and the kid would say, Oh! Father can take no less than half a crown. One time I was home on holidays, when Anne and Matthew were still babies, and I was up in the room when the collector came. I knew that my mother hardly had anything because my father was dead some years and I heard the kid say that Father wouldn't take less than half a crown. People were terrified of the priest in them days, if he was walking through the village, they'd all be running to their doors, you'd think it was God himself that was coming. If there is such a thing as a heaven, those people definitely must be there. I told my mother to put the two shillings back in her purse and I told the kid to get lost. I told him to ask the priest to send us down a loaf because we had nothing to eat all day. My poor mother was crying. Don't be so daft, I says, Almighty God knows that you haven't got anything. It's Him you account to. On a Sunday then, all the shopkeepers and all the big shots' names would be called out from the Altar, ten shillings, five shillings, fifteen shillings, and when it came down to the half a crowns, there was no names mentioned. Talk about hypocritical. Thank God all that has changed nowadays; Thank God that it's so different.

The bad things I like to forget; the good things I remember. It's a good place now, but it's also a bad place. I'm proud of Ireland the way it has changed, but it has lost its character from what I remember. The friendliness is gone and it's every man for himself now. Years ago the lads would all come down to our house at night to my brothers; they'd go to the neighbours another night where they'd be all sitting around the table playing cards and singing Irish songs. And it was good you know. We'd have little oil lamps hanging on the wall because there wasn't electricity. It was lovely in those days. You'd never have heard tell of murders and the things that's happening now. If the old people were to come back and see it now the way it is, they'd want to die all over again. Whatever has gone wrong with the people, I don't know. It's a shame really. But, where we are here in County Mayo, thank

God, this little village is so lovely and peaceful and quiet. The women in the shop over there won't let you come out if they know you've no family or no transport. Mary Doherty and Mrs. Daly won't hear of us coming out if there's snow or frost on the road. I just phone over my shopping and they bring it to the house. If its raining and they see you on the road, they'll give you a lift. There is everything here that everybody could wish for. To tell you the God's truth, we are the luckiest handful of elderly people that ever was born. St. Brendan's is like a little model village. You don't have to go out for nothing. You can get your lunch over in the Nursing Home or if you're not well, get on the phone and the girls will come over with it on a tray. If you are worried about your blood pressure one of the girls is over there to take it.

With Marty Whelan on *Open House* (RTE television programme)

Where could you get the care like that? You're left here as long as you want until the day that you die, but if you start falling around, you'll go over to the Nursing Home for your own safety. Otherwise you can stay here for the rest of your natural life. It's like a tonic. You feel so safe and secure. Living here makes you want to go on with your life; you don't get depressed or lonely because you know that you've got good people around. When I was in Manchester I used to pray to God to take me away in my sleep, but not anymore.

I could have been well married many times in the thirty-six years I've been a widow, but I was always frightened to take a chance again. What is the point in getting married anyhow? At the end of the day you're still left on your own. But, it's nice when your children come to see you and mine are never away from here. Even my grandchildren regard themselves as Irish and they tell everyone that their Granny comes from Achill. They're as happy as I am that I'm home because they used to worry about me in Manchester where there were people getting mugged all the time. At this time of the year you'd have to be in at four o'clock in the evening. They're doing it in Dublin now, mugging and even breaking into the houses and that, but not in Mulranny, or any other small village in Ireland. Oh! It's a lovely place here, a lovely place.

The young people now don't know they were ever born. They wouldn't survive a week of what we've been through. Away to foreign countries, working out in fields for half nothing, soaking wet coming in at night, but it hasn't done us any harm. It's all in the past now. At the time I had no option, because I was just a kid, but I am glad I went away for the simple reason that I wouldn't have liked to be stuck here all the time, because you don't get to know very much. You haven't seen anything. You don't know the other side of life. I can tell life from both sides now; I've seen the good parts and the bad parts, especially in Ireland. I can think back to the way things were in my day and the way they are now. This house is comfortable and it's clean and that's all that matters. I'm eighty-six years old and I do all my own cleaning and shopping. Dr. Cowley calls me a mighty lady. I tell him when I need home help he'll be the first to know. I really had a lovely life, to be quite honest with you. If I wrote a book it would be a bestseller. People have often said that to me that I've had a very colourful life. And it's had a lovely happy ending thanks to Dr. Cowley.

Interviewed at her home in Mulranny, County Mayo, November 26th, 2007

HOME WITH WILLIAM
by Frances Browner

"It's very quiet here, isn't it?" William is on his way to the post office to pay the rent. This was his third foray into Westport town that day. "There's nothing else to do, is there?" It's a blustery March afternoon and the wind whips around the corner of James Street onto The Mall. I assure him it was the time of year; that it would be much better when spring was here and the evenings longer. I had found that the previous year, I told him. January and February in Ireland were dull and dreary and I thought if I had to awaken one more time to the sounds of the wind howling; I would go mad. Now I don't notice it at all. "You found that too?" His eyes lit up and in them were pools of recognition that bond two people who had been through the same experience. Yes, I found that too and would have gone back any time during that first two months. The Safe Home team hear that all the time from people who are finding it hard to settle. Mary Ann reckons that many of them would bite a return ticket out of your hand during the first six months. Coming home is hard; like William said before, it's like emigrating all over again.

The flat on Altamount Street is warm and cosy. The kettle is on when I arrive and a fresh apple tart had been bought in from Annie's bakery. The television in the corner, which cost one hundred and sixty nine euros, isn't turned on very often because of the bad reception from the nearby railway. William listens to the radio instead and reads the newspapers. He didn't bother watching the rugby match between Ireland and Wales the previous Saturday. "They're not beating any-body, are they? I nearly bet on Wales that morning and the bookie got annoyed with me. Anyhow the odds weren't that good; you'd need to be backing hundreds." The kettle boils; the tart is cut and I settle into the tiny two-seater discarded by a cousin, which will be fine until the new beige suite is delivered from *Argos*. The shipment had arrived two days after Christmas, complete with music centre and a nice antique mirror situated over the fireplace. The next door neighbour donated a bookcase, complete with books and even told him where to place it in the sitting room. Pictures brought from London adorn the walls, as well as one of the Sacred Heart contributed by the cousin, and an old print of Westport purchased in a local antique shop. William seems to have a penchant for antiques, I note, and I wonder where the old gramophone ended up? Still in its box, I am told, even though there's a space carved out for it on the bookcase. Red and cream curtains protect the patio door and a fawn rug acquired for half-price in *O'Grady's* closing sale partially covers the porcelain tiled floor.

"I came at a bad time," William sips his tea, "hopefully it'll be better in the summer. Bad weather is distressing. It's a lot of pressure, moving. There were nights that I couldn't sleep." Is it the quietness, I wonder? I had found the silence surrounding my new home in Charlesland eerie at first. There's a huge difference between living in a small town in Wicklow or the West of Ireland and a cosmopolitan city in England or America. "I don't know what it was," William slices more tart, "but something was wrong because I couldn't sleep. Still I don't regret coming back even though I miss my friends in London. On Sunday nights I miss going up to *The Lion* with my mates. There's no *Lion* here. I was in *Hoban's* last night, but there was no music and only about eight or ten people there. It's very quiet when there's no music. There was a good crowd in *The Porterhouse*, but I didn't know anybody there. There was no music, only three televisions showing soccer. I watched it for a bit and then got out. The beer has gone up another thirty cents, I believe, but not all of the pubs have enforced it yet. When my sister and her friend were here, they preferred *Conway's*. There wasn't as many people in the town long ago yet all the pubs made a living. From here to the station there was three pubs one time. *Clarke's* was taken down about five or six years ago and apartments put up instead; *O'Brien's* then was closed down along with another one up at the station, *Ring's*. What I can't understand is that they've built homes for three hundred up this end of town, including that complex over there by *Tesco* and surely there'd be business for one pub. If only fifty customers went in a night. People living up here wouldn't have to drive, or walk into town. It would be nice and handy for me. I could pop up at ten o'clock for a pint before bed. If it's a bad night now, I can't walk into town. Do you hear that wind? They say it's going to be an awfully stormy night.

Take me home to Mayo

Ireland has changed so much. The people are different; they're not as friendly. They kept telling me that over in England too. Then again I don't know anybody around here anymore, and they don't know me. They're all driving around in big cars, aren't they? There's nobody walking; nobody to stop and have a chat with. Some of the pubs are awful noisy; full of youngsters and they talk awful loud. I used always go into *Toby's* when I'd be home on holidays, but its all youngsters there now and the noise is desperate. Maybe I should go back to England, but that would be a hard thing to do too. I'd have to wait for a flat and that. Ah! I'm too old for all that. If I was still in my forties I'd do it. It would be terrible embarrassing to have to admit to the mates that it didn't work out though, just like they said it wouldn't.

I've heard from Billy once. He's alright, doing a bit of gardening. Tom rang a few times and I had a Christmas card from Jerome in the Camden centre. I rang him to thank them and he was delighted. I miss the friends. You'd never see anyone around here; not even the neighbours. They're very nice, but I never see them. My sister has been down and her son, and the brother too. They thought it was lovely here, nice and quiet. It's alright. I don't like the curtains. My sister said there might be some bargains when *Arnott's* shuts down in Dublin. I hate looking out onto that wall; I wish I had a nicer view. Maybe I'll sow a few flowers in the summer and hang a few baskets or run climbers along the wall. I'll be able to sit out on the patio then.

Tesco is just across the road and you can get everything you want there. Their meat is the best. The bread is better here, I've found, especially that soda bread I get up in Annie's. I can't cut it though; it breaks away from the knife; it's so fresh. She does nice apple tarts too.

I eat about one a week. I used to visit my cousin, Tom, out in Hackne before he died and his wife baked the best apple pies.

I was in *Hoban's* one night and met local poet, Mick Lavelle, who sang a song about a returned emigrant. It was my first Saturday night and I said to myself, I must go and hear some music. It's a funny little pub. There's a bar in the front; a bar in the middle; and then a back bar where they do a bit of dancing. I had gone early to get a seat before the music started at ten and was sitting there by myself when Lavelle came in and sat beside me. He knew me, he said, and asked was I home on holidays. No, I said, I live here now. He sang the song anyhow and kept pointing at me and two other men who were also home from England. He's a good old singer for a man of seventy-eight and a poet too. I think he wrote a song about the lottery. It's fifteen million tonight, I believe. That would be a nice win.

There's a lot to do, but Noreen Mulrine from Safe Home has been a great help. I was getting pension credit in England but that stopped once I got home. I'm supposed to be getting something similar here, but they haven't been giving it to me. They were giving me a few bob to tide me over, but that's stopped too. Noreen is looking into all that. I've been up to Sligo several times to the Department of Social Welfare to show them my bank statements. Three months I was told it would take for the pension to come through; it must be that now. Maybe I'll take the auld accordion out and go busking down at the Mall. It's still in the box there. My sister's friend, Veronica, wanted to buy it off me. She thought it was mighty altogether. Noreen sorted out the telephone and the medical card and arranged for my bills to be paid through direct debit from the bank. The travel pass arrived here one day in the post and I didn't know what it was. I've been using it to take the coach up and down to Castlebar. The first time the driver looked at it and said that's new. It is, I said. When I was getting off I asked him what time was the bus back to Westport. It's written up on the stop, he said. Nothing for nothing from him, I'd say. I like shopping in Castlebar in *Heaton's* and *Argos*. There's more shops there than in Westport. My first electricity bill came to one hundred and sixty-two euros for two months. I'm waiting for Noreen to fix it because I know it shouldn't be that much. My sister says there's something wrong. A bloke came to the door then last Friday night looking for my television licence. It was about seven o'clock, but he said it was the only time he could catch people. I'm entitled to a free one, I told him and it's taking a while to come through. I hope I don't get a summons. I'll have to go back to the Community Welfare Officers again.

They don't get up around here for all hours. I'm awake at six some days and I get up around seven. I was too busy up to last week to join anything. Every day there was bits and pieces to be doing around the flat. I spent my time walking in an out of town shopping. I might have a little flutter in Cheltenham. I was at the races in Epsom a few times and at Ascot. Maybe I'll go to the Galway races this year. I often feel like jumping on a bus for Galway, but what time would it get back, that's the problem. The drivers will tell you nothing. There's other places I could go to on the coach I suppose, like the Foxford Mills and the Ceide Fields and the Famine Memorial on the road to Leenane, but maybe you'd need a car for those places. My brother offered to leave his *Ford Fiesta* here for me, but we were quoted nine hundred euros by a local buck to insure it for a year. My cousin said I should try a few other places like *Quinn Direct* where I might get a better price; the first time insuring it will cost a bit anyway.

I'd say to anyone if it's in your mind to come home, then come, but wait until the summer. I came at a bad time, didn't I? Christmas in itself is stressful; it's on your mind isn't it? Then the first three nights I spent here, the flat was like an icebox. It was too cold to go to bed even. Then there was no water. I had to boil a bucket from the mains here and use it to wash and flush the toilet. Even with the heat on it was cold. It took about four or five weeks to heat up. Never mind, I survived, but it was all a bit stressful at first. I'm here now. I meet up with Jim, a Clare man, who was away too. It's nice to meet up with people who know.

William and I march down Mill Street where we meet just as much traffic as on Junction Road in Islington, but not as many people. We encounter a lone jogger who passes us again on his way back up Bridge Street. There's a drizzle of rain; not clothes drying weather; it's just as cold as London in December and the wind blows our ears back. It's darker here with not as many street lights and no neon signs; not as many people to visit or stop and talk to either. Neither is there as much crime and William says he walks a lot more here than he did over there. The dampness gets to his arthritis though. It's far damper here than in it was in London, he admits.

We sit at the bar in *Matt Molloy's* where a session is in full swing. We order Guinness and a hot whiskey and become immersed in the music, which had started impromptu that afternoon the barman, Seamus, tells us. A few lads on guitar and a girl with Mary Black's voice harmonize: *And the holy ground took care of everything.* William reminisces about the premises that used to be a shop in his childhood and how his father would bring them there when he had business in town. He remembers the shop assistant dragging sacks of goods across the saw dusty floor while his mother shopped and his father traded in the bar at the back. The shop shelves are still evident and the till for the money. The last page in the calendar reads September 1937; a wireless is silent behind the counter and an old yellow photograph depicts the shop front with 'McGing' inscribed over the door.

A bus pulls up outside and the tourists spill out. Seamus bolts over the bar to join the revellers in *Raglan Road*. As the muse of Patrick Kavanagh and the voice of Luke Kelly resound I wonder aloud to William that surely he finds something warm and real about a place like this? Surely listening to his native music in his hometown has got to be preferable to a similar event in one of Ireland's adoptive enclaves around the world? "We used sing like this in *The Lion* too," he is reluctant to give in.

The pizza man arrives with two large pies and whispers, "If you're good you'll get some too." One of the songsters belts out *The Deportees* and a fellow appears behind the bar to fix the taps. He said he'd started the job a few days earlier, "And you came back to finish it?" William taunts him. He roars with laughter and joins us for a pint after addressing William as Willie, just like everyone else in town. I don't think people have changed here, I tell him. I think they're still lovely. I relate how the year before when I first came to Westport everyone on the street said hello. I couldn't get over it. Some of the returnees I interviewed said that they miss popping in and out of their neighbour's houses, but William and I agree we're glad they don't do that anymore. We're too used to our privacy now.

A girl slides onto the stool beside me and asks for a list of drinks, which of course is not available, so she settles for a glass of Guinness. I ask if she's going to sing, but she doesn't know any Irish songs she says, because she's from Belgium. "I too," shout a couple in the middle of the bar and they then proceed to converse in Flemish. William should come here more often, I tell him. In a place like this he would never be alone. I'm like the pint of Guinness there, he smiles, waiting to settle.

There's a hatch at the end of the bar opening out into a yard where the smokers gather and a few people approach to buy drink and take it through a door on the other side. They're the set dancers, Seamus tells us, and they have classes there every Monday night. There you go, I tease William. He was never a good dancer, he reminds me. 'I had it up here', he points at his head, 'but not down here', looks at his feet. 'The women would walk away and leave me on the floor. The only thing I got up for was The Siege of Ennis when I'd be drunk. (*I hope you find the feet of a dancer*, the songstress is right on cue.) I love the music though and I listen to *Céili House* on the radio if I stay in on a Saturday night. I prefer that, as if I have a late night, I have a hard time getting up for nine o'clock Mass the next morning. I always went to Mass all over the years except the odd Sunday in London. I go to half ten if I have a hangover; nine if I haven't. The priest nearly knows by now; he could set his clock by me. It was drilled into us back then; I'd feel awful guilty if I didn't go. I'd be afraid I'd go to Hell. Then there's lots of them going to Mass who'll end up in Hell too'.

The crowd is cramming in now. They must be breaking themselves in for Paddy's Day, William suggests. There's not as many as there used to be, according to Seamus. A Paddy Wagon of Australians used to pack the place every Monday night; now it's only every second Monday because their dollar is weak too. There's your man, Lavelle, now; he's at every gathering where there's music. A small, wiry man with glasses wanders through the door, slips in behind the bar and makes himself a cup of tea. William wonders will he sing the song about the emigrants. The group are just finishing Neil Young's *Only love can break your heart,* when Lavelle bursts into *Willie McBride;* his own version about the chap he meets in every bar who insists on singing this tune, *again and again and again and again,* he ends to rapturous applause. I love this place. There's such a sense of warmth and camaraderie and fellowship and fun. My enthusiasm is running away with me. 'It is a popular place', William agrees. 'There were a lot of people in London who just wanted to say they had a drink in Matt Molloy's pub, even though they never met the man himself. The real music starts at ten', he tells me; 'this is just the lead in, but we'll be gone home by then'.

I chat to Mick Lavelle beside the fire, but he can't remember the emigrant song. I must have about a thousand, he tells me, and Willie mustn't have given me enough money the last time. William laughs when I tell him. 'I'd like him to sing it, he says, but I wouldn't like him to come out and start pointing at me'. We can say it's for me, I decide, because I'm a returned emigrant too.

The musicians pack up their instruments and bid farewell. Their turn is over and they make way for the real session to begin. William and I decide on one for the road although he's tired now. "I did too much walking today; three times in and out of town. I'm not too bad now with the sleeping; but I'll be awake early in the morning. I'm not much gone on lying in bed; never was. My father used to say too much sleep will give you a big head."

We nurse our drinks and talk about music. William likes *The Eagles,* and *Dr. Hook and the Medicine Man.* "But I never liked *The Beatles,* isn't that strange? I preferred Simon & Garfunkel." We talk about American politics. "I don't like Hilary Clinton; I don't think she'll beat McCain; then again neither might Obama. I was surprised that the Kennedy's supported him and hope he doesn't suffer the same fate as them." We talk about life in Ireland versus elsewhere. "Did your friends want you staying in New York the last time you were back? Did they want you to admit that you'd prefer to be there, like my crowd will do me?" He asks me. I recalled the man I met on my last visit to New York who insisted that I must miss the good life in America? There's nothing shoddy about life in Ireland, I told him. William thinks those people would like to come back deep down. "I'm more relaxed here than I was in London," he confesses. "It's quieter I suppose and safer. I was more on edge in England. It wasn't my country; this is. I was lucky I was able to come back. It's worse for a couple when only one wants to come. They're both going in the opposite direction. I know a man who had to go back because his wife couldn't settle here. It's harder if you're not going back to your own home place, but to your partner's. It's hard if you've got a family over there too."

We decide to call it a night. "If I have another one anyhow I'll never get up that hill in the wind. Between that and the arthritis all I'm fit for now is a glass of milk and a digestive biscuit. After milking cows all my life, I never drank it for years and they say that whatever you ate or drank too much of in your youth could be the cause of arthritis." We break the door open out into a windy March night. *Is this the last call for Ellis Island?* Bid goodbye outside the *Clew Bay Hotel* and promise to meet soon, when the summer sifts in. Willie is right; it is nice spending time with people who know; with people who've been on the same journey.

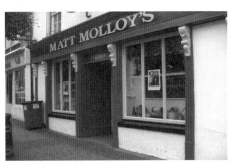

Matt Molloy's, Westport, Co Mayo

THE 'SAFE-HOME' PROGRAMME

As a child in Birmingham I recall attending a St Patrick's Day concert and hearing a priest tell the audience that, "Ireland's greatest export is men" and receiving a round of applause. I couldn't understand the reason for the applause then and I can't understand it now.

From the mid-nineteenth century until the early 1990s Ireland was a country of net emigration. It had become a way of life for the mass of its people reaching a low point in the 1950s when half a million mostly, young men and women departed these shores. They left in their droves, often forced out through dire economic circumstances in a State that was governed for the benefit of the few at the expense of the many.

It was almost a 'given' that across much of Ireland young people would have no alternative but to leave the country to find work and despite an often inadequate education that sentenced so many of them to a lifetime of unskilled manual labour (until ruined health brought an early end to their working life) these young migrants to Britain and the US sent money home to support those they left behind. Between 1939 and 1969 some £2.2 billion featuring as revenue in Government finances came from our emigrants abroad. The State's education budget in 1960 was £16 million. That same year Emigrant Remittances totalled £15.5 million yet 82% of emigrants to Britain in 1960 had left school by the age of fifteen.

However, despite the harsh circumstances that made emigration a necessity for so many there is something about the tie to home and country within the psyche of the Irish emigrant that you don't find (to anything like the same extent) in people who leave other countries. You'd see it in the group of lads, in 1960s London, standing at the base of a tree, a radio lodged high in the branches – for a better reception, listening to Micheal O'Heir's commentary on the All-Ireland final from Croke Park; the St Patrick's day parade in New York with the banners of the Ancient Order of Hibernians and each Province and County proudly held aloft; the Irish music and dancing passed down to second, third and fourth generation Irish children. And then there is the emigrant's dream of home that echoes in our poetry and song.

But coming home is not for everyone. No matter how heartfelt the wish might be for the majority of our emigrants their lives will be lived away from Ireland. Where they married, founded families and have children and grandchildren around them the tie to these loved ones would be very hard to break. Many emigrants happily settled into communities enjoy good relationships with great friends and neighbours and are content with their lives. Although not a subject that has attracted widespread publicity a significant number of Irish emigrants 'sell up' abroad and return home every year including our own Fran who returned to Ireland in 2007 after 20 years in New York.

However there was always the small minority who desired to return home but could not because they were unable to come back and buy a house for themselves. The aim of Safe-Home is to assist those older Irish emigrants to return to Ireland who, without us would not be able to do so and our objective is to ensure that they are able to settle successfully once they have come home.

In Ireland we are a national organisation and are active throughout the State. Outside of Ireland we are an international organisation receiving expressions of interest in coming home from our older emigrants on five continents.

Of-course the Ireland that our emigrants left 30 or 40 years ago is a vastly different country to the one they return to. While all of our cities and many of our rural towns have changed beyond recognition you might sometimes think that a lot of rural areas have gone backwards. Greater prosperity in recent years means that most households now have one or more cars and prefer to drive to a nearby town to shop. This has meant that small shops that may have been local enough to walk to have closed due to lack of patronage. Public transport in much of rural Ireland can range from poor to non-existent. The demands of the Celtic Tiger saw a huge increase in the number of women working and a spin off from this has been houses locked up and left empty during the day even in the most rural of spots. Gone are the days when there was a woman in every house and an old person propped up in a chair beside the range. Life is busier. The pace of life in rural Ireland may seem slow to those coming home from London or New York but it has become a great deal faster and "no one walking around that you can stop to have a chat with" is frequently remarked on by returnees.

But Ireland is beautiful for all that. It is home. It is the land that young men and women did not want to leave; the land they supported financially to the tune of many Billions of Euro in today's terms; the land that was celebrated in songs and in stories in homes, pubs, clubs and dancehalls wherever Irish men and women settled. It is the land they never forgot and the land a minority seek to return to in their twilight years.

Coming home is not easy. Settling your affairs in the country you are living in, travelling home, transferring pensions, arranging for services to be connected, opening a bank account etc would be stressful for a healthy young person let alone a man or woman in their 70s. We cherish our returnees and admire their strength of character in that, despite knowing all of the stress that lay before them, they trudged ever onwards in their determination to come home.

We welcome them, those who told their stories in this book and those who didn't; stories that were they to be told would be as fascinating as many contained here; emigrants who returned from Australasia, Africa, the Middle East, Europe and the America's north and south. We welcome them all and I pay tribute to our chairman, Dr. Jerry Cowley and the members of the Board, our two Development Officers, Brenda Fleming and Noreen Mulrine who carry out the support visits when they come home; Safe-Home's Administrator, Mary Ann Fadian who, based in our office in Mulranny, is often the first point of call for those contacting the programme and Fran Browner who interviewed returnees and crafted their stories.

Máirín Higgins
Programme director

SAFE HOME

Oh! Home at last
Relaxed and free
This is the only
Place to be.
It's in our minds
Our hearts and souls
We've dreamt for years
Of Coming Home

This lovely Isle
We left behind
Has changed so much
It blows our minds.
The cost of living
Is a pain
But, we won't emigrate again

And now at last
Our dreams fulfilled
Our work and worries over.
God Bless and Thanks
To the Safe Home gang
Who helped us all back over

Kathleen & Mickey Bradley
Lacken, Co. Mayo
Returned: January 2004

ACKNOWLEDGMENTS

I would like to acknowledge the Government of Ireland for their funding of this book. I am sincerely grateful to the Chairman of The 'Safe-Home' Programme, Dr. Jerry Cowley, and the Board of Directors for backing this project and for their assistance in realizing its publication. Thank you to my colleagues, Mary Ann, Brenda and Noreen for always being there to lend a hand. A special thanks to the Programme Director, Máirín Higgins, for initiating the recording of these historical memoirs and for her encouragement and support throughout the process. We are indebted to the production team at Original Writing, especially Garrett, Steven and Michal for bringing the publication to fruition and to those who offered their time and expertise, including Liam Kelly, National Transport Museum, the staff at National Photographic Archive, Piaras MacEinri, Irish Centre for Migration Studies, UCC, and Edward Donnelly, Tipperary GAA. We are also obliged to Kathleen Sweeney, Derreens, Achill for the Kirkintilloch pictures; Fr. Paddy Curran, PP, Castlebar, (RIP) for the centre piece collage and to Michael O'Leary, Ryanair, for permission to use their images. Finally, this work could not have been completed without the participants who were so generous in sharing their stories. I thank you for your patience and your hospitality; for your pictures and your mementos, but most of all for your memories - the most treasured gift of all.